# Reconstituting the Market

# Reconstituting the Market

## The Political Economy of Microeconomic Transformation

Edited by

### Paul Hare

*Centre for Economic Reform and Transformation*
*Heriot-Watt University, Edinburgh, UK*

### Judy Batt

*Centre for Russian and East European Studies*
*University of Birmingham, UK*

and

### Saul Estrin

*London Business School, UK*

**ho**
**ap** **harwood academic publishers**
Australia • Canada • China • France • Germany • India • Japan
Luxembourg • Malaysia • The Netherlands • Russia • Singapore • Switzerland

Amsteldijk 166
1st Floor
1079 LH Amsterdam
The Netherlands

---

**British Library Cataloguing in Publication Data**

Reconstituting the market : the political economy of
  microeconomic transformation
  1. Microeconomics   2. Europe, Eastern – Economic conditions –
  1989 –   3. Europe, Eastern – Politics and government – 1989 –
  I. Hare, P. G. (Paul G.)   II. Batt, Judy, 1955 –   III. Estrin,
  Saul
  338.5′0947

ISBN: 90-5702-329-6 (softcover)

# Contents

## PART V – OUTCOMES

# Notes on Contributors

**Judy Batt**, *Senior Lecturer in Politics, Centre for Russian and East European Studies, University of Birmingham, UK.*

**Anna Canning**, *Researcher, Centre for Economic Reform and Transformation, Heriot-Watt University, Edinburgh, UK.*

**Martin Cave**, *Professor of Economics and Pro-Vice Chancellor, Brunel University, Uxbridge, UK.*

**Marie Clark**, *Coopers and Lybrand, London, UK.*

**Junior R. Davis**, *Researcher, Centre for Economic Reform and Transformation, Heriot-Watt University, Edinburgh, UK.*

**Saul Estrin**, *Professor of Economics, London Business School, London, UK.*

**Paul Hare**, *Head of the School of Management, Professor of Economics and former Director of the Centre for Economic Reform and Transformation, Heriot-Watt University, Edinburgh, UK.*

**Otto Heinz**, *European Bank for Reconstruction and Development, London, UK.*

**Mohammed Ishaq**, *Researcher, Department of Management and Marketing, University of Paisley, UK.*

**Derek C. Jones**, *Professor of Economics, Hamilton College, Clinton, NY, USA.*

**Eugen Jurzyca**, *President, Centre for Economic Development, Bratislava, Slovakia.*

**Larisa Leshchenko**, *Economist, World Bank Office, Kiev, Ukraine.*

**Silvana Malle**, *Organisation for Economic Cooperation and Development, Paris, France.*

**Rasa Morkûnaitë**, *Economic Research Centre, Vilnius, Lithuania.*

**Domenico Mario Nuti**, *Professor of Economics, London Business School, London, UK and University of Rome "La Sapienza", Rome, Italy.*

**Alari Purju**, *Department of Economics, Tallinn Technical University, Estonia.*

**Valeriy Revenko**, *Professor Institute of Cybernetics, Glush Kora, Kyivi, Ukraine.*

**Adam Rosevear**, *PhD student, London Business School, London, UK.*

**Jon Stern**, *Senior consultant, National Economic Research Associates, London, UK.*

**Lina Takla**, *West Merchant Bank, London, UK.*

**Kataryna Wolczuk**, *Lecturer in Politics, Centre for Russian and East European Studies, University of Birmingham, UK.*

# 1
# Introduction

*Paul Hare, Judy Batt, Martin Cave and Saul Estrin*

## THE POLITICAL ECONOMY OF TRANSITION IN NEW STATES

Economic transition in the post-communist context involves not just a reduction in the role of the state, but a qualitative redefinition of it. The task is to transform states designed for the purposes of managing the socialist economy into ones capable of promoting radical economic reconstruction along liberal market lines. Post-communist economic transition amounts to a 'revolution from above', to create the institutions of a market economy from scratch. Clearly, this places extraordinary demands on the state, which is required to intervene actively in the process, but in a qualitatively different way from in the past, under the communist regime. There are important parallels in the tasks faced by Latin American and Third World states embarking on economic liberalization and structural adjustment (see Healey and Robinson, 1991). The literature on 'state failure' derived from the experiences in these countries has had an important influence on the design of strategies for post-communist economic transition (see, for example, Krueger, 1989), but it tends to be profoundly sceptical about the role of the state in economic reform, and to see the main problem in terms of 'rolling back' the state, minimizing its capacity to intervene in the economy. An alternative view is that of Joan Nelson, who argues that what is required is 'not so much a less powerful state as one that plays different roles and does so more effectively' (Nelson, 1989:10).

What has been most striking about economic transition in the post-communist context has been the peculiarly dramatic way in which it has thrust the problem of the state to the fore. All three of the multinational, communist federal states have collapsed, and economic factors played a major role in stimulating the nationalist resurgence which brought that about (see Batt, 1993; Bicanic, 1995). The nationalist resurgence, however, was by no means only a by-product of the strains generated by economic transition and economic crisis. It was an inherent part of the qualitative redefinition of the state and its relationship to society following the breakdown of communist dictatorship, when the reconstitution of the state on a democratic basis came onto the agenda. Democracy presupposes the existence of a coherent political community, a 'body politic' which the state is to represent and to which it is to be made accountable – in other words, a 'nation'. Where there is no agreed definition of the 'nation' and no consensus on the basic terms of political coexistence, the principle of majority rule will not generate collective decisions which can be generally accepted as fair.

In Central and Eastern Europe, the 'nation' has historically been understood primarily in ethnic and cultural terms. Nationalism first emerged as a powerful challenge to the nineteenth-century multinational Habsburg, Ottoman and Russian empires. In this context, the struggle for democracy became closely associated with the demand for separate nation-states, understood as the property of whichever ethno-cultural community was able to assert the strongest claim to a given territory. In this context, the collapse of the communist system was taken as a 'second chance' not only for democracy (which failed to establish itself securely after the collapse of the empires at the end of World War I), but for 'national self-determination' by those nations which had so far failed to achieve separate national statehood. Thus the advent of democratic politics was always likely to call the multinational federal states into question – especially the Soviet Union, inheritor of the Russian imperial tradition. Leaving aside the question of whether the collapse of all these federal states was 'inevitable', we can nevertheless note the interesting fact that none of them proved able to renegotiate the terms of the union to the satisfaction of their component republics. Notwithstanding their very different origins and problems, none was able to survive, let alone to muster the strength demanded by the task of economic transformation.

As a result, most of the post-communist states today are in fact new states. While the processes of economic transformation have been widely analysed already (see, for example, Bruno, 1993; Frydman and Rapaczynski, 1993; Williamson, 1993; Hare and Davis, 1997), much of this work simply takes for granted the existence of a well-established state apparatus capable of conceiving, developing and implementing reforms. It seemed to us a worthwhile question to ask whether economic transition would prove not only a more complex, but also a qualitatively different task in new states. Uncertain of their identity, insecure in their new borders, lacking many of the basic political and economic institutions of independent statehood, and deficient in qualified professional élites and experienced administrative staffs, new states seemed to us to face unique challenges in defining and implementing coherent policies for economic transformation. This was the starting point for the research project which produced the papers presented in this volume.

Our selection of 'new' states was confined to those former republics of the communist federations which did not inherit the central government institutions of the former federations, and the cases on which we focused were Ukraine, the Baltic Republics, Moldova, Slovakia and Slovenia. Our aim was to compare the varied experiences of combining state-building with economic transition in these new states. We also wished to contrast these cases with the experience in Russia and the Czech Republic, which had inherited more of the institutional structure of the former federal states, as well as with other post-communist states, such as Hungary and Poland, which have remained intact through the transition.

The issues we identified at the outset of our project as likely to affect new states most distinctively were as follows.

## Establishing the 'Rules of the Game'

Getting the constitutional framework right is a crucial precondition of implementing effective economic policies. The formation of a new state is likely to be accompanied by intensified conflict among competing élite groups over the basic constitutional 'rules of the game', which at best diverts energies from economic policy questions and at worst may lead to governmental paralysis and damaging economic drift. Key issues in this respect surround the definition of the terms of central executive authority both *vis-à-vis* parliamentary institutions and *vis-à-vis* regional and local power centres within the new state. The struggle over the definition of the terms of central executive authority could readily become intricately interwoven with the parallel struggle over the definition of the terms and strategy of the economic transition itself.

## Creating New Economic Institutions

By definition, the new states lack central economic institutions, such tasks having previously been undertaken in Moscow, Prague or Belgrade. They therefore have to develop such institutions as a central bank to operate an independent monetary policy, economic ministries and organizations to formulate and implement policies on competition, privatization and restructuring. In undertaking such tasks, they may have greater freedom yet face greater challenges than states inheriting central institutions from a previous regime. The less they inherit by way of an institutional legacy, the more there is to fight over. How rapidly would the new states develop their capacities to define and retain control over economic procedures, and develop appropriate regulatory frameworks? How effectively would the new state be able to contribute to the development and promotion of the new private sector? How willing would it be to exert pressure on former state-owned firms to reform and restructure?

## Nationalist Ideology and Economic Transition

The formation of a new state is invariably associated with an upsurge of nationalism, and nationalist ideology will remain central to the politics of new states as the main means of their legitimation. How would nationalist ideology shape the economic strategy and policy choices of the new government? However, we could see two quite different ways in which this could work. For example, in both Ukraine and Slovakia, the striving for self-rule had been closely associated with reluctance on the part of the respective élites and wider social constituencies in each country to implement a radical liberal model of economic transition. Economic nationalism in these cases seemed likely to take the form of searching for a 'third way' or more etatist economic model. In the Baltic Republics and Slovenia, by contrast, breaking away from the communist federations was closely linked with nationalist resentment at being 'exploited' by the federation and at the 'siphoning off' of republican resources to feed the insatiable appetites of the other members of the federation, which were economically weaker, and much less committed to consistent economic reform. So these new states started out life with a nationalist rhetoric which was much more favourable to the adoption of a consistent strategy of liberal economic reform. Insofar as legitimation of the new regime was bound up with the promise to 'return to Europe', this signified in the economic field its commitment to the market economy in order to be able to reintegrate economically with Western Europe. We were interested to see how these various forms of nationalism would affect the economic performance of the new states.

## National Conflict and Economic Transition

Most of the new states covered in our project had to cope with the reality of ethnic diversity, which sat uncomfortably with the nationalist rhetoric dominating the language of politics employed by the political élites. The ability to manage ethnic diversity, to preserve territorial integrity and to build a coherent 'body politic' by reaching an accommodation with ethnic minorities, would be an exceptionally important test of the political skills of the new governing élites. A new constitutional compromise might have to be hammered out to guarantee not only the minimal internationally-accepted standards of minority rights, but also to implement some degree of minority self-administration. In the cases of Estonia and Latvia, the basic issue of legal citizenship remained to be satisfactorily resolved, while in the other cases, citizenship in the broader sense of equal inclusion in the political life of the state had to be implemented.

This problem is inextricably linked with economics. Prolonged ethnic conflict would divert energies and attention away from the task of economic transition. Moreover, the economic strategies and the specific economic policies adopted by the new governments would affect different ethnic groups in different ways insofar as these groups are concentrated in specific sectors or occupations. Conflict over economic transformation in this case would become articulated in the language of ethnic politics. Nationalist governments' choice of economic policies might also be strongly conditioned by ethnic considerations, in order to favour the majority and/or exclude minorities. This could affect, in particular, privatization legislation. What impact might this have on the economic rationality of policy choices?

Having set out our starting assumptions and our hypotheses, now is the time to 'come clean' on some of the problems we encountered with them. While some of our assumptions were borne out, and some of our hypotheses proved fruitful, in the course of our research we increasingly came to question the usefulness of the distinction between 'new' and 'established' states in accounting for differences in performance in economic transformation. This led us to the following broad conclusions, set out as a series of linked points.

1) *Some of our new states were newer than others, and while this could play a significant part in explaining progress (or lack of it) in economic transformation in some cases, in others, the connection was less clear.*

The key contrast in our group of new states was between Estonia, the leading economic reformer in our group of new states, and Ukraine, the laggard. Estonia had enjoyed two decades of fully independent statehood between the two World Wars. One essential theme in its recovery of independence in 1991 was the assertion of legal continuity with the prewar republic. Estonia does not regard itself as a 'new' state, but one which had been illegally occupied and incorporated into the Soviet Union in the course of World War II. The claim to legal continuity was bolstered by the fact that the international community never formally recognised the Soviet annexation of the three Baltic Republics. 'State-building' in this case meant not the construction of something new but the restoration of much of the constitutional and legal *status quo ante*. This was highly advantageous from the point of view of rapidly gearing up the state for the purposes of implementing a coherent and effective programme of economic transformation. But it was bad news indeed for the Russian-speakers who had moved into Estonia in the Soviet period, who found themselves after 1991 relegated to the position of 'illegal immigrants'. As non-citizens, they were denied the right to participate in national political life; they were also excluded from participation in voucher privatization. Cynically one might argue that this has been an advantage from the point of view of Estonia's economic transformation: most of the Russian-speaking immigrants came to the country to work in enterprises set up in the Soviet period to meet the needs of the Soviet economy. These enterprises are the most vulnerable in the new market environment created by a government committed to reorienting trade to the West. While ethnic Estonians have also been hard hit by the rapid transformation (particularly in agriculture), unemployed Russian-speaking workers do not have the vote and are wary of openly protesting because they fear this would lead to their expulsion from the country.

Ukraine, on the other hand, found itself in a much less advantageous position. It had never existed as a modern state, and the very idea of Ukraine as a state wholly separate from and independent of Russia was controversial even among ethnic Ukrainians themselves. Ukrainian independence was the cherished goal of nationalists concentrated in Western Ukraine, a region only incorporated into the Soviet Union in the course of World War II. But insofar as Ukraine could claim the basic attributes of statehood – a clearly defined territory and set of distinct institutional structures – these were a product of the Soviet era. Correspondingly, its post-communist economic transition has been inconsistent and hesitant, bogged down in constitutional crises, the political paralysis of divided and only partially reconstructed ex-communist *nomenklatura* élites, and the lack of social and national consensus.

The ethnic issue has played out very differently in Ukraine and Estonia. From the start, the Ukrainian constitution avoided nationalist exclusivism, and citizenship was open to all permanent residents as of December 1991. Thus while there is a sizeable Russian minority in Ukraine, heavily concentrated in Soviet-era heavy industries in the east and south, it has not felt as threatened as its counterpart in Estonia. Indeed, Ukrainian governments have sometimes referred to fear of provoking ethnic conflict and Russian-backed separatism as a reason for going slow on economic transformation. In fact, the first nationalist government under President Kravchuk was too preoccupied with the symbolic politics of 'nation-state building' to pay much attention to economic transformation. Moreover, Russians have an important ally in the large group of ethnic Ukrainians who use Russian as their preferred language, and have common socio-economic interests and political values with the Russians, rather than with the more 'nationally-conscious' Ukrainians in the West. Thus the very incoherence of the concept of the Ukrainian 'nation' explains both the low level of ethnic conflict, and the slow pace of economic transformation in Ukraine.

While in these two cases, the connections between the 'newness' of the state and the progress of economic transition seem clear, in our other cases the picture is more obscure. Neither Latvia nor Lithuania has been able to capitalize upon its inter-war heritage to implement economic transformation with the same determination and focus as Estonia has. On the other hand, Moldova, if anything an even more ambivalent new state than Ukraine (see Batt, 1997) and the only one of our cases whose territorial integrity has come under armed threat, nevertheless seemed to have managed some aspects of the economic transition – namely, the introduction of a new currency and control of inflation – rather better than Ukraine, and, in the circumstances, remarkably well (see Ishaq, 1997).

Slovakia seems to be an intermediate case: its period of independent statehood under Nazi protection from 1939–45 had left an ambivalent legacy. While the experience confirmed for most Slovaks that they were capable of self-rule, the period was clearly too short and the wartime context too exceptional to leave an institutional legacy which would be of much use in the post-communist context. Moreover, the association of the first Slovak Republic with fascism was profoundly divisive, and remains so today. Attitudes to the wartime republic remain an important facet of the basic political cleavage in post-communist Slovak politics, reflecting deep divisions over the new Slovakia's orientation towards Europe and its commitment to democratic values (see Batt, 1996). Slovak economic performance since the split with the Czech Republic has been much more successful than expected, while its politics have been highly polarized and personalized. Uncertainty surrounds some basic constitutional issues, especially the position of the President. In part, Sloavkia seems to be an 'Italian case', where the economy somehow manages to avoid the worst consequences of a weak state. However, its macroeconomic performance can also be attributed to the inheritance of certain fairly effective institutions and competent professionals from its federal past. This brings us on to our next point.

2)   *None of our new states were totally new, in the sense of an institutional tabula rasa.*
What all three of the communist federations, from which our new states sprang, had in common was an elaborate constitutional 'superstructure' which already defined the constituent republics as national homelands and granted them most of the formal trappings of sovereign statehood. As one Russian has put it, 'The republics exhibit the full set of characteristics of independent states that have lost their independence.' (quoted by Zaslavsky, 1992:106). They had their own constitutions, national symbols, parliaments, governments, and many ministerial bodies; their own republican branches of the Academy of Sciences, education systems, cultural institutions and mass media. The real content of politics in these quasi-state structures of course had differed widely in the three cases: while the Soviet Union was *de facto* a unitary and highly centralised state, Yugoslavia in many respects seemed more loosely integrated than the European Community (see Rusinow, 1985; Steinherr and Ottolenghi, 1993). But in each case, as the respective Communist Parties' monopoly of power faltered and collapsed, these quasi-state institutions began to gather life of their own, and finally claimed the 'right to self-determination'. Thus in all our cases, independent statehood was fought for, won, and internationally recognised on the basis of institutions and borders laid down in the communist period. No national group or region which lacked the status of a federal republic has succeeded in forming a new state (although attempts have certainly been made, the only serious likelihood of an exception to this rule at present would be the partitioning of Bosnia). Thus in all cases, the new states were built on the rather extensive institutional foundations laid by the communist republics. Moreover, this institutional continuity had implications for the formation of the 'new' post-communist political élites, which in all our new states, albeit in varying proportions and with varying degrees of cohesion, represented an alliance between members of the ex-communist *nomenklatura* (reformist modernisers, pragmatic opportunists or genuine 'closet nationalists' from within the local Communist

Parties) and nationalist and/or democratic 'dissident' opponents of the communist system.

3)   *At this point, we were forced to recognise that the task of building 'new' states really has a great deal in common with the task of transforming post-communist states in general.*

In fact, we concluded that all post-communist states can be regarded as 'new' states, in the sense that the post-communist political and economic transformation involves fundamentally and qualitatively new definitions of what the state is, who it is for, and what purposes it serves. Many of the issues which we identified as likely to emerge in economic transitions in new states – constitutional wrangling, nationalist politics and ethnic conflict, institutional deficits, shortages of appropriately qualified personnel – are present to a greater or lesser extent in the other post-communist states.

For example, Romania, relatively one of the longest-established states of post-communist Europe, has exhibited many of the political symptoms we had expected to find in new states, and at the same time, its economic transformation has been almost as hesitant and inconsistent as that of Ukraine. This can readily be explained as a result of the peculiarly destructive impact on society and on the state itself of Nicolae Ceausescu's reign of personal despotism. When his regime collapsed in the revolution of December 1989, it left a power vacuum which was almost unavoidably filled by a hastily-improvised government largely composed of the more flexible former communists, and soon resorting to characteristic communist political habits. Nevertheless, elections were held, and in November 1996 both the Presidency and the parliament fell into the hands of the opposition Democratic Convention, and a new government has been formed which gives every sign of being committed to radical economic transformation.

A still more dramatic case is that of Albania, not a 'new' state in either a legal or territorial sense, but nevertheless in institutional terms a virtual *tabula rasa* when communist rule collapsed in 1990. With much Western help and support, Albania made rapid economic progress until 1996, apparently unencumbered by the obstacles presented elsewhere by more intact and resilient post-communist state structures. But this was not sustained. The flimsiness of its political reconstruction was exposed when President Berisha resorted to crude electoral fraud in the 1996 elections. In early 1997, the country slid back towards total political disintegration as Albanians took to the streets and seized arms in violent reaction to the loss of their savings (to the estimated equivalent value of one-third of GDP) in fraudulent pyramid investment schemes. The economy once again faced ruin.

The extension of the idea of 'newness' to cover all post-communist states does offer a general insight which, we believe, is helpful insofar as we are concerned with understanding what distinguishes post-communist (or post-totalitarian) transitions from post-authoritarian ones (for example, in southern Europe and Latin America). It does help to pinpoint what it is about the post-communist economic transition which makes it politically so much more complex than the implementation of economic reforms and structural adjustment programmes in other parts of the world.

However, what we also discovered is that, if all post-communist states are in some sense 'new' states, they are all new in different ways. Comparative analysis and explanation of their different politico-economic trajectories in the post-communist period requires close attention to their history as states, in both the pre-communist and communist periods.

Rather than organizing the materials presented in this volume on the basis of a distinction between 'new' and 'established' states, as had been our original intention, we have therefore grouped our country case-studies by regions, broadly defined by shared geopolitical predicaments, political cultures, and experiences of communist rule: the Baltic Republics; the Central Europeans; and the former Soviet Union.

## INSTITUTION-BUILDING AND THE RULE OF LAW

The simple, but very general idea underlying this section is the following: not only do states create nations (rather than the other way around), but they also create markets. Having already emphasized that all post-communist states should be regarded as new states, the particular aspect of this view most relevant here is that which links most directly to the core economic concerns of this book. This is the point that communist states were not states in the consitutional, rule-of-law sense that we often take for granted when discussing the established and economically developed Western democracies. Hence the project espoused by virtually all post-communist states of bringing about a transition from central planning towards some form of market-type economy (usually summed up as 'the transition to the market') is not merely a technical economic matter; nor is it a matter of *laissez-faire*, in the sense of removing all of the old constraints and restrictions on economic choices and activities, and allowing the market mechanism to blossom. Instead, the state itself has to be restructured in order to facilitate the creation of markets that could not exist at all under central planning and to carry out key functions necessary to the operation of a market-type economic system.

In other words, the state cannot simply withdraw from the economy, but its role in relation to economic processes needs to be redefined and reconstituted.

Of course, how any given state evolves depends on the internal political processes of the country concerned, and these need not yield outcomes especially conducive to the formation and sustenance of a well-functioning market system. Thus it is one thing for an outside observer to analyse and discuss the political-economic *desiderata* for a market economy, and the associated implications for the state, quite another for them to be put into effect; and even where apparently sound laws, regulations and institutions are established, there can still be a large gap between the formal structures and their practical implementation. Hence there are issues of the state's competence or capacity to undertake new tasks, and this inescapably political aspect of the transition must always be taken into account when assessing economic policies: some policies are only feasible with an already strong, competent state structure in place, others can create intolerable strains for a weak state (or simply fail, through incapacity), and yet others can actually assist the state-building process by strengthening certain institutions and practices that can then have beneficial spin-offs in other policy domains.

Nevertheless, we start here by identifying the markets and functions most crucial for building a market economy (most of which either did not exist, or only existed in a highly attenuated form under central planning).

## Markets

Banking and finance (the latter including insurance and pensions); labour; housing; foreign exchange; produced goods and services (technical standards, product safety, quality controls, etc.).

## Functions

Legal framework for private business (property rights, contracts, foreign trade and investment, etc.); competition policy; industrial policy; adaptation to the EU, WTO rules and other international obligations and practices; providing a stable environment for business (fiscal policy, social security policy, etc.); fostering savings, investment and economic growth.

This is not the place for an extended discussion of these points, since they are well known, and are widely understood and accepted (see Hare and Davis, 1997). What is particularly relevant here is their implications for the post-communist state, and for the nature of state-economy interactions and relationships in that context. For such a discussion, it is not necessary to dwell on the precise details of market structures and supporting institutions in each of the above areas, but a few general points need to be highlighted:

(i)    Constructing a market-type economy is neither costless nor automatic. New economy-wide and regional/sectoral institutions are needed and old ones (such as banks) have to function very differently from what was their normal practice under central planning; each individual firm also has to build up its links with suppliers and customers to enable it to function in the new conditions; and new mechanisms and procedures are needed to facilitate economic change and restructuring;

(ii)    It is not easy to ensure that the transactions which take place in various markets, and which private economic agents consider to be feasible, satisfy appropriate social criteria of acceptability;

(iii)    Much of what we think of as the institutional infrastructure of the market economy should be regarded as a public good (or, perhaps more accurately, as a long list of public goods). The supply of such goods is usually thought of as the proper province of the state, but this is not quite correct: rather, these 'goods' will either be provided by the state, or by private agents protecting their own (economic) interests, or through custom and practice (usually without formal legal enforcement), or not at all. The mix of provision in a given country will then determine how well or badly its economic system functions;

(iv)    Under conditions of extreme political/economic uncertainty, it is nearly always efficient for private economic agents either to delay investment or to persuade someone else (such as the state) to undertake the risks by meeting (or, perhaps, sharing) the costs.

To illustrate these points, we simply take two examples to explain how and where the state fits into the picture: reforming banks (the market for credit), and the establishment of institutions to implement competition policy.

## Reforming Banks

Under central planning, and even under its reformed variants that operated in countries such as Hungary, banks – or, in most countries, the single state-owned mono-bank – served as conduits for officially approved credits to firms and other agents engaging in activities approved under the prevailing plan. They were also commonly used as channels for the allocation of subsidies. Many of these credits were not expected to be profitable, and since enterprises were not generally permitted to fail (i.e., cease production and go out of business), additional credits were often made available to cover (or, in some cases, cover up) the losses resulting from earlier credits. This was an important aspect of the soft budget constraint concept discussed by Kornai (1980), associated by him with the notion of state paternalism.

In market-type economies, however, banks do not serve as a channel for subsidies, and when they provide loans, they do expect them to be profitable, and to be repaid in a timely way. Hence market-oriented, commercial banks engage in a number of important activities not found in the institutions with the same name operating under central planning. The activities include: selecting borrowers and allocating credits on the basis of the estimated profitability of their proposed production plans; monitoring loan performance, holding reserves to cover possible non-performing loans, and taking special measures to improve returns on loans not doing well; allocating and re-allocating depositors' funds across the economy on the basis of relative profitabilities. These functions are additional to the wider functions of the whole banking system (including the central bank) to provide the means of payment, stabilise its value so that it can serve as a store of value, and to manage foreign exchange transactions and reserves.

To convert 'socialist banks' into normal commercial banks, therefore, requires a number of different steps, some internal to the banks, some unavoidably involving the government in various ways. In the former category is included the huge task of reforming the banks' accounting and monitoring systems, retraining bank staff, and the technological upgrading of bank facilities and services. Much more difficult are the crucial steps that necessarily involve the government and its agencies. Of these, the design and implementation of bank licensing and regulatory arrangements (e.g., specification of minimum capital, reserve requirements, refinancing conditions, and the like) are amongst the most important. In many countries they are delegated to the central bank, though in a few, bank regulation is handled by a separate body, or even from within the Ministry of Finance: in any case, however bank supervision is handled, it can only be done on the basis of general legislation passing through the parliament or a decree issued by the government. Moreover, experience in many countries, including the transition economies, makes clear how important it is to get these matters 'right', in order to minimise the risks and dangers of large-scale fraud (such as the pyramid investment schemes that have taken off in several countries, and the unregulated formation of new banks), to preserve public confidence in the monetary and banking system (to discourage 'dollarization' and capital flight), and to encourage savings and investment. The market left to its own devices will not usually deal with these aspects of bank reform, but successful regulation demands both political will and competence, and a high degree of technical expertise: some of the transition economies have found it very difficult to bring these elements together effectively.

An even more complex aspect of banking reforms in the transition economies concerns the treatment of inherited or newly accrued bad debt. The temptation, often reinforced by vigorous sector-based lobbying of the government, is to cancel much of the old debt to give everyone concerned – both banks and the enterprises to which they lent – a fresh start. This is almost invariably a bad mistake for two reasons: (a) it sends out a signal that bad debts can be forgiven, and hence encourages both banks and firms to behave as badly in the future as they did in the past, in the expectation of a further rescue; and (b) it is costly, since governments are usually unwilling to write off the value of depositors' bank accounts at the same time as they cancel bad debts, and therefore have to inject a great deal of money to restore bank balance sheets. Of course, it is vital to avoid a general collapse of the banking system, and the banks alone cannot resolve such large-scale indebtedness. Hence the government has to do something, both to sustain confidence and to enforce better (i.e., more commercially oriented) behaviour in the future. Again, however, deciding how best to proceed is both technically difficult and politically risky, as the diverse experience across the transition economies makes abundantly clear.

## Implementing Competition Policy

Competition policy is, in some respects, a strange example to select for this section, since according to standard textbook market models, market equilibrium is generally efficient except in the special cases where a monopolist enjoys an entrenched position: hence at most one might need some policy tools to constrain the exploitation of monopoly positions. But in practice there is considerably more to competition policy than that, for even in markets where entry and exit are nominally free, the potential choice sets of the firms operating there are far wider than those that can be found in textbook models. For instance, it is clearly more profitable to create a monopoly position wherever possible – by merging with competitors, making exclusive contracts with suppliers or customers, fraudulent advertising. Similarly, profits can often be raised by lowering product quality or technical standards in ways which, in a mature market economy, might fail through the competitive entry of new suppliers. But in transition economies with weak or non-existent capital markets, such new entry cannot be relied upon and in any case, market information is often so poor (due to the absence or weakness of trade associations and similar bodies) that the problem might not be recognised very quickly. Lastly, many marketing networks in transition economies are hangovers from the linkages established under central planning, which may not be an efficient solution; and in some spheres proper marketing systems, such as wholesalers, might not even exist yet.

For all these reasons, competition policy in transition economies is vital. Even where its actual interventions are limited or indecisive, the operation of a competition policy agency helps to set the proper climate for market behaviour, defining what is acceptable or unacceptable market behaviour and hence inducing firms to seek profits through the former. At the same time, competition policy is a bit vague and is often seen by politicians as unnecessary 'froth' on the surface of the market economy. By underestimating it, though, politicians signal that forms of market behaviour that would not be remotely acceptable in mature market economies can be tolerated during the transition. In establishing such a policy, however, politicians do need to be able to resist the blandishments of sectors in 'need' of special help, and given the configuration of interest groups in the immediate post-communist period, this has often not proved easy. But the politicians cannot simply duck the issue by asserting that there is no problem in this area, and leave these issues to 'the market'.

## REDEFINING STATE-ENTERPRISE RELATIONSHIPS

We have seen that the process of transition is more than a simple reduction in the role of the state; it involves a reshaping of the functions that the state plays within the economy. In this section, we focus on how these changes affect the relationship between the state and the enterprise sector, notably with respect to privatization. This has been a surprisingly political process even by Western standards, with considerable variations across countries.

## The Reasons for Mass Privatization

Privatization in the West has been largely designed to improve company perform-ance and economic efficiency (see, e.g., Vickers and Yarrow, 1988). Principal-agent theory has clarified our understanding of the way that asymmetries of information between owners and managers create a conflict of interest in all firms where ownership has been separated from control. In the West, it is believed that these issues can be addressed by the effective operation of market competition, es-pecially in the capital market and the market for managers. These markets provide incentives for competing scrutiny of managerial performance, as well as mech-anisms to motivate managers to work in the interest of owners. These forces are argued to be deficient in state-owned firms, because governments have a variety of objectives for their ownership other than profitability – for example maintaining employment in areas of high unemployment, or keeping down the prices of neces-sities. The contradictory directives to managers which result provide leeway for managerial slack and inefficiency. Moreover civil servants do not have the same personal incentives to monitor managerial performance, nor the same levers to give incentives for company efficiency. For these reasons, it is usually argued that a shift from state to private ownership will improve enterprise performance.

The economies in transition face many of the problems that economic theory would predict from widespread state ownership, in terms of poor managerial per-formance and low levels of corporate governance. However, the economic envir-onment in most of Central and Eastern Europe does not leave one sanguine about the likely effects of privatization. Product markets in many countries are highly imperfect (see Estrin and Cave, 1993), capital markets are severely underdevel-oped and poorly regulated (see EBRD *Transition Report*, 1996) and managerial markets hardly function at all because of extreme shortages of key personnel (see Peiperl and Estrin, 1997).

In this situation, one might feel that immediate privatization makes little sense, especially since a generation or more of communism had left the general popula-tion with little savings, from which state owned assets could be purchased. Some early voices stressed an approach of slow institutional development based around encouraging free trade and product market competition, and only gradually pro-ceeding towards privatization as the legal and institutional infrastructure improved (see, e.g., Stiglitz, 1994; Murrell, 1996).

However, two factors have instead pushed reforming governments in the direction of rapid privatization. First, in most countries, though ownership was formally in the hands of the state, control was firmly with the managers or, in some countries like Poland, workers (Estrin, 1994). It was believed that a failure to pri-vatize quickly would lead to the rapid decumulation of these assets. They would ei-ther be consumed by the labour force in higher wages (or over-employment) or stolen by management to create new family-owned private business. The state did not have the political desire to reassert effective governance control over the firms that it nominally owned, because such a move could easily be interpreted as a reversion to the former communist system. In many countries, it was also unclear whether the governments had the administrative competence to reimpose effective control over the bulk of firms in the economy.

The second factor was a deep cynicism about the government's motives for ownership, and the uses to which government officials would actually put their interests in the enterprise sector. Western analysts such as Frydman and Rapaczynski (1993) or Andre Shleifer (see, e.g., Boycko, Shleifer and Vishny, 1995), expound the general mood among the reforming intelligentsia in the region that governments are inherently corrupt, and cannot be entrusted with the ownership of firms. From this perspective, the deep-rooted performance problems with state-owned enterprises were seen as deriving from the 'politicization' of company decision-making, associated with state subsidy and soft budget constraints (see also Kornai, 1980). Privatization was trumpeted as the solution to the problem. But it had to be all-encompassing and very rapid, to prevent the entrenchment of the new group of reforming politicians into the corrupting position of owning the corporate sector.

The immediate problem to be solved was therefore not company inefficiency, low productivity or the development of competitive markets; rather it was the 'depoliticisation' of the state enterprise sector. This meant that the speed and scale of privatization became virtually a litmus test of reforming zeal for post-communist governments, in some cases arguably to the detriment of policies with respect to other aspects of the market economy. 'Reforming' governments were for the most part governments with plans for far-reaching privatization. Laggards in the reform process could be identified by the lack of attention given in the government's programme to rapid widespread privatization.

## Methods of Privatization

We suggested above that transition governments would not be able to rely on the traditional Western methods of privatization: public offering, sealed bid auction or trade sale to other firms. These approaches face insurmountable problems as ways to privatize almost the whole economy in Central and Eastern European countries, because the stock of private domestic savings is far too small to quickly purchase such a large chunk of assets at prices which reflect future expected profitability. For example, it was calculated that at pre-reform savings rates it could take more than a century for the government to sell Czechoslovak industrial sector assets at their historic cost valuation! (See Estrin, 1994). There are also profound difficulties in valuation when there is not a proper record of the business accounts and when the transition process is fundamentally altering the pattern of competitive advantage in particular sectors and firms. Deficiencies in the legal infrastructure have also made it very hard for potential buyers to evaluate liabilities and risks, for example with reference to land tenure or the environment.

This has not ruled out the use of auction or public tender methods for a few selected firms. The most obvious customers are foreign multinationals, though the idea of selling the viable parts of the industrial sector to foreigners has given rise to considerable disquiet throughout the region. Some governments have also favoured the purchase of firms by their workers and/or managers (management employee buy-outs (MEBOs)), often with ownership rights concentrated on Trusts and the purchase being financed against future expected profits of the enterprise in question.

An alternative privatization method for transition governments has been restitution to former owners. This immediately recreates a property owning middle class, and re-establishes 'real owners'. However it is highly regressive, leading to instantaneous concentrations of wealth in the hands of people whose sole claim to such privilege is the circumstances of their parents or grandparents. It can also be very slow because, for example, suppose that a factory has been built on a plot of land formerly owned by a farmer. Does he receive the land? Or should he be compensated for the value of the property at the time of its seizure? It is not clear how valuations are to be made. Nonetheless, restitution has been an important element in privatization in several Central European countries.

In most transition countries, however, policy-makers concluded that conventional privatization methods could not deliver the required scale of privatization in the relevant time frame. They therefore innovated a new method of privatization: 'mass privatization'. This involves placing into private hands the 'savings' that would be required to purchase state assets in the form of publicly issued vouchers or privatization certificates.

Mass privatization avoids the problems of enterprise valuation. Most importantly, it allows large numbers of firms to be transferred from state hands quickly, while in principle permitting an egalitarian distribution of the former government assets. However, governments forego most if not all of the potential revenues from privatization.

Mass privatization schemes have differed significantly between countries (see Estrin and Stone, 1996 for summary). For example, considerations of equity imply that vouchers should be distributed to the entire population. However in the FSU (former Soviet Union), questions of nationality, ethnicity and seniority have also been relevant. The key issue, however, concerns the type of capital market institutions built into the mass privatization process. In the ambitious Czech and Slovak scheme, shares in enterprises were transferred in waves comprising hundreds of firms simultaneously. A computerized system was set up to mimic a general equilibrium market clearing process between the 1300 firms approximately in the first wave, and the more than 7 million private voucher holders. The vouchers could in principle be exchanged directly by individuals for shares in companies, but the government encouraged the development of financial intermediaries (Investment Funds), and by the end of the process these held the vast majority of shares (see Coffee, 1996). Funds also sprang up in Russia and Ukraine, though their impact has been more modest so far. However, in the Polish scheme, the vouchers could only be used to buy shares in government-created Investment Funds, which were initially allocated their shareholdings in companies.

Estrin and Stone (1997) describe the arrangements in the 18 transition countries with mass privatization schemes (significant countries which have not introduced mass privatization are Hungary, most of the former Yugoslav Republics and Uzbekistan). Two 'brand' models of mass privatization can be discerned. The three Baltic States, Slovenia and Ukraine broadly followed Russia with firms being privatized piecemeal rather than in waves, and with capital market institutions being allowed to develop in a largely *ad hoc* way. Bulgaria, Moldova and Romania have broadly followed the Czech and Slovak model, with firms begin privatized in waves using non-tradable vouchers and with capital market institutions typically being encouraged or developed as part of the process.

## Ownership Structures in Transition Economies

The concentrated effort to privatize quickly encapsulated in the mass privatization programmes across the region has led to an extraordinary growth in the private sector. From providing less than 10% of GDP in every country in the region except Poland and Hungary in 1989, the private sector share has risen to more than 50% in ten countries, and more than 33% in eighteen (see World Bank *Development Report*, 1996).

We noted above that most transition countries have used a variety of privatization methods. Only in Estonia and Hungary have sales to outsider owners represented significant privatization methods in terms of the proportion of assets transferred, and both of these countries have relied disproportionately on foreign direct investment to finance their privatization strategies. Elsewhere, mass privatization or buy-outs by managers and workers[1] have predominated.

The relatively high share of output supplied by the private sector appears to be largely independent of the privatization method adopted, or indeed of whether any sustained policy has been enacted at all. Thus, Poland, Hungary, the Czech Republic and Russia all have private sectors supplying more than 50% of output. However, Hungary did not have a mass privatization policy; the Polish programme has been modest in comparison with other privatization methods and as noted above the Russian and Czech schemes represent opposing modes of mass privatization. An important reason is that much private sector growth everywhere has been via the small scale privatization of shops, farms and workshops, as well as via the *de novo* growth of the small industrial enterprise sector.

## Implications of Mass Privatization Policies

The politics behind this variety of privatization policies and outcomes has been extremely complex. In Hungary for example, economic factors appear to have predominated over domestic political factors. Thus, the pressing need to meet foreign debt obligations and to balance the domestic budget deficit forced the government from 1991 to take control of the privatization process in order to reap the maximum revenues (see Canning and Hare, 1994). As a result, Hungary has obtained the largest share of foreign direct investment into the region (see Estrin, Hughes and Todd, 1997). However, this approach has caused some degree of domestic backlash against foreign-owned firms. Estonia has also relied on sales to foreign-owned firms but here the motive in part was perhaps to avoid voucher or MEBO privatizations which could have given significant ownership rights to Russian residents.

Voucher schemes in the Czech Republic and Slovakia were designed to transfer ownership to outsiders, with concentrated holdings in the hands of Investment Funds. However, it has been widely asserted that governance has been weak (see, e.g., Coffee, 1996; Takla, 1998). There are a number of reasons for this. The funds themselves are for the most part controlled by state-owned banks, so in one sense privatization is purely nominal. Moreover, capital market structures and regulations are very poorly developed in both countries (see World Bank, 1996; OECD Country Reports, 1996). Finally, there is at best modest evidence that the new owners are seeking to change the behaviour of managers, let alone to seek their replacement by more market-oriented personnel.

Most other mass privatization schemes have led primarily to insider ownership, either by workers, managers and both in combination. For example, according to Earle and Estrin (1996), 83% of privatized firms in Russia were majority owned by insiders in 1994. Of these, workers held a majority stake in 78%. Insiders' average holding was around 66%, as against 20% for outsiders (Investment Funds, other enterprises, banks, foreigners, etc.) and 14% for the state. Similar figures emerge from initial studies in Ukraine (see Rosevear, 1997).

## Conclusions

In summary, it was political factors that have drawn most reforming governments of Central and Eastern Europe to mass privatization. The policy has been very successful in terms of growth of the private sector; this has been rapid almost everywhere and there has been little variation according to whether countries are 'new' or 'old'. Thus in the area of privatization like that of other policies noted above, the collapse of communism and the process of economic reform makes all governments and countries 'new' in the relevant sense. This has led many of them to introduce a common policy like mass privatization, even though domestic political issues cause considerable variation in the detailed application of the programme.

However, mass privatization does not so far seem to be addressing the fundamental problems of inefficiency and managerial slack at the heart of the economic problems of the region. As yet, few studies reveal improved performance in privatized firms (see, e.g., Estrin, 1996; World Bank *Development Report*, 1996 for surveys).[2] It seems likely that this is because the new owners from the mass privatization process are either too dispersed, too weak or not motivated to change enterprise performance in a fundamental way (see Earle and Estrin, 1996). In particular, there is little reason to expect profound changes from insider owners – either managers or workers – whose jobs and livelihood will be put at risk by deep restructuring.

This is not necessarily inconsistent with the objectives of reforming governments, for whom mass privatization was more about 'depoliticization' than speedy improvements to corporate governance and performance. However, it suggests that the economic, if not the political benefits to privatization may take longer to appear than was first hoped. The important issues examined here arise in several of the country chapters that follow, notably those on Poland, the Czech Republic, Estonia, Russia, and to some extent Ukraine.

## INTRODUCTIONS TO EACH CHAPTER

In this section we briefly introduce the chapters that follow, with a view to guiding the reader across some difficult terrain, highlighting some of the linkages between chapters, indicating some of the major findings, and hence leading up to the closing section of this chapter.

Part I, on conceptual issues, comprises three chapters, namely those by Judy Batt and Kateryna Wolczuk on the political context; Martin Cave on the framework of telecommunications regulation; and Otto Heinz on competition law in transition economies.

Batt and Wolczuk highlight the peculiar problems of transformation in the new post-communist states, focusing on two sets of fundamental constitutional issues: defining the political community which the state represents and to which it is to be made accountable; and defining the checks and balances, the division of power within the state. Firstly, they focus on the dynamics of nationalism, which has provided the basic *raison d'être* of new state formation, in relation to the tasks of economic reform and political stabilization in multi-ethnic societies. Secondly, they look at the formation of the institutions at the centre, and in particular the problem of balance between legislative and executive power. The focus here is on the semi-presidential constitutional model characterized by an executive presidency, which has been widely adopted in the region, having undoubted attractions to new, weakly integrated states. Most of the issues introduced here arise in the subsequent chapters on Ukraine and Moldova, and to some extent Slovakia.

For all economies, the public utilities are not only large in terms of their demands for capital, but they also pose especially difficult regulatory concerns. These arise from the presence of increasing returns to scale in parts of the major systems (e.g., electricity generation), and from the inefficiency of duplicating core networks like the electricity transmission grid and the backbone of the telephone network, including the lines to individual subscribers. Of course, evolving technology does change the economics in this regard, as can be seen in the case of telecommunications with the development of mobile telephony and cable services (the latter often provided as a cheap by-product of the supply of entertainment services). Nevertheless, the regulatory issues associated with ensuring rapid investment while limiting the exploitation of monopoly power by incumbent firms remain problematic. These are the issues discussed both in general terms for the transition economies, and for the specific case of Slovakia, in Martin Cave's chapter. As he shows, in countries with fragile and sometimes unstable governments, and with democratic procedures and practices not yet firmly rooted, these problems are even more difficult to resolve than in more developed economies. Regulatory uncertainty is pervasive, and credibility hard to establish, in such conditions. Despite this, investors, including foreign investors, have proved surprisingly willing to take shares in the transition economies' telecommunications companies as they are privatized. Some of the later chapters, notably those on Hungary and Latvia, return to the issues introduced in this chapter.

The structure of Heinz' chapter consists of two main parts: on the one hand it examines the external challenges of competition law in the region, while on the other it takes a look at the internal challenges of competition law as it relates to economic transition. The main external challenge under discussion is integration into the European Union, but mention is also made of other, albeit less significant, external pressures for adjustment of competition law and policy such as membership of the Organization for Economic Cooperation and Development (OECD) or the Central European Free Trade Agreement (CEFTA). As for the internal challenges, the competition-related aspects of privatization and demonopolization are naturally in the foreground. These issues are in the background of several subsequent chapters, but are more prominent in the chapters by Jurzyca and Clark.

Parts II, III, and IV contain chapters grouped according to region. Thus Part II, on Central Europe, provides Mario Nuti's study of employee ownership in Polish privatization, the study by Anna Canning and Paul Hare on the political economy of privatization in Hungary, Lina Takla's chapter on privatization in the Czech Republic, and two chapters on Slovakia. These are Jon Stern's account of macroeconomic success and lagging microeconomic reforms in Slovakia, and Eugen Jurzyca's analysis of economic competition in the transitional Slovak economy.

According to Nuti, the privatization process in Poland was *slower* than planned. Second, privatization followed a *multi-track course* through the accretion of new methods adopted to overcome unexpected difficulties as they arose. Nuti quotes Janusz Lewandowski, twice Minister for privatization, *'In the transition, privat-*

*ization is a process whereby assets whose real owners are not known and whose real value is uncertain are sold to people who do not have the money to buy them'.* Third, *all Polish privatization tracks involved some form, often very significant, of employee ownership.* This unexpected and important feature of privatization in Poland, replicated almost everywhere else in transition economies except for the Czech and Slovak Republics (and therefore picked up in several other chapters), is the main object of Nuti's chapter, reviewing the modes and reasons for employee ownership, the implications predicted by theory, actual performance, problems and prospects. The unresolved problems of employee ownership in Poland, especially for its stronger version of MEBOs, include governance conflicts, financial constraints to growth, institutional instability.

The chapter by Canning and Hare focuses on the political economy of privatization in its second phase in Hungary, the country which, overall, has gone furthest in privatizing the public utilities, introducing elements of competition and setting up regulatory mechanisms and institutions to monitor them. The authors provide a brief review of the evolutionary path of Hungary's privatization 'vision', policy and strategy under the 1990–94 MDF government, and attempt to identify the factors influencing this evolution. Developments regarding privatization under the socialist/liberal coalition government which came to power in 1994 are also covered. The core of the study is a detailed examination of the privatization of the major utilities and the regulatory environment now in place.

Hungary's privatization made a slow start and then accelerated dramatically in 1995 as a range of legal and political issues were resolved, many public utility companies were sold off, and many other components of the privatization programme bore fruit. However, it is also important to refer to important financial constraints, both internally, from the Ministry of Finance, and externally from the IMF (among others) which almost certainly contributed greatly to focusing the government's mind and hence allowing the recent progress to be achieved. It is unlikely that progress with privatization in 1996 and beyond will prove to be as rapid as in 1995, partly because there are simply fewer firms left to privatize, and in particular relatively few of the attractive utility companies that did so well in 1995. Moreover, many of the firms still in complete or partial state ownership are in poor economic shape and urgently need either drastic (and presumably expensive!) restructuring, or closure. Either of these options raises difficult and so far unresolved issues about how to pay for restructuring, and how to keep down the social costs of major closures. Finally, Hungary remains unique in the region in the extent to which its privatization has relied upon sales rather than the free distribution of state-owned assets.

Takla's chapter on the Czech Republic reviews the main issues involved in privatization, examining its preconditions, outcomes and aims, as well as the theoretical and policy debates which surrounded the drafting and subsequent implementation of privatization programmes. The chapter then describes the privatization process and evaluates the alternative privatization methods in the context of the country-specific experience of the Czech Republic, with occasional reference to Hungary and Poland. Hence there is a great deal of attention to the process of mass (voucher) privatization in the country, and the way that this ensured the predominance of outsider ownership. However, the widespread emergence of Investment Funds brought its own problems for corporate governance. The chapter finds that privatization was rapid, though slower than planned, and that much private sector growth, as elsewhere, was due to the growth of *de novo* firms.

The chapter by Stern shows that the growth and trade performance of the Slovak economy has been good and much better than expected, in particular relative to the Czech economy. The only area in which the Czech economy has clearly done better is on unemployment. The chapter also clearly demonstrates the relatively slow pace of microeconomic restructuring and the unwillingness of the current and previous Meciar governments to establish an economy based on competition. So far, sound monetary and fiscal policies plus an open trading environment have been sufficient to result in good growth and trade performance. The key question is whether it will continue to be sufficient. Stern argues that the constraints from the reluctance to trust markets and institute thoroughgoing microeconomic reform will become progressively more important. Thus, under current policies, one should expect a slowing down of the growth rate and trade growth, although not necessarily in the next year or so.

Jurzyca describes, in his chapter, the main philosophy, developments, special features and practical experience linked to particular areas in which the Anti-Monopoly Office of the Slovak Republic (AOSR) has been involved. Based on that experience, he then formulates some recommendations for the proper functioning of competition policies in transitional countries. From the very beginning of the transition process, he concludes that greater emphasis should have been put on intensive *education about the principles of economic competition*. He shows that the awareness about this of the public, government officials and business-persons in Slovakia was relatively limited. There are significant differences between transitional and developed economies not only in their legal framework, distribution of ownership, and structure of government, but also in the culture of the people. Nations recognizing the importance of unrestricted competition are doing better economically than those which accept its distortions. The most difficult part of market economies to implement in some post-socialist countries would appear to be the way of thinking, especially in regard to the rules of competition and market behaviour.

Focusing on the three Baltic States, Part III includes Alari Purju's study of the political economy of privatization in Estonia, Junior Davis's detailed examination of privatization and regulation of public utilities in Latvia, and Rasa Morkûnaitë's review of capital concentration in the process of voucher privatization in Lithuania.

Purju's chapter surveys the preconditions for privatization in Estonia and the respective concepts of different governments. The methods and results of small-scale privatization, large-scale privatization, restitution and land reform are also discussed, as are the Estonian voucher scheme and the privatization of dwellings. Privatization in Estonia has many features which are similar to the same process in other Eastern European countries. However, there are also some preconditions for ownership reform specific to Estonia. These include extensive migration from other republics of the former Soviet Union; only regaining independence from the former Soviet Union in August 1991; an initial commitment to the rouble zone (the national currency, the Estonian kroon, was only introduced in 1992); and the predominant role of state ownership in housing. All the Estonian governments since 1990 have declared privatization to be the central issue of the continuing reforms. Two approaches can be distinguished: (i) the so-called restitution approach, which gave priority to restitution and also distribution by vouchers; and (ii) the entrepreneurial approach, which stresses the role of core investors and management in the process of privatization. During the period 1990–96, seven governments preferring one or other of these approaches have been in office. However, though some changes of emphasis on different methods have occurred, the privatization process continued along basically the same path.

The privatization and regulation of public utilities in the Baltic States generally, and Latvia in particular, have occupied centre stage in the political and economic debates concerning the development of the region. In Latvia, political and economic considerations concerning especially public utility regulation, but also privatization, have coalesced around both interest and political groups with their own agendas. The most contentious issues regarding the effective regulation and privatization of public utilities in Latvia concern: (i) the appropriate ownership of the utilities; (ii) the nature of the regulatory structure, in particular whether regulation should be conducted by an independent agency, a branch of the Ministry of Economy, Finance or Transport, or the enterprise itself; (iii) the desirability of allowing entry and competition; and (iv) the choice of procedures for the control and setting of prices.

An analysis of these issues within the prevailing political economy environment is the subject of the chapter by Davis. The problems that have constrained progress in both developing and introducing effective public utility regulation and privatization in Latvia are due to: (i) a lack of policy consistency on the part of the government; (ii) the recent banking crisis and economic recession; (iii) inadequate anti-trust (competition law) and legal environment; (iv) the *ad hoc* development of complex and non-independent public utility regulatory structures; and (v) effective political resistance by particular interest groups both within the Saeima (Latvian parliament) and among public utility managers.

According to Morkûnaitë, Lithuania, too, was strongly committed to carrying through a comprehensive programme of privatization, though not without much debate on the methods, speed and priorities. On the whole, the privatization programme in Lithuania resulted in too little corporate governance by strategic owners with the necessary skills and financing to bring about enterprise recovery. As it was supposed that insider-owned firms would perform better than outsider-owned firms, the vast majority of all voucher-privatized assets ended up in the hands of employees and management. The third major ownership group emerging from privatization in Lithuania comprised investment companies. Evidently, the formal ownership transfer that first takes assets out of state hands is unlikely to be the end of the story, since the next stage of enterprise restructuring will probably follow further concentration of private ownership in organizations capable of providing effective corporate governance.

Next, Part IV covers three of the member states of the CIS, namely the two largest – Russia and Ukraine – and a small one that turned out to be politically extremely interesting – Moldova. The resulting five chapters present a great deal of novel material. They comprise Derek Jones' chapter on privatization and restructuring in Russia, drawing on a survey of St Petersburg, Larisa Leshchenko and Valeriy Revenko's study of privatization and restructuring in Ukraine, the first detailed study of that country's microeconomic transformation. Following these chapters, Marie Clark presents a practitioner's view of competition policy and price regulation in Ukraine, and Adam Rosevear discusses the initial results from an interview-based study of enterprise restructuring in Ukraine. Finally, Judy Batt, Mohammed Ishaq and Paul Hare study the political economy of state-building in Moldova.

The aim of Jones' chapter is to present evidence drawn from recent surveys in Russia in two areas – corporate governance and the new trade unions. The chapter makes a modest step in the direction of extending our empirical knowledge by drawing on this survey data to report new findings for both privatized and non-privatized firms on the nature and effects of different structures of ownership and control. There does not appear to be much support for the claim that either state-owned firms or employee-owned firms are worker-controlled. Our findings suggest that in transition economies privatization does not produce fundamental changes in inherited patterns of corporate governance but rather has served to strengthen managerial control. There is no strong evidence that the key obstacle to enhanced performance is employee ownership. A related set of issues concern the nature and the role of trade unions (and, more generally, the preferred form of industrial relations), and the chapter finds that successor unions are capable of reform.

Turning to Ukraine, Leshchenko and Revenko discuss the initial legal framework and the peculiarities of the first stage of the privatization process, i.e., 1991–93, which may be described basically as a case-by-case phase. The year 1994 is treated by authors as the second phase of the privatization process in Ukraine since it stands apart in terms of new actors and institutions; it was the peak period for the use of non-competitive methods and at the same time saw a moratorium on all sale-purchase agreements. Ultimately, the 'rules of the game' were drastically changed and new ones imposed at the end of the year. This year could be considered as a transition period in the shift from a case-by-case approach to the mass privatization stage.

A revised mass privatization programme was launched at the very end of 1994 and characterizes the third, most probably the last phase of Ukrainian privatization. Despite some side-effects, by the end of 1996 privatization in Ukraine resembled an assembly line with around 400 enterprises supplied monthly and, as a result, in the ownership structure of almost 4000 companies a dominant stake is in private hands.

The issue of monopoly pricing is a high priority for the Anti-Monopoly Committee of Ukraine (AMC) and in 1995 they requested assistance from the UK's Know How Fund. The resulting work was carried out by Coopers and Lybrand, and Clark's chapter reports on some aspects of this. Monopoly pricing is not only a concern in Ukraine, of course, but is also a major issue in other transition economies. In Russia, for example, the UK's Office of Fair Trading worked with the Russian competition authorities on their guidelines. The chapter provides some background information on the competition law in Ukraine and the Anti-Monopoly Committee of Ukraine. It then considers why the AMC should be involved in the investigation of prices, some of the key problems that the AMC will need to face and the recommended approach. For both economic and political reasons, our view is that the AMC should investigate allegations of excessive prices despite the technical difficulties, due to the cultural history of co-ordination between firms and high barriers to entry. The conditions under which price control might be acceptable would seem to be: no effective competition between current producers; evidence of significant barriers to entry; and no scope in the short to medium term for lowering the barriers to entry. In these circumstances, there is either little scope for competition or competition might be very slow to develop.

Theoretical considerations suggest that private and privatized firms would be likely to restructure more than state-owned firms, and that the pace of restructuring would also depend on the ownership structure and corporate governance of the firms concerned. Specifically, there would be an expectation that insider-ownership would be less conducive to restructuring than outsider ownership. To a modest extent, these prior expectations are tested and to some degree supported for the firms reviewed in the chapter by Rosevear. The firms concerned are a pilot sample of Ukrainian firms interviewed in the first half of 1997.

Though geographically small, Moldova turns out to be an interesting country to study for both political and economic reasons. The chapter by Batt, Ishaq and Hare aims to identify the factors which have propelled Moldova's evolution away from the nationalist unitary state formula, and then studies some key features of Moldova's early post-communist economic development in the light of the country's difficult political background. It is crucial to start by reviewing the peculiar history of the territory on which the Moldovan state now stands, and the ambivalence of the Moldovans themselves as to their political identity. The Moldovans' propensity for compromise was greatly reinforced by their weakness in the face of the challenges to their independence from the simultaneous revolts of the Gagauzi and the Russian minority, who formed the Transdniester Moldovan Republic

(TMR), backed by communist 'neo-imperialists' and 'Great Russian' nationalists in Moscow. The chapter then discusses the post-communist economic situation and recent performance of Moldova, and some of the country's more striking reform achievements, linking these back to the political context. There is no doubt that the Republic of Moldova has made significant progress on macroeconomic stabilization since 1994. The break up of the Soviet Union meant the loss of previously secure markets, the exposure of the economy to severe shocks, and the emergence of economic problems such as unemployment and open inflation, with neither the networks or the 'culture' to deal with these problems adequately. However, despite these initial problems the benefits of reform have begun to materialize. Inflation has come down dramatically since 1994, an outcome in which the exercise of a restrictive monetary policy had no small part to play. Progress with inflation, however, has not yet been matched by correspondingly positive progress in the area of growth, though sectors are starting to grow again and at least the declining path of GDP has been arrested. Nevertheless, Moldova's unusually creative approach to finding a 'political settlement' in the country gives grounds for cautious optimism about the country's prospects in the economic sphere as well.

The last part of the book, Part V, consists of just one chapter, that by Silvana Malle, presenting an overview of the issues covered at the original conference which gave rise to this book. Some of the points identified in that chapter are referred to in the closing section of the present one, below.

## CONCLUDING OBSERVATIONS AND ISSUES FOR FURTHER STUDY

There are many possible lessons to be derived from the studies reported in this volume, and what follows is only a small sample of the most significant ones. They are grouped according to four broad headings: (i) the state and its political structures; (ii) competition policy; (iii) privatization; and (iv) regulation of utilities. Since a great deal of detail can be found in the subsequent chapters, we confine attention here simply to an identification of key topics, themes and conclusions. Most of what is listed below is still not sufficiently well understood, so there is scope for a great deal of further research.

### The State and its Political Structures

The key lessons were the findings that all states undergoing transition to a market-type economy are new states in a very significant sense, and that the nature and definition of the state itself – in terms of boundaries, ethnic composition and the political 'place' of ethnic minorites, and the relationships between state and economy – would be called into question by the end of communism. The implications of these observations are still unfolding, and our conceptual understanding of the processes involved is itself in need of much development. The relevant chapters in this book have only made a start.

## Competition Policy

It turned out that, while it is very important to provide *strong protection of economic competition* in transition economies, the *main restrictions on competition are not in the standard areas* like mergers, abuse of dominant position, agreements restricting competition*, since these are greatly influenced – and moderated – by the pressures resulting from globalization.* Instead, a greater danger in regard to distortions of economic competition is presented by the behaviour of the executive and legislative branches of the new governments, as a result of their lack of knowledge and experience of a market economy, or as the consequence of a balance of power biased in favour of particular interest groups.

In the initial stages of dismantling the centrally planned economy it was necessary principally to *create competition* by privatizing 'easy-to-privatize' firms, allowing private entities to do business, opening the borders to international trade, adopting a basic legal framework for business (price liberalization), etc. Then, in the second phase, the main accent has been on *promotion of competition,* represented by the adoption of specific laws designed to strengthen competition in those areas where it already existed, by requiring administrative bodies to remove any measures limiting competition, by privatization of 'hard-to-privatize' firms (natural monopolies), by intensive education of business persons, government officials, and the general public, by further liberalization of foreign trade, etc. In the last stage of transition, *protection of economic competition* will be of prime importance. The main activities will be dealing with state aids, refining the legal framework, restructuring government, and the standard activities familiar in developed market economies.

## Privatization

Privatization programmes have had diverse objectives: to ensure equity, to depoliticize the economy, to stop the appropriation of assets by insiders, to increase government revenues, to harden budget constraints and finally to raise efficiency and to speed up restructuring. In practice, however, privatization has entailed a number of controversial and complex decisions at every stage of the operation. Delays in decisions can often be attributed to protracted policy debates, as well as numerous institutional and technical problems regarding implementation. Nevertheless, some general conclusions are possible.

(i)   First, given that the starting position was that of near total state ownership of industrial assets, we find that ownership was successfully transferred out of state hands albeit at a differing pace and using very different methods.

(ii)  Second, if speed is a reflection of depoliticization, the actual speed of privatization did not correspond to the projected timetable and unforeseen obstacles have tended to slow down the process.

(iii) The implementation of privatization schemes generally reveals that the state remains an important player in the privatization process in the form of residual owner. New private enterprises share their markets with old state enterprises, privatized firms, joint ventures, and increasingly with foreign competitors.

(iv)  It has proved very hard for the state bodies still running the remaining SOEs to step back. Similarly, the role of government in the whole privatization process has been extensive, and continues to be important, probably too important.

## Regulation of Utilities

At the start of transition, this was undoubtedly regarded as a low priority area, yet the companies providing energy supplies (gas, oil, electricity, etc.), transport services, water supplies, and telecommunications are usually among the largest companies in any given country, and their performance has a huge impact both on the production costs of most other economic sectors, and on consumer welfare. Hence the ownership and regulation of these companies is increasingly seen as extremely important for the further development of the transition economies, especially for those already furthest along the path of economic reform. At the same time, economic policy regarding these sectors is inescapably political, and this has made it very hard for governments to establish independent regulatory authorities to supervise their behaviour. There is a dangerous temptation, in this area, to run before learning to walk, in the sense of seeking to implement technically complex and politically threatening regulatory schemes before either the market infrastructure, the administrative capacity or the political environment are ready for it. Several countries have made this mistake, sometimes on the basis of well-meaning western advice based on the experience of developed western countries such as the US or the UK. Finding approaches that are politically feasible as well as economically sound remains a difficult, and at times quite delicate, problem.

## NOTES

1. Russia's mass privatization fell somewhere in between: it enabled many managers and workers to buy the enterprises in which they were employed.

2. Though the picture may be beginning to change according to some very recent work (see e.g., Köllö, 1997; Kohl *et al.*, 1997).

## REFERENCES

Batt, J. (1993), 'Czecho-Slovakia in Transition: from Federation to Separation', *RIIA Discussion Paper* No. 46, London: RIIA.

Batt, J. (1996), 'The New Slovakia: National Identity, Political Integration and the Return to Europe', *RIIA Discussion Paper* No. 65, London: RIIA.

Batt, J. (1997), 'Federalism and Nationalism in Post-Communist State Building: the Case of Moldova', *Regional and Federal Studies* (forthcoming).

Bicanic, I. (1995), 'The Economic Causes of New State Formation During Transition', *East European Politics and Societies*, 9(1), pp. 2–21.

Boycko, M., Schleifer, A. and Vishny, R. (1995), *Privatizing Russia*, Cambridge, Mass.: MIT Press.

Bruno, M. (1993), 'Stabilisation and the Macroeconomics of Transition: How Different is Eastern Europe?', *Economics of Transition*, 1(1), pp. 2–21.

Canning, A. and Hare, P. (1994), 'The Privatization Process – Economic and Political Aspects of the Hungarian Approach', ch. 9 in Estrin (1994), q.v., pp. 176–217.

Coffee, J., Jr. (1996), 'Institutional Investors in Transition Economies: Lessons from the Czech Experience', in: *Corporate Governance in Central Europe and Russia, Vol. 1. Banks, funds and foreign investors*, edited by R. Frydman *et al.*, Budapest: CEU Press, pp. 111–186.

Earle, J.S. and Estrin, S. (1996), 'Employee Ownership in Transition', in *Corporate Governance in Central Europe and Russia, Vol. 2. Insiders and the State*, edited by R. Frydman *et al.*, Budapest: CEU Press, pp. 1–61.

Estrin, S. (ed.) (1994), *Privatization in Central and Eastern Europe*, London: Longman.

Estrin, S. (1996), 'Privatization in Central and Eastern Europe', *CERT Discussion Paper* 95/6, Edinburgh: Heriot-Watt University.

Estrin, S. and Cave, M. (eds) (1993), *Competition and Competition Policy: A Comparative Analysis of Central and Eastern Europe*, London: Pinter.

Estrin, S. and Stone, R. (1996), "A Taxonomy of Mass Privatizations", in *Transition*, Washington, DC: World Bank.

Estrin, S., Hughes, K. and Todd, S. (1997), *Foreign Direct Investment in Central and Eastern Europe*, RIIA, London: Pinter.

Frydman, R. and Rapaczynski, A. (1993), 'Insiders and the State: Overview of Responses to Agency Problems in East European Privatization', *Economics of Transition*, 1(1), pp. 39–60.

Hare, P.G. and Davis, J. (eds.) (1997), *Transition to the Market Economy*, 4 volumes, London: Routledge.

Healey, J. and Robinson, M. (1991), *Democracy, Governance and Economic Policy: Sub-Saharan Africa in Comparative Perspective*, London: ODI.

Ishaq, M. (1997), 'Macroeconomic Stabilisation in Transition Economies – the Moldovan Experience', Edinburgh: Heriot-Watt University, mimeo.

Köllö, J. (1998), "Employment and Wage Setting in the Three Stages of Hungary's Labour Market Transition", in *Enterprise Restructuring and Unemployment in Models of Transition*, edited by Commander, S., Washington, DC: World Bank.

Kornai, J. (1980), *The Economics of Shortage*, 2 volumes, Amsterdam: North Holland.

Krueger, A. (1989), 'Government Failures in Development', *Journal of Economic Perspectives*, 4(3), pp. 9–24.

Murrell, P. (1996), 'How far has transition progressed?', *Journal of Economic Perspectives*, 10(2), pp. 25–44.

Nelson, J. (1989), 'The Politics of Long-Haul Economic Reform' in *Fragile Coalitions: the Politics of Economic Adjustment in the Third World*, Washington, DC: Overseas Development Council.

OECD Country Reports (1996), *Reports on Czech Republic and Slovakia*, Paris: OECD.

Peiperl, M. and Estrin, S. (1997), *Managerial Markets in Transition in Central and Eastern Europe: A Field Study and Implications*.

Rosevear, A. (1998), 'Enterprise Restructuring in Ukraine', this volume.

Rusinow, D. (1985), 'Nationalities Policy and the National Question', in P. Ramet (ed.), *Yugoslavia in the 1980s*, Boulder, Colorado: Westview Press, pp. 131–65.

Steinherr, A. and Ottolenghi, D. (1993), 'Yugoslavia: Was it a Winner's Curse?' *Economics of Transition*, 1(2), pp. 209–243.

Stiglitz, J. (1994), *Whither Socialism?*, Cambridge, Mass.: MIT Press.

Takla, L. (1998), 'Privatization in the Czech Republic', this volume.

Vickers, J. and Yarrow, G. (1988), *Privatization: An Economic Analysis*, Cambridge, Mass.: MIT Press.

Williamson, J. (1993), *The Economic Consequences of Soviet Disintegration*, Washington, DC: Institute for International Economics.

World Bank (1996), *World Development Report 1996: From Plan to Market*, (Washington, DC: World Bank).

Zaslavsky, V. (1992), 'Nationalism and Democratic Transition in Post-Communist Societies', *Daedalus*, 121(2), pp. 97–121.

# Part I

# Conceptual Issues

# 2
# The Political Context:
# Building New States

*Judy Batt and Kataryna Wolczuk*

## INTRODUCTION

The majority of post-communist states are new states, formed as a result of the collapse of all three of the multi-national communist federal states, the USSR, Yugoslavia and Czechoslovakia. In contrast to previous examples of the breakdown of authoritarian rule and the transition to democracy (in, for example, southern Europe and Latin America), the post-communist transitions appear to expose the state itself to the most profound challenge. As Claus Offe has pointed out:

> *'At the most fundamental level a "decision" must be made as to who "we" are, i.e., a decision on identity, citizenship and the territorial as well as social and cultural boundaries of the state.'*[1]

The purpose of this chapter is to highlight the peculiar problems of transformation in the new post-communist states, focusing on two sets of fundamental constitutional issues: defining the political community which the state represents and to which it is to be made accountable; and defining the checks and balances, the division of power within the state. Firstly, we focus on the dynamics of nationalism, which has provided the basic *raison d'être* of new state formation, in relation to the tasks of economic reform and political stabilization in multi-ethnic societies. While the nationalist assumptions of the dominant majority and the demands of effective economic policy both seem to point to a centralized model of the nation-state, this model is likely to provoke resistance and non-compliance on the part of ethnic minorities, generating tensions which may both obstruct economic reform

and threaten the whole project of state-building. Secondly, we look at the formation of the institutions at the centre, and in particular the problem of balance between legislative and executive power. The focus here is on the semi-presidential
constitutional model characterized by an executive presidency, which has been
widely adopted in the region, having undoubted attractions to new, weakly integrated
states. This model is contested by proponents of the alternative, parliamentary
constitutional model, who argue that in the post-communist context presidentialism
is both a threat to democracy and no guarantee of stable and effective government.
However, parliamentarism itself also has difficulties in living up to the claims of
its defenders, and can easily degenerate into a recipe for political paralysis.

## THE DYNAMICS OF NEW STATE FORMATION: FEDERALISM, NATIONALISM, DEMOCRATIZATION AND ECONOMIC TRANSFORMATION

The resurgence of nationalism has been a ubiquitous feature of post-communist
politics. This has often been interpreted as a 'disease', a symptom of the patho-
logical condition of societies traumatized and disoriented by decades of totalitarian
rule. The demise of communism left a 'moral vacuum' readily filled by nationalism, which simply substituted one myth of collective identity with another.[2] But
eastern Europe does not have a monopoly on nationalist politics: it is nationalism
which has provided the basic definition of political community and of the legitimacy of the state in modern Europe. Correspondingly, nationalism retains a pivotal
role in European political discourse, despite – and in part because of – the intensifying pressures towards European integration and 'globalization'. The emergence
of new states in the post-colonial Third World was also accompanied by a new
wave of nationalist ideology dedicated to 'nation-building' and socio-economic
modernization; more recently, the failures of these states to fulfil their promises
has prompted a further round of separatist ethnic-nationalist challenges.

Nationalism is inseparably linked with the demand for 'democratization' of the
state. While nationalism certainly may take on authoritarian forms which undermine democracy, democracy itself depends on the existence of some prior general
consensus on *who* in fact constitutes the political community to whom the state
'belongs', to whom it is to be made accountable, and on what terms. As Sir Ivor
Jennings pithily put it, 'The people cannot decide until someone decides who are
the people.'[3]

The collapse of the multi-national communist federations indicates the failure
of these states to generate a common political identity transcending the multiple
national identities which they contained. These federations were fatally flawed by
their combination with communist rule. A true federation is built on a *foedus* or
contract, based on the assumption of the equality and autonomy of the parties involved. Daniel Elazar defines federalism as a combination of 'self-rule' with

'shared rule', a 'partnership established and regulated by a covenant, whose internal relationships reflect the special kind of sharing that must prevail among the partners, based on mutual recognition of the integrity of each partner and the attempt to foster a special unity among them.'(Elazar, 1987:5.) Federalism is thus inextricably linked in principle to constitutionalism and the rule of law.

Communist rule was fundamentally incompatible with these principles. The communist federal structures remained largely a formality as long as the communist Party maintained its monopoly of political power and its own centralized internal discipline.[4] While all manifestations of 'nationalism' outlawed as a threat to the unity of the state, the communist Party itself became associated with the interests of the dominant ethnic group – of Russians, Serbs and Czechs. For the lesser nations, communist rule was resented as much for its national oppressiveness as for its inherently undemocratic character.

But the formal structures of the federations were not wholly without meaning for the national communities they purported to represent. Quite apart from the symbolic recognition they gave to the existence of different national identities, the national republics also provided benefits in the form of mother-tongue education, privileged access to high status posts in the governmental and administrative structures. And for the poorer republics, the centralized redistribution of resources promoted social and economic modernization in line with the communist Party's objectives. Paradoxically, while suppressing nationalist ideology, communist rule also promoted the formation and development of distinct national élites in the republics. These élites' interests were tied to the Communist Party, on whom they depended for their power, and to the federation, which provided economic resources and outlets for the production of their enterprises. From the point of view of the non-dominant nations, all of this was, to some extent, an improvement on what had previously been offered under the unitary states of the pre-communist era. But this still did not constitute an authentic 'contract' between free and equal peoples. It was at best a covert 'deal' struck between the centre and dependent local élites.

While initially set up as the means of controlling national aspirations, the republics began to take on a life of their own as soon as the centre weakened and communist rule began to decay. That process was closely linked to economic reforms, initially sponsored by the Communist Party itself with the express aim of strengthening communist rule. This was to be achieved by introducing greater flexibility, initiative and responsiveness into the economic system. All of these necessarily implied some decentralization of control, and so had inescapable political ramifications, whether the Party wished to recognize it or not. In the more homogeneous national states such as Poland and Hungary, economic reforms were accompanied by a diffusion of political power to regional and sectoral lobbies, which then proved able to stymie reforms when they threatened their interests.[5] In the federal states, the same diffusion of power took place, but it also acquired a national dimension insofar as it affected the interests of the republics, their relationships with the centre and with each other. Poorer republics, now under increased competition for resources, felt that the centre was reneging on its side of the 'deal', while richer republics, usually the more ardent proponents of economic reforms, felt freer to express their frustrations at the inefficiency of resource transfers and subsidization of the poorer republics.

The translation of these economic tensions into full-blown nationalism was greatly facilitated by the existence of republican institutions. In all communist states, the introduction of market-type pressures revealed regional economic disparities, but where these regions corresponded with national territories possessing a formal organizational structure, it was much easier for economic inequalities to become articulated politically as nationalist resentments. But the resurgence of nationalism cannot be reduced to economic factors alone, and was by no means at the outset spearheaded by disgruntled republican *nomenklatura* élites. That role was played by nationalist intellectuals, some of whom were more or less closely associated with the Communist Party, but some of whom were anti-communist dissidents. The crucial step was when the reformist central leadership of the Communist Party decided to bolster economic reform in the face of resistance from conservative bureaucratic forces by introducing political reforms, to relax controls on the press, open the way to criticism of the 'mistakes of the past', and encourage the participation of the masses, long excluded from any role in political life.

While this was expected to strengthen the hand of party reformers at the centre, what happened everywhere was that the criticism and mass participation rapidly burst through the bounds of reform 'from above'. In the more homogeneous national states, the demands centred on the democratization of the state, to transform it from the instrument of the single party backed by a foreign power – the USSR – into the authentic representative of the national will. To the extent that the state itself within its existing borders was basically accepted as given, nationalism and democratization of the state could work together.

In the multi-national federations, however, political relaxation served to reveal long-smouldering national resentments, which were only exacerbated by free discussion. Criticism was aimed not only at conservatives at the centre, but often focused its most bitter attacks on the local, republican party élites. What they were charged with was not so much 'conservatism' on the question of economic reform, but slavish subordination to the centre and betrayal of the national interest. It was at this point that, if it had not already occurred to them, it finally became clear to the republican élites that in order to survive, they should jump on the nationalist bandwagon. It was to be the defection of key sections of the republican élites to the nationalist cause that transformed intelligentsia-led revolts into a potent political challenge to the centre, eventually leading to dismemberment of the federal states. It was only where national identities had been given institutionalized form, in the republics of federal states, that the nationalist revival acquired the organizational resources necessary to the formation of new states. Nowhere (with the possible exception of Bosnia) have national minorities which did not enjoy institutionalized recognition in the communist state structure been able to redraw state borders.

This brings us on to the awkward fact that most of the new states formed out of the collapsed federations are themselves multi-national, containing sizeable, and usually disaffected, national minorities within their populations. The break-up of the federations has thus not 'solved' the national problem, but reproduced it in a new context. The formation of new states has satisfied the aspirations of the titular majorities of the former federal republics, but it has not created coherent political communities including all inhabitants of the territory. This has major implications for the institutional structure of the new states.

'State-building' in the modern era has been strongly associated with the drive for centralization and the extension of state power uniformly across a given territory. The model of statehood favoured by the builders of new states in post-communist Europe is a unitary one, which owes much to the French Napoleonic tradition, idealized by many intellectuals in the region as the epitome of modern liberalism and rationality. It has many attractions in the post-communist context, particularly for the purposes of implementing economic transformation. Too often, this has been seen in terms of 'rolling back the state', reducing its powers and the scope of its intervention in the economy, in line with the trends towards liberalization, deregulation and privatization in western economies. But the task of post-communist economic transformation is of a qualitatively different order: it amounts to the implementation of a 'capitalist revolution from above'[6], in which the state is bound to play the leading role. What is needed, in the words of Joan Nelson (writing of the politics of economic adjustment in the Third World), is 'not so much a less powerful state as one that plays different roles and does so more effectively' (Nelson, 1989: 10). The question is whether the centralized-unitary model is the only, or the most appropriate, basis on which to build strong states in the post-communist context.

The demands of economic transformation seem at first sight to dictate the choice of a unitary and centralized constitutional model as the framework for clearly-defined authoritative leadership, coherent and co-ordinated policy-making, and uniformity in policy implementation. The paucity of able and suitably qualified administrative personnel further strengthens the arguments for a concentration of forces at the centre. However, unitarism and centralization do not automatically guarantee effective economic transformation – they are just as likely to be exploited by ex-communists to justify minimal change in the structures of the state and its relationship to the economy. Rather than providing a formula for state transformation, unitarism and centralization may simply preserve the weaknesses of the communist state. As one major comparative study found, the most formally centralized of the post-communist states also tended to show the least progress in economic transformation, and 'the avoidance of substantive devolution may be rationalized as a means of pushing through economic reform, in countries where reform is not, in fact, being successfully pushed through.' (Gibson and Hanson, 1996: 307.)

Moreover, there is a further reason why the adoption of the centralized-unitary model may not produce strong states in post-communist eastern Europe. It is attractive to state-builders in the region not only as a means of preserving communist structures, but also as a means of entrenching the dominant position of the national majority in whose name the state was originally founded. The claim to 'national self-determination' is based on the principle that each nation has a right to a state of 'its own'. The state is correspondingly assumed to be the property and embodiment of the majority nation in the given territory. But where – as in most of the new states of eastern Europe – the territory has historically been inhabited by more than one nation, the unitary and centralized 'nation-state' is a recipe for conflict. While the majority may be prepared to concede 'minority rights', this rarely goes as far as recognizing minorities as 'nations' with equal 'state-forming' status, which would imply a right, if not to secession, at least to an institutionally-entrenched, guaranteed, proportional 'share' in state power. Recognizing the right of minorities to 'self-determination' is difficult because it is readily seen as a threat to the territorial integrity of the new state, and even to the very existence of that state as an independent entity.

On the other hand, the failure of the majority nation to come to terms with the reality of ethnic diversity can itself become a threat to the survival of the new state. A doctrinaire, exclusive nationalism on the part of the majority, insisting on deference on the part of others to symbols confirming its 'right of possession' of the new state, and entrenching its hegemony in a centralized and unitary constitution, can provoke the very dangers of secession that the majority itself most fears. The most extreme case, which well illustrates the costs involved, is that of Moldova, where two secessionist entities have successfully contested the right of the Moldovans to monopolize the state. One of the them, the Russian-dominated Transdniestrian Moldovan Republic, has also succeeded in limiting Moldova's sovereignty by directly involving Russia in the conflict. A similar threat has also loomed over the establishment of independent states in Estonia and Latvia. A less extreme case is that of Slovakia, where independent statehood has been accompanied by heightened tensions between Slovaks and the Hungarian minority.

Where national minorities are large, and especially where they are geographically concentrated, the implementation of a unitary state threatens to relegate national minorities to the status of 'second class' citizens. Guarantees of 'minority rights', limited to measures aimed at protecting the rights of individuals, are unlikely to be enough to satisfy the aspirations of national communities to collective recognition. In these circumstances, a convincing argument can be made that the full political equality of citizens not only as abstract individuals but as members of distinct national communities requires a more pluralistic form of state, with institutionalized forms of power-sharing including autonomous territorial self-government. Implicitly or explicitly, federalism reappears on the political agenda as an alternative formula for state-building.

But federalism is by now a 'dirty word' in the post-communist world, having proved ineffective as a means of managing national diversity. Far from mitigating national conflict, the federal institutionalization of national diversity only seemed to exacerbate conflict by providing the constituent national units with the political resources which enabled them to paralyse federal government, and eventually to secede. If it could be proven that the failure of past federations was due to their communist flaws, there might be grounds for hope that the transition to democracy would provide the conditions for a more acceptable and workable federalism. But the case of Czechoslovakia is not encouraging. The collapse of the Czechoslovak federation – in contrast to that of the USSR and Yugoslavia – occurred *after* the collapse of communist rule. The Czechoslovak communist regime steadfastly resisted all economic and political reforms to the end, thus postponing the emergence of the centrifugal dynamic until after the sudden final demise. Democracy in itself did not promote the successful re-negotiation of the contract between Czechs and Slovaks which would have preserved the federation. A crucial motor of the collapse were the tensions generated by economic transformation, which only began after 1989. These tensions were exacerbated by the role played by former communists in Slovak politics, but this is not the whole story. Economic transformation was seen as a threat by large segments of the Slovak population, and the demand for Slovak autonomy was inextricably linked with the desire of Slovaks to implement a different, 'gradualist' economic policy very much at odds with that thrust upon them by Prague.

The challenge facing the builders of new states in post-communist Europe is thus an enormously complex one, involving a delicate balancing act between the demands of economic transformation, which seem to require a strong state in the sense of an authoritative and effective centre, and the demands of managing multinational societies, which seem to point towards a more pluralistic and devolved state structure. There are no ready models to prescribe the appropriate institutional framework. Each state will have to hammer out its own eclectic formula in an extended and open-ended process of negotiation and compromise.

## INSTITUTION-BUILDING AT THE CENTRE: PRESIDENTS AND PARLIAMENTS

The distinction between 'new' and 'old' states is less obvious when we turn to look more specifically at the processes of institution-building at the centre, as new states vary greatly in their choice of governmental arrangements, which range somewhere between parliamentary and semi-presidential systems. As is clear from the previous section, the 'new' states were anything but an institutional *tabula rasa*. As the existing state institutions acquired greater importance after the collapse of the Party, they found themselves in a strange new political environment with new roles and, most significantly, under much greater strain. New states shared with old states the task of the radical reconstruction of the state as a whole, in order to transform it from an executive instrument by which the Communist Party exerted its will into an autonomous set of institutions capable of aggregating and implementing in a coherent and acceptable form the will of society. In this sense, all post-communist states are 'new', although, as will be argued, the new states may illustrate the problems in a more acute form. This applies in particular to the former Soviet republics. There, despite the new-found assertiveness of the republican institutions towards Moscow in the final days of the USSR, the essentially superficial nature of republican institutions was only too evident: they were not designed to function independently, let alone operate under the strains of socio-economic crises or mediate between conflicting views as to what construes a collective identity. Renewal of legislative-executive structures immediately came to the top of political agenda.

In the mid-1980s Daniel Elazar felt compelled to restate the 'truism' that constitution-making is an 'eminently political act'. This has been amply demonstrated by the constitution-drafting process in post-communist states, which has been thoroughly politicized because it is being carried out by the same people and bodies that are to be governed by the new rules. As a result, prevailing conditions have not allowed the luxury of detailed and detached debate and the implementation of rationally coherent constitutional blueprints, as advocated by some political scientists.[7] The constitutional division of authority turned out to be a by-product of a political 'tug of war' rather than purposeful planning.

During the self-determination struggle, when the indigenous élites shifted their allegiance from the federal centres to the republics, legislatures usually acquired a genuine popular legitimacy as they were transformed from mere extensions of the federal centre to symbols of national sovereignty. Parliaments, as the highest state institution, assumed full and extensive powers after the demise of the communist parties and federations, and they immediately confronted the task of adopting new constitutions. Once they found themselves taking on the role of a Constitutional Assembly, it is not surprising that they strove to retain their power, especially their control over the formation and dismissal of the executive branch; the usually indirectly-elected presidents were relegated to a figurehead role.

The preservation of the role of parliament as the highest representative state body in the new constitutions (as in, for example, Slovakia, Latvia, Estonia), in preference to some form of semi-presidentialism, can be interpreted as a commitment to the European model of parliamentarism: democratic, consociational and liberal. According to Lijphart, parliamentarism is the cornerstone of the consensus model of democracy, which prevents majority rule and distributes power through multi-party systems, coalitional government and more equal executive-legislative power relations (Lijphart, 1991:73–84). Therefore, being conciliatory and representative, PR (proportionally representative) parliamentarism is perceived as particularly suited to multi-ethnic societies, precluding what can be an egoistical and blatant majority rule.

Yet, parliamentarism in new post-communist states has proved to be anything but a recipe for a plural and consociational model of state. As titular ethnic majorities dominated legislatures, the new states turned into exclusive republics or nationalizing instruments. In Latvia and Estonia, for example, representative democracy has only been achieved at the cost of disenfranchising a section of society.[8] And in Slovakia, while 'normal' electoral rights have been granted to all citizens, parliament and government have pursued nationalizing policies against numerically disadvantaged ethnic minorities. The abstract model of proportional representation failed to contribute to an all-inclusive polyarchy, based as it was on exclusive definition of the political community. This adds weight to Donald Horowitz' argument that 'there are many institutions compatible with democracy in the abstract, but not all of them are conducive to multi-ethnic inclusiveness' (Horowitz, 1993:28); this can only be ensured by *purpose-built* institutional arrangements.

The development of a multi-party system (which parliamentarism nevertheless fosters) as a forum for participatory politics is one of the cornerstones of post-communist transformation. Yet, in some Soviet successor states, rather than consolidation of political parties, it is the endurance of the bureaucratic 'parties of power', comprising state enterprise directors, collective farm chairmen, central and regional state apparatuses, which characterizes the political process. This casts a shadow over the prospects for a successful transformation, which envisages a shift towards more open and democratic channels of political participation. The former party and state *nomenklatura*, by joining the 'national liberation struggle' led by the cultural intelligentsia and former dissidents, ensured that they were not disenfranchised in the new states and were accommodated in the legislatures. They subscribed to nationalism and became versatile in the rhetoric of state-building in order not merely to survive politically, but to expand their dominance. Effectively, they monitored and controlled the pace and speed of economic reforms, so that it did not jeopardize their immediate interests; for the same reasons they insisted on preserving centralized state structures.

Nevertheless, their commitment to nationalism is suspect and thus extends only as far as needed to avoid radical change. At the same time, the imperative of nation-state building, so dear to the hearts of the nationalist intelligentsia, was essentially lost on them. This made them more accommodative and less doctrinaire in terms of their views on policy relating to ethnic minorities. Their pragmatic outlook, paradoxically, counterbalanced that of the native cultural intelligentsia, which saw the role of the state as an instrument of nation-building. Where bureaucratic elites were still well represented in parliaments following independence, as in Moldova and Ukraine, they supported the construction of a territorial framework for ethnic minorities such as Gagauz autonomy and the Crimean Autonomous Republic.

The strength of the bureaucracy *vis-à-vis* the nascent political parties and the alliances built by those political actors, affected the choice between a parliamentary or a semi-presidential system of government. On the eve of independence, new presidential offices were created almost everywhere, as an extra guard against the federal centre and/or the symbolic continuation of pre-communist national traditions. Then the particular choice between a ceremonial head of state or a chief executive, and the resulting executive-legislative relations, reflected the balance of power amongst the political actors – those forces with higher expectations of success usually insisted on direct elections and wider powers.

One of the most compelling arguments for an executive presidency was that of the urgent need for rapid decision-making in the face of the economic impact of 'going independent' – high inflation, collapse of trade, falling GDP – and the deficiencies of the inherited state institutions. The evident inadequacies of administrative capacities added weight to arguments for shifting decision-making powers to a singular leader and for tighter control over the periphery. The stability and predictability associated with a fixed-term presidency were viewed as indispensable virtues during the chaotic period of state-building, and which parliament-dependent governments could not guarantee.

However, presidential systems are not the choice endorsed by political scientists. 'Zero-sum' elections, which are an almost universal feature of directly-elected presidencies, are one of the many cited perils of presidential systems.[9] The high stakes in such elections, in which the 'winner takes all', are believed to encourage polarization of the electorate and are, for that reason, especially undesirable in ethnically heterogeneous societies, where incumbents may be tempted to exploit ethnic divisions to secure a victory.[10] However, there is limited evidence that directly-elected post-communist presidents have resorted to exploiting ethnic cleavages and/or promoting the interests of dominant ethnic majorities. The drive to broaden their popular mandates seems to be a more widespread strategy, rather than identifying with any particular section of the electorate, cultivating the extremes and pursuing anti-minorities policies. Even more, by adopting the symbolic role of father-figure in what are essentially weakly integrated societies, presidential leadership has provided a much-needed sense of purpose and destiny. The Ukrainian and Moldovan Presidents – both members of the former *nomenklatura* – at the head of countries divided over both past and future, created a vital link between the new state and its people, by focusing on economic reform and material well-being as the vehicle which would deliver loyalty to the new state.

However, if presidents' symbolic roles enhance the legitimacy of new states, in terms of economic efficacy the shifts of power between parliaments and executive presidents fail to produce results. Overall, presidential control over government has not proved to be particularly successful in combating socio-economic crises: decisiveness at the centre (where it indeed exists) tends to be only part of what economic reform requires. The main barriers to crisis resolution tend to be the anonymous 'parties of power' – the bureaucrats, whose expertise, commitment and, ultimately, interests all have a role to play.

At the same time, the creation of an executive presidency often implies a trade-off between assumed yet rarely realized policy-making efficacy and political accountability. The sense of urgency resulting from socio-economic crises and state weakness creates a faith in the extraordinary application of political power and rules of governing. Where a strong presidency is seen as the remedy to institutional disarray, the political process inevitably centres on the president, who comes to be perceived as the personification of the nation and the sole protector of its interests. The resulting feelings of 'being on a special mission' erode the incentive to compromise with other representative institutions and/or to comply with the decisions of the constitutional review body. As there are two directly elected institutions, there is no democratic principle on how to decide on which of them 'really' represents the popular will.[11] The usually very low opinion rating of legislatures encourages presidents to revert to direct links with the electorate through referenda, thereby further undermining the sovereignty of parliament. In Ukraine President Kuchma has resorted to a threat of referendum twice, not only to push the long delayed constitutional changes through an obstructive parliament but also to acquire extensive powers.

Ultimately, elevating the presidency above other institutions hampers the very process of democratizing new (or even existing) states and inhibits attainment of the primary objective of democratization, which is locating power in an impersonal set of rules, procedures and routines rather than personalities, however benevolent they may seem. The de-personalization of political interactions touches upon the fundamental issue in transformations, which is what Przeworski refers to as 'institutionalizing uncertainty'. The element of uncertainty is built into the democratic system when no political force has the monopoly of means to control outcomes, and when there are 'checks and balances' reducing the scope for arbitrary decision-making. Transformation implies a shift from power being vested in personalities to the fulfilment of accepted rules and procedures, through which outcomes are sanctioned and validated. Until there exists an overarching adherence to such rules, accompanied by readiness to accept the results of their application, the institutionalization of democracy is not achieved.

Nevertheless, as the 'newness' of the state and its perceived vulnerability tends to legitimize the investment of authority in specific individuals (such as the president), the pressures for decisive national leadership clash with the imperatives of democratization. Therefore, even if the precise impact of presidency, along with the merits and perils of particular constitutional arrangements cannot be debated in isolation from other characteristics of each polity, the lingering danger of personalization of political power remains a feature of systems with executive presidencies who enjoy popular mandates.

At the same time, however, during periods of volatile transition, presidents, although suitably placed to undermine democratic consolidation, hardly have a monopoly on the usurpation of power. Under favourable circumstances, prime ministers have also aspired to the role of charismatic leader with authoritarian connotations. In Slovakia, as determined by the constitution, the prime minister and government are both weak and dependent upon a powerful parliament (National Council), which can sack individual ministers against the wish of the prime minister. Yet, in practice Prime Minister Meciar's populist appeal and support in parliament have made him a much more powerful actor than provided for by the constitution. The bitter struggle to unseat the indirectly-elected President (which incidentally stemmed from personal rivalry and animosity) was led by the Prime Minister. By transferring some presidential powers to the parliament and government, he aimed to eliminate opposition to his populist, nationalistic policies. Such policies are well served by direct democracy such as referenda, which rely on emotional arousal, and easily stirred nationalist sentiments. Being a plebiscitarian mode of decision-making, they serve the interests of any – including ethnic – majority. Recognizing their power, Meciar removed a degree of control over the rights on referenda from President Kovac.

In analysing the formation of political regimes in post-communist states, we look for evidence of the two principal modes of separation of power prevailing in the West: functional (between an executive presidency and legislature) or political (between government and opposition). Each is associated with a specific system of checks and balances, as well as channels of political accountability. Yet a neat separation of powers either along institutional or partisan lines is only rarely evident in post-communist states. Overall, the weakness of legislatures has resulted in an increased burden on presidencies, regardless of their constitutionally-determined powers, as they engaged in negotiations between parliamentary majorities, governments and oppositions to overcome policy-making impasses. But while often facilitating consensus, presidents can simultaneously contribute to the complexity of the process by pursuing their own agenda. Executive presidents – by default – are more involved in day-to-day decision-making. In such systems political configurations are more complex and political outcomes cannot be easily deduced from the institutional layout. The overlapping multiple cleavages defy a simplistic functional/ institutional or political/partisan division. In Moldova, President Snegur's alliance with the Popular Front was followed by a switch to ex-communist bureaucrats, whose vested interests in preserving Moldova's independence rather than integrating with Romania, he shared. In Ukraine President Kuchma strategically allied himself with the national democrats (who voted for his rival in the presidential elections) in order to outmanoeuvre the leftist forces entrenched in parliament during the constitution-making process and obtain support for his economic reforms.

Nevertheless, despite the inadequacies of constitutional arrangements, the very establishment of constitutional rules of political bargaining is at the core of democratization and state-building. Such a recognized and mutually acceptable set of rules, even if flawed and occasionally challenged, provides a degree of stability and predictability. Some observers argue that although there is no direct correlation between the type of executive-legislature relations adopted and pace of economic recovery, there is a relationship between the absence of a constitutionally-sanctioned framework, which leads to overlapping competencies and undefined rules on the one hand, and a corresponding lack of economic reform on the other.[12] Constitutions *per se*, however imperfect, appear to contribute to political stability and the capacity to adopt economic reform measures.

To this end, the example of independent Ukraine clearly illustrates the intertwined problems of constitutional confusion, institutional stalemate and economic drift. The conundrum for Ukraine was that because of the historical divisions within society, there was not even a shared ideal of statehood around which the constitution could be created. The fundamental question of collective identity had to be addressed and the question of whether 'ownership' of the state lay with 'the peoples of Ukraine' or the 'Ukrainian people'. The lack of agreement on the definition of 'political community', accompanied by the intense conflict over the delineation of authority, hindered the constitution-drafting process and interfered with the process of creating the instruments for effective everyday economic decision-making. Effectively, Ukraine experienced one of the gravest cases of economic collapse amongst post-communist states.

## CONCLUSION

When analysing the relationship between economic transformation and state-building in new states, we encounter a striking variety of outcomes. In Estonia and Latvia, we find a state-led policy of ethnic exclusion along with commitment to, and, in the case of Estonia, remarkable progress in economic reform, which stands in direct contrast to the ethnic 'truce' and protracted economic decline in Ukraine. Thus, the whole configuration of pre-existing conditions – interethnic relations, the degree of national consciousness in the native majority, élite alliances, the residual administrative capacity, pre-communist past and aspirations for a return to Europe – all have to be taken into account in explaining the diverging political and economic trajectories of new post-communist states.

Although the key to successful state consolidation lies in establishing institutions and structures which provide incentives to compromise and consensus, the extent to which a particular constitutional framework can effectively mediate the tensions in society depends on a wide variety of factors. Each new state seeks a balance between the competing demands of this multi-faceted project and has to work out its own model. Designing and constructing a state framework that is democratic, efficient and promotes interethnic harmony in post-communist conditions is not a straightforward matter and is hardly likely to be achieved at the first attempt. A long process of conflict, mutual accommodation, and constitutional revision is inevitable, and will decisively affect the pace and shape of the economic transformation in each case.

## NOTES

1. C. Offe (1991), p. 869.
2. This interpretation has been put forward most coherently by George Schöpflin. See for example Schöpflin (1993).
3. Quoted by J. Henderson (1991), p. 50.

4. For a comparative analysis, see R.H. Dorff (1994), pp. 99–114.
5. On Hungary, see J. Batt (1988); on Poland, see K. Poznanski (1986).
6. For further discussion of this, see Offe, *op.cit.*
7. See, for example, Sartori (1994a); Shugart and Carey (1992).
8. The concept of the exclusive republic has been applied to post-Soviet states by P.G. Roeder (1994), pp. 61–101.
9. However, Donald Horowitz and Giovanni Sartori are amongst those who oppose an unmitigated condemnation of presidentialism. See, for example, Horowitz (1990), pp. 71–79; Sartori (1994b).
10. For an analysis of that and other perils of presidentialism, see Linz (1994).
11. Ibid.
12. See Hellman (1996), p. 56. In a similar vein, J. Zielonka (1994, pp. 87–104) argues that even imperfect constitutions have an overall beneficial stabilizing effect.

# REFERENCES

Batt, J. (1988), *Economic Reform and Political Change in Communist States*, London: Macmillan.

Dorff, R.H. (1994), 'Federalism in Eastern Europe: Part of the Solution or Part of the Problem?', in *Publius: the Journal of Federalism*, Vol. 24, Spring, pp. 99–114.

Elazar, D. (1987), *Exploring Federalism*, Tuscaloosa, AL: University of Alabama Press.

Gibson, J. and P. Hanson (1996), 'Decentralization and Change in Post-Communist Countries', in Hanson, P. and J. Gibson (eds), *Transformation from below: local power and the political economy of post-communist transitions*, Aldershot: Edward Elgar.

Hellman, J. (1996), 'Constitutions and Economic Reform in the Postcommunist Transitions', *East European Constitutional Review*, Vol. 5(1), Winter.

Henderson, J. (1991), 'Legal aspects of the Soviet federal structure', in McAuley, A. (ed.), *Soviet Federalism, Nationalism and Economic Decentralization*, Leicester University Press.

Horowitz, D.L. (1990), 'Comparing Democratic Systems', *Journal of Democracy*, Vol. 1(4), Fall.

Horowitz, D.L. (1993), 'Democracy in Divided Societies', *Journal of Democracy*, Vol. 4(1), October.

Lijphart, A. (1991), 'Constitutional Choices for New Democracies', *Journal of Democracy*, Vol. 2(1), Winter 1991.

Linz, J.J. (1994), 'Presidential or Parliamentary Democracy: Does It Make a Difference', in Linz, J.J. and A. Valenzuela (eds), *The Failure of Presidential Democracy*, Baltimore and London: The John Hopkins University Press, pp. 3–90.

Nelson, J. (1989), 'The Politics of Long-Haul Economic Reform', in Nelson (ed.), *Fragile Coalitions: Politics of Economic Adjustment in the Third World*, Washington DC: Overseas Development Council.

Offe, C. (1991), 'Capitalism by Democratic Design? Democratic Theory Facing the Triple Transition in East Central Europe', in *Social Research*, Vol. 58(4), Winter 1991.

Poznanski, K. (1986), 'Economic Adjustment and Political Forces: Poland since 1970', in Comisso, E. and L. Tyson (eds), *Power, Purpose and Collective Choice*, Ithaca and London, Cornell University Press.

Roeder, P.G. (1994), 'Varieties of Post-Soviet Authoritarian Regimes', *Post-Soviet Affairs*, Vol. 10(1), pp. 61–101.

Sartori, G. (1994a) *Comparative Constitutional Engineering*, Basingstoke and London: Macmillan.

Sartori, G. (1994b), 'Neither Presidentialism nor Parliamentarism', in Linz, J.J. and A. Valenzuela (eds), *The Failure of Presidential Democracy*, Baltimore and London: The John Hopkins University Press.

Schöpflin, G. (1993), *Politics in Eastern Europe*, Oxford: Blackwell.

Shugart, M.S. and J.M. Carey (1992), *Presidents and Assemblies: Constitutional Design and Electoral Dynamics*, Cambridge University Press.

Zielonka, J. (1994), 'New Institutions in the Old East Block', *Journal of Democracy*, Vol. 5(2), April, pp. 87–104.

# 3
# Regulatory Institutions and Regulatory Policy for Telecommunications in Economies in Transition: Some Issues and an Illustration

## Martin Cave

This chapter is concerned with the problems which arise in promoting efficiency in the utilities sector in economies in transition. The illustrations are based on the telecommunications sector, although they apply more broadly to electricity, gas, transport and water utilities, or to any other sector where production is characterized by substantial sunk costs and relatively small scope for competition.

The first section discusses the problem of regulatory design in general terms, but with a special focus on economies in transition. The second section reviews problems of adjustment related to the telecommunications industry, and the regulatory framework in which they are being addressed. The third section discusses the example of Slovakia in more detail. The final section contains conclusions.

## DESIGNING REGULATORY INSTITUTIONS

### The Problem

Many mass-market network industries (which I shall refer to as utilities) share three critical technical and economic characteristics which make their regulation a matter of some difficulty (see Levy and Spiller, 1994):

- Utilities are capital intensive and the assets which they require are both durable and – in many cases – sunk, not in the sense of lying underground, although this is true of many of them, but in the sense of not being capable of sale and redeployment. As a result, such assets are something of a hostage to fortune made by the providers of the investment.

- Many, if not all, network utilities are characterized by economies of scale, which place a limit on the number of firms which can efficiently provide service to any particular area. These economies of scale typically apply primarily (but not invariably) to distribution networks, rather than to activities such as extraction of energy and generation of electricity (at one end of the supply chain) and to retailing and 'supply' (at the other). In between, however, there is likely to be scope for only one, or a limited number of networks. As a consequence governments cannot rely upon the operation of the competitive process to police incumbents. Secondly, some network industries are characterized by economies of scope, which may add further to the concentration of market power in the hands of the incumbent.
- The services provided by network utilities, especially transport, water and energy, but to an increasing extent telecommunications too, are consumed by and necessary to the welfare of a large proportion of the population and, at any approximately cost-based prices can represent a significant proportion of household budgets, especially in the case of poorer families. Utility pricing thus has a major impact on real incomes and price changes have major redistributive effects. Utility services are also of fundamental importance as an intermediate input into almost all other sectors of the economy. Their pricing and the financial policies used to support them thus have a major impact on such things as international competitiveness.

These three characteristics have had a major influence upon the organization of the sector. Over the last century, an 'American' model was developed of investor-owned monopoly utilities, whose activities – especially pricing – were regulated through politically accountable regulatory authorities which, were, however, often captured by the regulatee. The traditional 'Western European' model is of a state-owned monopoly utility, acting either as a government department or as a commercialized enterprise subject to controls imposed by government on its pricing and investment policy. Both of these models have changed radically in the past twenty years with privatization, the introduction of competition and new forms of incentive regulation, and it is towards this new model that many economies in transition now aspire to move. However, their starting point has been an even more centrally controlled and heavily distorted variant of the Western European model.

## Utilities under Central Planning

In most East European countries, national networks were created from regional utility companies in the later 1940s and early 1950s (see Cave and Valentiny, 1994). Because of their size and importance, public utilities became departments of ministries or even constituted a whole ministry. The ruling ideology required that their services should be cheap and available to all. However, only the first part of this injunction was fulfilled. Tariff structures typically favoured households so that residential consumption was constantly under-priced compared to industrial use, and cross-subsidization of consumers became a permanent feature of the tariff structure. Moreover, tariffs in general failed to cover economic costs. This was sustainable due to the lack of a feedback mechanism between prices and investment. As occurred generally in these economies, investments were covered by the central budget through taxation without any reference to revenues raised by the utilities; the Planning Office's choices among new projects were not based on rate-of-return analysis but on administratively set output targets.

Prevailing economic doctrine and the needs of industrialization resulted in the separation of 'productive' and 'non-productive' activities within the economy. The former were assumed to create wealth, while the latter were assumed to consume it. Giving preference to 'material' production or 'material' services was a characteristic feature of economic policy under central planning. Although most public utilities fell into the category of 'productive' activities, some of them were considered less productive than others.

Energy industries (gas and electric utilities) were in a more advantageous position as they provided an input central to material production. In the early stages of industrialization, energy shortages created bottlenecks and 'black-outs' in periods of rapid growth. Subsequently, the problem became one of extravagance in energy use. The transport and particularly the telecommunications industries suffered more from the rules of central allocation of investments, as planners first satisfied the requirements of 'material production' and services only received residual financial resources.

An equivalent hierarchy of customers could also be detected within each sector. While network expansion in electricity or gas supply already showed some signs of preferential treatment of industrial or bulk consumers, the development of transport and telecommunication services made the distinction between industrial and residential consumers more directly.

As a result, public utilities, with the exception of energy, were relatively weak sectors in the centrally planned economies. Because of their low prestige, reflected in the investment allocation system, they were provided with fewer and fewer resources. Their performance lagged behind that of utilities in market economies. In many areas their relative backwardness became a major factor contributing to the inefficient use of resources. At the same time, inflexible and relatively low tariffs led to excess demand, and the intensity of service utilization was much higher in Eastern Europe than in Western economies.

In telecommunications, particularly, Eastern Europe was at the bottom of the European league, in terms of installed telephone lines per 100 population. The networks also suffered from technological backwardness due to autarchic development. The lack of technology transfer eliminated competitive pressure, often raised costs and cut Eastern public utilities off from the rapid changes in technology in the

West. The annual loss of GDP in Hungary due to the low level of telecommunications was estimated as 4 to 5 per cent GDP (Major, 1992: 78).

Thus severe shortages, poor quality of service and lack of investment characterized the public utilities as they entered the era of transition to a market economy. The bureaucratic style of government of the previous system had affected utilities in fundamental ways.

What problems are likely to arise in moving from this traditional arrangement of utility sector in a centrally planned economy towards the dominant regime emerging in the rest of the world, which, as noted above, is characterized by privatization, the development of competition and the introduction of more economically efficient pricing policy?

As far as pricing and the development of competition are concerned, we discuss in more detail below the policies adopted by economies in transition in relation to the telecommunications and electricity sectors. Such separate treatment is necessitated by major differences in the characteristics of these industries. However, all utilities sectors share the first of the characteristics noted at the start of this section – the necessity for substantial levels of investment in assets which are non-salvagable, or sunk, and which therefore make the investor vulnerable to some form of expropriation. This could simply be achieved, for example, by tightening price controls so that the investor in the utility receives just sufficient revenue to cover its operating costs, but neither earns a rate of return on its investments, nor has the value of them returned to it through the incorporation in prices of depreciation charges. That this is more than a theoretical possibility is shown by the experience of telecommunications in Jamaica, noted below.

## Enforcing the Regulatory Contract

Such 'regulatory taking' is a much discussed problem, a frequently proposed solution to which is by means of the so-called regulatory contract. This legendary instrument is an informal agreement between, on the one hand, government and regulators acting as agents for their principals, consumers and citizens and, on the other hand, the management of the regulated firm acting as agents for their principals, the stockholders. Under the contract, the regulatory body commits to providing an adequate rate of return on investments, if those investments are efficiently chosen and managed; at the same time, to protect consumers from exploitation, it further commits itself to some form of control over prices and related areas such as quality of services, although the details of the arrangements, notably the power of the incentive mechanisms built into them, may involve significant departures from simple remuneration of cost.

The necessity for some quasi-contractual relationship of this kind seems obvious. If it is absent, firms will either refuse to invest or require a return on their investment so high as to make it even more likely that the regulator will not accede to it by authorising the corresponding prices. A major crux of the problem of regulatory design therefore becomes how best to structure arrangements for the specification and – even more importantly – the enforcement of the regulatory contract. The major contribution of Levy and Spiller and their associates to this debate has been their attempt systematically to identify alternative methods for implementing the regulatory contract (Levy and Spiller, 1996). Helpfully, they view the problem as one of choosing from amongst a range of alternatives, characterized by different ways of providing the crucial enforcement mechanism. We first review this work in general terms, before applying it to the circumstances of economies in transition.

To be reassured that their assets will not be expropriated, private investors require the existence of regulatory arrangements which impose some restraint on the regulators' discretion in operating a given system, restraints on changing the system, and institutions to enforce those restraints. Satisfying these requirements involves demands upon three types of agents:

- the parliament, which enacts primary legislation governing the allocation of regulatory functions and the duties and powers of the various regulators,
- the administration, including officials in government departments or appointees to more or less independent regulatory bodies, which implement the legislative arrangements
- the Courts, to whom aggrieved parties can appeal in the event that they believe that the administration is not acting in accordance with the legislation.

Designing an efficient regulatory mechanism involves allocating functions among the three sets of agents in order to provide the necessary comfort to investors, while at the same time discouraging regulatory capture.

As far as the *Parliamentary system* is concerned, two key distinctions are whether the system of government is unified or whether it constitutes a federal system in which power is distributed between federal and sub-federal levels, and whether the voting system leads to radical alternations of Government, rather than more minor adjustments of coalitions. Thus federal systems such as the United States, Australia and the European Union generate frameworks in which regulated industries are controlled by legislation originating from a number of sources. This makes sudden and radical change less likely. Equally, voting systems such as first-past-the-post accentuate changes in popular preference and are likely to lead to relatively radical changes in government, as compared with proportional representation which tends to generate coalition governments.

As far as the *administrative system* is concerned, countries differ considerably in the capacity, tenure and degree of independence of their public servants. Thus in some countries, a change of government will lead to a major change in administrative personnel, including those involved in quasi-judicial functions, as well as ministers' policy advisors. In other countries, the bureaucratic system will demonstrate greater inertia, and key regulatory appointees may have been placed by Statute in positions of independence. Thus Directors General of UK regulatory agencies are appointed by the Secretary of State, generally for a five year period, and may not be dismissed except in the case of incapacity or malfeasance. As a result, the change of government in the UK in 1997 did not lead to any immediate change in the composition of the regulators. If, on the other hand, regulatory functions are discharged by departmental officials subject to rotation at will, this safeguard does not exist. This important distinction is quite separate from one based upon the level of competence of the officials involved, which places a limitation upon the degree of complexity of the regulatory issues which can be made subject to their discretion.

As far as the *legal system* is concerned, a country's regulatory endowment can differ in a number of important ways. They key element is, of course, the independence or lack of independence of the judiciary. Absent judicial independence, no legal safeguard is of value. Other important distinctions concern the development of administrative and contract law. A highly developed system of administrative law will diminish the risk of abuse of the administrative process. Equally, the availability of contracts between the government and the regulator, enforced by the Courts, is an alternative route to providing security for investors.

For illustrative purposes, we now describe some of the permutations of the Parliamentary, administrative and legal institutions which can be found in three countries outside Eastern Europe, as a prelude to discussing the problems which exist in relation to economies in transition.

The United Kingdom exhibits a highly centralized system of government, although increasingly subject to restraints imposed by its membership of the European Union. It is subject to radical alternations in the governing party. This is compensated to some extent by assigning substantial independence through existing legislation to independent regulatory agencies. But the independent regulators (single individuals) thus appointed have considerable discretionary power. They do not have to follow precedent, nor are they tied to any particular 'rate base' in setting prices. Although the system of administrative law is relatively undeveloped, there is little doubt about the independence of the judiciary. The contractual option described below has not been implemented. The overall framework is thus vulnerable to Parliamentary changes, but protected to some degree by the nonpartisan nature of the public service.

Jamaica, on the other hand, is also subject to swings in government composition, but lacks a tradition of independent regulation, although an Office of Utility Regulation has recently been established, with limited powers. The most dramatic events in Jamaica have concerned telecommunications regulation, where private investors in the 1970s were subject to what Spiller and Sampson (1996) refer to as quasi-expropriation. Following the withdrawal of the private operator, a new company, Telecommunications of Jamaica, was created, subject to licences which formalize a system of rate of return regulation subject to arbitration in the event of disagreement. In other words, the system relies primarily upon operating licences with an automatic arbitration procedure, supervized by an independent judiciary with a history of protection of property rights to give investors comfort.

In the United States, as a first approximation the system of sharing of powers between Congress and the Executive, and between Federal and State levels of government generates a degree of stability and inertia not found in either the United Kingdom or Jamaica. At the same time, the courts play a fundamental role in regulatory processes – not only policing procedural issues as in the UK, but enforcing property rights and an adequate return on capital, and in many cases taking over the substances of regulatory decision-making. The independent regulatory agencies themselves are, however, in some cases directly politically accountable, leading to a situation in which short-run political considerations may sometimes lead to breaches of the regulatory contract.

## Regulatory Design for Economies in Transition

What lessons does this analysis have for economies in transition? Clearly, as well as suffering from the weak infrastructure referred to above, such economies also have to develop institutional arrangements against a background of lack of trust and the absence of a properly developed 'civil society'. In terms of the characteristics of the three types of agent identified above, economies in transition typically have centralized states inherited from their previous existence, and electoral systems which, when combined with a relatively volatile electorate, produce transfers of power between rival parties or coalitions. In some states, notably Russia, this instability is blunted by the separation of powers between president and Parliament. Transfers of power do not necessarily mean a radical overhaul of policy towards utilities, nor to expropriation of private investors. Militating against this is a common desire among governments of all kinds to secure significant revenues, including foreign direct investment, from their highly valuable utility assets.

As far as the judiciary is concerned, economies in transition naturally vary in the degree of independence enjoyed by the judges and in the stability and level of development of their legal codes. As a generalization, however, it is unlikely that much reliance can be placed upon the judiciary to uphold property rights, especially in circumstances where commercial and property law are in a relatively early stage of development.

These two characteristics impose a heavy burden on the administrative system in generating favourable expectations on the part of investors concerning the security of their assets. Much of the discussion on this issue has revolved around the desirability of establishing independent regulatory agencies, which are capable of implementing necessarily somewhat vague legislative principles in a manner consistent with the implicit regulatory contract. This is contrasted with the alternative of regulation undertaken directly by Government departments, whose decisions are inseparable from those of the governing party.

Experience teaches, however, that there may be no real difference between these alternatives, unless the 'independent regulator' really enjoys security of tenure and an assured level of funding for him/her and others. However, the fact that independence can in some circumstances be subverted does not automatically undermine all arguments in its favour (Stern, 1997). In particular, independent regulators have more opportunities than a government official to gain legitimacy and power by seeking an independent political constituency for themselves by developing mechanisms for accountability to bodies other than the Government departments with which they are associated, and by seeking to protect their independence by developing transparent procedures. The first task would naturally be achieved by appealing to the constituency of consumers (as regulators in Western countries have done), although the task is made more difficult for regulators in economies in transition by the pricing policies likely to be required of them, discussed in the following sections. Alternative routes of accountability will depend upon the details of the legislation, but an independent regulator has an opportunity to develop a direct link with Parliament, which is absent when regulation is administered within a Government department. Thirdly, an independent regulator often has the capacity to develop its own procedures, which ideally will involve such familiar methods for publicizing decisions as a consultation process, open hearings, and the giving of reasons for decisions. Such procedures can make it more difficult for Governments or regulated firms to suborn the regulatory process for their own ends.

The analysis in this section has underlined the fragility of regulatory processes throughout the world. Because of uncertainties about the future, all long term contracts tend to be incomplete. Where they involve relations between investors in sunk assets and a second contracting party which is in some degree politically accountable, the uncertainties multiply. Perhaps a more surprising finding is that, as the evidence below shows, a number of alternative regimes exist which make it possible to implement the regulatory contract in a workable fashion.

But even against this general background of difficulty, the situation in economies in transition is particularly fraught. Their Parliamentary and legal systems are often embryonic, and their administrative capacities limited. The risk of loss of credibility is always present. Moreover, the decisions to be taken in relation to utilities are often hard and unpopular. We now illustrate these problems further with respect to the two sectors of telecommunications and energy.

## POLICY AND REGULATION TOWARDS TELECOMMUNICATIONS

### Policy Options

The telecommunications sector of economies in transition in Central and Eastern Europe and the former Soviet Union exhibited a discouraging picture in the early

1990s, with penetration rates of less than one-third the average of the OECD countries, and payphone access also extremely poor. Waiting lists for telephone lines were considerable, and in many countries average waiting times were between 5 and 15 years. Even those who had lines enjoyed very patchy service, with high levels of fault incidence and of call blocking. Some of these problems may be attributed to the outdated equipment to be found in the region, itself partly the consequence of Western technology embargoes that remained in place until the early 1990s.

Tariffs were also low and unbalanced, although comparisons of tariff are bedevilled by problems in obtaining meaningful exchange rates. At nominal exchange rates revenue per line in the former Soviet Union was only US$15 per year in 1992, compared with an average of US$1030 in the OECD countries. As in most European countries, but to an even greater degree, tariffs were unbalanced, with residential line rental typically less than US$40 per year and long distance and international call rates exceptionally high.

According to estimates made at the time, the attainment of Government objectives by the year 2000 would require an annual rate of line growth of 11 per cent and investment of over US$100 billion over the 1993–2000 period. This would raise penetration to roughly one-half the OECD average. It was clear that the internal resources of the region were quite inadequate to achieve these objectives. The shortfall not only covered finance but also the necessary technology and management skills. In the circumstances, designing a regulatory framework capable of encouraging the necessary investment became a key priority.

The strain placed upon the regulatory system would, however, depend upon the nature of the strategy employed. Given that the *status quo* was unacceptable, governments in economies in transition were faced by two main options – a radical strategy of immediately liberalizing markets or a more conventional strategy of allocating a temporary monopoly to the incumbent, accompanied by privatization through a trade sale to a consortium of overseas operators. Both of these will involve use of radio-based technologies (fixed or mobile), which can speed up the provision of service, diminish up-front investment, generate significant revenue given the high willingness to pay when waiting lists for fixed line service are high, and generate revenue for the government through the sale of franchises.

A study undertaken for the EBRD has evaluated these two alternatives, the characteristics of which are shown in Table 1 (Davies *et al.*, 1996). The study concluded that the desirability of the two alternatives in terms of standard welfare analysis depended significantly on the extent of network externality. The fast track privatization option gives the government an opportunity to require high levels of network build in the early stages which confer major benefits if there are network externalities. Clearly, however, any such comparisons depend critically upon the detailed assumptions made in the analysis.

A review of policies adopted in a sample of economies in transition shows a preference for the fast track privatization option. Table 2 indicates the nature of the policies adopted, in a selection of countries. All of them have adopted, or intend to adopt, a policy of privatization involving a strategic partner.

**Table 1.    The Two Principal Options**

| 1.  Competition |
| --- |
| • Immediate liberalization of all telecoms markets, including local and long distance telephony: mobile telephone, cable TV service providers, utility companies and others permitted to supply fixed telephony services. <br> • One-off increase in average price levels at the time of liberalization. <br> • TO prices remain subject to regulation until active competition erodes its market power. <br> • Rapid rebalancing of TO prices towards cost. |

| 2.  Fast-track Privatization |
| --- |
| • Fast-track privatization of TO. <br> • Sale of controlling interest in TO to a consortium including a western telecoms operator. <br> • Rights and obligations of privatized operator specified in licence or concession. <br> • TO retains a monopoly over telephony for 5–10 years; all other telecom markets opened up to competition. <br> • TO commits to ambitious targets for network expansion and service quality improvement. <br> • One-off increase in average price levels prior to privatization. <br> • TO subject to price cap regulation. <br> • Gradual rebalancing of prices towards costs. |

*Source*:    Adapted from Davies *et al.*, (1996).

In terms of the stresses placed upon the regulatory regime, fast track privatization requires the conclusion of a contract between the strategic investor and the regulatory body, the main elements of which cover pricing, the timing of the introduction of competition, and the speed of network build up. This contract can clearly go wrong in a number of ways. First, the network operator may exercise excessive control over the agreement reached, or to defer unnecessarily the introduction of competition. Alternatively, the government or regulatory may pratice an opportunistic policy of enforcing high network build targets, during which the operator incurs losses, and then reneging on agreements to defer competition, especially in profitable long-distance and international calls.

Table 2.　**Regulation and Privatization Strategies in Selected Countries**

| Country | Independent sector-specific agency | Strategy |
|---------|-----------------------------------|----------|
| Czech Republic | Yes | Strategic partner |
| Hungary | Yes | Strategic partner |
| Poland | No | Various |
| Slovakia | No | Strategic partner may be sought |

## The Regulatory Framework

The development of regulatory regimes to deal with these issues is still at an early stage. As Table 2 indicates, some countries have retained the sector-specific regulatory function within the relevant government department, where others have allocated it to an agency enjoying a degree of indpendence but largely confined to an advisory capacity. It is too early to say how these arrangements will work out.

In some countries the anti-monopoly authority has been more influential in the regulation of the sector than any sector-specific regulator. For example, in Poland, the anti-monopoly office has made a number of interventions in telecommunications markets. These include action requiring the dominant operator to provide access to underground telephone lines to potential competitors (Fingleton *et al.*, 1996, p. 120).

In summary, the design of a regulatory framework for telecommunications in economies in transition presents considerable challenges. Massive levels of investment are required, and a significant increase in the level and change in the structure of tariffs. In preference to using competition as an enforcer and demanding immediate rebalancing, governments have generally preferred the more gradual approach which relies upon an arrangement with a strategic partner, who makes a commitment to invest in the return for a temporary monopoly. Because of the potentially high profits available from the industry, there has been no shortage of strategic partners, and heavy competition among them for the franchise. This suggests that, so far, lack of certainty about the regulatory arrangements has not discouraged investment, although it may of course have increased the cost of capital. This is despite the fact that, on the face of it, the degree of protection provided to investors through the Parliamentary process, the administrative system and the Courts, is not particularly high.

## THE CASE OF SLOVAKIA

This section takes Slovakia as a case study for the relationship between regulatory policy, the transfer of ownership from the public to the private sector and the design of regulatory institutions intended to resolve the problems set out in Section 1 above. Slovakia is chosen as an example, because of a general recognition that its political, administrative and judicial circumstances create particularly stony ground for the achievement of a credible regulatory contract.

A variety of evidence can be provided to support this proposition. Firstly, the government created following the election in 1994, led by Prime Minister Meciar, has used its powers to attack the president, to weaken the opposition, and to pursue a limited policy of privatization which is widely regarded as furthering the private or partisan interests of government members (see Butora and Huncik 1997).

Because the regulation of utilities has continued to be carried out by the government, rather than by an independent agency, no attempt has yet been made to create an administrative framework for regulation free from direct government control. However, an attempt of this kind has been made with respect to competition, or, where an Anti-Monopoly Office was established to implement a competition law based, like those of many countries seeking accession to the European Union, on the competition provisions in the Treaty of Rome. Slovak arrangements were thus not dissimilar from those of the other three CEE countries examined in a careful comparative study by Fingleton *et al.*, (1996). However, the outcome in Slovakia differed from those in the other three countries. In those other countries, the President of the Office enjoyed comparatively long tenure and came to exercise a degree of authority in the field of economic policy-making. In Slovakia, by contrast, there is a quick turnover of officials, with four holders of the post of President in a four year period. In effect, the AMO, although nominally independent, found itself quite incapable of resisting government policy when that policy conflicted with the Office's interpretation of its legislative mandate. The ability of the government summarily to fire the President effectively made any apparent independence quite worthless.

This evaluation of the political arrangements in Slovakia is reinforced by the opinions of the European Commission published in mid-1997 concerning the applications for membership to the European Union presented by the ten candidate countries. In summary, Slovakia scored relatively highly against the economic criteria and in its capacity to assume membership obligations by assimilating the *acquis communautaire*. It scored poorly, however, on the political criteria, with the Commission judging that the Slovak government does not sufficiently respect powers devolved by the constitution to other bodies, and too often disregards the rights of the opposition. The report also notes that the fuller independence of the judicial system would ensure its functioning in satisfactory conditions, and that the fight against corruption needs to be pursued with greater effectiveness (*Transition* 1997).

This, then, was the rather inauspicious institutional background against which Slovakia has been attempting to promote further investments in its telecommunications network. Its situation is characteristic of the region, with low penetration rates, a significant waiting time, and relatively low productivity. Like other economies in transition, Slovakia has an ambitious plan, approved in 1995, to develop the sector by 2000. This should increase penetration to two-and-a-half times the 1991 level, and produce a predominantly digital network. Waiting times would be eliminated. The extent of progress to date towards these objectives is shown in Table 3.

**Table 3.   The Expansion of Slovak Telecommunications – 1993–96**

|  | 1993 | 1994 | 1995 | 1996 |
|---|---|---|---|---|
| Residential subscribers on analogue exchanges | 631,881 | 648,694 | 647,185 | 613,966 |
| Business subscribers on analogue exchanges | 214,729 | 205,070 | 184,037 | 162,341 |
| Residential subscribers on digital exchanges | 30,298 | 99,515 | 183,228 | 306,694 |
| Business subscribers on digital exchanges | 15,858 | 50,550 | 104,036 | 163,470 |
| Total | 892,766 | 1,003,829 | 1,118,468 | 1,246,471 |
| Number of employees | 15,491 | 15,367 | 15,306 | 15,374 |
| Revenue per Employee ($) | 14,700 | 17,100 | 19,400 | 26,200 |

*Source*:   Jurzyca, 1997.

As far as liberalization is concerned, the principles of the new law on telecommunications lay down that basic voice services will be liberalized from the beginning of 2003. Mobile competition already exists among three licensees, with Slovak Telecommunications playing a role both in the analogue system and in one of the two GSM licences granted in 1996. The other GSM licence is a joint venture of France Telecom mobile telecommunications and a number of Slovak firms, predominantly utilities. Competition in value added services already exists.

The reservation of the voice telephony service as a monopoly until 2003 clearly indicates that the Slovak government, like other governments, has not followed the path of immediate liberalization. Regulation is undertaken by the Ministry of Transportation, Post and Telecommunications of the Slovak Republic, with a telecommunications office undertaking some functions. Prices are regulated by the Ministry of Finance, which regulates prices for voice, data and value added services. The current government has the intention to turn over regulation to an independent agency, the powers and the composition of which have not yet been established.

In summary, the regulatory environment of the telecommunications sector in Slovakia is unstable and unpredictable. Despite this, however, a number of European operators have expressed a willingness to become a strategic partner in Slovak Telecommunications. According to Jurzyca (1997), citing a newspaper source, these include companies from the UK, Germany, The Netherlands and Denmark.

However, the company which has expressed the greatest interest is France Telecom, which already exercises some influence with the company and the Ministry. Despite the fact that any investment made by the strategic partner would be in a highly uncertain environment, there appears to be no shortage of candidates.

## CONCLUSIONS

This chapter began by utilizing the helpful framework developed by Spiller and his associates to identify the potential strength of institutional arrangements to sustain the regulatory contract in industries characterized by durable sunk investments. On the face of it, the requirements for this problem to be solved satisfactorily are fairly stringent: the contract has to be enforceable, must be invulnerable to post-contractual opportunism by one of the parties, and, for this reason, must be relatively explicit. Strict satisfaction of all these conditions is likely to be unattainable, not least because in the limit a government with control over parliament can enact legislation which overturns any contractual underpinnings to a regulatory contract, or, where enforcement is through administrative procedures rather than through a legal contract, a government may be able in practice to subvert the administrative process by personnel changes. By this standard, the development of satisfactory regulatory arrangements seems highly problematic even in countries like the United Kingdom or the USA which are often regarded as exhibiting relatively stable regulatory contracts which provide a reasonable amount of security to investors.

When the analysis is applied to economies in transition, the difficulties multiply. They are exacerbated by two forms of inheritance from the previous regime. One concerns weaknesses of the infrastructure built under socialism, which is inadequate in some sectors and poorly designed and operated in others. On top of these technical difficulties are inherited prices which are not only below cost but are also unbalanced, both with respect to groups of customers and with respect to the services provided.

The second damaging inheritance takes the form of new and untried parliamentary procedures, administrative personnel untested in the operation of market systems and a system of law which has to establish its independence as well as develop the statutes corresponding to a market economy. By any count, the task of developing regulator institutions in such economies seems an unusually difficult one.

Yet, despite these difficulties, economies in transition have so far encountered relatively few difficulties in attracting foreign direct investment. This applies both to the telecommunications sector and the energy sector, the experiences of which have been briefly summarized above. One would expect the return required from such investments to be higher than would apply in traditional market economies. But that still leaves open the question of why investors have been willing to invest at all, given the apparent risks of expropriation which they face.

A number of possible explanations can be found to this puzzle:

- In the case of the energy sector, over-capacity and massive waste of energy under the old regime has limited the need for further investment. As a result, Western investors have been able to limit their risks. This does not apply, however, to telecommunications where massive additional investments are required. But international experience shows that telecommunications is potentially a highly profitable industry. Investors must therefore balance the downside risk of expropriation against considerable upside opportunities.
- Many economies in transition are so large and have such potential for growth that companies are willing to take risks even against a background of regulatory uncertainty. A massive investment made by George Saros and his associates in the Russian long-distance operator Svyazinvest falls into this category. It is also noticeable that Western firms are eager to invest in China, despite continuing uncertainties concerning the country's commitment to privatization of the infrastructure, and a regulatory regime which is extremely opaque.
- All countries and governments will also be aware of reputational effects. A single blatant breach of the regulatory contract involving expropriation of foreign investors' sunk assets may jeopardise future prospects of foreign investment in all sectors subject to similar risk or even more broadly. So far, governments in economies in transition have apparently been prepared to preserve their countries' financial reputations, even in the case of short-term temptations in particular industries. Some firms may also be able to take retaliatory measures in the event of expropriation, in the limit by withdrawal of necessary technical inputs or by making it difficult for the networks concerned to get access to spare parts or upgrades.

These considerations still leave a number of countries potentially outside the fold. Such countries would typically be small, subject to economic stagnation, owning networks requiring considerable investment flows and having already lost their reputations for adhering to the regulatory contract, probably in the interests of short-term political or financial gain. The interesting thing is that Slovakia and its telecommunications sector appear to fit this picture very accurately, given the government's past behaviour in matters of privatization and the regulation of competition, and the bitterness of its domestic politics. The forthcoming privatization of Slovak Telecommunications will therefore be of greater than normal interest, for the information which it will provide on the availability and cost of foreign investment in privatized utilities. So far, however, foreign investors seem willing to make such investments, suggesting that the expected returns must at least equal their perception of the cost of capital. This may demonstrate that the problem of designing regulatory institutions can be more easily overcome than the analysis of Section 1 suggests. However, a longer period of experience is needed to resolve this issue in relation to economies in transition.

# REFERENCES

Botora, M. and Huncik, P. (eds). *Global on Slovakia*, Sandor Matai Foundation, Bratislava.

Cave, M. and Valentiny, P. (1994), 'Privatization and Regulation of Utilities in Economies in Transition' in S. Estrin (ed.). *Privatization in Central and Eastern Europe*, Longmans, London.

Davies, G. *et al.*, (1996), 'Technology and Policy options for the Telecommunications Sector. The Situation in Central and Eastern Europe and the Former Soviet Union', *Telecommunications Policy*, Vol. 20, No. 2, pp. 101–124.

Fingleton, J. *et al.*, (1996), *Competition Policy and the Transformation of Eastern Europe*, CEPR, London.

Jurzyca, E, (1997), *Prospects for Privatization of Slovak Telecommunications*, Mimeo, CFD, Bratislava.

Levy, B. and Spiller, P. (eds) (1996), *Regulations, Institutions and Commitment*, Cambridge University Press, Cambridge.

Major, I. (1992), 'Private and Public Infrastructure in Eastern Europe' *Oxford Review of Economic Policy*, Vol. 7, No. 4, pp. 76–92.

Spiller, P. and Sampson, C. (1996), 'Telecommunications Regulations in Jamaica', pp. 36–78 in Levy, B. and Spiller, P. (eds) *Regulations, Institutions and Commitment*, Cambridge University Press, Cambridge.

Stern, J. (1997), 'What Makes an Independent Regular Independent', *Business Strategy Review*, Vol. 8, No. 2, pp. 67–74.

Transition (1997), 'The Commission's report Card', *Transition*, Washington, DC: The World Bank, August, pp. 5–8.

# 4
# The Present Challenges of Competition Law and Policy in Central Eastern Europe

*Otto Heinz*

## INTRODUCTION

The following will try to show the challenges that competition law and policy have had to face – and indeed still face – in Central-Eastern Europe.

As regards the geographical scope of this chapter, two qualifications must be made: one is that most of the following will be confined to the countries of Central-Eastern Europe, including the Baltic States, as opposed to the countries of the former Soviet Union. Although a significant number of the challenges which are connected with the transformation of the economy are relevant throughout the whole region, the extent of these problems is rather different in the two parts of the region; and, most importantly, there is a considerable difference relating to possible EU integration as a relevant factor in shaping competition policy. The Czech Republic, Hungary, Poland, Slovakia, Slovenia, Romania, Bulgaria and the Baltic States have all concluded a so-called Europe Agreement with the European Union and its Member States. These documents envisage the possibility of a future EU accession, and give a quite detailed set of rules in preparation for this process. This has a significant impact on competition law and policy. This is not to say, however, that the efforts made by the states of the former Soviet Union in introducing competition legislation (competition law has been introduced, for example, in Georgia, Belarus, Ukraine and Kazahstan) are in any way insignificant; it simply means that the scope and nature of the problems are often different, and this chapter will focus more on the first group of countries.

The second qualification relating to the geographical scope of this chapter is that even though there will be constant references to other countries, and even though the problems mentioned are of a general nature, as a matter of consistency and transparency the following discussion will cite examples principally from one country, namely Hungary. Moreover, one of the central themes of the present chapter is the need for an integrated approach to competition law, and it is significantly easier to illustrate this using the example of one system. Again, however, the problems and the solutions are clearly of a general nature.

As for the time-scale covered, this chapter tries to summarize the experiences of the last six or seven years since the introduction of competition laws, and an attempt will be made to point out that there is a new stage being introduced after the first period. This requires some changes in the established approach towards competition law. This will partly be demonstrated by reference to the contemplated amendments of Hungarian competition law.

The structure of this chapter consists of two main parts: on the one hand it examines the external challenges of competition law in the region, while on the other it takes a look at the internal challenges of competition law as it relates to economic transition. The main external challenge under discussion is integration into the European Union, but mention will also be made of other, albeit less significant, external pressures for adjustment of competition law and policy such as membership of the Organization for Economic Cooperation and Development (OECD) or the Central European Free Trade Agreement (CEFTA). As for the internal challenges, the competition-related aspects of privatization and demonopolization will be in the foreground.

## EXTERNAL CHALLENGES

### Integration into the European Union

*Europe Agreements*

As mentioned above, most of the Central-Eastern European states concluded almost identical Europe Agreements with the EU and its member states in the course of 1994 and 1995 or, in the case of Slovenia, in 1996. To comply with these agreements, in return for the possibility of becoming full EU member states upon the expiry of these ten-year agreements, the associated countries must open up their markets to the EU and harmonize their laws with EU law, with special regard to EC competition and trade law. These provisions have, in fact, been in force through interim agreements since 1992.

The Europe Agreements, together with the subsequently enacted rules governing their implementation, are of relevance for competition law and policy in Central-Eastern Europe in two principal respects: on the one hand they serve as a basis for the harmonization of domestic competition laws with those of the EU, and on the other hand they lay down the basis for co-operation between the competition authorities of the EU and those of the associated states. This will be examined in what follows.

## i) Harmonization of competition laws

In the legal sphere, the Europe Agreements require the associated states to strive for complete harmonization of their respective national laws with EU law within ten years. This is regarded as a major condition for these countries' EU integration. The ten-year period is divided into two consecutive stages of five years. During the final year of the first stage, the respective Association Councils established under these agreements must decide upon the transition to the second stage of the harmonization programme. With regard to the timetable for such harmonization, mention must be made of the so-called White Book issued by the Commission in May 1995 and which, in the form of recommendations, contains an exact timetable for the implementation of EU legislation that is strictly related to the internal market.

As for competition law, the Europe Agreements directly incorporate the competition provisions of the Treaty of Rome, with special regard to Articles 85, 86 and 92. In strictly legal terms it has been uncertain to what extent secondary legislation of the EU relating to competition law should also be considered in the implementation of the Europe Agreements. However, it has become increasingly clear – especially since the issue of the White Book – that it was pragmatically and politically desirable to interpret the aforementioned obligations in an extended way, and also to incorporate the relevant directives and regulations into the legal order of the associated states. This of course means a very detailed harmonization process, and even includes the adaptation of the jurisprudence of the European Court and the European Commission.

In Hungary, for instance, the Act of Parliament[1] which promulgated the Europe Agreement imposed an obligation on Government to inform Parliament whenever a draft law is presented which falls within the scope of the Europe Agreement. Proposals are scrutinized to determine whether they are compatible with Community legislation and/or whether they achieve approximation to EU rules. There is a Government Resolution[2] which sets out a work plan based on a comprehensive law harmonization programme. In the area of competition law, the Law on Competition of 1990,[3] which was already based on EC competition law, has recently been amended[4] to reflect further requirements dictated by EC law. The government is at present contemplating issuing eight block exemptions exactly covering the areas covered by the block exemptions issued by the Commission under Article 85(3)EC.

## ii) Co-operation between the EU and the associated states

As a result of the legal reforms inspired by the Europe Agreements, the competition laws of the associated states will increasingly resemble the competition laws of the EU and its member states. However, it is also vital that the reform is implemented and there is institutionalized co-operation between the EU and the associated states. The Europe Agreements foresaw this need when they envisaged that the Association Councils should adopt measures implementing the competition provisions of the Europe Agreements within three years after the entry into force of these agreements. Indeed, the lack of such measures has made it extremely difficult up until now to interpret the competition provisions of these agreements properly, and to put them into practice. These implementing rules are being adopted this year by the Association Councils under the different Europe Agreements.[5] Although adopted separately, these rules are expected to be identical.

At the heart of the implementing measures are the rules regulating the methods of co-operation. The forms of co-operation are dependent on how competence is distributed between the competition authorities of the EU and the associated states. As a general rule, the competition authorities of both sides (DG IV of the Commission and the competition authority of the associated states) shall deal with cases involving any breach of the competition provisions of the Europe Agreements according to their own rules.

In cases that may affect both the Community and the market of the associated states, and which may fall within the competence of both competition authorities, the competition authorities are required to notify each other, allowing the other authority sufficient time and providing sufficient information to facilitate comments or consultations and to enable the proceeding authority to take into account the other authority's views, as well as to take such remedial action as it may find feasible under its own laws. Whenever one of the authorities considers that anti-competitive activities carried out on the territory of the other authority substantially affect important interests of the party in question, it may request consultation with the other authority, or it may request that the other party's competition authority initiate any appropriate procedures in order to take remedial action under its legislation. The competition authority so addressed should give full and sympathetic consideration to such views, and a mutually acceptable solution must be sought.

In cases falling within the exclusive competence of one competition authority, whenever the proceeding competition authority finds that the case affects important interests of the other party, it shall notify the other authority without formal request by the latter. The latter authority may request information about this case – unless it is contrary to the significant interests of the authority possessing the information.

A further important provision of these rules is that they make it a legal obligation that the block exemption regulations in force in the Community be applied in full. The competition authority of the associated state shall be informed of any procedure relating to the adoption, abolition or modification of block exemptions by the Community.

Finally, it is to be noted that these implementing rules also play a role in merger cases. If a merger case falling under the EC Merger Regulation[6] has a significant impact on the economy of the associated state, the competition authority of this state shall be entitled to express its views in the course of the procedure, taking into account the time limits as provided for in the Regulation. The Commission shall give due consideration to such views. This provision – if properly applied – is significant because it gives to the associated states the possibility of influencing to some extent competition decisions in the EU.

## Possible Conflicts of Interest
### i) State aid

One understandable source of conflict in the area of competition law is state aid. State aid has possibly greater significance in the case of a former socialist country, where reallocation of income was the organizing principle of the economy.[7] Under the Europe Agreement the associated states undertook the obligation to follow the principles of Article 92(EC) relating to state aid. However, recognizing the difficulties of transition, the Europe Agreements provide that, during the first five years, any public aid granted by the associated states will be assessed under Article 92(EC) as aid to 'promote the economic development of areas where the standard of living is abnormally low or where there is serious unemployment.' In EC law this does not automatically exempt such aid from the prohibition of Article 92(1)EC; rather, it gives the possibility to the Commission to exempt such aid. The area of state aid is likely to remain the area where there will be the most conflict between the EU and the associated states.

### ii) Vertical restraints

Another point where there has been conflict in competition policy between the requirements of EU integration and the needs of market economy development in the associated states is the question of vertical restraints.[8] There has already been a great deal of debate about the question of whether it is desirable in EC law itself to prohibit vertical agreements too. There are several economic arguments supporting the view that, while the prohibition of horizontal restraints is desirable, such a prohibition relating to vertical agreements is not justifiable.[9]

However, the Commission added an unusual objective of competition policy: the promotion of single market integration. There is considerable political pressure on the part of the Commission to make the associated states amend their competition laws in such a way as to prohibit vertical agreements too. This would certainly serve the objective that businesses should face very similar rules in the field of competition both inside and outside the EU. Especially initially, however, when transition required the possibility of establishing new distribution networks and vertical co-operation, it was desirable that vertical agreements were not prohibited. Furthermore, the strength of the political argument for integration was also weaker when it came to such concessions, until the real political will to allow accession to go ahead in the foreseeable future could be felt from EU side. In the meantime, however, the situation seems to have changed in some of the Central-Eastern European countries. Arguably, vertical links between the new enterprises are already formed, and politically there seems to be a readiness that was not there before regarding the accession of the associated states. This is also reflected in the amendment of Hungarian competition law already mentioned, which would prohibit vertical agreements. This, however, makes the simultaneous introduction of block exemptions into the system essential in order to ensure that justifiable vertical agreements are granted exemption. Since in the EU, Community law enjoys priority over national law, and it also has direct applicability in member states, which is not the case in the case of associated states, it is therefore fair to say that sometimes a stricter harmonization of domestic competition laws is necessary in the case of the associated states in contrast to member states.

## Other International Co-operation

### CEFTA

The Central European Free Trade Agreement was entered into by the Czech Republic, Hungary, Poland, Slovak and Slovenia. Romania, Bulgaria and Lithuania have officially submitted applications to join the Agreement. Even though the main concern of CEFTA was obviously trade liberalization, it also contains provisions on competition law. Thus Article 22 of the CEFTA provides that it is incompatible with the Agreement if – to the extent it affects trade between the parties – there is such an agreement or concerted practice between companies, the objective or effect of which is to restrain or distort competition. The abuse of dominant position by one or more companies in the whole or a significant part of the territory of the parties is also considered to be incompatible with the Agreement. These provisions also include rules on state enterprises and companies entrusted with special rights. Article 23 deals with state aid, and declares that any aid provided from state resources, in whatever form, that distorts or threatens to distort competition by favouring certain firms or the production of certain goods, is incompatible with the Agreement to the extent it affects trade between the parties.

All these provisions follow closely the relevant provisions of the Europe Agreement, and apply them in the context of the CEFTA States. This is definitely a very positive sign because, besides the enhancement of trade between these countries which have a very similar level of development, the enhancement of co-operation in preparation for EU integration in – among other areas – the area of competition law, would also be very important. Unfortunately, the solution adopted in the case of the EFTA states in the European Economic Area Agreement, where a common EFTA Surveillance Authority was set up to monitor the implementation of the competition provisions of the EEA Agreement, did not take place in this instance. This was not realistic due to the lack of institutionalized co-operation between the CEFTA countries in contrast to that existing among the EFTA states.

### OECD

Mention must also be made of the fact that the accession of the Czech Republic, Hungary and Poland to the OECD also contributed to the reform of the competition rules of these countries. The OECD has played an active role in initiating co-operation between Central-Eastern European countries in the area of competition law. Furthermore, competition law also had to be taken into account when the application of these countries was accepted by the OECD.

# INTERNAL CHALLENGES

## Privatization

### *Merger Control*

Privatization can bring about the creation of increased market concentration. There is therefore an obvious problem that competition law has a role in tackling. The market structures in these countries with formerly centrally planned economies are often very concentrated anyway, and if state monopolies are sold as a whole this concentration is preserved. Sometimes it may happen that competing firms are sold to the same investor. Foreign investors are willing to pay a premium for such a position, and the need for extra income from privatization could create a dangerous conflict of interests. On the other hand, however, privatization may even be used to reduce concentration through decentralized selling, which demonstrates the significance of an appropriate privatization policy as a part of competition policy. It causes an additional difficulty, from the point of view of competition, that there is a strong need to generate as much revenue as possible from privatization regardless of the consequences in connection with market concentration at times. There are also efficiency considerations that could conflict with competition during privatization. Because of the small size of the Hungarian market, for example, economies of scale exceed the national borders in the case of several products. In other words, the minimum efficient scale of production is often much larger than what would correspond to serving the domestic market alone.

It is interesting to examine the argument according to which the success story of Hungary as a destination for foreign direct investment (FDI) is due to the fact that the country gave away dominant positions during privatization. This view seems to be supported by the fact that as regards the traditional motivating aspects of FDI, the Czech Republic and Poland are clearly in a better position, yet there is significantly more FDI coming to Hungary. However, analysis of the markets in Hungary does not seem to support this view. Privatization did not, in fact, bring about market concentration. This is partly due to increased trade liberalization (brought about by the Europe Agreement, CEFTA and the GATT) that dismantled existing barriers of entry. The analysis of FDI in Hungary from the point of view of market concentration shows the following result (Table 1):[10]

**Table 1. FDI and Market Concentration in Hungary**

| | |
|---|---|
| Because of the nature of the market concentration could not be created: | 42% |
| Natural monopolies: | 29% |
| Market power could have been created or inherited but it did not take place: | 14% |
| Market power was created or inherited | 15% |

This table shows that only in 15 per cent of the cases did FDI create or inherit a dominant market position, which certainly does not justify the hypothesis mentioned above about FDI in Hungary. Even so, it cannot be denied that competition policy has to tackle this issue, especially in countries with a less liberal trade policy. In Hungary, although representatives of the Office of Economic Competition (OEC) are able to make their voice heard when privatization decisions are made, their real opportunity to intervene is when it comes to merger control. Having analysed the experiences of merger control in Hungary, however, competition policy has clearly not been effective enough in this regard. This is largely because of a shortcoming of the present Law on Competition.[11] In most of the cases of mergers relating to FDI it was established that these do not fall within the scope of Hungarian competition law because control was acquired by a foreign investor who had not previously carried on economic activity in Hungary. There were several such cases in the course of the privatization of the energy sector.[12] The recent amendment to competition law[13] overcomes this problem since it introduces the doctrine of effect: even if the activity of a company is exercised abroad it can be caught by Hungarian competition law in the event that it has an effect in the territory of Hungary.[14]

Despite the aforementioned constraint on competition policy, there had also been merger cases previously in the practice of the OEC that involved issues of privatization. In the Balatonboglár Case,[15] Company A, as the winner of the tender, was expected to buy 51 per cent of the shares of Company B from the State Property Agency. As the transaction exceeded the thresholds fixed by the competition law, the parties therefore applied for the permission of the OEC. Similarly to the practice of the Commission, the decision whether to permit a merger to go ahead is based on an evaluation of the positive and negative effects of an actual merger on competition. In the present case it was established that the high market share of Company A would be further enhanced by the acquisition of control in Company B. However, the OEC attached importance to the fact that the acquisition of decisive influence would take place through privatization. Also taken into consideration was the fact that in the event of permission not being granted Company B would most likely go bankrupt, and that it was therefore not possible to conclude that refusing permission would have a better effect on competition than letting the merger go ahead. Based on these considerations the OEC decided to grant permission.

It is interesting to contrast this decision with another one relating to merger control and privatization. In the Gasztrolánc Case[16] the situation was similar to the previous case: Company A intended to buy 51 per cent of the shares of Company B from the State Property Agency as the winner of a tender. However, the main difference between this and the Balatonboglár Case was that in the present case the companies were by far the two strongest competitors in their market. It was concluded by the OEC that it would seriously harm competition if Company A were to acquire decisive influence in its biggest competitor, even if, as a result, Company

B were prevented from being privatized. The granting of permission would, according to the OEC, only be justifiable if the firm to be privatized went bankrupt, as was the situation in the Balatonboglár Case. Company B, however, was a well functioning state enterprise that had been able to develop in response to growing competition in recent years, even in state ownership. By granting permission competition would be considerably reduced. Therefore, permission was refused.

Considering the two cases together one can conclude that privatization as such does not enjoy priority over competition. Privatization is certainly a factor to consider in merger cases but the principles of merger control apply to issues of privatization too.

## State Aid

Privatization can also be problematic from the point of view of state aid. As mentioned earlier, the Europe Agreements contain a commitment on the part of the associated states not to follow practices that are incompatible with the principles laid down in Article 92(EC). According to the practice of the Commission there are two main sources of conflict concerning state aid during privatization. The first case is when the state uses state aid to make its firms saleable, the second is when the state-owned firm is sold under value, thereby providing state aid. Since there is usually no specific domestic legislation on state aid, it is therefore worth having a look at the policy framework created by the Commission on the issue.

### i) State aid to shape up firms

It is very common to provide help to firms to be privatized through capital injection, debt write-offs or conversion of debt into equity. The standpoint of the Commission is that the most important issue is whether the actual selling takes place according to standard market practice. If this is ensured then it is possible to negotiate with the Commission[17] about state aid provided to shape up firms before privatization. In the light of the practice of the Commission[18] it seems that privatization itself does not directly justify state aid measures. However, it does enjoy a favourable attitude on the part of the Commission, and state aid of this kind during privatization may be exempted under Article 92(3)(b), promoting the execution of an important project of common European interest.

### ii) State aid by selling under value

The standpoint of the Commission in this regard is that 'the sale of public enterprises may give rise to aid if it is not carried out in a fully transparent manner and in particular if bids are not invited or conditions are imposed on the sale by public authorities.'[19] In other words no aid is involved where shareholdings are sold to the highest bidder as a result of an open and unconditional bidding procedure. The following requirements can be set out in this regard:

- the sale should be effected in a public tender;
- the sale should be effected under transparent and non-discriminatory conditions;
- the valuation of the company should be carried out by independent advisors;
- if the public tender procedure fails, the Commission must receive prior notification of any negotiated procedure for the sale of ailing companies.

This practice of the Commission reflects the market economy investor principle applied by the Commission. It can be regarded as rational marketing behaviour on the part of the state to make the firms to be sold more attractive to potential buyers, even through subsidies. However, selling under value cannot be regarded as the rational market behaviour of a private investor. It is important to note that in the light of experience not even the first phase is exempted automatically from EU state aid rules, it is only assessed more favourably by the Commission.

### Anti-Cartel Regulation

Another special consequence of predominant state ownership is that competition law cannot properly apply the economic unit concept, which is the usual approach to groups of companies under the same ownership. It has been indispensable for agreements between state-owned companies also to be subjected to strict scrutiny to ascertain whether they constitute a cartel, despite the fact that parties to the agreement belong to the same economic unit. Now that, in some of these countries, privatization is close to being completed, this is no longer necessary and it is possible to switch to the usual approach and exempt these agreements. This development is reflected in the recent amendment of Hungarian competition law.

## Other Challenges

Mention must also be made of a number of further challenges that competition law and policy have faced, and must still face, in economies in transition besides the problems mentioned earlier.

One such aspect is the extensive black economy. It is questionable to what extent one can expect companies to abide by higher standards in their market behaviour when they have to face strong competition from rivals who do not undertake to comply even with the basics of market regulation.

Another particular aspect is the increased need for foreign investment. There is an incentive, therefore, to enforce or regulate more leniently or to put aside considerations of competition when privatizing, especially when a foreign investor might be involved.

In a market economy which is in the process of being formed the need for consumer protection is increasingly present. This is reflected, for example, in the Hungarian Law on Competition, since a significant part of its provisions contain rules prohibiting fraud against consumers.

In almost all of these countries there has been relatively high inflation. In the uncertain environment of high inflation it is more difficult to distinguish between purely parallel behaviour and concerted practice.[20]

A similar problem in transition economies is the unavailability of data. As business contacts are being broken up and statistical and other information systems being transformed dramatically, it is increasingly difficult to obtain proper data; and this applies also to the competitors in given markets, and to the competition authorities.

## SUMMARY AND CONCLUSIONS

In conclusion, it is clear that there are several challenges that competition law and policy have to face in Central-Eastern Europe which are different from the usual challenges facing competition law in traditional market economies. The two most important such challenges are European integration and privatization. This also means that sometimes it is not possible to give solutions based solely on classical competition theories.

It is a very important conclusion that in the highly concentrated, closed and turbulent economies of the post-socialist countries there is a strong need for an integrated, broadly defined competition policy which also includes privatization policy, trade policy and to some extent even foreign policy. Only a consistent and long-term approach can help to achieve the desired results.

It is also to be pointed out that competition law seems to have arrived at a milestone, at least in Central Europe. This is reflected, for instance, in the recent amendment of Hungarian competition law. The first, introductory phase of establishing competition law is over. Most importantly, the two dominant elements of the environment of these competition laws seem to have changed. Privatization is close to completion,and this takes a great burden off the shoulders of competition policy. Also significant is the fact that the market players have by now established themselves, set up their distribution networks, and the environment is considerably less turbulent than it was. As for the external side of the environment, the European integration process has also arrived at a new stage. The first years after the changes in the early 90s were years of waiting. Even though such important arrangements were made as entering into the Europe Agreements, it was nevertheless unclear what weight these documents can carry, how they will be interpreted and, in general, what are the chances of accession of the associated states.

Even though many details are still unclear, there now, however, seems to be at least a clear political will and a decision about the accession of the Central-Eastern European states may be expected in the foreseeable future. The acceptance and the nature of the implementing rules of the Europe Agreements, and the issue of the

White Book are all signs of this development. This also has important consequences for competition law in the region. It is significantly more justifiable to make competition law and policy more EU-oriented, even making more concessions, when the rewards and the objectives of these efforts are reasonably clear.

## NOTES

1. Law No. I of 1994.
2. Government Resolution No. 2174/1995 (15 June).
3. Law No. LXXXVI of 1990 on the Prohibition of Unfair Business Practices.
4. Law No. LVII of 1996 on the Prohibition of Unfair Business Practices and Restriction of Competition.
5. For example, Decision No. 1/96 (of 30 January 1996) of the Association Council of the European Communities and their Member States, on the one hand, and the Czech Republic on the other. (OJ L 31/21 of 9.2.1996.)
6. Council Regulation (EEC) No. 4064/89 of 21 December 1989.
7. Kovács (1996).
8. For more detail see: Sárai (1996).
9. Wish (1994).
10. For details see: Kovács and Pogácsás (1996), p. 50.
11. See note 3.
12. See: Annual Report of the Office of Economic Competition to Parliament in 1996. Cases Vj-224/1995, Vj-239/1995, Vj-241/1995, Vj-242/1995, Vj-243/1995, Vj-244/1995.
13. See note 4.
14. Article 1 of Law No. LVII. See note 4.
15. Case Vj-236/1994.
16. Case Vj-172/1994.
17. XXIst Commission Report on Competition Policy, point 251.
18. European Business Law Review, March 1992, p. 78; XXth Commission Report on Competition Policy, point 251.
19. XXIInd Commission Report on Competition Policy, point 464.
20. Vissi (1991).

## REFERENCES

Hampton, C. (1992), 'Commission Examines a Series of Aids in the New German Länder and Berlin', *European Business Law Review*, March, p. 78.
Kovács, C. (1996), 'Hungarian Competition Policy during Transition and Competition Policy for the Integration', paper for the Conference on 'Rules of Competition for the Economic Integration of Countries in Transition into the EU', Freiberg, Germany, July 5–6.
Kovács, C. and Péter P. (1996), 'Szépek és erösek?', Figyelõ (tr. = Observer), 13 June, p. 50.

Sárai, J. (1996), 'Some Questions of the Introduction of Prohibition on Vertical Agreements into the Hungarian Competition Act', conference paper, May.

Vissi, F. (1991), 'A versenypolitika', in *Versenypolitika és Arszabályozás*, Budapest.

Wish, R. (1994), *Competition Law*, 1994.

**Part II**

**Central Europe**

# 5
# Employee Ownership in Polish Privatizations

*Domenico Mario Nuti*[1]

## POLISH PRIVATIZATIONS

Large scale privatization of state assets is *the* distinctive feature of the recent transformation of Central Eastern European economies, with respect to *all* earlier attempts at reforming the Soviet-type system. Poland was among the first in announcing it (September 1989) and launching it (with the Law on Privatization of State Enterprises, 13 July 1990); Hungary's earlier initiative (1988) was designed to regulate spontaneous private appropriation by insiders rather than to radically transform the system, while Yugoslavia's 1989 privatization law applied to a different ownership regime. Poland already had a significant private sector on the eve of transformation, not only in agriculture but also in non-agricultural sectors. In 1989 private agriculture amounted to 75 per cent of the land, about 10 per cent of GDP and 21 per cent of employment (see Rapacki and Linz, 1992); in the 1980s non-agricultural private activities trebled to about 10 per cent of GDP and employment, including manufacturing as well as traditionally private activities such as trade, catering, services.

In 1990–96 the Polish private sector expanded fast, reaching over 65 per cent of employment, but primarily through what has been variously called 'organic growth' or 'grass-roots privatization', i.e., the growth of existing private activities and the rise and growth of *de novo* firms, rather than through the fast transfer of state assets to new private owners, domestic or foreign. In many ways such transfers have followed a different course from that originally anticipated.

First, the privatization process has been *slower* than planned. The early 1990 target of privatizing 50 per cent of state enterprises by the end of 1992, later moved to the end of 1995 (Rapacki, 1995, p. 57; Monkiewicz, 1996), has not been achieved. By end-1995 there were still over half of the initial state-owned enterprises (4,563 out of 8,453), not to count wholly Treasury-owned joint-stock and other limited liability companies (*jednoosobowa spolka Skarbu Panstwa*, or jsSP) and incomplete privatizations; completed privatizations amounted to only about one fifth (see Table 1). The market value of the residual state sector is controversial, but its book value is of the order of 75 billion zlotys[2]; in 1995 among the 100 largest Polish enterprises, 19 were state-owned, 35 were wholly Treasury-owned joint stock companies, and 17 were mixed ownership companies with dominant state ownership (OECD, 1997).

Second, privatization has followed a *multi-track course* through the accretion of new methods adopted to overcome unexpected difficulties as they arose. Initially the dominant method was to be a western style 'indirect' or 'capital' privatization, involving open sales of shares and the search for a strategic outside investor. This proved to be slower, costlier and harder than anticipated: in the words of Janusz Lewandowski, twice Minister for privatization, '*In the transition, privatization is a process whereby assets whose real owners are not known and whose real value is uncertain are sold to people who do not have the money to buy them*'. To resolve the problems of lack of liquid savings – pulverized by high inflation at the inception of the Polish transformation – and of asset valuation, a mass privatization scheme was devised, which technically is another form of 'capital' privatization. This track was held up by political and technical delays (see Nuti, 1994), launched by the Law on National Investment Funds (NIFs) and their privatization (30 April 1993), and implemented in 1996. It involves the distribution to adult Poles, on request and for a token payment, of certificates in 15 NIFs, to which 60 per cent of the shares of 512 'commercialized' state enterprises have been allocated (see OECD 1997, Annex IV)[3].

Meanwhile, many insolvent state enterprises were being closed down and sold off to private buyers, as a whole or in bits and pieces, according to art. 19 of the old Law on State Enterprises of 25 September 1981.[4] Other, economically viable state enterprises were being sold or leased, also as a whole or in parts, to private buyers and consortia of buyers, with priority granted to new companies formed with employee participation; this was allowed by the 1990 Privatization Law, art. 37 (enterprise assets could also be contributed to a new company, without preference for employees). The two processes reflected radically different, indeed opposite, underlying economic situations; however they had in common the so-called 'liquidation' of state enterprises, in the literal technical sense of their cancellation by the Tribunal from the registry of state enterprises. This is why these two forms of 'direct' privatization are often lumped together in Polish classifications.[5] A significant difference between the two kinds of 'liquidation' is the much higher rate of completion for art. 37 privatization (92 per cent *versus* 29 per cent of art. 19 procedures, see Table 1).

Further channels of privatization were opened by the Law of 3 February 1993 on Financial Restructuring of State Enterprises and Banks,[6] which leads to privatization through debt-equity swaps, often as a pre-condition of access to central funds; technically this is yet another form of 'capital' privatization. A Law on the Commercialization of state enterprises, involving their generalized transformation into joint stock companies, regardless of their privatization prospects, has had a difficult course and by mid-1996 was not yet operational: approved by Parliament, hit by a Presidential veto overturned by Parliament, successfully denounced to the Constitutional Tribunal, this law is to be reconsidered in a new draft.

**Table 1.   Progress of Ownership Transfer, Poland 1990–96 – Cumulative Number of Enterprises at the End of Each Year**

| | 1990 | 1991 | 1992 | 1993 | 1994 | 1995 | 1996 I–IX |
|---|---|---|---|---|---|---|---|
| Total number of state-owned enterprises | 8453 | 8228 | 7245 | 5924 | 4955 | 4563 | 3993 |
| Liquidation | | | | | | | |
| Started | 49 | 989 | 1576 | 1999 | 2287 | 2507 | 2708 |
| Completed | 0 | 201 | 561 | 893 | 1248 | 1450 | 1656 |
| Article 19 of the SOE Law | | | | | | | |
| Started | 18 | 540 | 857 | 1082 | 1845 | 1358 | 1428 |
| Completed | 0 | 19 | 86 | 186 | 303 | 396 | 518 |
| Article 37 of the Privatization Law | | | | | | | |
| Started | 31 | 449 | 719 | 917 | 1042 | 1149 | 1280 |
| Completed | 0 | 182 | 475 | 707 | 945 | 1054 | 1138 |
| Converted into joint-stock companies of which: | 38 | 260 | 480 | 527 | 723 | 958 | 1049 |
| NIF programme | 0 | 0 | 0 | 0 | 0 | 321 | 512 |
| Capital privatization | 6 | 27 | 51 | 99 | 134 | 160 | 180 |
| Public offerings | 5 | 11 | 12 | 15 | 19 | 22 | |
| Trade Sales | 1 | 16 | 39 | 81 | 110 | 132 | |
| Mixed methods | 0 | 0 | 0 | 3 | 5 | 6 | |
| Total | | | | | | | |
| Started | 93 | 1276 | 2107 | 2625 | 3144 | 3625 | 3770 |
| Completed | 6 | 228 | 612 | 992 | 1382 | 1610 | 1872 |
| Revenue from privatization (flows, mn zl.) | ... | 170.9 | 484.4 | 780.4 | 1594.8 | 2641.7 | 3115 |
| In per cent of GDP | ... | 0.21 | 0.42 | 0.50 | 0.76 | 0.91 | 1.15 |
| Leasing and sale of liquidated assets | | 46.4 | 171.8 | 287.0 | 322.9 | 406.2 | 640 |
| Capital privatization | | 124.5 | 308.7 | 439.4 | 846.7 | 1714.2 | 2285 |
| Bank privatization | | 0.0 | 3.9 | 54.0 | 425.2 | 521.3 | 830 |

*Source*:   Ministry of Ownership Transformation. From OECD, 1997.

In Polish practice, state enterprises 'involved in ownership transformation' are defined to include those registered as jsSPs, those whose art. 37 liquidation has been initiated (regardless of approval by the Ministry for Ownership Transformation or MPW), and those whose art. 19 liquidation has been initiated by their Founding Organization. At the end of 1995 the relative weights of the three categories was 26.8 per cent, 33.2 per cent and 40 per cent (see also Table 2, from MPW, 1996, whose data have been slightly revised by the Ministry with respect to those in Table 1).

Third, *all Polish privatization tracks involved some form, often very significant, of employee ownership.* This unexpected and important feature of privatization in Poland, replicated almost everywhere else in transition economies except for the Czech and Slovak Republics, is the object of this paper, reviewing the modes and reasons for employee ownership, the implications predicted by theory, actual performance, problems and prospects.

## EMPLOYEE OWNERSHIP: MODES AND MOTIVES

Employees of enterprises privatized following the 'indirect' or 'capital' track were offered 20 per cent of capital equity at half price, subject to a maximum of one year's wage; this was later transformed into a 10 per cent free share, subsequently raised to 15 per cent. Moreover, four such enterprises were the object of Managers' and Employees' Buy-Outs (MEBOs). In general 15 per cent of the capital of state enterprises privatized through mass privatization, as well as other commercialized enterprises, is reserved to employees (and in some cases also to farmers and fishermen who had a contractual relation with the enterprise – an interesting protection of 'stakeholders' other than employees).

'Direct' privatization, sometimes called 'restructuring' privatization, also led to employee ownership. By the end of 1994, 9 enterprises were sold/leased to employees and managers under Art. 19 liquidation, but the most common channel for employee ownership was art. 37 liquidation, which turned out to be the single fastest privatization track (see Gomulka and Jasinski, 1994). Typically these MEBOs were management-led, rather than pure employee or management buy-outs (Filatotchev *et al.*, 1996, p. 68). Out of a total of 140 enterprises sold under article 37, employees became sole owners of 9 enterprises and dominant shareholders of a further 20 (Filatotchev *et al.*, 1996, p. 72). Mostly, however, MEBOs took the form of a lease-purchase agreement, or rather a lease with an option to purchase, by a company established by at least 50 per cent of employees; ownership would be transferred after cumulative rentals matched the stipulated capital value and interest. *'Being the least conflictual, this [employee leasing] was the most frequent form of direct privatization. To the end of 1995, 788 enterprises followed this track, corresponding to 68.6 per cent of directly privatized enterprises'* (MPW, 1996, p. 24).

The most significant aspect of these MEBOs is credit, both by 'Founding Organs' agreeing on delayed payments, and by others for the provision of employees' initial down payment of 20 per cent of the book value of the enterprise. Apart from employee savings, this down payment was financed from a variety of sources: banks and non-bank financial intermediaries (such as venture capital firms), credit from enterprise own funds, special enterprise funds set up to support employee ownership.[7]

In general, the sectors more significantly affected by MEBOs and other forms of employee ownership have not been those which required restructuring most badly, such as mining, metallurgy and power generation, but instead those more traditionally favourable to employee ownership and participation, such as construction, trade and services (see Jarosz, 1994a and b; Table 2 also provides some indication of sectoral trends, incomplete due to excessive aggregation of the industrial sector).

Table 2.  Enterprises Involved in Ownership Transformations by Sector, Poland End 1995, and their Growth Rates in 1995

| Sectors | Total | | Art. 19 Liquid. | | Art. 37 Liquid. | | jsSP | |
|---|---|---|---|---|---|---|---|---|
| | n | growth % | n | growth % | n | growth % | n | growth % |
| National economy | 3465 | 15.1 | 1358 | 9.1 | 1149 | 10.3 | 958 | 32.5 |
| Industry | 1594 | 19.5 | 411 | 3.8 | 388 | 10.9 | 795 | 35.2 |
| Construction | 861 | 10.2 | 367 | 15.0 | 383 | 5.8 | 111 | 11.0 |
| Agriculture | 340 | 12.6 | 270 | 9.8 | 67 | 24.1 | 3 | 50.0 |
| Forestry | 18 | 5.9 | 9 | 0 | 6 | 0 | 3 | 50.0 |
| Transport | 175 | 9.4 | 126 | 2.4 | 30 | 30.4 | 19 | 35.7 |
| Communications | 1 | 0 | 0 | – | 1 | 0 | 0 | – |
| Trade | 311 | 12.7 | 99 | 8.8 | 189 | 10.5 | 23 | 64.3 |
| Other | 165 | 18.7 | 76 | 24.6 | 85 | 13.3 | 4 | 33.3 |

See text for the definition of headings.
*Source*:  MPW, 1996.

Polish experience with employee ownership matches that of most transition economies. The last thing that the new post-communist leaders everywhere – from Balcerowicz to Gaidar – wished to promote was precisely the emergence of significant forms of employee ownership. This was reminiscent of Yugoslav self-management, western socialist programmes and the search for a 'Third Way' – intermediate between straight capitalism and the old Soviet type system – which they firmly rejected. Thus in 1990 the Polish Privatization Minister, Krzysztof Lis, actually wrote to the British Embassy complaining that the support given by the British Know How Fund to employees' companies was against Polish government policy (Kowalik, 1994). In June 1991 Leonid Grigoryev and Evgeny Yasin regarded the birth of an employee-controlled economy as one of the dangers of voucher privatization (quoted by Sutela, 1994). The Russian Privatization Minister, Anatoly Chubais (1993), stressed that the Russian government was strongly opposed to any privatization procedures that would imply a give-away of enterprise shares to insiders. At the Davos Forum of March 1994, Grigory Yavlinsky could refer to Russian mass privatization, dominated by employee and managerial ownership, as 'a form of socialization'.

After all, wage employment – as opposed to workers' ownership/entrepreneurship, whether full or partial – was one of the few features of a market economy that was already in place under the old system. All that was needed to turn the existing near-market for labour[8] into a genuine market was to remove *de facto* 'job rights protection' (i.e., entitlements to existing jobs, which were never a legal right and therefore could be removed without any change in legislation) and create large scale unemployment in order to discipline wage demands and introduce flexibility in labour redeployment. In spite of free trade unions, collective bargaining, income policies and social pacts, sooner or later this was done, or is being done, practically everywhere.

Yet significant, large scale, unexpected forms of employee ownership emerged in the transition, with few exceptions such as the former Czechoslovak Federal Republic and its successor Republics – in spite of its pre-War tradition and the impressive intellectual input of Jan and Jaroslav Vanek.[9] Partly this unexpected development was the result of public policy measures forced on the new governments by the need to implement a quick and smooth transition, partly it happened purely by default (specifically on employee ownership in the transition, see Smith, 1993; Schaffer, 1996).

Employee ownership had to be introduced for a variety of reasons:

i) to reverse the effects of earlier attempts at reforming the old system that had introduced employee self-management, notably in Poland and to a smaller extent in Hungary (of course in addition to Yugoslavia; in Romania self-management had been formally introduced but had remained a dead letter).

Paradoxically these earlier attempts at reform became an obstacle to the subsequent transition, which could only be overcome by converting self-management into co-ownership. Privatization of state enterprises with self-management provisions required employees to surrender their 100 per cent entitlement to, say, 20 per cent of property rights (i.e., that part of property rights that involved the right to appoint and dismiss managers, to use and control capital, and the right to appropriate some of the results). For them to do so willingly employees had to be given instead, say, 20 per cent of full property rights (i.e., including the entitlement to any increase in capital value and the free disposal of capital, which they did not have before).

ii) as a natural consequence of transition, employee ownership was also introduced with the transformation of former pseudo-co-operatives, i.e., public sector co-operatives, into genuine co-operatives run by elected officials and independent from central organs; this was an early development in the Polish transition (which will not be considered here).

iii) to win over employee support for the transition in spite of concern for its short-run adverse effects on real wages and on mass unemployment.

In addition, unintended employee ownership also happened, by default, given:

i) the low and often negative value (at the ruling fixed wage rates but not for more flexible participatory earnings) of some state enterprises for which there could not have been other takers. In Polish parlance this is the case of enterprises 'liquidated' under art. 37 of the Privatization Law, which, otherwise, would have been liquidated for insolvency under act. 19 of the old Law on state enterprises;

ii) the shortage of domestic capital, which placed employees (especially in view of their inside information) in a good position with respect to domestic outsiders, while alternative external buyers frequently evoked xenophobic reactions;

iii) employees' and managers' natural inclination, in the absence of information about other enterprises and other localities, simply to automatically select the one which they knew best and was most important for their livelihood, or at most enterprises in the same locality – what Peter Murrell (1994) calls the 'balkanization of ownership'. In Poland this was a much less important factor than in those transition economies – like Russia – where mass privatization vouchers could be used to buy an interest in one's enterprise on privileged terms.

## THEORETICAL PREDICTIONS

From the theoretical literature on various forms of employee ownership a number of ready-made predictions can be drawn which will be listed here before reviewing their verification in the Polish case.

In general, the acquisition of a non-controlling interest by managers and employees in their own enterprises can be regarded as a positive development, which encourages productivity, better labour relations, economic democracy; the diffusion of employee ownership is encouraged in the European Community (Uvalic, 1991). The acquisition of a *controlling* interest, however, is capable of having devastating effects on earnings, employment, efficiency, restructuring.

First, employees may use their controlling power to maintain employment levels higher than those compatible with profit maximization at the going wage rate. When this happens workers will be dismissed only if their wages are higher than the value of their average product, not necessarily if wages are higher than the value of their marginal product. On the positive side there will be a lower unemployment level than otherwise, as a result of what is effectively a form of work-sharing within worker-controlled enterprises. On the negative side, such work-sharing at the microeconomic level will be less efficient than economy-wide work-sharing, because there will be no tendency for the value of labour's marginal product to be equalized throughout the economy; indeed employees might be kept on even when their marginal product is negative.

Second, employees may use their controlling power to raise earnings (including fringe benefits in kind, individual and collective) above the going wage rate to the point of bringing profits down to zero or even incurring losses, eating up equity capital right down to the point of bare solvency, i.e., of zero capital value of the enterprise – even if budget constraints are hard (if they are not, losses may also be inflicted on suppliers). Other shareholders can be effectively disenfranchised and expropriated. No additional equity capital will be available from outside on that basis; the enterprise will have to rely on internal finance for its growth, and naturally its viability will be limited to the sectors or techniques with less than average risk, size or capital per man.

Capacity restructuring, if any, will be much slower than otherwise, in the short run because of obstacles to labour shedding, in the medium-long run because of lower self-financed investment, lower access to loans and no access to external equity capital. If the resulting trade-offs between employment, efficiency and capacity restructuring – which ultimately involve a trade-off between lower short-term social costs and higher cost and longer duration of necessary restructuring – were actually acceptable to governments, all would be well in the best of all possible worlds. The trouble is that such trade-offs are uncontrollable and unpredictable, and therefore unlikely to coincide with government preferences; they are the result of an *absence* of government policy, without the justification of a *laissez-faire* approach because such phenomena are policy-induced and interfere with market processes rather than being their natural result.

The probability of such adverse implications of employee ownership is not an increasing function of the degree of their ownership and/or control. Nuti (1995 and 1997) has shown that such adverse implications are the 'catastrophic' consequence of *a controlling interest being exercised – whether individually or collectively – by those employee-shareholders who individually hold a share of equity capital smaller than their share in wage labour.* Only those employee-shareholders, in fact, gain more as employees from higher wages and continued employment than they lose as shareholders; other employee-shareholders have no incentive to behave any differently from other shareholders.

Predicting what might happen in a given enterprise with employee-ownership thus meets considerable difficulties. First, whether or not a given share of the votes is a controlling interest is not always known *a priori*: over 50 per cent of the votes may not be enough if the vote is dispersed among disinterested holders, while considerably less than 50 per cent may be sufficient to exercise control when the rest of the votes are dispersed or disinterested; in other words, a potential controlling interest may remain unused. Second, available information about share distribution is never related to earnings distribution, in the only way that would indicate whether employee-ownership can make a difference, even potentially. As far as one can see, no empirical investigation to date – east or west – has collected information about the relative size of individual employee shares in equity and in earnings. *For both reasons, we should expect empirical studies of enterprises with significant employee ownership to be fairly inconclusive.*

In these conditions the best we can do is to venture some plausible conjectures.

First, since as a rule managers are bound to hold higher individual shares than other employees, and enjoy incentives unrelated (or indeed negatively related) to the level of earnings of other employees, managerial holdings are best excluded from aggregate employee shareholdings for the purposes of assessing whether they can amount to a controlling interest diverting the company away from profit maximization.

Second, more generally, the higher the concentration of employee share ownership, the less likely it is that an enterprise with substantial employee ownership will behave differently from otherwise equivalent enterprises.

Third, in the course of time the employee-controlled enterprise is bound to easily revert to an ordinary company, when a sufficient number of employee-shareholders raise their equity stake over their share in total earnings, or cease to be employees, or shareholders.[10]

It should be stressed that the problems that might arise with an employee-owned enterprise are the same that would arise with shareholders who have another stake in the company besides their equity, e.g., as suppliers, buyers, creditors, debtors, competitors, etc. (see Nuti, 1995 and 1997). At the same time, such problems should not be confused with those of the standard co-operative or self-managed firm, where members are not full co-owners but only share the right to use enterprise capital and to appropriate net value added. The only features co-operatives and employee-owned enterprises have in common are a greater suitability to activities characterized by a lower than average capital intensity, riskiness and enterprise size, and a restricted access to risk capital. Otherwise employee-owned enterprises, unlike co-operatives or self-managed enterprises, do not have an incentive to restrict employment, to over-exploit a monopoly position, to respond sluggishly and possibly 'perversely' to price changes, to distribute rather than reinvest profits, to exhibit a bias for labour-saving projects (see Nuti, 1992).

## ACTUAL PERFORMANCE

Evidence on the impact of employee ownership on actual enterprise performance in Poland is practically limited to MEBOs, since other forms of privatization have led to weaker forms of employee ownership, fairly uniformly distributed among privatized state enterprises at the time of privatization and not yet sufficiently diversified. Neither standard Polish classification (exemplified in Tables 1 and 2), nor major studies of Polish privatization such as Belka *et al.*, 1994, single out enterprises characterized by significant employee ownership. Nevertheless a number of empirical studies are available on Polish MEBOs: Jarosz 1994a and b; Szomburg, 1994; Estrin *et al.*, 1994 (a comparative study of an enterprise sample from Poland, Hungary and Czechoslovakia); Rapacki, 1995; see also Estrin, 1996; Filatotchev *et al.*, 1996; Woodward, 1996.

Profitability of Polish MEBO enterprises appears to have been relatively better (though not very significantly) than that of other enterprises, whether otherwise privatized, or still in Treasury ownership, or in the traditional state sector. Thus in 1994 MEBOs recorded a profit rate on current costs of 7.4 per cent as opposed to 7.2 per cent for capital privatization, 6.2 per cent for Treasury owned enterprises and 5.1 per cent for the public sector as a whole. Net profit margins bear identical relationships, correspondingly 3.7 per cent, 2.9 per cent, 2.8 per cent, 2.5 per cent (Rapacki, 1995).

It would be rash to conclude, from these data, that Polish employee-owned firms are more efficient than residual state enterprises or traditional private firms. First there is a generalized consensus that the higher margin is due not to MEBOs better performance but to the fact that MEBOs were self-selected by employees precisely on the basis of their prospective cash flow being sufficiently attractive (Rapacki, 1995; Estrin, 1996; Filatotchev *et al.*, 1996). Indeed, gross mark-ups differ significantly, being much higher for MEBOs, presumably in order to enable them to bear the burden of lease/purchase costs. Second, on average the performance of MEBO companies deteriorated over time; the number of loss-making enterprises rose from 4.4 per cent in 1991 to 13.2 per cent in 1992 (see Filatotchev *et al.*, 1996). Third, there was considerable variability in such firms' performance, from the 4 very successful firms now listed in the Warsaw Stock Exchange to 7 leased firms which went bankrupt before the end of 1994. By and large the more successful have been medium-size (over 300 employees) industrial enterprises less exposed to competition, whereas small firms (under 100 employees) operating in a very competitive environment such as trade have experienced severe difficulties (Filatotchev *et al.*, 1996; Jarosz, 1994a and b; Szomburg, 1994; on the employment size distribution of privatized enterprises, see Table 3).

In the MEBO samples available, wages appear to have risen, initially, faster than in similar firms, only to be more contained than average in subsequent periods. Contrary to expectations, employment has been considerably more flexible than in other state firms, whether privatized or not, and in the economy as a whole, also falling faster than prior to privatization (although often employment fell significantly immediately before privatization). The highest wage increases have been obtained in the enterprises that experienced the largest employment decline (Jarosz, 1994a and b, Filatotchev *et al.*, 1996). This combination of employment, wage levels and trends, suggests that budget constraints have hardened just as in other privatized firms (which is not a surprise because they have hardened also in state enterprises, see Belka *et al.*, 1994); that causality may have gone from labour shedding to higher wages, rather than the other way round; that employee control – if present – has not dominated wage and employment policy, apart from a possible initial over-generosity which may have been due to an accommodating managerial attitude rather than to opportunism by employee-shareholders.

Investment in the MEBO enterprises was generally lower than in similar enterprises, due to the burden of lease payments, high interest and the inability to offer enterprise assets as collateral before the ownership transfer (see Jarosz, 1994 a and b). Financial institutions appear to have been aware of the greater risk of lending to enterprises controlled by insiders (see the previous section): apparently the nine main Polish commercial banks usually rated exclusive insider ownership as a greater risk than partial ownership with foreign or other outsider participation (Solarz, 1994).

**Table 3. Ownership Transformations in Poland According to Privatization Method and Employment Size at End-1995**

| Number of Employees | Total | jsSP | | | | Liquidation | | |
|---|---|---|---|---|---|---|---|---|
| | | Total | art. 5 | art. 6 | art. 7 | Total | art. 37 | art. 19 |
| Total | 3465 | 958 | 387 | 230 | 341 | 2507 | 1149 | 1358 |
| Up to 50 | 299 | 1 | 0 | 0 | 1 | 298 | 52 | 246 |
| 51–200 | 1495 | 42 | 16 | 0 | 26 | 1453 | 597 | 856 |
| 201–500 | 663 | 184 | 77 | 19 | 88 | 479 | 309 | 170 |
| over 500 | 1008 | 731 | 294 | 211 | 226 | 277 | 191 | 86 |

*Source*: MPW, 1996.
*Note*: Wholly Treasury-owned joint stock companies (jsSP) have resulted from art. 5 and 6 of the July 1990 Law on the privatization of state enterprises, and from art. 7 of the Law on National Investment Funds. 'Liquidation' took place under art. 37 of the July 1990 Law (restructuring privatization) and art. 19 of the old Law on state enterprises of September 1981.

## PROBLEMS AND PROSPECTS

Unresolved problems of employee ownership in Poland, especially for its stronger version of MEBOs, include governance conflicts, financial constraints to growth, institutional instability. Prospects for a further growth of employee shareholding in Poland are poor.

Governance problems here concern not so much, or not only, owners' control over managers, but the resolution of possible conflicts between those shareholders who are also employees or managers and other shareholders who are not. The government, even when retaining an interest as lessor, seems unsuitable to resolve these conflicts, since the lease or sale has occurred precisely because of its earlier inability to exercise effective control. The best solution is perhaps the reduction of the total share held by small insiders; a recent proposal to make at least 20 per cent of the capital available to outside investors (Filatotchev *et al.*, 1996, p. 82) is a move to add an external voice and reduce the weight of all insiders, but does not discriminate between small and large inside shareholders and, given such neglect, does not go far enough.

Access to finance, both for funding a MEBO and financing subsequent investment, is particularly difficult and costly. From the point of view of externally financing a MEBO, 'the appropriate candidate for such a transaction is an enterprise in a mature industrial sector, with stable and significant cash flow and with low investment needs' (Filatotchev *et al.*, 1996, p. 79); other enterprises are much less attractive candidates. Internal investment finance is greatly squeezed by the financial burden of leasing, exceptionally heavy in spite of privileged interest rates, due to the exceptionally high, nominal and real, basic interest rates in the transition in general and in Poland in particular (see Nuti, 1996). External finance – as noted above – is discouraged by the inability to offer enterprise assets as collateral before the ownership transfer which only occurs at the end of the purchase-lease agreement. Here it should not be difficult to transfer ownership after cumulative payments have covered, say, half of the enterprise capital value, after which point the value of employees' equity stake should be sufficient to raise and secure a matching amount of external finance (a MPW proposal reducing to one-third the minimum repayment sufficient to transfer ownership should be enacted in the near future).

Table 4.    **Change in Ownership Structure in Polish Enterprises Leased by Employees**

| Type of owner | Average holding end-1991 % | Average holding mid-1993 % |
|---|---|---|
| Employees | 75.4 | 66.9 |
| Managers | 9.8 | 12.0 |
| Outside investors | 14.8 | 21.1 |

*Source*:    Jarosz, 1994b; from Filatotchev *et al.*, 1996.

There is not only an *a priori* presumption but also empirical evidence, that a controlling employee ownership is a tendentially unstable institution. Table 4 for Poland, and even more so Table 5 for Russia, clearly demonstrate how the pattern of ownership i) shifts from insiders to outsiders, and ii) becomes more concentrated among insiders. As small employee shareholders cease to be small (relatively to their share in labour earnings), or employees (through retirement or turnover), or shareholders (through sales to outsiders), the employee-controlled enterprise will tend to behave as an ordinary capitalist enterprise with only the small though non-negligible net advantages from employee participation. Partly these trends are affected by limitations to share tradeability, with pre-emption rights by insiders and the need for transfers to outsiders to be approved by managements and other enterprise organs; but share liquidity naturally increases with the termination of employment (Filatotchev *et al.*, 1996). Ultimately, '...buy-outs, which have been a highly pragmatic means of effecting initial privatization, increasingly need to be viewed as a *transitory form of organization*' (*ibidem*, emphasis added).

**Table 5.   Shareholders by Ownership Type in Russian Joint Stock Companies
(Per cent of Equity, 1994–95)**

|  | April 1994 | Dec. 1994 | March 1995 | June 1995 | June 1996 forecast |
|---|---|---|---|---|---|
| Insiders (total) | 62 | 60 | 60 | 56 | 51 |
| of which:employees | 53 | 49 | 47 | 43 | 35 |
| directors | 9 | 11 | 13 | 13 | 16 |
| Outsiders (total) | 21 | 27 | 28 | 33 | 45 |
| of which:large | 11 | 16 | 17 | 22 | 32 |
| small | 10 | 11 | 11 | 11 | 13 |
| Government | 17 | 13 | 12 | 11 | 4 |
| TOTAL | 100 | 100 | 100 | 100 | 100 |

*Source*:   RF State Committee for Property Management, 1995. From: S. Mizobata, 1996.

From several view points – suitability for external financing of MEBOs, sectoral and size suitability – employee ownership does not appear to be a universal solution, in Poland as anywhere else. The downside of its high initial incidence and rate of completion in Poland is the current low rate of new starts; potential candidates and takers have been virtually exhausted. The direct privatization track in general and MEBOs in particular are now regarded in Poland as a *'dead end'* (Monkiewicz, 1996). More promising developments in current privatization policies in Poland are represented by generalized commercialization, debt for equity swaps, linking privatization with pension fund reform, raising revenue for the state budget (which in the past has meant capital privatizations with increasing participation of foreign buyers[11]) – rather than the further development of MEBOs and other forms of employee ownership.

# NOTES

1. An earlier draft was published in: Uvalic and Vaughan Whitehead (1997).
2. All zloty values given here are in post-denomination units, i.e., pre-1995 zlotys have been divided by 10,000.
3. Past commitments to mass privatization have been honoured, after an initial delay due to Premier Pawlak's qualms about national control of crucial sectors. By the closing date of 22 November 1996, as many as 25.7 million Poles, or 95 per cent of those eligible, have claimed their privatization vouchers; a year earlier only one in ten Poles said they would claim, while the government expected only 10 million participants. Vouchers were

distributed by the state bank PKO at zl 20 fee (US$7), selling for as much as ten times that fee on the Stock Exchange; in March 1997 they were exchanged for shares in 15 National Investment Funds (NIFs), controlling 512 companies formerly in state ownership, covering a cross section of industry. NIF shares, tradable beginning in June 1997, should massively enhance the capitalization of the Warsaw Stock Exchange.

4. Insolvent state enterprises can also be made bankrupt (art. 24 of the Law on state enterprises) on the basis of bankruptcy procedures (Decree of 24-10-1934 of the President of the Polish Republic). Art 19 liquidation differs from bankruptcy procedures primarily because it can only be applied if there are 'grounds for stating' that liquidation net revenues are sufficient to satisfy all creditors' claims.

5. By the end of 1995, out of all enterprises privatized under art. 37, 18.8 per cent were sold (mostly quick sales of bad enterprises otherwise subject to art. 19 liquidation); 5.6% were contributed to new companies; 68.6 per cent were leased and the remaining 7 per cent used a mixture of these methods.

6. At the initiative of either creditors or the debtor enterprise, in case of actual or prospective inability to service outstanding debt.

7. Apparently 30 per cent of initial finance came from such special funds (Filatotchev *et al.*, 1996, from a study of 142 companies reported in *Zycie Gospodarcze* n. 14, 1994)

8. Even at the height of stalinism state enterprises had to offer a wage level and structure matching their labour demands; they were subject to wage-bill ceilings but had a fair amount of flexibility in their wage policy, through the grading of jobs and of employees and through fringe benefits as well as in wage-fixing. The difference with respect to capitalism was primarily in the state of the labour market, i.e., the full and often over-full employment which prevailed in the centrally planned economy. While undoubtedly consistent with government policies, this was obtained as a by-product of 'tight' or 'taut' planning, i.e., endemic excess demand for goods and services at administered prices fixed below market-clearing levels, rather than as a result of specific measures of employment creation and protection. Apart from full/over-full employment, the wage contract in the traditional Soviet-type economy was basically the same as in the market economy.

9. See Kotrba, 1996. On general trends in other transition economies see the other contributions to this volume by Munteanu, Lissovolik, Rock and Klinedinst, Uvalic; Estrin 1994, and in particular chapters by Gomulka and Jasinski on Poland, Carlin on Germany, Ben-Ner and Montias on Romania, Canning and Hare on Hungary, Bim *et al.*, on Russia (see also Lissovolik, 1995).

10. Unless employee-shareholders happen to sell their stock to employees who still fail to reach an equity stake at least as high as their share in earnings – a fairly contrived supposition.

11. On the increasing importance of privatization revenue see Table 1. In 1995 two thirds of such revenue came from foreign buyers (see OECD, 1997).

## REFERENCES

Aslund, A. and R. Layard (eds) (1993), *Change of Economic System in Russia*, London.

Belka, M., S. Estrin, M. Shaffer, I.J. Singh (1994), 'Enterprise Adjustment in Poland: Evidence from a Survey of 200 Firms', LSE-CEP Working Paper no. 658, London.

Ben-ner, A. and J.M. Montias (1994), 'Economic System Reforms and Privatization in Romania', in Estrin (1994).

Bim, A.S., D.C. Jones and T. Weisskopf (1994), 'Privatization in the Former Soviet Union and the New Russia', in Estrin (1994).

Blejer, M.I. and M. Skreb (eds) (1997), *Macroeconomic Stabilisation in Transition Economies*, CUP 1997.

Blommestein, H. and M. Marrese (eds) (1991), *Transformation of Planned Economies: Property Rights Reform and Macroeconomic Stability*, OECD, Paris.

Canning, A. and P. Hare (1994), 'The Privatization Process-Economic and Political Aspects of the Hungarian Approach', in Estrin 1994.

Carlin, W. (1994), 'Privatization and De-industrialisation in East Germany', in S. Estrin (ed.), 1994.

Chubais, A. (1993), 'Main Issues of Privatization in Russia', in Aslund and Layard (eds), 1993.

Daviddi, R. (ed.) (1995), *Property Rights and Privatization in the Transition to a Market Economy. A Comparative Review*, Maastricht, EIPA.

Earle, J.S. & S. Estrin (1995), 'Employee Ownership in Transition, in C. Gray *et al.*, 1995.

Estrin, S. (ed.) (1994), *Privatization in Central and Eastern Europe*, Longman Group UK, Harlow.

Estrin, S. (1996), 'Privatization in Central and Eastern Europe', LBS and CEP-LSE, London.

Estrin, S., A. Gelb and I. Singh (1994), 'Shocks and Adjustment by Firms in Transition: A Comparative Study', LSE/LBS/World Bank, March.

Filatotchev, I., I. Grosfeld, J. Karsai, M. Wright, T. Buck (1996), 'Buy-outs in Hungary, Poland and Russia: Governance and Finance Issues', *Economics of Transition*, Vol. 4(1), pp. 67–88.

Frydman, R., E.S. Phelps, A. Rapaczynski and A. Schleifer (1993), 'Needed Mechanisms of Corporate Governance and Finance in Eastern Europe', *Economics of Transition*, Vol. 2, June 1993, pp. 171–208.

Gomulka, S. and P. Jasinski (1994), 'Privatization in Poland 1989–93: Policies, Methods and Results', in Estrin (ed.), 1994.

Gray, C., R. Frydman and A. Rapaczynski (1995), *Corporate Governance in Transitional Economies*, World Bank, Washington.

Jarosz, M. (ed.) (1994a), *Employee-Owned Companies in Poland*, PAN-ISP, Warsaw.

Jarosz, M. (ed.) (1994b), *Pracownicze Spolki Leasingujace*, MPW, Warsaw.

Jones, D. and J. Svejnar (eds) (1992), Advances in the Economic Analysis of Participatory and Labor-Managed Firms, Vol. 4, 1992, JAI Press, Greenwich and London.

Kotrba, J. (1996), 'Employees and Managers Ownership, Participation and the Czech Privatization Programme', published in Uvalic *et al.*, (1997).

Kowalik, T. (1994), 'The Social Costs of Liberalisation and Privatization in Poland' (mimeo), Warsaw.

Lissovolik, B. (1995), 'Special Features of Russian Privatization: Causes and Consequences', in R. Daviddi (ed.), 1995.

Lissovolik, B. (1996), 'Employee Ownership in Privatized Russia', published in Uvalic *et al.*, (1997).

Mizobata, S. (1996), 'Characteristics of Capitalism in Russia', CREES, Birmingham University.

Monkiewicz, (1996), 'W poszukiwaniu strategii przeksztalcen wlasnosciowych', mimeo, Warsaw.

MPW – Ministry of Property Transformations (1996), Dynamika Przeksztalcen Wlasnosciowych, nr. 27, Warsaw.

Munteanu, C. (1996), 'Employees and Managers' Share Ownership in Central Eastern European Privatization, The case of Romania', published in Uvalic *et al.*, (1997).

Murrell, P. (1994), 'Peremptory Privatization', AEA Annual Conference, Boston, 3–5 January.

Nuti, D.M. (1991), 'Privatization of Socialist Economies: General Issues and the Polish Case', in H. Blommestein and M. Marrese (eds), 1991, pp. 51–68.

Nuti, D.M. (1992), 'Traditional Co-operatives and James Meade's Labour-Capital Discriminating Partnerships', in D. Jones-J. Svejnar (eds), 1992, pp. 1–26

Nuti, D.M. (1994), 'Mass Privatization: Costs and Benefits of Instant Capitalism', CISME-LBS Working Papers no. 9, London, also in R. Daviddi (ed.), 1995.

Nuti, D.M. (1995), 'Corporate Governance et Actionnariat des Salaries', *Economie Internationale* no. 62.

Nuti, D.M. (1996), 'Inflation, Interest and Exchange Rates in the Transition', *Economics of Transition*, Vol. 4(1), pp. 137–158.

Nuti, D.M. (1997), 'Employeeism: Corporate Governance and Employee Share Ownership in Transition Economies', in Blejer and Skreb (eds) 1997, pp. 126–154.

OECD (1997), *Poland Survey 1996*, Paris.

Pagano, U. and R.E. Rowthorn (eds) (1996), *Democracy and Efficiency in the Economic Enterprise*, Routledge Studies in Business Organisation and Networks, London and New York.

Rapacki, R. (1995), 'Privatization in Poland: Performance, Problems and Prospects – A Survey Article', *Comparative Economic Studies*, Vol. 37 no. 1 Spring, pp. 57–75.

Rapacki, R. and S.J. Linz (1992), 'Privatization in Transition Economies: Case Study of Poland', Econometric and Economic Theory Papers, no. 9011, Department of Economics, Michigan State University.

Rock, C.P. and M.A. Klinedinst (1996), 'Workers Ownership and Participation in Enterprises in Bulgaria, from 1989 to 1995, and Future Prospects', in Uvalic *et al.*, (1997).

Schaffer, M. (1996), 'Worker Participation in Socialist and Transitional Economics', in U. Pagano and R.E. Rowthorn (eds), 1996.

Schliwa, R. (ed.), *Bottom-up Privatization, Finance and the Role of Employers' and Workers' Organisations in the Czech Republic, Hungary, Poland and Slovakia*, ILO, Geneva.

Smith, S.C. (1993), 'Employee Ownership in Privatization in Developing and Reforming Countries', George Washington University, April, mimeo.

Solarz J. (1994), 'The Financial Sector and Bottom-up Privatization', in Schliwa (ed.), 1994.

Sutela, P. (1994), 'Insider Privatization in Russia: Speculations on Systemic change', *Review of Economies in Transition-Idantalouksien Katsauksia*, no. 1, Bank of Finland, pp. 5–26.

Szomburg, J. (1994), 'Prywatyzacja w trybie leasingu', IBGR, Gdansk.

Uvalic, M. (1991), 'The PEPPER Report: Promotion of Employee Participation in Profits and Enterprise Results in the Member States of the European Community', revised edition, *Social Europe*, Supplement no. 3.

Uvalic, M. (1996), 'Insider privatization in the Countries of Former Yugoslavia', published in Uvalic *et al.*, (1997).

Uvalic, M. and D. Vaughan-Whitehead (eds) (1997), *Privatization Surprises in Transition Economies – Employee Ownership in Central and Eastern Europe*, Edward Elgar, Aldershot.

Woodward, R. (1996), 'Management-Employee Buy-outs in Poland', Studies and Analyses no. 69, CASE-Center for Social and Economic Research, Warsaw.

# 6
# Political Economy of Privatization in Hungary: A Progress Report

*Anna Canning and Paul Hare*[1]

## INTRODUCTION: A BRIEF REVIEW OF THE ISSUES

'Stabilize, liberalize, privatize!' declared the International Monetary Fund and the World Bank, along with most western analysts, when the communist regimes collapsed in Central and Eastern Europe (CEE) in 1989–90 and these countries embarked on a process of transformation from central planning to market economy. The CEE countries without exception set about putting these three precepts into practice as key policy objectives, albeit with significant differences between countries in speed, sequencing and in the actual methods adopted.

At root, the transformation from socialist central planning to a market economy entails a radical adjustment in order to create a 'new balance of power between the state and civic society, in favour of the latter' (Havas, 1996). In this light, privatization is arguably the most important, and probably the most complex element of the transformation process. This is because privatization, broadly defined as the transfer of state-owned assets to private ownership, alongside the creation and fostering of *de novo* private businesses, is about the (re)distribution of property (wealth) and the means of generating wealth. Hence, ultimately, it is about the longer-term distribution of economic and political power. Decisions related to privatization impinge on almost every aspect of the transformation process. They profoundly affect the future shape of the country's economy and its performance both on the domestic and international markets. In the CEE context, privatization involves a huge upheaval at every level of society: changes in regional patterns of economic activity, in the labour market, and, at the same time as a new class of entrepreneurs, property owners and shareholders emerges, some social groups will almost inevitably find themselves excluded or marginalized. Policy misjudgements or mismanagement could have grave consequences for social cohesion, threaten the consensus for reform as a whole and seriously undermine the country's political stability. Privatization thus brings a myriad of interest groups to the fore and into confrontation with each other.

The state itself must be regarded as a conglomeration of different interest groups, comprising the political forces in power (dominant ideological bias); the ministries (industry lobbies); the state bureaucracy (which exercises influence *via* the collection and processing of information and through the implementation of government decisions). The willingness of the state to relinquish ownership (control) of corporate assets and its ability to manage this process in a transparent and even-handed manner are thus also a litmus test of the credibility and efficiency of the fledgling democratic regimes' decision-making systems and implementation structures.

If these observations regarding privatization in transition economies are valid in general (and they are echoed by numerous analysts, e.g., Voszka, 1994; Havas 1996; Canning and Hare, 1994) nowhere are they more pertinent than in the 'second phase' of privatization, whose central element has been the fate of 'strategic companies', most notably the public utilities in CEE countries. Why? Because sectors such as energy generation/production and supply, transport, telecommunications, water, along with the large commercial banks, sections of the chemical industry, and in the case of Hungary, the aluminium industry, formed both the ideological core and the economic power base of the socialist economies. Their ideological importance derives from the fact that these sectors were crucial in order to be able to deliver on various social (political) objectives: e.g., ensuring availability of energy to all at low prices (energy prices to domestic consumers were kept lower than in the case of industrial consumers, and notoriously far below the marginal costs of supply); or to be able to control, in the case of telecommunications (including broadcasting), the flow of and access to information. Their economic importance stems from their character as vital inputs into almost all other productive activities and, in the case of the public utilities (including transport), from their direct contribution to consumer well-being.

This paper focuses on the political economy of privatization in its second phase in Hungary, the country which, overall, has gone furthest in privatizing these sectors, introducing elements of competition and setting up regulatory mechanisms and institutions to monitor them. The background to Hungary's reform path, the antecedents to privatization, the debate on the issues, the institutional framework and the progress of privatization in Hungary up to late 1993/early 1994 are well-documented elsewhere, including by the present authors[2]. Section 2 therefore confines itself to giving a brief review of the evolutionary path of Hungary's privatization 'vision', policy and strategy under the 1990–94 government of József Antall and his successor, Péter Boross, and attempts to identify the factors influencing this evolution. Developments regarding privatization under the socialist/liberal coalition government led by Gyula Horn, which came to power in 1994, are described in Section 3. Section 4 forms the core of this study, examining in detail the privatization of the major utilities and the regulatory environment now in place. Section 5 sets the above in the context of the overall development of the private sector in Hungary, and some conclusions are drawn in Section 6.

# EVOLUTION OF PRIVATIZATION IN HUNGARY 1990–94

Attitudes to and understanding of the issues underlying the privatization of state-owned enterprises (SOEs) in transition economies have evolved and changed since 1990[3], bringing concomitant changes in the focus of privatization policy and continuous modification in the strategy, pace and methods adopted. While many of these changes were pragmatic and well-founded (in response to changes in the broader economic environment; realization that targets set were unrealistic, etc.), other developments may be attributed at least in part to political influences and/or social pressures.

The privatization policy initially adopted by Hungary's first post-communist government (led by the centre-right Hungarian Democratic Forum), which came to power in May 1990, was characterized by the following principal features:

- emphasis on *economic* efficiency gains rather than political goals, e.g., in the immediate term, to reduce subsidies and increase revenues, thus easing the budget deficit; and, in the longer term, to improve microeconomic efficiency (and thereby the performance of the economy in general) through the introduction of 'genuine' private owners (profit motivation, competition, innovation, expansion of the private sector);
- emphasis on *commercial* privatization (i.e., sale of assets rather than free distribution to the public), maximizing revenues to the treasury; reorganization (i.e., demerger or separation of non-core activites or physical assets for sale separately) was not initially given much consideration; restructuring (i.e., internal organization, staffing, technology and processes, product profile, etc.) was deemed best left to new private owners;
- emphasis on involving larger (strategic corporate; institutional) *investors*, and attracting *foreign investors*, with a view to bringing in the capital and the technological and managerial know-how required in order to achieve the economic goals outlined in the first two points above;
- emphasis on relatively *gradual* privatization of state-owned corporate assets: the target set was to privatize 50 per cent of these assets (by value) by 1994.
- emphasis on *transparency* and accountability, in a *decentralized* framework where privatization could be initiated by: (1) the State Property Agency (SPA, set up in March 1990 under the reform-communist government of Miklós Németh to act on behalf of the state as owner in the supervision of transactions – e.g., incorporation, privatization – related to state-owned assets); (2) the enterprises; or (3) potential investors.

As early as July 1990, the government's position had altered in at least one significant respect: the SPA was made directly accountable to the government (rather than, as previously, to parliament) and decisions made by the SPA could not be appealed against through the courts. Enterprise councils (a form of self-management established in around 70 per cent of enterprises in the mid-eighties as part of a package of initiatives aimed at decentralizing economic decision-making and giving enterprises more autonomy) were to be abolished; all enterprises were to undergo 'transformation' (incorporation) by mid-1993, and the ownership/control rights transferred to the SPA. Although on the one hand this served to clarify ownership rights prior to privatization, it was also seen in some quarters – notably among economists in the liberal camp – as being a step backwards, amounting almost to 'renationalization' of enterprises. Privatization was, in effect, to be centrally managed. The first 'showcase' privatization programme, launched by the SPA in September 1990, involving 20 major companies with reasonably good balance-sheets and prospects, was a resounding failure. While some of the lessons drawn from this led to modifications of other aspects of privatization strategy, centralized state control of asset-management and privatization in Hungary have remained significant. Renowned Hungarian commentators on the political economy of privatization such as Éva Voszka (see, e.g., Voszka 1991, 1994, 1996) have argued vociferously and, in the main, credibly against some of the negative aspects of this tendency (e.g., lack of transparency; unwieldy bureaucratic procedures; vulnerability to party-political pressures, etc.). However, it is perhaps not out of place to ask to what extent such views are influenced by a deep – and widespread – suspicion of state control (and of the state administration), a legacy of the communist era (see Canning and Hare, 1994). Indeed, was there any other option open to the government at that time? It is worth bearing in mind that the institutional and legal framework (which could have permitted some dispersal of responsibility for the supervision and regulation of privatization) was yet in its infancy, while earlier abuses of power by SOE managers had shown thast uncontrolled 'privatization from below' would serve the interests only of very few.

Other changes: from 1991, the emphasis (both in legislation and in practice) gradually shifted towards 'safeguarding' state-owned assets, modernization, restructuring ('dirty dozen' – later 13 – firms granted special treatment; see OECD, 1994); the need to accelerate privatization of state-owned assets came increasingly to the fore, and the political aim of creating and fostering a property-owning middle-class was mentioned for the first time.

The emphasis on maximizing budget revenue diminished and the use to which revenues from privatization were put shifted increasingly towards restructuring and financing schemes to foster smaller, domestic investors (away from easing the state debt and the budget deficit). Compensation (to individuals whose property or land had been confiscated for political reasons under the previous regime(s)[4] ) and restitution (of church property) came on the agenda; municipalities were to be allocated properties/stakes in companies[5]. Favourable loan schemes were initiated to enable individuals to participate in the privatization process (e.g., the so-called Existence (E-) credits), especially the 'small' privatization programme (also termed 'pre-privatization' in Hungary) involving principally retail and catering outlets. Perhaps significantly, in the latter period of the Antall government's term in office, employee share ownership was given higher priority (initally only 5–10 per cent of company shares were set aside for purchase at preferential rates by employees) and supported by preferential loans. The terms attached to E-loans were eased considerably in 1993, and their use extended to cover participation in this and other schemes aimed at supporting local investors. Yet other schemes, e.g., 'leasing' (amounting to privatization by instalments at a zero nominal interest rate, circumventing the need to take on a commitment to loan repayments) and management buy-out/buyin opportunities were created or extended. Finally, in late 1992, with the next general election (May 1994) less than eighteen months away, the government annnounced plans for a privatization scheme based on credit vouchers open to all Hungarian citizens over the age of 18, without risk to their personal assets, with the avowed aim of creating 'the widest possible range of domestic owners'.[6] In the end, after long and impassioned debate, this so-called Small Investor Share Purchase Programme (KRP) was not implemented.

The government's seemingly dramatic shift in policy in favour of 'domestic owners' coincided with the decision to abolish, with effect from January 1994, the considerable tax relief which had been available to foreign investors since the late 1980s. Given the relative proximity of the next general election, and coupled with growing pressure from the right of the HDF, these moves were perceived by some observers as 'populist', pre-election mood-sweeteners, and a dangerous signal to the international business community. It is worth noting, however, that during 1991 and 1992 participation of the domestic population, lacking capital or access to loans on affordable terms and cautious in the extreme about the privatization process, had been very limited (see Table 1); at the same time, the aforementioned tax concessions had largely outlived their usefulness (that of offsetting the risks of investing in the pre-reform environment) and gave foreign investors an unwarranted advantage over their Hungarian counterparts.[7] Tax incentives were not, however, removed altogether. Instead a system offering tax concessions to companies – domestic or foreign – investing in specific activities or designated (depressed) areas was introduced. These issues were clearly reflected on the political front, some of the most divisive issues in this period being those related to privatization (notably that of land), and particularly the participation of Hungarian citizens in the process. It is not insignificant that from late 1992 and throughout 1993 serious rifts appeared between the three coalition parties, while acrimonious in-fighting took place between moderate and hard-line factions within their ranks, leading to a number of defections, a split in the Smallholders Party, and the ousting from the HDF of extremist demagogue István Csurka and a number of his followers in late 1993.[8]

It was not until July 1992 that the Antall government passed legislation on privatization and management of state-owned assets to replace the 'Temporary Asset

Policy Guidelines' in force since 1989. For the most part, policy and strategy were developed and modified during the intervening period on an *ad hoc*, piecemeal basis. Under the new Privatization Act (Act LIV of 1992), the envisaged extent of state ownership was widened. Around half the assets (in terms of value) originally slated for privatization were transferred to a new organization, the State Holding Company, established in October 1992 to manage assets which would remain partially or wholly in state ownership in the longer term for strategic reasons or, as in the case of the utilities, until such a time as the appropriate legislative and regulatory framework was in place and decisions had been reached regarding the most appropriate form of privatization (strategic or portfolio investors, etc.) and its scope.

Overall, between 1990 and 1994 a shift from decentralized to centralized privatization may be perceived; from strictly economic goals to more or less overtly political aims: creating a local property-owning class and (from 1993) winning electoral loyalty for the ruling parties, whose image had been tarnished by internal strife, extremist polemics and a number of scandals involving property deals.

Despite the problems, however, (and it should also be borne in mind that Hungary's economy was in the midst of recession during this period) the achievements of the first post-communist government in privatizing state-owned corporate assets and fostering development of the private sector in Hungary were far from paltry. Between December 1992 and December 1993, the private sector's estimated contribution to GDP rose from around 25 per cent to 65 per cent (UN/ECE), while its share in employment was estimated at around 53 per cent at the end of 1993 (see also Section 5, below). The momentum and volume of privatization *per se*, following a lethargic start in 1991–92, picked up in 1993 with the introduction of preferential schemes for domestic investors and the launch of the 'self-privatization' programme for small to medium firms.[9] The biggest single boost (in terms of revenue and prestige) to privatization in this period was the sale of a 30 per cent stake in the state telecommunications company, Matáv, to an American-German consortium in

Table 1.    **Privatization revenues, SPA and SHC 1990–95; APV Rt 1996 (HUF bns)**

|  | 1990 | 1991 | 1992 | 1993 | 1994 | 1995 | 1991–95 | 1996 |
|---|---|---|---|---|---|---|---|---|
| Cash: | 0.53 | 24.61 | 40.98 | 110.67 | 10.95 | 412.05 | 599.79 | 77.50 |
| • Hard currencies |  |  |  |  |  |  |  |  |
| • HUF | 0.14 | 5.74 | 24.92 | 22.96 | 35.41 | 39.52 | 128.69 | 36.39 |
| – of which dividends | – | 0.93 | 7.41 | 5.41 | 7.8 | 13.79 | 35.34 | 8.15 |
| – other | – | – | – | – | – | – | – | 3.16 |
| Privatization loans HUF | 0 | 1.01 | 9.07 | 21.72 | 29.27 | 3.92 | 64.99 | 2.44 |
| Compensation vouchers | 0 | 0 | 2.26 | 14.56 | 64.20 | 18.48 | 99.50 | 41.63 |
| Privatization loans in hard currency | 0 | 0 | 0 | 0 | 16.84 | 0 | 16.84 | n.a. |
| **Total** | **0.67** | **31.36** | **77.23** | **169.91** | **156.67** | **473.97** | **909.81** | **157.96** |

*Sources*:    APV Rt. 1996; Privatizációs Monitor, 1996; Voszka, 1996.

December 1993 (see Section 4 below). The revenues accruing to the two asset management bodies (Table 1) reflect the dynamics of privatization over this period.

## DEVELOPMENTS UNDER THE HORN GOVERNMENT, 1994–95

When the new coalition government (composed of the Hungarian Socialist Party, with the Alliance of Free Democrats as its junior partner) took office in summer 1994, its stance on privatization comprised the following principles:

- acceleration of privatization (without prior restructuring of the enterprises concerned by the state asset management organizations);
- sale of assets rather than distributive methods (free or on preferential terms) of privatization;
- increasing the role of enterprise management and independent consultancy companies, as opposed to centrally-managed privatization;
- transfer of management of state-owned assets (exercise of ownership rights) to commercial firms rather than state-run organizations.

In addition, the new government envisaged the merger of the SPA and the SHC, and proposed to bring the privatization process under the control of the Finance Ministry. These last two elements attracted immediate criticism; whilst in opposition the coalition parties had argued consistently in favour of restoring parliamentary control of privatization and against the creation of the SHC, which they considered a dangerous concentration of assets, its operations lacking in transparency and, as an organization, potentially vulnerable to politically motivated intervention (Voszka, 1996).

Draft legislation was already in preparation when the new government took office, but progress was delayed by seemingly interminable debate and dispute, not only between the coalition and opposition parties, but also between national and local government, and within the government itself. The trade unions and management representative bodies flexed their still powerful muscles against the perceived threat to their membership of the government's preference for cash sales to outside investors over preferential schemes supporting 'insider' privatization (ESOP, MBO, 'Leasing', etc.). There was vehement opposition among the ministries as regards the new powers to be assigned to the Finance Ministry as overseer of the privatization process, and each of the sectoral ministries battled hard to institutionalize its role (see Voszka, 1996). Finally, at the end of 1994, parliamentary debate on the 1995 budget took precedence, and the discussion on privatization legislation was postponed till early 1995. In this environment of uncertainty, progress with privatization slowed markedly, calling into question not only the government's ability to reconcile the various interest groups and temper the influence of its ideological allies, the trade unions, but its commitment to privatization as such.

The credibility of the Horn government's commitment to continuing privatization was further undermined by the row over the Prime Minister's personal intervention prohibiting the SPA at the last possible moment from going ahead with the sale of a majority stake in Hungar-Hotels (to American General Hospitality) in January 1995. This affair led to the immediate resignation of privatization commissioner Ferenc Bártha, followed by that of Finance Minister László Békesi at the end of January; this in turn resulted in a succession dispute which very nearly upset the stability of the coalition agreement. The debate on new privatization legislation began at the end of January, but stalled again while the new Finance Minister, Lajos Bokros' radical macroeconomic stabilization plan took shape, and with it a drastic overhaul of the state budget which would significantly influence the focus of privatization policy (e.g., budgeting for privatization revenues of HUF 150 bn). Not all of Bokros' proposals regarding privatization were accepted, however, including that of retaining two separate state asset management institutions, and that concerning scrapping the transfer of state-owned assets to the Social Insurance organizations. On these issues, as well as on the question of assigning the principal role in the supervision of privatization to the Finance Ministry, he was obliged to compromise.

The Privatization Act (Act No. XXXIX of 1995) was finally passed on May 9, 1995, after no fewer than 486 amendments had been debated (Mihályi, 1996), and came into effect the following month. On June 17 the government formally established the new State Privatization and Holding Company (SPHC), which although legally the successor of the SHC, in fact mirrored more closely the SPA's organizational structures (e.g., division into sectoral units), albeit with more centralized decision-making procedures (increased powers of the Board of Directors). The shift towards greater bureaucratic control of privatization transactions was reflected also in the emphasis on 'individual considerations' (Section 2(2) of the Act), and the scope for case-by-case evaluation of companies' privatization proposals granted to the SPHC under the so-called 'simplified privatization' scheme introduced in the Act (see also Section 5 below). At the same time, the Act no longer provides for privatization led by approved independent consultants, the decentralized mechanism known as 'self privatization' which operated under the earlier legislation.

The Act reflects substantial compromise (and, according to several observers – e.g., Voszka, 1996; Mihályi, 1996 – a dangerous lack of clarity, even contradiction, on a number of points) by comparison with the government's original stance. While cash sales are emphasized on the one hand, the Act continues to allow considerable leeway for all the earlier preferential schemes supporting employees and small domestic investors (with the exception of the Small Investor Share Purchase Programme). It is the declared objective of the Act to provide for the 'most rapid possible sale of state assets to private owners' (Section 1(1)), but few if any mechanisms are provided in the Act to ensure the realization of this objective.

Overall, while the passing of legislation on privatization did little to quell the debate on the underlying issues, which has continued both in the political and in the public domain, analysts and those involved in privatization appear to have reached consensus on one point: that the merger of the SPA and SHC has proved more advantageous than disadvantageous (Mihályi, 1996). Of greatest significance, however, is undoubtedly the fact that the new Act provided the legal framework for the privatization of the strategic sectors, to be discussed in depth in the next section.

## PRIVATIZATION AND REGULATION OF STRATEGIC SECTORS

Public (state-owned) corporations, notably in the network utilities, where there is some element of natural monopoly,[10] can (and do) function reasonably efficiently in many western economies, given the appropriate legislative and regulatory framework, good governance and competitive environment as regards product markets.[11] None of these were present in former centrally planned economies, or only to a very limited degree. Even if these conditions had been fulfilled, however (and beyond the general consideration that the post-socialist era governments of CEE countries had to make a credible commitment to disengage from political intervention in the management of enterprises), there were several cogent arguments in favour of privatizing the infrastructure industries in the special circumstances of CEE. Ordover, Pittman and Clyde (1994: 320–323) provide a useful summary:

- *ability and incentive to raise prices*: elimination of dramatic price distortions from the socialist era (politically sensitive);
- *ability and incentive to raise capital*: infrastructure utilities are capital-intensive industries; the transition economies of CEE, meanwhile, were characterized by a lack of capital (demands on state budget, embryonic capital markets), certainly on the scale required to upgrade and expand run-down, underdeveloped networks and services – especially telecommunications and transport infrastructure (essential for a functioning market economy); in the case of energy (from the 1970s through to 1990 Hungary depended increasingly on imports,[12] mainly from the former Soviet Union), the cost of diversifying sources;
- *ability and incentive to utilize an efficient mix of inputs*;
- *adaptability to change in future*.

The main strategic sectors/companies in Hungary are:

- MATAV – telecommunications
- Antenna Hungaria – radio and television broadcasting
- MOL – oil and gas industry
- MVM (and subsidiaries) – electricity generation/distribution
- 5 regional gas supply companies
- OTP, MHB, BB, K&H – commercial/retail banking sector.

## Privatization Issues

The strategic sectors were not priority candidates for privatization (with the exception of telecommunications, in view of the sector's significance in economic regeneration and its pressing development needs); most of the companies in these sectors were transferred to the portfolio of the SHC in 1992[13] as assets to be retained at least partially in state ownership in the longer term (in the majority of cases, a stake of 50 per cent + 1 was envisaged), with plans to allocate a further stake to the local municipalities, but not ruling out the possibility of eventually involving an element of private capital. Despite substantial reorganization and cost-cutting in the energy sector companies, modernization efforts stagnated and profits plummeted, principally due to the continued distortions in price structure. The deteriorating macroeconomic situation (external and internal debt, budget deficit) was an additional source of pressure, and it was becoming apparent that there were ever fewer 'privatizable' assets remaining in state ownership which would attract substantial foreign investment revenues.

Utilities assets were considered a good investment, but the prospect of rival privatizations, in both western and eastern Europe, placed the government in Hungary under considerable pressure to refocus its policy and accelerate the process of preparing the regulation and privatization of these sectors. Preparations for privatization began in 1993, and although progress seemed to have stalled indefinitely following the general election in spring 1994, the new government finally gave its approval in principle to the partial privatization of the energy utilities (as well as to the second phase of telecoms privatization) in November 1994.[14] There were a number of issues which were of particular significance in determining the most appropriate strategy for the privatization of the strategic sectors:

### Appropriate Type of Investor

In the majority of cases, foreign, strategic investors were preferred (in the case of consortia, the strategic partner(s) had to have a stake and controlling rights equivalent to at least 50 per cent). In addition, potential strategic investors had to fulfil a number of financial and technical criteria to ensure that they had adequate capital and experience to meet the privatization and investment commitments required of them. There were, however, two important exceptions where financial (portfolio) investors were sought: that of the oil and gas conglomerate, MOL, and the National Savings Bank (OTP), the biggest bank in Hungary in terms of assets (31 per cent of total bank assets) and number of branches nationwide, as well as having the largest share (two-thirds) of the retail market.

In the case of MOL, the shift away from seeking a strategic investor occurred after prolonged negotiations; potential investors appeared interested only in some of MOL's operations, while the industry itself lobbied hard to retain its autonomy, reluctant to be subsumed into one of the big multinational oil companies. In the end, 18.5 mn shares with a nominal value of HUF 1,000 were sold in autumn 1995 *via* private placement (on the US, Luxemburg and London stock markets) to foreign institutional investors; at the same time, 5.4 mn shares were sold to MOL employees and 492,000 to management on preferential terms. In December 1995 a further 3.5 mn shares were sold on the domestic stock market.

As regards OTP, the debate was even more sharply polarized (see Mihályi, 1996; Várhegyi, 1996); finally, in February 1995, it was decided that OTP should remain principally a Hungarian-owned bank; its position (in terms of capital and market share) was sufficiently stable to do without the help of a strategic investor, and yet prove attractive to portfolio investors. Accordingly, 20 per cent of OTP's shares were sold by private placement to foreign institutional investors; 20 per cent was transferred to the two Social Insurance organizations, 5 per cent was sold to employees and 8 per cent *via* public offering on the domestic stock market. These two transactions alone doubled the capitalization of the Budapest Stock Exchange.

## Whether to Sell a Majority or Minority Stake

In cases where a strategic investor was involved, it was clear that a controlling interest would have to be offered. However, plans to reduce the state holding to a minority in strategic companies met with vociferous opposition both in parliament and beyond. The question was finally resolved in summer 1995 by an amendment to the Privatization Act (which had only just been passed) introducing the concept of the 'golden share', which the state would retain in the case of the 5 regional gas supply companies, 8 electricity generation companies, 6 electricity transmission companies and the national electricity grid (OVIT). Economists have evinced some scepticism regarding the usefulness of the golden share clause. Given that the state, *via* the SPHC, is able to use its bargaining position to influence the terms of the concession contracts and operating licences granted to the companies investing in the utilities, the actual need for a golden share in the Hungarian case appears somewhat overstated.[15]

## Whether to Sell Whole Companies or Separate Parts

Most of the utilities had undergone substantial reorganization since 1990, for the most part converting the vertically-integrated monoliths created in the late 1950s/early 1960s into multi-enterprise structures composed of a number of joint-stock companies. The issue arose again, however, in the context of privatization – with particular force in the case of the national monopoly electric utility, MVM, and its subsidiaries, the national network operator (OVIT), the power stations, electricity supply companies and maintenance companies. Plans for the partial privatization of MVM and its subsidiaries were already well under way in accordance with the original concept outlined in the government resolution of November 1994;[16] pressure from the then Minister for Industry and Trade, László Pál (summer 1995), backed by the trade unions, to keep the companies in majority state ownership, stalled the process and finally cost Pál his ministerial portfolio. Finally, plans were modified and it was decided to sell a minority stake (but close to 50 per cent) in the power generators and distributors, giving investors the option of converting to a majority stakeholding in 1997.

In the case of MOL, a general consensus emerged on the benefits of keeping MOL as an integrated, unitary company following its earlier reorganization (1991), when the 5 regional gas supply companies were separated from MOL's predecessor, the oil and gas conglomerate OKGT.[17] The question here was rather whether to merge the company with Mineralimpex, and thus integrate Hungary's gas import/export trade (principally the former Soviet supply contracts) into the company profile. Mineralimpex was finally transferred to MOL in May 1995, increasing the company's registered capital from HUF 97.6 bn to 98.4 bn. It is recognized, however, that MOL's monopoly position as sole producer and wholesaler of gas, as well as owner of the transmission network, will have to be reviewed in the coming years in the light of EU plans for the future liberalization of European energy markets.[18]

### Whether the Sale Should Include Equity Raising

The socialist/liberal coalition government's privatization strategy placed considerable emphasis on raising the companies' equity. However, some of the arguments voiced in relation to the concept were rather woolly, not to say misleading, e.g., in the case of the energy utilities, that it would reduce the pressure to raise prices.[19] On the other hand, in the case of industries facing massive development commitments (e.g., telecommunications), capital raising can avert major solvency problems. Such was the case in the first phase of Matáv's privatization. Similar considerations were at work in the proposals for Antenna Hungaria, and in the case of the power generators (likewise the subject of intensive development programmes), acquisition of a majority stake was made conditional on capital raising.

### Timing

In the case of the strategic sectors, successful timing of privatization has more to do with the regulatory environment than the financial indicators of the companies concerned. The SPA issued tenders for the privatization of minority stakes in the regional gas companies as early as April 1992, and one year later launched a similar initiative for the electricity distributors. The tenders for the electricity distributors were withdrawn, however, since the bids received, proved unacceptably low (equivalent to between 6–60 per cent of the nominal value of the shares), underscoring the significance for potential strategic investors of legislative and regulatory conditions being clarified prior to privatization.[20]

## Regulatory Issues

### The Legislative and Regulatory Environment [21]

The Act on Concessions (Act No. XVI of 1991) provided the basic framework for the granting of concessions, mainly by public tender and subject to payment of a fee, to developers/providers of public infrastructure services including highways, road and rail transport services, telecommunications, and extending to mining activities (exploration and exploitation) and the transmission *via* pipelines of oil and gas. Under the Act, concessions are granted for a specified period (with a maximum of 35 years) and may only be extended once without issuing a new public tender, and then only for half of the originally specified period.

**Table 2.  Privatization of the Energy Utilities (Main Indicators)**

| | Equity (HUF bns) | Registered capital (HUF bns) | Stake sold % | Price (HUF bns) | Price (USD mns) | Share price (relative to registered capital) | Share price (relative to equity) | Investor |
|---|---|---|---|---|---|---|---|---|
| MOL Rt | 263.59 | 97.56 | 18.96 | 20.86 | | 112.76 | 41.74 | 150 institutional investors[a] |
| Gas distributors | | | | | | | | |
| DDGÁZ | 7.35 | 5.09 | 50+1 | 7.0 | 52 | 275.05 | 190.48 | Ruhrgas/VEW Energie |
| DÉGÁZ | 15.31 | 12.45 | 50+1 | 12.5 | 92 | 200.80 | 163.29 | Gas de France |
| ÉGÁZ | 7.04 | 4.73 | 50+1 | 10.4 | 77 | 439.75 | 295.45 | Gas de France |
| KÖGÁZ | 10.55 | 6.37 | 50+1 | 9.1 | 67.2 | 285.71 | 172.51 | Bayernwerk/ EVN |
| TIGÁZ | 24.41 | 15.94 | 50+1 | 23.4 | 171.8 | 293.60 | 191.72 | Italgas/SNAM |
| Total gas | 64.66 | 44.58 | 50+1 | 62.4 | 460 | 279.95 | 193.01 | |
| Electric utilities:[b] | | | | | | | | |
| ELMÜ | 61 | 62 | n.a. | 49.5 | | 174.9 | n.a. | RWE Energie/EV Schwaben |
| TITÁSZ | 34.16 | 34.16 | 49.23 | 17.90 | | 106.44 | 106.44 | ISAR Amperwerke |
| ÉMÁSZ | 30.50 | 30.50 | 48.81 | 22.47 | | 150.91 | 150.91 | RWE Energie/ EV Schwaben |
| DÉMÁSZ | 39 | 37.03 | 47.98 | 21.23 | | 119.53 | 113.47 | EDF International |
| ÉDÁSZ | 51 | 46.88 | 47.55 | 26.99 | | 121.07 | 111.30 | EDF International |
| DÉDÁSZ | 31 | 29.80 | 47.25 | 14.80 | | 105.09 | 101.02 | Bayernwerk |
| Dunamenti Power Stn.[c] | 36 | 33.54 | 48.76 | 19.33 | | 118.18 | 110.14 | Powerfin/ Tractebel |
| Mátrai Power Stn.[c] | 36 | 34.25 | 38.09 | 10.14 | | 77.74 | 73.96 | RWE Energie/ EV Schwaben |
| Total electric | 318.66 | 308.16 | 46.81 | 181.91 | | 126.11 | 121.96 | |

*Notes*:
a)   Mainly US and UK investment funds.
b)   The successful bidders also have the right to convert their stake to a majority one after two years (i.e., in 1997).
c)   7 power stations were put up for sale (the eighth, the nuclear power station at Paks, was excluded), but the bids received in all but the above two cases were judged unacceptable by the SPHC.
*Source*:   Mihályi (1996); Voszka (1996), Heti Világgazdaság 1996/5, February 3.

Telecommunications and frequency management legislation were passed in 1993, and the tariff regime overhauled in line with international practice with effect from January 1994 (see case study below).

The Act on Mining (Act No. XLVIII of 1993) is of considerable significance in the context of energy regulation and privatization. It makes detailed provision for the granting of concessions for mining and related activities, including exploitation of domestic oil and gas fields, and for the distribution and storage of hydrocarbons. Of special significance for the gas supply industry is the provision of open access to the natural gas transmission pipelines (owned by MOL) where there is extra capacity (this applies only to natural gas produced in Hungary), thus preparing the way for the de-monopolization and introduction of competition in gas supply.

By far the most important pieces of legislation as regards regulation of the energy sector are the Act on Gas Supply and the Act on the Generation and Distribution of Electrical Energy (Acts Nos: XLI and XLVIII of 1994), whose scope includes not only regulation of the transmission, supply and sale of gas and electricity, and the obligation to meet reasonable demand for a supply, but also safety provisions and provision for environmental and consumer protection. The Gas Act also makes provision for establishing the Hungarian Energy Office (MEH), a government agency under the supervision of the Ministry of Industry and Trade, and defines its regulatory functions, which include the issue of licences, e.g., for the supply of gas.[22] MEH also has the power (both under the Act and in the terms of the operating licences) to inspect installations (including consumer appliances) and their operation and maintenance, and may require licenced supply companies to seek authorization in the case of certain commercial decisions which could affect their ability to supply (e.g., mergers, demergers, reduction of equity and 'sale of a significant stake').

## Price Regulation

In the case of oil and oil derivatives, government price controls were removed with effect from 1991, since when both retail and wholesale prices have been market-driven. Ex-refinery prices are set by MOL in accordance with world market levels to compete with imports. Price controls for coal, coal-related products and Propane-Butane gas were also removed from March 1992.

Until December 31, 1996, the maximum official prices for natural gas are regulated by the Pricing Act (Act No. LXXXVII of 1990), with a phased increase beginning in 1995,[23] in accordance with the rules for price formulation and application established by MEH, as stipulated in the Gas Act.[24] Pricing from 1997 is subject to a government resolution (Resolution No. 1075/1995 (VIII.4)), which stipulates that both wholesale and retail prices must fully reflect justified operating costs and investments (including environmental commitments), and allow for an 8 per cent return on equity to ensure operational continuity. Prices are to be set by the Ministry of Industry and Trade, on the recommendation of the MEH, in accordance with an escalation formula (indexed to CPI) annexed to the resolution.

As in the case of gas, increases in electricity prices were introduced in three stages from September 1, 1995;[25] under the Electricity Act, charges for electricity from 1997 must contain justified costs and allow for an 8 per cent return on equity. Charges for district heating (including hot water and steam to industrial consumers), following a 1995 amendment to the Pricing Act, are determined by the Ministry for industry and Trade in consultation with MVM (in the case of power stations owned by MVM), on the basis of actual costs, and by the Municipalities in the case of district heating companies. (Comprehensive legislation and regulation of heat supply is pending.)

The regulatory system in Hungary is undoubtedly still in its infancy, and analysts are quick to point to actual or potential shortcomings. While legal loopholes may present problems of interpretation, however, and it may yet be some time before the institutions monitoring the operations of the regulated utilities develop the mechanisms for smooth and clear communication between the various groups whose interests they are designed to protect, such problems do not necessarily represent an insurmountable risk to investors in the utilities, while consumers in Hungary and other CEE countries have yet to develop adequate representative mechanisms. A far more important question, certainly as far as the investors (and the companies themselves) are concerned, is the credibility of the government's commitment to maintaining an 'arm's-length' relationship with the regulatory framework it has put in place.

Incidents such as the Prime Minister's personal intervention in the privatization of the Hungar-Hotels chain in January 1995, effectively annulling the transaction, brought considerable scepticism from within Hungary and abroad concerning the Hungarian government's commitment to continued depoliticization of the economic sphere, and fears that party-political forces still retained the upper hand in the state apparatus. On August 22, 1996, the government announced its decision – over the head of Industry Minister, Imre Dunai (who immediately tendered his resignation) – to postpone the third stage of energy price increases (scheduled for October 1, 1996) till January 1997, despite its legal obligation and pledge to investors to implement the increases. Again, confidence in the current government was undermined, and share prices were dealt a severe blow (shares in MOL fell by 9 per cent within one day on the Budapest and London Stock Exchanges, trading in MOL shares was suspended for a day, and trading on OTC markets of shares in the regional electric utilities came to a standstill). In addition to the potential losses to the investors,[26] such incidents call into question the stability of the regulatory system and are likely to jeopardize further privatization of the strategic sectors in particular (and thus also the revenues to the state).

## Case study: Privatization and Regulation of Telecommunications

Reform and privatization of telecommunications was given priority over that of other utilities in Hungary and in most of the transition economies in CEE for several reasons.

- the extreme backwardness of the existing network and services,[27] starved of investment under socialism (due to emphasis on 'material' production sectors; ideological control of information), presented a serious **barrier to economic regeneration**, especially to the development of the private sector, to competitive foreign trade and thus to prospects of integration into the world economy. It was also the major technical impediment to the development of other services and institutions essential to a market economy, e.g., banking and financial services, business information services, data processing, as well as to the modernization of the state administration.

- the **scale of investment** (much of it, moreover, long-term, sunk investment) required to extend and modernize the sector to bring Hungary's telecoms network up to the average 1990 EU level (38 per cent penetration) by the end of the century,[28] was beyond the scope of domestic investors and of the hard-pressed central budget. Domestic investment resources had shrunk due to the fall in GDP (–3.5 per cent in 1990; –11.9 per cent in 1991) and to the imposition of monetary and fiscal controls in order to stabilize the economy and curb inflation; Hungary was both internally and externally indebted, and the transition placed extra burdens on the budget (e.g., unemployment benefits), further constraining investment; due to their high subsidy content, rapid liberalization of charges for telecommunications services in order to raise revenue for investment was politically infeasible within the state sector.

- investment in telecommunications development has significant externality effects (especially for an economy in transition) which made it an **objective of economic regeneration** in itself: creation of new employment (absorption of unemployed labour, reducing welfare burden); it is a growth industry, attractive to investors and resilient to recession (inward investment, for exrevenues); technology transfer, with its attendant benefits; increasing the value of human capital (technical, management skills); multiplier effects (creation of new service industries, businesses).

The Hungarian Telecommunications Company (Matáv), the national telecoms provider, among the five largest companies in Hungary in terms of capital and turnover, was founded in 1990 when the Hungarian Post Office was divided up, separating its constituent operations, postal services, telecommunications and broadcasting. Regulation of telecommunications was transferred to the Ministry for Transport, Telecommunications and Water Management (MTTW). Corporatization of Matáv was completed in July 1991, when the company was registered as a joint-stock company wholly owned by the state (which exercised its ownership rights through the SPA, until the SHC was established in late 1992 to manage strategic assets of the state). As the groundwork was being laid for a partial privatization of Matáv involving a strategic foreign investor, the company embarked on a massive programme of network development, raising funds in the form of development loans from multilateral organizations such as the World Bank and the EBRD, commercial bond issues, incentive schemes for potential subscribers, and – in an innovative move – launched its own (joint venture) investment company, Investel.

Partial liberalization of its pricing regime, including consumer tariffs, in 1991, increased revenues and opened further external credit lines, as well as enhancing the sector's attractiveness to foreign investors poised to enter the potentially lucrative CEE telecommunications markets as soon as the legislative and regulatory environment became more transparent. Earlier liberalization of other segments of the market, e.g., equipment manufacture, had led companies such as Siemens and Ericsson into the arena from 1990 with major joint ventures, providing much of the hardware required for the first phase of modernization, the installation of a new digital overlay backbone network and digitalization of exchanges (despite CO-COM restrictions, which were only eased in February 1992). By 1993, significant progress had been made; over half a million new lines had been installed and waiting times for potential subscribers had been halved in many areas (see Table 3). Matáv reorganized and decentralized its operations, setting up a number of subsidiaries and joint ventures to carry out diverse activities ranging from network construction to international trading, and in summer 1991 launched Westel, the first (analogue) mobile telephone service in CEE, in a joint venture with US West.

**Table 3.  Data on Telecommunications in Hungary (1991–94)**

|                                        | 1991      | 1992      | 1993      | 1994      |
|----------------------------------------|-----------|-----------|-----------|-----------|
| Main lines                             | 1,128,129 | 1,291,133 | 1,497,577 | 1,731,502 |
| Main lines per 100 inhabitants         | 10.92     | 12.52     | 14.57     | 17.3      |
| Public payphones                       | 26,725    | 28,321    | 30,631    | 33,700    |
| Card phones                            | 300       | 1,218     | 8,500     | –         |
| Exchanges                              | 1,710     | 1,680     | 1,735     | 1,829     |
| automatic (%)                          | 93.2[a]   | 95.2      | 96.5      | –         |
| – of which digital (%)                 | 7.4[a]    | 16.5      | 33.0      | 47.0[b]   |
| Telefax stations                       | 14,580    | 24,721    | 29,388    | –         |
| Telex stations                         | 14,213    | 13,296    | 11,664    | –         |
| Waiting list (potential subscribers)   | 657,796   | 753,079   | 771,873   | –         |

a. 1990
b. 1995; Business Central Europe (1995): 43.
*Sources*:   Matáv Rt.; UK Government OTS (1994); Hunya , 1995.

While network development and the diversification of value-added services proceeded at a remarkable pace, progress with legislation on telecommunications and resolving regulatory uncertainties was much slower. The Telecommunications Act was passed in November, 1992, but did not come into force until July 1993, following the passage of companion legislation on frequency management. The Act was accompanied by a policy document setting out the government's strategy for development of the various segments of the telecommunications market, defining policy principles on the granting of concessions for the provision of telecommunications services, outlining the regulatory regime and plans concerning Matáv's privatization.

These two documents represented something of a compromise on the key issue of Matáv's monopoly as the national services provider. Initial drafts, envisaging the introduction of competition only in value-added services, but retaining exclusive use of the base network (on grounds of natural monopoly) showed the influence of the telecommunications industry. Months of debate moderated the policy finally adopted; liberalization was envisaged for an extensive range of telecommunications services and, significantly, competition was to be introduced in the regional telephone markets. On the other hand, Matáv would retain its monopoly over the national network (on the grounds of its 'obligation to supply' and to prevent 'cherry-picking' in the development and provision of services); its monopoly in the international and domestic long-distance market would also be retained until 1999, in order to secure (via continued cross-financing) the revenues necessary for the 'stable' completion of network modernization and development, and enhance the company's eventual privatization prospects (and thereby also the likely revenue to the treasury from privatization). Although the abolition of Matáv's monopoly in the provision of local services was a significant step (and unique in the region),[29] and the gradual phasing out of its monopoly in other segments of the market was in accord with EU policy concerning telecommunications monopolies in its own member states, the dominant position of Matáv remained secure, especially given that many value-added services also rely on access to the base network.

Under the Telecommunications Act, the market is divided as follows:

- **services subject to concession agreements** (under the provisions of the Act on Concessions): these consist principally of those services which the state has an obligation to supply, e.g., public telephony serviecs, public mobile telecommunications services, public national paging systems, and both national and regional television/radio broadcasting. The Telecommunications Act stipulated that, from April 30, 1994, public telephony services could only be provided by concession-holders. Local concessions were to be put out to tender if a majority (50 per cent) in the local municipality so requested, and Matáv would be allowed to bid on the same terms as other would-be service providers.
- **services subject to licence**: e.g., public switched data transmission, cable television.
- **services not requiring authorization**: e.g., proprietary, private or closed group networks within the premises of any organization or business.

There is no unitary regulatory authority; instead, different functions are assigned as follows:

- the **Communications Supervisory Authority**, with regional offices throughout the country, holds responsibility for issuing licences for the provision of telecommunications services;
- the **Telecommunications Conciliation Forum** has as its principal function to 'protect the public interest', liaising between national and local government bodies, industry representatives and consumers and asrbitrating in case of disputes between them;[30]
- the **Ministry of Transport, Telecommunications and Water Management (MTTW)**, to which the other two bodies are accountable, has overall regulatory responsibility, notably for formulating and implementing policy and regulating prices.

A radical and necessary overhaul of price regulation was carried out, and a new tariff regime was introduced with effect from January 1, 1994, replacing administratively set (by ministerial decree) maximum charges for individual services with a price-capping system in the case of most tariffs. Not unlike the system in operation in the UK, the cap applies to the rate of increase in total revenue earned from a group of services, but in Hungary it is indexed to producer prices (PPI) rather than consumer prices (the CPI, as in the UK). The regime is designed with the intention of gradually eliminating the long-standing price distortions resulting from cross-subsidization and bringing charges, especially for local calls, into line with costs by the end of the decade. In real terms, the cap (shown in Table 4 below) is expected to mean an annual price increase of 15–20 per cent in the case of local and zone I calls, and a reduction of approxiately 10 per cent per annum in charges for domestic long-distance (zones II and III) and international calls.

**Table 4.   Telephone Tariff Regulatory Regime**

| Tariff | Pre-1994 | Post-1994 |
| --- | --- | --- |
| Connection | administratively fixed charge | administratively set maximum charge |
| Repair | based on actual cost | unrestricted |
| Line rental | administratively set maximum charge | price cap |
| Local calls | administratively set maximum charge | price cap (PPI+7%) |
| Domestic long-distance calls – zone I | administratively set maximum charge | price cap (PPI+7%) |
| Domestic long-distance calls – zones II and III | administratively set maximum charge | price cap (PPI–4%) |
| International calls | unrestricted | price cap (PPI–4%) |

*Source*:   MTTW, Heti Világgazdaság, 1993/32, August 7: 45.

Potential investors appeared undeterred by the delay in implementing the new price regulation mechanism and establishing the regulatory institutions. 14 major telecommunications companies (or consortia) submitted bids in August 1993,[31] when the tender was issued for the privatization of a significant minority stake (at least 30 per cent) in Matáv, along with a concession for the provision of public international and domestic long-distance services and local services in 29 areas (see endnote 29). The duration of the concession was to be 25 years, renewable for a further 12.5 years, with a clause granting 8 years' exclusivity and committing the concession-holder to a development plan including a minimum 15.5 per cent annual increase in the number of telephone lines and elimination of the waiting list by 1997. Four bidders were short-listed to participate in the second round, the outcome of which was announced in December 1993: the German-US consortium, MagyarCom (comprising Deutsche Telekom and Ameritech) had acquired a 30.2 per cent stake, along with operational and financial control of Matáv, for the sum of USD 875 mn, surpassing the expectations of the most optimistic analysts.[32] USD 400 mn was to be used to raise the company's equity; USD 133.25 mn in concession fees was to be paid to the Ministry (and ultimately into the Telecommunications Fund); USD 6.5 mn covered the privatization consultants' fees, while the remaining USD 335.25 mn was paid to the SHC in exchange for Matáv shares.

The second phase of Matáv's privatization was beset by delays and uncertainties related to the protracted debate on privatization policy and legislation under the new socialist/liberal government which was elected into office in summer 1994. A decision in principle was announced at the end of 1994 to reduce the stake to be held long-term in state ownership to 25 per cent + 1 vote. Regarding the nature and timing of the sale of a second tranche of shares, a number of issues arose which focused sharply the interests of the government (via the State Privatization and Holding Company (SPHC), which took over the functions of the SPA and SHC following the passage of the new Privatization Act in summer 1995) and those of the incumbent stakeholder, MagyarCom.

First, there was the question of whether to target the sale at portfolio or strategic investors; since seeking a strategic investor other than MagyarCom itself would have been out of the question, the debate revolved around whether the sale should take place by means of public offering and/or stock market flotation, or by inviting MagyarCom to convert its minority stake to a majority one. MagyarCom clearly had an interest in increasing its stake to at least 50 per cent + 1, and there were strong arguments for postponing any share issue or flotation until the company was in a stronger financial position.[33] The position of the SPHC, on the other hand, reflected the government's need for privatization revenue – if possible by the end of 1995 – if the budget deficit was to be kept under control and the targeted figure for revenues from privatization (HUF 150 bn) for 1995 was to be met. In effect, the state asset management company increasingly aligned itself with Matáv/MagyarCom representatives in favour of the more rapid and straightforward option: allowing MagyarCom to increase its stake. However, the SPHC was keen to sell the maximum possible stake; MagyarCom had to be persuaded, since the acquisition of more than 50 per cent + 1 voting share would not significantly increase its control over the company (Mihályi 1996). Finally, in late December 1995, it was announced that MagyarCom was to purchase a further 37 per cent stake in Matáv for the sum of USD 852 mn, thus giving it a total stake of just over 67 per cent.[34]

# PRIVATIZATION AND GROWTH OF THE PRIVATE SECTOR IN HUNGARY

## Competition Policy[35]

The importance of competition policy as part of the institutional framework for a market-type economy, reinforcing privatization and the formation of new private businesses, has long been recognized in Hungary. The current Act on competition policy has been in force, virtually without amendment, for 5 years, but a new draft law was laid before parliament in June 1996. One major change will be the widening of the scope of the act to cover not only businesses and business activities, but any person or organization (e.g., professional associations) whose actions are deemed to undermine competition. A company's behaviour abroad can also be taken into account under the amended law, in cases where the company's activities abroad will have an effect on competition in Hungary. Consumers will also be given more extensive protection from misleading marketing practices (which accounted for the largest number of fines against companies in the past five years). Company mergers – expected to increase in numbers in Hungary over the next few years – will also come under closer supervision in future.

The most significant changes to be brought about by the new Act are listed below:

- broader range of legal and natural persons falling within the scope of the Act;
- application of the general clause (forbidding unfair market practices) will become a matter for the courts instead of the Competition Office;
- regulations governing practices which mislead the consumer are modified and extended;
- prohibition of 'vertical cartels' between market agents not in competition with each other;
- removal of prohibition of cartels formed between companies under the same ownership (i.e., not independent);
- government may grant exemptions from cartel prohibition at its discretion, including overriding an earlier decision by the Competition Office;

- definition of types of merger requiring authorization has been broadened (i.e., acquisition of controlling rights, not only structural fusion);
- ceiling on market concentration of companies to be determined on the basis of revenue from sales (set at HUF 10 bn), not market share;
- a market share of over 30 per cent will not be assumed *per se* to imply market domination;
- the Competition office will have greater control over decisions to take legal action (via the Competition Council) in cases of alleged violation of competition law or unfair practice;
- decisions to initiate proceedings under the law must be made public by the Competition Office;
- the proceedings of the Competition Council (court) are to be public;
- the Competition Council may declare its judgement (including payment of any fines) to be effective immediately;
- interest to be charged at twice the current central bank rate on any overdue fines;
- where a decision of the Competition Office is found to be in breach of the law, the CO will pay any fine, plus damages incurred, with interest at the same rate as above.

## Institutions Managing Privatization

The 1996 budget provided for the establishing of the Treasury Property Directorate (Kincstári Vagyoni Igazgatóság), under the direct supervision of the Finance Ministry. However, the precise role and functions of this body remain undefined – especially with regard to the 'division of labour' between this and the State Privatization and Holding Company (APVRt). At some time in the future, a decision must be reached with regard to the future of the APVRt. If privatization of state-owned corporate assets is completed in 1997 (as planned), will the APVRt be disbanded? What form of institutional management will be put in place to look after the shares remaining in state ownership in the longer term (e.g., 25 per cent stake in MOL and in the electricity companies)? Some observers think it possible, even likely, that a third institution – the investment arm of the Hungarian Investment and Development Bank (there are plans to split the bank in two) – will be given charge of this task. Others do not rule out the possibility that – depending on the political environment – responsibility will revert to the relevant ministries.

Table 5 shows how the portfolio of state asset management companies changed between 1990 and 1995. It can be seen that at the end of 1995 Hungary only had 12 completely state-owned companies, but there were still several hundred companies with majority state ownership. Table 6 shows the flows of income and expenditure generated by the privatization and other trans-actions of the asset management companies. Clearly, 1995 was a very successful year for Hungary's privatization, as we discuss more fully in the next sub-section.

**Table 5.   Changes in the Portfolio of the State Asset Management Bodies**
**(to 31.12.1996)**

| State-owned enterprises<br>As of January 1, 1990 | Number<br>1,857 |
|---|---|
| Changes (from January 1, 1990) | |
| • Transferred from other asset management org. | 1 |
| • Transferred to other asset management organization | 84 |
| • In liquidation | 342 |
| • Dissolved | 115 |
| • Closed down | 13 |
| • Incorporated | 1299 |
| State-owned enterprises as of 31 December 1996 | 5 |
| Companies – total | 1691 |
| • Established *via* incorporation | 1299 |
| • Founded or acquired | 362 |
| • Transferred from other asset management bodies | 30 |
| Changes | |
| • Transferred to other asset management organizations | 62 |
| • In liquidation | 137 |
| • Dissolved | 38 |
| • Closed down | 21 |
| • 100% privatized (sold) | 915 |
| • Under asset management | 11 |
| Current number of companies* | 507 |
| of which • in majority state ownership | 245 |
| • in minority state ownership | 262 |

*Note*:   *The state retains a long-term stake in a total of 109 companies, including a golden share in 20 of these.
*Source*:   Privatizációs Monitor, 1996.

## Progress with Privatization

1995 set a record for the privatization of state-owned assets in Hungary; in terms of book value, HUF 481 bn state-owned assets were transferred to private owners, 20 per cent more than in the previous 5 years taken together. Cash revenues were also correspondingly high, at HUF 438 bn (60 per cent higher than the total until that time). Thus despite a slow start, numerous disputes and the apparent stagnation of privatization initiatives in the first three-quarters of the year, November and December brought some real successes. However, the 15 headline-stealing strategic sector transactions deflected attention from other developments in the privatization process. Other important transactions included the completion of the privatization of Hungary's pharmaceutical firms: Egis, Biogal, Chinoin, Richter and Humán, to a mixture of institutional and strategic investors, bringing revenues totalling more than HUF 18 bn. A number of these large transactions (though fewer in total than in the previous year), as well as the sale of MOL and OTP shares took place on the Budapest Stock Exchange, greatly boosting its capitalization. Towards the end of 1995, the long-delayed privatization of Budapest Bank (an earlier contender, Credit Suisse, had withdrawn in March) was successfully resolved with the sale of a 60 per cent stake to General Electric Capital Services for the sum of nearly USD 90 mn.[36]

**Table 6.   Income and Expenditure of the State Asset Management Institutions 1990–95 (in HUF bns)**

| Expenditure | 1990 | 1991 | 1992 | 1993 | 1994 | 1995 | Total |
|---|---|---|---|---|---|---|---|
| Directly related to privatization and asset management (incl. operational costs) | – | 1.14 | 6.16 | 7.56 | 25.26 | 14.78 | 54.90 |
| Payments to municipalities and companies required by legal provisions | – | 2.29 | 4.30 | 3.42 | 6.04 | 6.07 | 22.12 |
| Payments and reserves related to guarantees | – | – | 5.78 | 7.79 | 7.01 | 3.65 | 24.23 |
| Payments related to reorganization of assets (companies); investments in preparation for privatization | – | – | 8.70 | 49.53 | 8.03 | 17.38 | 83.64 |
| Payments to budget (total) – of which: | 0.51 | 22.37 | 51.51 | 57.45 | 151.67 | 176.37 | 459.88 |
| • direct payments to budget | 0.51 | 9.36 | 24.53 | 2.61 | 39.57 | 150.00 | 226.58 |
| • contributions to special government funds | – | – | 4.50 | 7.22 | 17.95 | 0.24 | 29.91 |
| • payments in respect of state commitments | – | – | 22.48 | 47.62 | 94.15 | 20.57 | 197.83 |
| • dividend payments | – | – | – | – | – | 5.56 | 5.56 |
| Other | – | – | – | – | – | 23.69 | 23.69 |
| TOTAL* | 0.51 | 25.80 | 76.45 | 125.75 | 198.01 | 241.94 | 668.46 |
| **Income** | | | | | | | |
| Convertible currencies | 0.53 | 24.61 | 40.98 | 110.67 | 10.95 | 412.05 | 599.79 |
| Forints | 0.14 | 5.74 | 24.92 | 22.96 | 35.41 | 39.52 | 128.69 |
| – of which income in respect of assets | – | 0.93 | 7.41 | 5.41 | 7.8 | 13.79 | 35.34 |
| Credit | 0 | 1.01 | 9.07 | 21.72 | 29.27 | 3.92 | 64.99 |
| Compensation vouchers | 0 | 0 | 2.26 | 14.56 | 64.2 | 18.48 | 99.50 |
| Convertible currency credit | 0 | 0 | 0 | 0 | 16.84 | – | 16.84 |
| Total | 0.67 | 31.36 | 77.23 | 169.91 | 156.67 | 473.97 | 909.81 |

*In January 1996, HUF 192 bn was paid to the budget from the surplus privatization revenue in 1995.

*Source*:   APVRt,1996; Heti Világgazdaság, June 8 1996: 100.

Sales of small and medium-sized firms, on the other hand, totalled only 119 in 1995, compared with 228 in 1994 and 230 in 1993.[37] The so-called pre-privatization, affecting retail, catering and small service establishments, which was launched in 1990[38] as one of the earliest privatization initiatives, had not yet reached completion at the end of 1995. Some 350–400 cases still await resolution (out of a total of approximately 10,700), the long delay in most cases being due to legal disputes related to past anomalies in practice regarding land registration and leasehold rights. Total revenues to the state from pre-privatization are in the region of HUF 20 bn, so the sale of the remaining outlets is unlikely to swell the state coffers to any great extent.

The 'simplified privatization' scheme[39] for small and medium businesses (with assets of less than HUF 600 mn and fewer than 500 employees), was initiated by the socialist/liberal government in 1995 (under the new Privatization Act) in the interests of speeding up privatization and increasing cash revenues. A crucial distinction between this scheme, which aimed to include 300–400 firms, with the minimum involvement of the SPHC, and the earlier 'self-privatization', was that it was managed largely by the senior management of the firms themselves. Firms were expected to recommend a sale price (set on the basis of prescribed criteria), which was then approved or amended by a specialist committee set up for the purpose by the SPHC, following which a batch of firms would be listed and memoranda issued. If the firm failed to attract a purchaser in the first round, the task of privatizing would fall to the management. As of December 1995, out of 73 firms advertised, 37 firms were sold, principally to Hungarian investors, using this technique, while 34 were unsuccessful. A second, and much larger batch of firms was expected to be announced late in 1995, but was delayed until March 1996 – and then only included 48 companies. Among the reasons for the delay, analysts cite legal problems, but also the fact that the need for a case-by-case decision by the SPHC 'expert' committee on the minimum asking price for individual firms, has in effect made the procedure more bureaucratic than was intended (Voszka, 1996).

HUF 18.5 bn worth of assets were exchanged in 1995 for compensation vouchers with a nominal value of HUF 10.6 bn.[40] Between 1991 and 1995 vouchers with a total nominal value of HUF 70 bn were accepted by the state asset management bodies in payment for shares (34 per cent) or assets sold *via* tender or auction (64 per cent). Prospects of absorbing the compensation vouchers still in circulation or yet to be issued (the total estimated nominal value is HUF 81 bn), look increasingly difficult, given the greatly reduced number of privatizable assets remaining and the state's as yet only partially fulfilled commitment to transfer substantial assets to the Social Insurance organizations.[41] This was reflected in the decision, announced in March 1995, to permit voucher holders to convert their entitlement into a life pension.

Contraction of the state sector, vitally important to the relative expansion of the private sector, has been substantial in Hungary, although it is still far from completion. Hungary has remained an attractive destination for foreign investment; with total inflows of almost USD 13 bn up to the end of 1995, Hungary alone accounts for nearly half of total FDI in the CEE region. While around USD 5 bn of this was related to privatization of state-owned assets, an even larger share (USD 8 bn) of total foreign investment went into greenfield projects. The US and Germany are the leading investors in Hungary, both in privatization (see Table 7) and overall, with total investments (to end-1995) of USD 5.2 bn and USD 4 bn respectively. According to Ministry of Industry and Trade figures, foreign-owned and joint venture companies (which total around 25,000), are estimated to account for around 25 per cent of privately-owned entrepreneurial assets,[42] and produce 70 per cent of Hungary's export income.

Table 7.   **Foreign Investment in Privatization, by Country (Cumulative Totals from 1990 at Market Prices)**

| Country | No. of companies | | HUF bns | | Percentage of total | |
| --- | --- | --- | --- | --- | --- | --- |
| | end-1995 | end-1996 | end-1995 | end-1996 | end-1995 | end-1996 |
| Germany | 96 | 101 | 270.75 | 288.14 | 36.74 | 34.50 |
| USA | 34 | 39 | 143.00 | 167.82 | 19.40 | 20.10 |
| France | 41 | 41 | 102.00 | 102.00 | 13.84 | 12.21 |
| Austria | 112 | 116 | 46.75 | 52.06 | 6.34 | 6.23 |
| Belgium | 9 | 9 | 33.93 | 33.93 | 4.60 | 4.06 |
| Italy | 22 | 28 | 27.28 | 34.76 | 3.70 | 4.16 |
| UK | 33 | 33 | 19.64 | 19.64 | 2.67 | 2.35 |
| Netherlands | 14 | 16 | 19.45 | 24.86 | 2.64 | 2.98 |
| CIS | 16 | 16 | 10.45 | 10.46 | 1.42 | 1.25 |
| Sweden | 11 | 11 | 10.04 | 5.73 | 1.36 | 0.69 |
| Switzerland | 16 | 18 | 7.86 | 18.41 | 1.07 | 2.20 |
| Other | 47 | 51 | 45.80 | 77.31 | 6.21 | 9.25 |
| • of which international public offerings | 19 | 20 | 40.18 | 68.64 | 5.45 | 8.22 |
| Total | 451 | 479 | 736.95 | 835.12 | 100.00 | 100.00 |

*Note*:   Table does not include greenfield investment.
*Source*:   ÁPV Rt., Mihályi, 1996.

The MIT put the share of the private sector as a whole in GDP at around 60 per cent at the end of 1995 (UN/ECE survey estimates give a higher figure (70 per cent, end-1994)[43]. Also at the end of 1995, 60 per cent of Hungary's banking sector was estimated to be in private hands (Voszka, 1996). Estimates from the MIT on the weight of private sector involvement in various industries in 1995 included: trade (90 per cent), construction (75–80 per cent), textiles (75 per cent, with 25 per cent foreign capital), paper industry (60 per cent, including 50 per cent foreign involvement), and printing (55 per cent).[44]

# CONCLUSIONS

Hungary's privatization made a slow start and then accelerated dramatically in 1995 as a range of legal and political issues were resolved, many public utility companies were sold off, and many other components of the privatization programme bore fruit. In the early months of the present government's life there were serious doubts about Hungary's commitment to privatization and, correspondingly, there was notably slow progress with new legislation. It also proved unexpectedly difficult and contentious to settle the terms of the merger between the SPA and the SAMC to form the SHPC. Once resolved, rapid progress became possible.

However, it is also important to refer to important financial constraints, both internally, from the Ministry of Finance, and externally from the IMF (among others) which almost certainly contributed greatly to focusing the government's mind and hence allowing the recent progress to be achieved.

It is unlikely that progress with privatization in 1996 and beyond will prove to be as rapid as in 1995, partly because there are simply fewer firms left to privatize, and in particular relatively few of the attractive utility companies that did so well in 1995. Moreover, many of the firms still in complete or partial state ownership are in poor economic shape and urgently need either drastic (and presumably expensive!) restructuring, or closure. Either of these options raises difficult and so far unresolved issues about how to pay for restructuring, and how to keep down the social costs of major closures. Hungary's earlier policy of getting on with privatization and leaving it to new owners to manage restructuring – the new owners paying the necessary costs and also keeping the social consequences of their decisions somewhat removed from government – might simply be unworkable for many of the remaining firms. But no new strategy is yet in sight.

As far as the public utilities are concerned, a great deal of progress with privatization has been achieved after a somewhat hesitant and uncertain start. For the energy sector and for telecommunications, regulatory bodies have been established to govern pricing policy, various licensing issues, access to networks, investment policy, and related issues, though unlike in the UK the regulators are quite closely associated with the relevant sector ministries. The main issue for regulation has not been the precise details of this or that specific measure (though many questions could be asked about that), but whether the Hungarians would succeed in establishing a regulatory framework that commanded the respect and confidence of the firms being regulated, the population in general, and the government. Unfortunately, as we have seen, the attempt to establish regulation that would function at 'arms length' from the government has not yet succeeded, and episodes of undesirable government intervention have been very damaging for regulatory credibility. Even worse, such episodes not only upset the stock market and reduce prices of existing privatized public utility shares (hopefully only temporarily), but the resulting regulatory uncertainty probably serves to lower the price at which subsequent public utility sales will be feasible. There could therefore be a high price to pay for at best very modest gains from the intervention.

Finally, Hungary remains unique in the region in the extent to which its privatization has relied upon sales rather than the free distribution of state-owned assets.

Hungary's approach has succeeded to a far greater extent than many observers expected and the country deserves credit for that. However, while one important function of privatization is to 'distance' former state-owned enterprises from the state, and to depoliticize business decisions, in this respect Hungary has not quite succeeded yet and further progress is needed.

# NOTES

1. The authors are indebted to Attila Havas, Pál Valentiny, Éva Voszka, Péter Mihályi, József Balogh, Marcella Niklós, Ernö Zalai, Péter Ákos Bod, Klaus Meyer and Tamás Révész, for their invaluable comments and suggestions.
2. Canning and Hare, 1994; Hare, 1994; See also Estrin, 1994; Voszka 1991, 1994.
3. Not only in the CEE countries themselves; western analysts have constantly had to revise and refine their views on privatization since 1990 as the complexities of privatizing in the transition economies have become apparent.
4. Act No. XXV of 1991 on Partial Compensation for Damages Unlawfully Caused by the State to Properties Owned by Citizens, in the Interest of Settling Ownership Relations. This Act covered damages occurring under the socialist regime (from 1949); further legislation was passed in 1992 awarding compensation for damages suffered between 1939 and 1949, and in cases of persons deprived of their lives or liberty for political reasons.
5. Act No. XXXIII of 1991 on the Transfer of Certain State Assets to the Ownership of Local Municipalities.
6. Tamás Szabó, Minister without portfolio responsible for privatization, in a document introducing the voucher scheme, 'Strategy for a breakthrough in privatization' (October 1992). See Canning and Hare, 1994, for more detailed discussion.
7. Tax concessions (of up to ten years) already granted to foreign investors before the end of 1993 were not revoked. Although some Hungarian observers claim that official policy documents of the period showed a clear distancing from the aim of attracting foreign investors, and there was some concern at the time that such policy shifts would deter investors, FDI nevertheless continued (and continues) to play an important role, both in privatization and in greenfield investment in Hungary. Hungary has remained the largest recipient of FDI of all the transition economies in CEE, with an estimated total of USD 14bn between late 1989 and mid-1996 (compared, for example, with Poland's USD 9bn, Russia's USD 6.6bn and the Czech Republic's USD 6bn) (OMRI Daily Digest, Part II, February 20, 1997).
8. Csurka later went on to found the right-wing nationalist Hungarian Justice and Life Party (MIÉP), but his supporters, though vocal, have not been sufficient in number to gain him a seat in parliament.
9. The self-privatization scheme was in part a response to the lack of success of earlier, heavily bureaucratic privatization methods; firms eligible to participate in the scheme entered into a transformation/privatization contract with a consultancy firm selected from a list approved by the SPA. Privatization proposals thereafter only required formal 'rubber-stamping' by the SPA in order to go ahead. (See e.g., Canning and Hare, 1994, for detailed discussion.)

10. See, e.g., Newbery (1994); Ordover, Pittman and Clyde (1994) for definition and detailed discussion of the issues surrounding natural monopolies.
11. Ordover, Pittman and Clyde (1994) give a useful summary of the literature on these issues.
12. See Valentiny (1994). Energy imports increased from 37 per cent in 1970 to 54.6 per cent in 1990.
13. Some, however, remained in the hands of the SPA, e.g., the power stations and the regional electricity supply companies. This was to lead to some embarrassment in 1993 when the Ministry for Industry and Trade and the SHC began privatization negotiations for MVM; the two agencies appeared to be acting at cross-purposes when almost simultaneously the SPA prematurely (and unsuccessfully) initiated the sale of 15 per cent of the shares it held in the supply companies.
14. ÁVÜ Közlöny (SPA Gazette), December 6, 1994: 14.
15. See also Mihályi, 1996: 731.
16. For example, to privatize MVM together with OVIT and the Paks nuclear power station, targetting principally smaller domestic investors, compensation voucher holders, and domestic and foreign institutional investors; a majority stake in the 6 electricity distributors and 7 power stations was to be sold to strategic investors.
17. National Mineral Oil and Gas Trust.
18. See Valentiny, 1994.
19. As Mihályi (1996) points out, the purchase price of fuel represents 70–90 per cent of overall costs in the energy sector; reducing capital costs therefore has little, if any, affect on energy prices.
20. See, e.g., Voszka (1996) for detailed analysis.
21. This section draws heavily on the analysis of Zoltán Faludi (1995).
22. In the case of the regional gas companies, which previously enjoyed exclusive rights to supply in their respective geographical areas, the new licencing rules allow for competition to take place between suppliers applying for a licence to operate in areas not already served by a gas supply; MEH issues licences for such areas to the company offering the highest standard of service at the lowest cost.
23. A three-stage increase in prices was envisaged, commencing with an 8 per cent increase effected on September 1, 1995; and increase of 25 per cent on March 1, 1996, and culminating with a further increase taking effect on October 1, 1996, the level of which was to be determined later. At the end of 1994, consumer prices for natural gas remained below the import price.
24. Magyar Energiahivatal, 'A földgáz árkiigazítási rendszere 1997-ig' (Structure for the adjustment of prices for natural gas up to 1997), March 20, 1995.
25. In the case of electricity, average consumer prices as of end-1994 were estimated to cover only 50 per cent of costs.
26. OMRI Daily Digest, August 23, 1996; OMRI Economic Digest, August 29, 1996 (electronic sources). The delay in raising energy prices was expected to cost the energy companies between HUF 100mn and HUF 1 bn (USD 660,000 – 6.6 mn), according to estimates published in the Hungarian dailies on September 2. The electricity companies feared that they would be hardest hit; MOL Director, Zoltán Mándoki pointed out that MOL's market value fell by HUF 16 bn as a result of the government's decision, and the company expected to lose revenues of between HUF 2 and 4 bn. (OMRI Economic Digest, September 2, 1996).

27. In 1990, Hungary had fewer than 10 main lines per 100 inhabitants, among the lowest penetration rates in Europe, and even by comparison with the former socialist countries of CEE (the figure for the Czech Republic was 16; in Slovenia, 21, compared with 33 in Spain, and 44 in the UK). Potential subscribers could expect to wait on average 12 years for a line to be installed; 10 per cent of exchanges were still operated manually and as many as 30 per cent of rural communities had no private telephone lines at all. (See Canning, 1996.)

28. A ten-year development plan drawn up by Matáv itself in 1990 estimated the investment required to reach this level of penetration at around USD 2bn (at 1990 prices); in 1992, a survey published by the International Telecommunications Union put Hungary's investment needs over the eight years to the end of the decade at USD 3.5bn. (Heti Világgazdaság, Telecommunications Supplement, April 29, 1994.)

29. Constraints of space prevent detailed discussion of developments related to the provision of local services. A brief outline is warranted, however, to give an indication of the market position of the local companies *vis-à-vis* Matáv. Under the Telecommunications Act, Hungary was divided into 56 (later 54) so-called primary regions. Local authorities in 25 regions submitted applications which met the eligibility criteria for tendering for concessions to supply local telephone services, subject to similar terms and conditions (duration, exclusivity for a limited period, development commitment) as in the case of the concession for international and long-distance services. Regions not applying automatically remained in the hands of Matáv. Bids were actually received (February 1994) for only 23 of the eligible regions, 8 of which were awarded to Matáv and 15 to independent operators, predominantly US and French-led consortia, some to local government companies (in a number of cases with a foreign partner). The outcome: including the 29 uncontested regional concessions, and the two which failed to attract bidders, Matáv gained control over 39 local networks; these represented an estimated 80 per cent of Hungary's local telephone market (see Canning, 1996).

30. The TCF is a non-profit making, non-political council. It receives funding from membership subscriptions and from the Telecommunications Fund. The Fund was set up by the MTTW for the main purpose of channelling resources (mainly concession fees, along with some central budget funding) into telecommunications modernization in less developed regions of Hungary.

31. In accordance with the government's policy decisions regarding the type of investor and commitment sought for Matáv, eligibility criteria included: operating experience (provision of telecommunications services to at least 1 mn subscribers); solvency (gross revenues from public telecommunications services of at least USD 1 bn in the previous 2 years); network development experience in the past 5 years.

32. Matáv's financial indicators were relatively poor, with productivity well below that of telecoms providers in many developing countries, and low profitability (its debt ratio was equivalent to almost half its registered capital). Its position improved, however, as a result of a timely capital injection (less than one month before the privatization deal was concluded) of HUF 8.55 bn, giving the International Finance Corporation (IFC) and the European Bank for Reconstruction and Development (EBRD) a stake of 0.99 per cent and 1.97 per cent respectively in Matáv (post privatization and capital-raising), and in part substituting earlier loans.

33. As a result of its massive investment and development commitments, Matáv's profits fell to a mere HUF 97 mn in 1994, extremely modest given that its equity is around HUF 185 bn (Mihályi, 1996). Moreover, the value of Matáv shares (traded on Hungary's secondary markets) had fallen from 280 per cent at the time of the first phase of privatization (December 1993) to 160–180 per cent in summer 1995. The company also suffered heavy losses when the court, arbitrating in a dispute between Matáv and 13 regional concessionaries over the value of assets transferred by Matáv, found in favour of the regional companies.
34. Smaller stakes in Matáv (totalling around 5 per cent) were transferred to employees, local municipalities and compensation voucher holders.
35. On the general issues of competition policy, see Fingleton *et al.*, (1996)
36. For detailed discussion of privatization and changes in ownership in the banking sector, see Várhegyi, 1996.
37. These figures do not include sales below HUF 50 mn (e.g., under pre-privatization).
38. Act No. LXXIV of 1990.
39. See Voszka, 1996; Mihályi, 1996 for details.
40. Principally Pannon Váltó and the ERAVIS hotel chain. Most of the shares thus issued on the stock exchange were in fact bought by voucher-holding funds rather than individuals. (Mihályi, 1996.)
41. The two bodies were to receive assets totalling HUF 55–65 bn; as of the end of 1995, only around HUF 10 bn had been transferred.
42. See Mihályi, 1996.
43. UN/ECE Economic Survey of Europe in 1994–95, Table 3.2.6.
44. These data are taken from the Internet (URL: http://www.ikm.hu/english), and should be regarded as approximations only.

# REFERENCES

ÁPV Rt (1996),'Összefoglaló az Állami Vagyonügynökség és az Állami Vagyonkezelö Rt. 1990–1994 közötti privatizációs tevékenységéröl, a bevételek és kiadások alakulásáról, valamint az 1995. év végére kialakult vagyoni állapotról', (Summary of the privatization activities, income and expenditure of the State Property Agency and the State Holding Company between 1990 and 1994, and the assets held as of the end of 1995), ÁPV Rt, January 1996.
Canning, A. (1996),'Privatization and Competition in Hungarian Telecommunications', in Ryan, D. (ed.), *Privatization and Competition in Telecommunications:*, Westport, CT: Praeger/Greenwood Publishing.
Canning, A. and P. Hare (1994),'The privatization process – economic and political aspects of the Hungarian approach', in Estrin, S. (ed.), *Privatization in Central and Eastern Europe,* Harlow: Longman, pp. 176–217.
Estrin, S. (1994),'Economic transition and privatization: the issues', in Estrin, S. (ed.), *Privatization in Central and Eastern Europe,* Harlow: Longman, pp. 3–30.
Faludi, Z. (1995),'A gázipar privatizációjának jogi problémái' (Legal problems related to the privatization of the gas industry), Gazdaság és Jog, No. 10, October 1995.
Fingleton, J., Fox, Eleanor, Neven, Damien and P. Seabright (1996), *Competition Policy and the Transformation of Central Europe,* London: CEPR.

Hare, P. (1994), 'Privatization in comparative perspective: an overview of the issues', in Estrin, S. (ed.), *Privatization in Central and Eastern Europe,* Harlow: Longman, pp. 31–53.

Havas, A. (1996), 'Privatization in Hungary', draft study prepared for Project Syndicate, Central European University, Budapest, mimeo.

Hungarian State Holding Company (1994), Annual Report 1994.

Hunya, G. (1995), 'Transport and Telecommunications Infrastructure in Transition', *Communist Economies and Economic Transformation,* Vol. 7(3), pp. 369–384.

Mihályi, P. (1996), 'Privatizáció 1995', in Kurtán, S., S. Péter and L. Vass (eds), Magyarország politikai évkönyv (Political Yearbook of Hungary), Budapest: Demokrácia Kutatások Magyar Központja Alapítvány, pp. 727–772.

Newbery, D.M. (1994), 'Restructuring and privatizing electric utilities in Eastern Europe', *Economics of Transition,* Vol. 2(3), Oxford University Press, pp. 291–316.

OECD (1994), *Review of industry and industrial policy in Hungary,* Paris: OECD

Ordover, J.A., Russell W. Pittman and P. Clyde (1994), 'Competition policy for natual monopolies in a developing market economy', *Economics of Transition,* Vol. 2(3), Oxford University Press, pp. 317–343.

Privatizációs M. (1996), WWW information website of the ÁPV Rt. http://www. apvrt.hu/ pmh1.htm

Valentiny, P. (1994), 'Energy regulation in Hungary', ESRC East-West Programme, Working Paper No. 3/94, Edinburgh: Centre for Economic Reform and Transformation, Heriot-Watt University.

Várhegyi, É. (1996), 'A bankrendszer átrendezödése' (Reorganization of the banking sector), in Petschnig, M.Z. (ed.), Jelentések az alagútból – Töréspontok (Reports from the tunnel – Breakpoints), Pénzügykutató Rt.: Budapest, pp. 88–99.

Voszka, É. (1991), 'A spontaneitástol a központontosításig – és tovább?' (From 'spontaneity' to centralization – and where next?) Pénzügykutató Rt., Budapest, Évkönyv 1991.

Voszka, É. (1994), 'A tulajdonosi szerkezet változása' (Changes in the structure of ownership), in Petschnig, M.Z. (ed.), Jelentések az alagútból, (Reports from the tunnel), Pénzügykutató Rt.: Budapest.

Voszka, É. (1996), 'A tulajdonosváltás jellemzöi' (The characteristics of the ownership reform), In Petschnig, M.Z. (ed.), Jelentések az alagútból – Töréspontok (Reports from the tunnel – Breakpoints), Pénzügykutató Rt.: Budapest, pp. 153–181.

## COMMENT ON 'POLITICAL ECONOMY OF PRIVATIZATION IN HUNGARY: A PROGRESS REPORT' BY ANNA CANNING AND PAUL HARE (Klaus E. Meyer)

Privatization in Hungary always has been a special case among the countries of Central and Eastern Europe. While others discussed and partially implemented mass privatization schemes, the Hungarian authorities focused on attracting outside investors. Any discussion of privatization in Hungary invariably led to foreign direct investment (FDI).

Times have moved on. Again, Hungary presents the observer with a completely different set of policy issues. Most chapters in this volume discuss issues such as creating effective corporate governance after mass privatization led to diffuse ownership. Yet, current Hungarian policy debates the regulation of privatized natural monopolies. It seems that Hungary is one step ahead again, or is it?

The excellent and very detailed account by Anna Canning and Paul Hare illuminates the volatility of the Hungarian privatization policy from 1989 to 1996. Throughout this period, the dominant policy has been to attract outside investors taking controlling stakes, apart from a set back after the election of 1994. Yet, the various privatization schemes developed at any stage, implemented or not, and often discontinued before long, have been written under the influence of the political moods of the day.

It is instructive to relate the changes in the privatization policy to the flows of foreign direct investment. Privatization started gradually with the first cases in late 1990. Many manufacturing enterprises were sold over the next three years. FDI inflows rose from US$ 215 million in 1989 to almost US$ 1.5 billion in 1991 and 1992. In 1993, privatization shifted towards restructuring and financing schemes to foster domestic investors. Yet, the first privatization of a 'strategic' company, MOL, and a December rush before the expiration of preferred tax treatment, raised FDI even further to US$ 2.4 billion. In 1994, privatization seemed to be on hold as the new government had to sort out its new institutional framework. FDI fell back to US$ 1.1 billion. In 1995, the privatization of natural monopolies again attracted foreign investors in a number of major projects. FDI rose to a new record high of US$ 3.4 billion. In *per capita* terms, Hungary is now one of the prime destinations for foreign investment, not far behind Singapore.

This close relationship of foreign investment and privatization raised a number of questions. Firstly, is this trend sustainable? Canning and Hare consider it unlikely that progress with privatization can be as rapid as in the past. There is simply not much left that would not only attract investors interest, but their willingness to pay substantial amounts of money for it. This suggests that the remarkable flow of FDI to Hungary is not sustainable, even in the medium term. For lack of acquisition targets, investors may increasingly turn to greenfield projects. This makes a different contribution to industrial development, but would attract smaller amounts of investment capital and government revenues – greenfield projects are by their nature initially small.

Secondly, how much did Hungary gain from its widely acclaimed lead as FDI host? As argued above, the investment capital is concentrated on a small number of major projects. These make the difference between FDI capital flows between Hungary and its Visegrad partners, Poland and the Czech Republic. In terms of the number of projects, multinational enterprises are equally present in all three countries, as reported by survey studies. However, the Hungarian privatization policy led to a distinct difference in the industrial structure: Major foreign ownership in some selected industries and key companies. The general expectation is that this should benefit the restructuring of these industries and companies, with consequent spill-over effects for the economy at large.

Thirdly, privatization generated more revenues for government budgets than in other countries of the region. Indeed, the chapter argues that financial constraints faced by the government have been a driving force behind the privatization policy, and particularly its timing. Is this a virtuous pressure? If one argues that privatization is desirable, but inhibited by bureaucracy or lack of political consensus, such budgetary pressure would indeed be helpful in bringing about privatization. Yet, if the budgetary needs determine the timing of privatization, this may lead to suboptimal outcomes. For instance, privatization without the prior establishment of the appropriate regulatory framework can lead to unsatisfactory outcomes: Canning and Hare report the withdrawal of tenders for regional gas and electricity distributors because of unsatisfactory bids.

Privatization revenues may also delay the development of a sustainable budgetary policy. The officially reported balance deficit is not in line with the long-term fiscal conditions. The problem equally emerges in Western Europe, where privatization revenues are used to make budgets 'fit' for the Maastricht criteria in the base year, 1996. In Hungary, the government has to find new ways of balancing its budget once all attractive enterprises are sold. If, as is hoped, the economy recovers and the tax collection system improves after the transition recession, then this may be a merely theoretical concern. Yet, the cash revenue may also delay reforms in other parts of the budget, such as pensions, subsidies to industry or social welfare. While softening the initial impact of capitalism, it could require more painful adjustment measures later.

The chapter moves on to discuss the privatization of natural monopolies, especially utilities and telecoms. Whereas the mass privatization or the small privatization could hardly draw on any Western experiences, this privatization needs to tackle many issues of very current concern in the UK and elsewhere. The establishment of independent regulatory authorities has been a major challenge in the UK. The debate on the appropriate methods and criteria for regulation is ongoing, and continuously reassessed based on recent experiences. Challenges of regulators from the political sphere are not uncommon. Yet, the concept of an independent authority gains increasing acceptance in society.

In Hungary, these institutions are far more difficult to establish. Even though the legal framework may be established, a regulatory body needs a political and social environment that respects its independence. In Central Europe, the general respect for any governmental institution is not very high after the experiences of central planning. Nor do politicians recognise the need to stick to a committed policy to maintain credibility with the business community. Credibility of the regulatory authorities, as well as political institutions with the power of changing the rules of the game, will only emerge over time. (Even the most respected of independent agencies, the Deutsche Bundesbank did not gain its reputation over night).

In this light, incidents such as the postponement of agreed energy price increases are discouraging. They reduce the credibility of future policy commitments, and thus potential privatization revenues. Other countries of the region may face even more regulation-related questions by potential investors once they reach this stage of privatization. On the other hand, they have the opportunity to learn from the Hungarian experience and set up their institutions right from the start.

MATAV is the crown-jewel in the new wave of privatization. Since the telecommunications sector is becoming increasingly competitive, its leading service providers are first in line for privatization, not only in Central and Eastern Europe. The natural monopoly applies only to the basic, local network as such, rather than to end-user facilities and long-distance calls. Even local networks face challenges from mobile phones. In fact, the transition countries have an opportunity to jump various stages of telecoms development by moving to mobile networks before sinking cables into the ground. Unfortunately, the chapter has little to say about the legislation and liberalization of the mobile phone industry. It may be that desire for profitable privatization of MATAV led to undue protection of its monopoly, and a delay in legislating for competing sectors. Hungary may have missed opportunity to take two steps of development at once.

Overall, Hungary has been successful in bringing in outside investors, and was first to privatize the so-called strategic industries. Thus Hungarian industry should have more access to financial and technological resources, and fewer problems with diffuse ownership and weak corporate governance. Yet all is not well in Hungary, which despite its commitment to privatization and foreign investment is slower than its neighbours in resuming a positive growth path. As these comments should illustrate, the devil is in the details.

# 7
# Privatization in the Czech Republic

*Lina Takla*

## INTRODUCTION

Privatization is the mechanism which redefines property rights and should thus in transitional economies bring about *'de novo* the basic institutions of a market financial system including corporate governance of managers, equity ownership, stock exchanges and a number of financial intermediaries' (Lipton and Sachs, 1990). We can distinguish between 'small' and 'large' privatization. 'Large' privatization mainly involves industrial enterprises and utilities, while 'small' privatization generally relates to smaller units in services or retailing sectors. The former Czech and Slovak Federal Republic[1] (CSFR) led the way with voucher privatizations for large firms in 1991, based on (virtually) free distribution of shares to the population at large. Hungary's privatization path is also unique. Unlike Poland and the Czech Republic, Hungary explicitly opted from 1990 to sell its productive assets instead of giving them away. Because of balance of payments difficulties, Hungary also chose to sell assets to the highest bidder, typically foreigners. In Poland, despite an early intention to rely on free distribution of assets, the most important element behind private sector growth has been what is termed in the Polish context as *organic privatization.* Gomulka (1993)[2] defines this as a form of privatization from below where new businesses are established by both domestic and foreign investors sometimes as a result of *asset privatization.* All three privatization paths have achieved a rapid change in the shares of output nominally in state hands although the resulting size distribution of firms in the private sector is very different. This provides us with the opportunity to evaluate the link from ownership change to the establishment of corporate governance and financial market institutions.

The next section of this chapter reviews the main issues involved in privatization examining its pre-conditions, outcomes and aims. We survey the theoretical and policy debates which have surrounded the drafting and subsequent implementation of privatization programmes. Section three describes the privatization process and evaluates the alternative privatization methods in the context of the country-specific experiences of the Czech Republic, with occasional reference to Poland and Hungary (on which, see Chapters 5 and 6 in this volume). Finally, we draw out the main conclusions.

## THE ISSUES

The concept of privatization is deceptively uncomplicated: a simple transfer of property from state-hands into private hands (Vickers and Yarrow, 1991), in the West relying on the public sale of assets, e.g., the experience of countries such as the UK where 'there were only 24 major privatizations in the first decade of the Conservative administration, 1979–89' (Estrin, 1991). In practice, privatization debates have flared and the implementation of privatization has turned out to be a complex procedure. In this section, we first survey the definitions of privatization and summarize the privatization debate to date.

## Pre-Conditions

Differences in privatization policies and in the differential outcomes of privatization policies across Poland, Hungary and the Czech Republic can be explained by each country's initial economic situation, differences in their economic progress thus far and contrasting political developments. Central European countries were broadly similar in their industrial structure prior to reform, but varied in initial macro-economic conditions, economic performance during transition and the degree of political stability and continuity.

At the outset of reform, the majority of GDP in the Czech Republic was provided by state firms. Poland and Hungary were exceptional by Eastern European standards because their private sectors already accounted for about 18 per cent and 30 per cent of output respectively in 1989. The share of the state sector in the economy reflected these differences in management and employee autonomy at the enterprise level. It ranged from nearly 100 per cent in the Czech Republic to about 65 per cent in Poland.

Unlike Hungary and Poland, the CSFR could not build on substantive earlier reforms and had to perform complete transformation (overnight). The whole debate about gradualism *versus* big-bang reforms (see earlier section) arose from a comparison of the merits of Hungarian reforms versus Czech and Polish style macro-stabilization programmes[3]. In the Czech Republic, centralization persisted as the dominant influence up until 1989. Reforms in the 1980s had thus been less comprehensive than those of Poland and Hungary. Hungarian 'reforms' started after the restoration of communism in 1956, when the government became more open. Reforms were partial as the government sought to avoid any serious threat to the Communist Party. However, Hungary's reforms in the 1980s were *'the most far reaching in the socialist world, with the possible exception of China'* (Hare and Revesz, 1992).

The Czech Republic only started significantly granting enterprises greater decision-making power in 1990. Prior to 1990, Czechoslovakia's market structure was less decentralized and competitive than that of Poland's and Hungary's because planning persisted for a longer time (see Estrin and Takla, 1993). Plan targets were detailed, determining the physical quantities that each firm was to produce and the inputs and financial resources which were to be made available to it (see Ellman, 1987). From March 1980, the socialist government applied a succession of cosmetic reforms, merging firms horizontally (Koncern) or vertically (Kombinat).[4] These reforms did not affect decision-making at the enterprise level. Tentative measures toward decentralization of decision-making occurred in the late 1980s because of the impact of Gorbachev on Czechoslovakia.[5]

These experiments involved major decentralization, with a firm's economic and technical decisions being made by its management. Ministries were to be confined to investment projects affecting the industrial branch as a whole and faced constraints. They were supposed to refrain from distribution of profits from successful to less successful firms, for example. A Law on State Enterprises was passed in 1988, but was not supposed to come into effect until 1991. It implied reductions in subsidies and the possibility of liquidation for the first time.

In the Czech Republic, although firms had been under tight state control until 1989, macroeconomic stability was maintained throughout most of the communist period. Czechoslovakia inherited a system which was characterized by fiscal conservatism reflected in restrictive macroeconomic policies. Important contrasts between the three countries are highlighted in their inflation and current account records prior to reform. Inflation had never emerged as a serious problem in the Czech Republic, being 1.4 per cent in 1989 and averaging less than 2 per cent from 1980 to 1989 (OECD 1991), with hidden inflation estimated at 2.5 per cent per annum over the same period. In 1989, Hungarian inflation stood at 11.6 per cent and Poland was heading towards hyperinflation (351.1 per cent). Poland therefore had a bigger macroeconomic problem to contend with and its reform programme relied heavily on price stabilization measures.

Previous policies left the new Czechoslovak regime in 1990 faced with neither the external debt nor the monetary overhang of Poland and Hungary. In 1990, external debt as a per cent of GDP was 65 per cent in Hungary and 80 per cent in Poland, while it stood at only 19 per cent in Czechoslovakia. The CSFR also weathered the deterioration in terms of trade and external financing difficulties of the 1980s better than other countries in the region. External debt service obligations and external debt[6] in convertible currencies remained in the 1980s well below those of Hungary and Poland.

The difference in debt situations pre-reform further emphasises the different methods which were incorporated into the privatization schemes of all three countries. The decision of whether to distribute assets freely was easier for Czechoslovakia then it was for Poland and Hungary. This has meant that subsequently the Czech Republic could afford not to rely on the direct sale of its assets in order to finance its budget deficit. Czech foreign direct investment policy – which did not offer special incentives to foreign investors and which relied on a low wage stance – could be sustained, as there was no crisis over their foreign reserves requirements and no threat of a foreign debt crisis. The Czech Republic paid back its IMF standby loans well ahead of its allotted time period.

To sum up, whatever the divergence in past performance, all three Central European countries faced similar problems at the outset of change: how to initiate competition and how to change the ownership structure of the economy, while preserving macroeconomic stability. This background has in part shaped privatization debates and conduct in all three countries. For example, the issue of insider control was not a major stumbling block in the Czech Republic. In Poland, where the decentralization of decision-making at the enterprise level started in 1981, employees had to be incorporated into privatization legislation as they held effective control over enterprise assets. In Hungary, managers and/or employees guided – at least at the beginning of the process – the conduct of many privatization initiatives regardless of actual government legislation and debates. Pre-conditions were, however, not the only factor that shaped individual privatization packages. Academic and political debates about the aims of privatization were also crucial in shaping adopted policies.

## The Aims of Privatization Policy

Privatization can take several forms, from direct sales of all or part of state-owned firms, public offerings, and various forms of voucher-based privatization. The arguments for voucher privatization are best summarised in Nuti, (1994) as intentions to:

- ensure *equity*

As industrial assets are assumed to have belonged to the population at large under the previous system, privatization methods that insured some form of fair initial distribution of wealth were advocated by certain reforming governments (Czechoslovakia in 1990/91, President Walesa in his September 1993 campaign). It was held that adult citizens have equal claims on state assets and that capitalism should start with an egalitarian distribution of this wealth. Equity considerations not only focus on the population at large; they have also been used to bolster the position of certain groups in society.

- *depoliticize the economy*

The major difference between West European governments grappling with the privatization dilemma and former socialist countries is that in the latter countries the share of the state sector in the economy at the start of transition far exceeded the western average which ranged from 1.3 per cent of total output in the United States in 1983 to 16.5 per cent in France in 1982 (Milanovic, 1989). Reformers concluded that their previous economic system meant that the behaviour of the state as owner would always lead to active interference in enterprise activities and thus obstruct competition. The speed of privatization has been linked to the need for quick depoliticization of the economy, (Lipton and Sachs, 1990). The new ownership structure should be installed fast in order to minimize 'the probability of degeneration in the sense of devolution to state ownership, assuming this would represent a step backward rather than forward'.

The formation of *new* post-communist states is challengingly described in Batt (1996). Post-communist states are viewed as opting for a model of statehood built upon the Napoleonic tradition '*particularly for the purpose of implementing economic transformation. Too often, this has been seen in terms of "rolling back the state", reducing its powers and the scope of its intervention in the economy, in line with trends towards liberalisation, deregulation and privatization in Western economies.*' But, the task of economic reform is one where the state cannot take a back seat position. It has to implement '*capitalism from above*' (Ofer, 1991) and what is needed is not the disappearance of the state or a less powerful state, but a state which '*plays different roles and does so more effectively*' (Nelson, 1994).

- *stop the appropriation of state assets by insiders*

This aim is a political objective where privatization is a sufficient end-result in itself. It is not the economic effect of privatization that matters, but the fact that by turning property into mainly *outsider* private hands you remove it from the control of its former Communist management. This was a major motivation in the Czech Republic and is demonstrated in its choice of voucher privatization with coupon sales to the population at large at a nominal price. Other political motivations mentioned in the literature include the fact that privatization should help prevent a reversion to the old system and ensure that reforms are virtually irreversible.

- *to increase government revenues*

The financial aim of privatization is prevalent in western economies where it was viewed as a means of raising government revenue. The governments in Eastern Europe could opt for measures based on the sale of assets for reasons such as financing their foreign debt or increasing costs of unemployment and other social benefits as restructuring begins. This financial aim has only been actively aspired to by Hungary where the government initially decided to sell rather than give away property.

- *to harden budget constraints*

Firms under the old-planning system are assumed to have operated under *soft-budget constraints*. They were heavily subsidized by the *Centre* through the pricing system, the willingness of governments to cover company losses and the investment allocation mechanism. Soft budget constraints meant that demand for inputs such as labour had a 'tendency to grow without limits' given that financial constraints on managers were virtually non-existent. Budget constraints will however harden with the move from planning to market through price liberalization as well as through a decision by the government to privatize firms and cut subsidies and thus sever the direct link between the government's budget and the enterprise sector. It is even more widely argued that public ownership favours intervention.

- to raise *efficiency* and *speed up the physical and financial restructuring* of enterprises[7]

The main objective of mass privatization in the Czech Republic was purely the transfer of property out of state hands. In the words of Vaclav Klaus (1993) *'We consider it unnecessary to design techniques and legislation with respect to the objective of selecting perfect owners. An objective like this is far beyond the capacity of post communist governments and first (initial) owners may not be the final ones... it is the economy as a whole, not a particular state-owned firm or firms that calls for transformation. In other words, however efficient or inefficient, financially healthy or unhealthy individual businesses may appear, it is not them, but the whole economy, which requires a change.'*

The change in management incentive structure is the key to linking privatization to increases in productive efficiency. The problem of Creating effective corporate governance has been raised by many observers (Aoki and Kim, 1995; Dittus and Prowse, 1996; Berglof, 1994). If privatization leads to control by a private non-bank entity, then managerial incentives will be checked through the stock exchange and the market for corporate control. A private owner is more likely than a state owner to design managerial reward schedules in order to fulfil its profit maximization objective.

The key point is that the nature and speed of privatization leads to different ownership configurations which in turn lead to a range of incentives to restructure. For example, through its choice of mass privatization, the Czech Republic had privatized around half of its large enterprises by mid-1993, with most of the other half being subsequently privatized in 1994. Although the intention might not have been fast restructuring, privatization in this case is postulated as likely to lead to restructuring because the new external environment is more likely to enforce a bankruptcy threat on enterprises. Private enterprises will notionally be monitored through the market for corporate control *via* the stock exchange, through lending arrangements with the new private commercial banks or equity stake holdings by these same banks. Active involvement of funds as owners will increase the weight placed on the profit motive.

## DESCRIPTION OF PRIVATIZATION

Table 1 charts privatization plans as perceived in 1991 and contrasts them with actual outcomes. In 1991, all three countries aimed to privatize a large bulk of their

Table 1.   Privatization Plans in the Czech Republic, Hungary and Poland in Mid-1991 Versus Privatization Outcomes

| | Czech Republic | Hungary | Poland |
|---|---|---|---|
| **Period to Privatize** | | | |
| **1991 plan** | over 5 years | in 5 years | in 3 years |
| **1994 outcome** | | | |
| **Share of Private sector in GDP** | over 60% in 1994 | over 60% | 55% |
| **Share of Private Sector in total employment** | over 60% | around 50% | 60% (end 1993) |
| **Privatization Institutions** | Ministry of Privatization National Property Fund | State Property Agency State Asset Management Company | Ministry of Privatization |
| **Privatization Method Planned** | mass privatization through the emission of vouchers used to purchase shares or entrusted to investment funds in the period, 1990 | mass privatization through the distribution of shares on subsidized credit from 1992 sale primarily through the stock exchange also auction and tender 1990 | mass privatization through emission of certificates in investment funds set up by the state |
| **1996 outcome** | voucher privatization mixed with other methods 1992–94 | 'spontaneous' 1990–91 case by case on the capital market 1993–95 direct sale to foreign investors 1990–96 | 'liquidation' 1990–95 mass privatization 1996 |

*Source*:   EBRD (1994), Estrin (1991), Lavigne (1994) + EBRD (1997).

industrial assets within the next five years. By mid-1994, the share of the private sector in GDP was above 50 per cent in all of them. This rise in recorded private sector shares can be initially attributed to an increase in trade and services activities, but later to other sectors as well (Balcerowicz and Gelb 1994). The extent to which this private sector growth can be directly attributable to the privatization of state enterprises will be examined later. Table 1 also reveals that the Czech Republic and Poland both assigned the task of privatizing the economy to a newly created state organ the 'Privatization Ministry'. The Czech Republic created an additional state body, the National Property Fund (NPF) – where the shares of enterprises 'to be privatized' were held. The NPF also received the income from privatization sales. It was also intended to manage the state's stake in enterprises in the interim period, before these share holdings were turned into a private entity

The state had to take two important considerations into account when implementing its privatization programme. First, it had to decide the mechanics of privatization (property to be allocated, timetable, choice of enterprise and choice of industries, type of privatization). Second, when opting for a privatization strategy, the state had to address the outcome of privatization for the allocation of power between the different economic actors at the onset of privatization (the state and its various ministries, the managers and the employees, the investment funds and the banks).

Table 1 indicates that the initial plans of both Poland and the Czech Republic favoured privatization based on give-away schemes. The *equitable* intent, as described earlier in the section, of mass privatization was prevalent in all three programmes. In practice, in all three countries, mass privatization has been implemented/done in conjunction with other schemes namely restitution. In the Czech Republic, 3 per cent of property was set aside for restitution; in Hungary former owners have been given vouchers instead of physical assets. Mass privatization was further politicized in Hungary, as vouchers were also used to compensate political persecution victims.

In Central Europe at the onset of reform, capital markets were under-developed and the levels of savings were such as to leave the population unable to purchase the majority of state assets. In addition, even if purchase of the assets were possible, mass privatization only requires simple valuation techniques and minimal financial and physical restructuring prior to *auction*. Privatization methods as perceived in the earliest plans, all encompassed a mass privatization element. This element was emphasized strongly in the Czech and Polish case and less so in the Hungarian. Privatization outcomes in all three countries exhibit a mixture of methods. We next provide a step-by-step description of the evolution of privatization in the Czech Republic.

## Czech Republic – Mass Privatization and the Emergence of Funds

The process of Czech privatization has been amply surveyed (see, Singer and Svejnar, 1995; Takla, 1994; Coffee, 1994; Mejstrik *et al.*, 1994). The techniques and decisions most identified with Czech privatization are namely: '(1) the use of vouchers to effect a rapid disposition of state property; (2) the free entry permitted to privately formed Investment Privatization Funds (IPFs); and (3) the use of such IPFs as a corporate governance solution to dispersed ownership[8].' Kenway and Chlumsky (1995) identify 'three salient facts' about Czech privatization, namely; 'Firstly, funds have emerged from the voucher privatization as holding the majority of shares sold by voucher: 73 per cent in the first wave (1992) and 64 per cent in the second wave (1994). Secondly, although there are hundreds of them, the few largest funds have an enormous weight; thus the funds founded by the top six investment companies acquired over 40 per cent of the vouchers in the first wave and 24 per cent in the second. Thirdly, a single fund could hold up to 20 per cent of a firm's equity, while funds founded by the same investment company could jointly hold up to a maximum of 40 per cent.'

The Czech Republic is the only one out of our three cases where mass privatization has been effectively adopted. The voucher scheme was intended to ensure the rapid transfer of state-owned property to the private sector and to offer the Czechoslovak citizens a stake in the reforms. Funds were privately set up by domestic and foreign banks to act as possible intermediaries for citizens' investments. Czech privatization is thus an often quoted 'successful' example of mass privatization, '*understood as offering the free or very heavily subsidized transfer of a large proportion of state assets to the whole population*' (Nuti, 1994). Voucher privatization[9] is a component of 'large-scale Privatization' aimed at manufacturing, banking and insurance organizations which often have a domestic monopolistic character and invariably operate on a large scale. The option of privatization method also determines the state's interest in managing ownership changes. In both Poland and the Czech Republic mass privatization has been heavily managed by the government. The emphasis on mass privatization has differed across the three countries and although in the Czech case, voucher privatization was a high profile activity, it is important to note that it was only a component in a multi-track approach to privatization.

The Czech Republic benefited during the period 1990 to early 1996, from a stable government and broad political support. This allowed the government substantial leverage in the conduct of its privatization policy. Once discrepancies between parties were resolved in Parliament, the government was able to pursue its policy without recourse to further substantial political compromises. The involvement of the government was central to 'large privatization'. The state took an active role in the privatization of enterprises by managing the process through its approval of privatization projects. The inherited coalitions and hierarchies between the government and state enterprises were and still are largely in place. Branch ministries were sometimes at odds with the Privatization ministries in their evaluation of projects, and have often supported existing management.

Excluded from the impact of the Large-Scale Privatization Act 27 February 1991[10], were properties to be restored to former owners by special legislation and all Church property confiscated after 25 February 1948 [Restitution Act 22 February 1991]. The corporatization of SOEs was a precondition for their inclusion in the voucher privatization programme. Corporatization entailed the transfer of 100 per cent of the share capital of enterprises to National Property Funds (NPFs).

There were three such funds: one for the Czech republic, one for the Slovak republic, one for the federation. While the organization and activity of the Federal National Property Fund was determined by the Act, it left the republican legislatures to determine the legal relations and activity of the Republican National Property Funds. The federal and republican governments had a time period to issue guidelines for ministries and local government which were called upon to submit (for governmental approval) lists of enterprises which should be privatized.

By the end of 1995 most enterprises had been privatized; (see Table 2). 49.3 per cent of firms with over 25 employees were in private hands as against 6.4 per cent in state-owned hands.

Table 2.   Distribution of Enterprises by Ownership type, End 1995

|  | % of enterprises |
| --- | --- |
| Private | 49.3 |
| Co-operative | 6.4 |
| State | 13.7 |
| Municipal | 0.1 |
| Owned by Associations, Political Parties and Churches | 0.1 |
| Foreign | 3.2 |
| Joint venture between domestic and foreign partners | 7.1 |
| Mixed domestic (private + state + other) | 20.1 |

*Source*:   Monthly Statistics of Czech Republic, CSO, 2–96.

'Large-scale Privatization' employed a broad range of privatization methods, apart from voucher privatization. The nature of the enterprise involved and the 'time factor' were the decisive influences when deciding the method. Heavy reliance on the voucher method was chosen by the enterprise management in four types of firm: companies that were financially 'troubled' and too large for alternative methods; where workers saw privatization as a form of worker buy-out as they could choose to place their points in their own firm; where managers sought the voucher method as a way of maintaining control ; and where management could not find an alternative to the voucher scheme (e.g., could not find a foreign partner) (see Takla, 1994 for further details).

Most enterprises used corporatization as a first step in their privatization project. Through their projects enterprises were also able to divide up their shares between different privatization methods, including standard options such as direct sale, public auction or more unique measures such as vouchers. Table 3 charts the progress of large scale privatization up to the end of 1993. It shows that 23.6 per cent of companies were sold or transferred as shares of joint stock companies, direct sales accounted for 22.3 per cent and free transfer accounted for 30.8 per cent. In the privatization of shares of joint-stock companies nearly 52 per cent of shares were privatized through vouchers and 31.5 per cent of shares remained in the hands of the NPF (Kotrba, 1994). Table 4, charts the progress up until end 1994 and reveals that most units were sold through direct sale to an outside investor. However, Table 4 shows that the percent of nominal stock value of property sold using direct sales was only 7 per cent, while entities privatized *via* vouchers represented around 51 per cent of the nominal stock value.

**Table 3.   Distribution of Shares by 31/12/1993**

| Approved Privatization Method | Number of units % of total | Number | Value of property | % of total |
|---|---|---|---|---|
| Public Auctions | 6.8 | | | 0.7 |
| Public Tenders | 6.7 | | | 2.2 |
| Direct sales | 22.3 | | | 5.3 |
| Sold or transferred as shares of joint-stock companies | 23.6 | | | 86.5 |
| Free transfers | 30.8 | | | 3.4 |
| Restitution | 8.1 | | | 0.8 |
| Restitution with buy-in | 1.7 | | | 1.1 |
| Total | 100.00 | 7,533 | 871.6 bn Kcs | 100.00 |

*Source*:   Pistor and Turkowitz, 1994 .

**Table 4.   Privatization of Stocks**

| | December 1994 % nominal stock value |
|---|---|
| Secondary Markets | 3.7 |
| Voucher Privatization | 50.7 |
| Direct Sale | 7.0 |
| Free Transfers to Municipalities, Pension Funds, Banks or Savings Banks | 7.2 |
| Restitution or Restitution Investment Fund | 3.2 |
| Stock Held by the NPF long-term | 9.8 |
| Stock Held by the NPF temporarily | 18.4 |

*Source*:   The Privatization Newsletter of the Czech Republic, February 1995.

## Mass Privatization

The 'Large-Scale Privatization Act' came into force on 1 April 1991. In the context of the voucher scheme, shares were to be acquired by voucher holders (individuals or investment funds) through a complex bidding process. A basic privatization project (submitted by the enterprise management) included a statement of the proposed disposition of shares: the proportion available through voucher privatization, the proportion for direct sale etc. The government decided centrally the allocation of property for mass privatization. It was the enterprises' responsibility to submit their projects and *outsiders'* prerogative to present their own competing projects. The *winning* project was decided upon chiefly by Privatization Ministry officials. The project specified the amount of shares allocated to voucher privatization. Although drafted by the enterprise, a privatization project was the responsibility of the 'founder'. The founder selected the project it deemed to be most suitable and recommended it for approval.

The winning privatization project was generally chosen by a team consisting of officials from the Ministry for privatization and officials of the relevant founder ministry under whose jurisdiction the particular enterprise initially found itself. Exceptions to this rule were instances where the selected project recommended the sale of some or part of the property to a private owner or any sale to a foreign investor. In these cases, it was the national government which made the final decision. This principle also applied to the sale of enterprises with a large number of employees (over 3,000 workers). The founder also had to submit to the ministry those projects it did not recommend. Projects which recommended the break-up of enterprises were approved. Most competing projects proposed the break-up of the existing SOE. This could be viewed as a positive development if it created medium and small enterprises. On the other hand, some projects have sought to divide indivisible property.

Foreign buyers were also allowed to collaborate with Czech firms in the formulation of the basic project. If the enterprise was too slow, it could be given a time limit by the Supervisory State Agency, described in the Act as the 'founder' (usually a ministry responsible for a particular sector of industry). Not surprisingly, management was reluctant to deliver the necessary information for outside parties to develop their own competing projects and withholding information was made illegal by the amendment to the law on 'large-scale Privatization', passed in February 1992. This legislation also corrected a loophole which had allowed existing management to sign long-term rental agreements. Such agreements would *de facto* predetermine the fate of the property before privatization. Management and worker ownership was thus not explicitly encouraged in the Czech case although management took part in the privatization process as it was in charge of submitting basic plans of privatization.[11] Privatization of large enterprises has rarely involved leveraged buy-outs. Management buy-outs were only common in 'small-scale privatization' because managers took long-term leases in 1990, so 'a buy-out was a logical solution to avoid a gridlock'.

Prior to initiating the process of 'large-scale Privatization', enterprises were divided up into three broad categories. The first category contained enterprises included in the first wave of privatization, characterized by the perceived relative ease and speed of their privatization. The second category was second-wave enterprises, dominated by large engineering, chemical and metallurgical companies. Also included in the second wave were key branches of the power sectors as well as public utilities and infrastructure. Finally, the third category contained businesses to be kept in state hands for at least another five years, for example railways and airports. These shares were to be formally held by the National Property Fund, although rights are entrusted to other state bodies (for example, ministries).

**Table 4.    State led Restructuring as Part of the Privatization Programme**

| Industry | Number of enterprises prior to the approval of privatization projects | Number of enterprises after the approval of privatization projects | % increase in number of firms |
|---|---|---|---|
| Ferrous metallurgy | 20 | 51 | 155 |
| Non-ferrous metallurgy | 16 | 50 | 213 |
| Chemicals and rubber | 57 | 131 | 130 |
| Machinery | 303 | 676 | 123 |
| Electronics | 74 | 212 | 187 |
| Building materials | 119 | 280 | 135 |
| Wood-processing | 81 | 230 | 184 |
| Metal products | 18 | 41 | 128 |
| Paper and cellulose | 22 | 84 | 282 |
| Glass, china and ceramics | 55 | 159 | 189 |
| Textiles | 94 | 409 | 335 |
| Apparel | 23 | 72 | 213 |
| Leather | 19 | 72 | 279 |
| Printing and publishing | 31 | 50 | 61 |
| Food-processing | 198 | 683 | 245 |
| Others | 49 | 93 | 90 |
| **Total** | **1179** | **3293** | **179** |

*Source*:    Zemplinerova (1994).

'Large-Scale Privatization' was a two-stage programme (preparation and implementation), with the second stage having started in 1992. Privatization was compulsory and in the first wave 1,700 enterprises in the Czech Lands, 700 firms in Slovakia and one 'federally owned' firm had until the end of 1991 to submit business plans to their 'founder' sponsoring ministries.

Adult citizens, over 18 years of age, were allowed to buy a 14 page book of vouchers entitling them to 1,000 shares in at most 10 listed privatized enterprises for about US$ 30.[12] They had the alternative of turning the vouchers over to mutual funds which would then bid for shares. The voucher book came with a 30 page instruction book. Most of the eligible population, about 8.5 million adults, purchased these books. Vouchers were not transferable, though they could be transferred to heirs. They could not be used as security for a loan. The obvious problem with this scheme lay in the fact that voucher holders would need information to appraise the enterprises on offer. Property to be privatized was separated into joint-stock companies; a list of enterprises involved in voucher privatization was published along with basic data on the share of stock offered for voucher sale. Balance sheet information was also printed in daily newspapers. Individual investors could place their vouchers with the funds in return for certificates. The issue of how many funds to set up, and the issue of whether funds were to be active or passive investors was removed from government responsibility. The private voucher holders could independently decide whether to bid for shares by themselves or to place their shares with investment funds.

The exact number of bidding rounds within each wave was not predetermined. Rather it was anticipated that the process would end 'when a decisive share of the property would be sold and further continuation would not lead to the sale of the remainder'. Bidding for shares proceeded as follows. First, shares of all enterprises were offered at the same 'nominal' value, expressed in investment points per share. In the first wave, this price was set at 100 investment points per three shares. As the bidding process proceeded, the demand of shares by investors was supposed to reveal the 'true' value of the firm. Bidders knew the calling price of a share of an enterprise (in terms of points) and bid accordingly. If the supply of shares exceeded the demand for shares, shares were exchanged for points. When demand exceeded supply by 25 per cent, shares were first allocated to the bidding individuals and the remainder was rationed amongst bidding IPFs. If excess demand was over 25 per cent, points were not converted into shares and the price of shares was raised by the government before a new round of bidding; the process continued until excess demand was below 25 per cent.

Once initiated the first wave of voucher privatization proceeded relatively fast (see Svejnar and Singer, 1993 for details). Progress was slower than expected; investors received their shares from the first wave of privatization in the summer of 1993. Their decision to purchase was taken 12–15 months earlier, and on the basis of 1991 balance sheets. Around ninety-three per cent of total share supply in the first round of privatization was sold and ninety-nine per cent of all disposable voucher points were used. In the first round, bids were mainly oriented to high value companies. Ninety-two per cent of disposable points were bid, indicating a high participation rate. Only about thirty per cent of the shares bid for were sold. The success rate plummeted in the third round, as the price of shares was set too low at the start of the round. Only 24.5 per cent of shares ordered in this round were sold.

In the first wave of Czech privatization, property valued at US$ 23 bn was put up for sale, US$ 7 bn of which through vouchers. Only 7.2 per cent of shares remained unsold and 277.8 million shares were sold to private investors. Of 1,471 companies, 291 were fully sold. The unsold shares are temporarily being held by the National Property Fund, which will dispose of them mainly by arranging direct sale through an intermediary.

As a by-product of voucher privatization, a large number of Investment Privatization Funds were established voluntarily with most funds sponsored by commercial banks with several banks sponsoring more than one fund. The relationship between funds and banks is the following; banks have established a 'management company' which runs the fund. Many of the funds are affiliated to a single *founder*. Investicni Banka, for example created twelve different funds in the first wave. Five of the top seven fund groups were founded by banks.

## The Role of the State

The Ministry of Trade and Industry, the Consolidation Bank (responsible for bad debts), and the National Property Fund (NPF), and in the medium term, the Privatization Ministry are likely to remain in control of government management of industry and enterprises.

Forty-eight percent of Czech enterprises which existed in 1989 were privatized by the end of the second round of voucher privatization. The number of enterprises remaining in the state sector was estimated at no more than five hundred as early as the end of 1995. These enterprises were ones held by their 'founding' ministries, with the Ministry of Trade and Industry holding the bulk of enterprises. By the end of March 1994, it held 316 firms in thirteen 3 digit industries, employing 2.1 per cent of the total workforce. These firms were on average *medium sized* (337 employees) with the largest firm, a uranium mining company, employing 7,000 workers.

The state also retained 20 per cent of the value of property privatized through vouchers *via* the National Property Fund. The NPF emerged as the single largest shareholder after the first wave of privatization. At the end of the first wave of voucher privatization the NPF still held a stake of 10 per cent or more in more than fifty per cent of voucher privatized companies. The NPF also kept a *golden share* option in thirty-seven companies in the first wave. Forty approved privatization plans in the second wave stipulated that golden shares should be used. The state also holds some property indirectly through the NPF. The NPF owns between 34 to 45 per cent of the main banks involved in founding the bank-backed investment funds. The NPF is gradually selling off or otherwise disposing of its stakes in Czech firms.

## CONCLUSIONS

Privatization in practice has entailed a number of controversial and complex decisions at every stage of the operation. Delays in decisions can be summarized as stemming from protracted policy debates and institutional and technical problems regarding implementation (see Nuti, 1994) including:

1. the inclusion of foreign capital;
2. the inevitable mix of political and economic methods of privatization and the interaction of mass privatization with the other methods (restitution, direct sale to domestic and foreign buyers, allocation of shares to employees, management buy-outs etc.);
3. the regulation of the process and the fast establishment of a legal institutional framework to consolidate the transfer of ownership;
4. the inception of capital markets.

The evaluation of the comparative experiences will be done in part in the light of some of the objectives proposed above. To recap, these normative objectives are: to ensure equity, to de-politicise the economy, to stop the appropriation of assets by insiders, to increase government revenues, to harden budget constraints and finally to raise efficiency and to speed up restructuring. All three privatization programmes scrutinized in this chapter have faced the dilemma of deciding between some of these sometimes divergent objectives. There may, for example be contradictions between the best restructuring outcome and equitable schemes based on restitution or vouchers. The new owners might not have the required level of know-how or capital backing to undertake the restructuring required.

From our descriptions we can draw the following conclusions. First, given that the starting position was that of near total state ownership of industrial assets, we find that ownership, in all three cases (Czech Republic, Hungary, Poland), was successfully transferred out of state hands albeit at a differing pace and using very different methods. Second, if speed is a reflection of depoliticization, even in the Czech case, the actual speed of privatization, did not correspond to the projected timetable and unforeseen obstacles have tended to slow down the process. The implementation of privatization schemes in the three countries surveyed reveals that the state remains an important player in the privatization process in the form of residual owner. New private enterprises share their markets with old state enterprises, privatized firms, joint ventures and increasingly with foreign competitors. Second, our examination of the nature of the state apparatus still running the remaining SOEs, reveals that in all three cases it has been very hard for these bodies to step back. It is hard for the Czech NPF to give up control of the banking sector and to privatize banks fully without encountering the bad debt problem. The Hungarian government did not part with its control over major utilities willingly.

The role of government in privatization cannot be ignored. Mass privatization in both the Czech Republic and Poland was very much a policy implemented from the top. Its meaning and conduct has however differed greatly between both countries. In the Czech Republic, it was administered quickly and found to be an easy solution to transfer property out of state hands. It led to the predominance of investment funds, a large number of individual minority shareholders, the rapid creation of a stock market and the predominance of a state organ, the NPF. In Poland, it was a slow process and was until recently overshadowed by privatization through liquidation and subsequent employee ownership and the quick proliferation of *de novo* private firms. Hungary, on the other hand put little emphasis on mass give-away schemes and preferred to sell its assets to foreign buyers. The participation of foreign investors has differed between countries. Nevertheless, a small number of large sales to foreign buyers has contributed to keeping the budget balanced even in the case of the Czech Republic. Receipts from the National Property Fund covered the budget deficit in 1993. Foreign direct investment in all three countries represented a high percentage of the total for all of Eastern Europe (76.5 per cent), the share of Hungary being the highest (36 per cent) (Hughes, 1994).

Mixed ownership is therefore a common feature of ownership patterns in all three countries and new state institutions have sprung up to fill the role of managing state interests in the enterprise sector. This renders the separation between state and private ownership difficult. All three governments have attempted to create new systems of management of state property. These efforts have revolved around changing the legal structure of state enterprises (commercialization or corporatization), altering the governing structure of enterprises and designating a body to manage state interests and finally altering the legal and regulatory framework under which state enterprises operate. The stake of the Czech, Hungarian and Polish government in industrial enterprises is of two kinds: enterprises that have been classified as 'of national interest' and firms that have been difficult to sell or auction away. The first category of firms has been intentionally kept in state hands, while the second could be described as 'residual' holdings (Pistor and Turkowitz, 1994) that the state intends to be rid of. There has been a tendency for state shares to move between classifications and between different state owners (between Treasury-owned and non-Treasury-owned, between different state organs and ministries, between different privatization agencies). In addition, what is strategic at one point in time (utilities in Hungary in 1995) can become less so when the *cash generation requirement* starts to bind because of a budgetary crisis.

Privatization debates in Central and Eastern Europe have thus in practice been highly politicized and lengthy. The preparation of schemes on the political level has involved protracted discussions about objectives, welfare, and allocation of power in the industrial and financial sectors. Some of the problems encountered during the process of privatization could have been avoided, if a number of implementation issues had been discussed beforehand. Many of these problems might have been attributed to the fact that privatization has been proceeding in parallel with the evolution of various market economy institutions. Governments have had to build up relevant institutions and legislation while undertaking the transfer of property. It would have been very difficult for them to announce simultaneously their privatization plan with all its relevant contingency clauses and its implementation timetable, and adhere to their schedule. Other problems faced when implementing privatization were due to the conflict between objectives and interest. And finally, realistically many problems arose because of the inherently political (and politicized) nature of the privatization process. Governments have generally enacted privatization policies which have thus at times been inconsistent with their overall policy. This has led to a series of amendments to privatization legislation, delays in the implementation of schemes and paralysis in state enterprises. Some of the delays encountered were inevitable given the complexity and magnitude of the task. In practice, government policy has been interactive with changing conditions and unforeseen hiccups. Although some of these problems were predictable, it is unlikely that these *new* governments would have been able to cover all eventualities. In general, their response to unanticipated problems has been *ad hoc* and improvised. Other delays in implementation have occurred either because of technical problems with the mechanisms of privatization, or legal loopholes which have had to be remedied quickly or lastly because of political problems which have necessitated the amendment or reversal of programmes.

## NOTES

1. On 1st January 1993, the Federal Republic of Czechoslovakia was separated into two constituent parts: Czech Republic and Slovakia. There were economic difficulties associated with this division, some were connected with the privatization process; the continuation of voucher privatization and solving the repercussions of the fact that the first wave of privatization took place at a Federal level, with cross-republican investments.
2. Gomulka 'Poland: Glass Half Full', in Portes R. (ed.) 1993.
3. Bruno (1992) and Balcerowicz and Gelb (1994) provide a full and comprehensive comparative discussion of the stabilization policies adopted by East and Central European countries.
4. This was a result of a 'Set of Measures to Improve the System of Planned Management of the National Economy after 1980', introduced in March 1980.
5. In 1987, there was a scheme for 'the Comprehensive Restructuring of the Economic Mechanism'; thirty-seven principles of restructuring were laid out in January 1987 and adopted in December 1987. Experiments began in 1987 with 22 enterprises which constituted almost 8 per cent of the output of the centrally controlled economy, mostly in the export-oriented consumer goods branches. In January 1988, a further 38 enterprises – or more than 19 per cent of output – were placed under the new system.
6. Domestic debt was even more insignificant. The government budget was close to balance; net government debt in 1989 stood at less than 1 per cent of GDP.
7. We visit this topic in depth in the next two chapters of the thesis.
8. Coffee (1994).
9. Note : No fixed equity was set aside for the voucher programme. However, all equity not sold to a buyer had to be privatized through the voucher programme. Besides, three per cent of equity automatically went to the restitution fund.
10. The Federal Ministry of Finance classified firms at the inception of the programme as follows. **Category A** consisted of public utilities and other regulated SOEs which were not to be privatized in the near future. This included at the federal level 30 per cent of state-owned companies in sectors such as defence, some public utilities. **Category B** covered state-owned medium to large heavy and light industry firms. These firms took

part in the large-scale privatization process. **Category C** covered property which took part in the small-privatization or 'municipalization' process (restaurants, local services, flat rentals etc.).

11. See Coffee (1994) for an account of management privatization proposals.
12. In the first quarter of 1992 the average monthly wage was US$ 135.9, the average weekly salary was thus about US$ 34.

## REFERENCES

Aoki, M. and Kim, H-K (eds) (1995), *Corporate governance in transitional economies: Insider control and the role of banks*, EDI Development Studies, Washington, DC: The World Bank.

Balcerowicz, L. and Gelb, A. (1994), 'Macropolicies in Transition to a Market Economy: a Three-Year Perspective', World Bank Annual Conference on Development Economics, Washington D.C., April.

Batt, J. (1996), 'The New Slovakia: National Identity, Political Integration and the Return to Europe', *RIIA Discussion Paper* no. 65, London: RIIA.

Berglof, Eric (1994), Corporate Governance in Transition Economies: The Theory and its Political Implications, Universite Libre de Bruxelles, Discussion Paper, July 1994.

Bruno, Michael (1992), 'Stabilization and reform in Eastern Europe', *IMF Staff Papers*, 39(4), Washington, DC: IMF.

Coffee, J. (1994), 'Investment Privatization Funds: the Czech experience', paper presented at a Joint Conference of the World Bank and the Central European University Privatization Project, Washington D.C. 15–16 December.

Dittus, P. and Prowse, S. (1996), 'Corporate control in Central Europe and Russia: Show banks own shares?' In Roman Frydman, Cheryl Gray and Andrzej Rapaczynski (eds), *Corporate governance in Central Europe and Russia. Vol. 1: Banks, funds and foreign investors*, Budapest: Central European University Press.

EBRD (1994), *Transition Report*, London: EBRD.

EBRD (1997), *Transition Report*, London: EBRD.

Ellman, M. (1987), *Socialist Planning*, 2nd edition, Cambridge University Press, Cambridge.

Estrin, S. and Takla, L. (1993), 'Competition and Competition Policy in the Czech and Slovak Republics', in Estrin, S., Cave, M., (eds), *Competition and Competition Policy: A Comparative Analysis of Central and Eastern Europe*. London: Pinter.

Gomulka, S., 'Poland: Glass Half Full', in Portes R. (ed.) 1993.

Hughes, K. (1994), 'The Development of Industrial Policy in Transition Economies: A Comparative Analysis', paper presented at a Conference at Chatham House and prepared as part of an ACE funded project by the European Commission.

Lavigne, M. (1995), *The economics of transition from socialist economy to market economy*, New York: St Martin's Press.

Lipton, D. and Sachs, J. (1990), 'Creating a Market Economy in Eastern Europe: The Case of Poland', in Lipton and Sachs, eds, *Brookings Papers on Economic Activity* 2: 293–341.

Mejstrik, M., Lastovicka R. and Marcincin, A. (1994), 'Privatization and Opening the Capital markets in the Czech and Slovak Republics', Working Paper No. 54, IES, CERGE, EI, Prague.

Milanovic, B. (1989), *Liberalization and Enterpreneurship: Dynamics of Reform in Socialism and Capitalism*, Armonk, N.Y. and London: Sharpe.

Nelson, Joan, M. (1994), *A precarious balance: Democracy and economic reforms in Eastern Europe,* vol. 1, San Francisco: International Center for Economic Growth.

Nuti (1994), 'Mass Privatization: Costs and Benefits of InstantCapitalism', CIS-ME-LBS Working Papers no. 9, London.

Ofer, G. (1991), *The Service Sector in Soviet Economic Growth: A Comparative Study*, Harvard University Press, Cambridge, MA.

Svejnar, J. and Singer, M. (1995), 'Using vouchers to privatize an economy: the Czech and Slovak case', *Economics of Transition*, 2(1), 43–70.

Takla, L. (1994), 'The relationship between privatization and the reform of the banking sector: the case of the Czech Republic and Slovakia' in Estrin, S. (ed.), *Privatization in Central and Eastern Europe*, Longmans, London.

Vickers and Yarrow (1991), Economic Perspectives on Privatization, *Journal of Economic Perspectives*, Spring.

# 8
# The Slovak Republic: Macroeconomic Success and Lagging Microeconomic Reform – How Long Can it Last?

*Jon Stern*

## INTRODUCTION

When the Slovak Republic became an independent state at the end of 1992, outside commentators were very pessimistic about its economic prospects both in absolute terms and relative to those of the Czech Republic. It was the Czech Republic that appeared to have all the advantages in terms of industrial structure, foreign direct investment and tourism inflows. In addition, it was the Czech Republic that appeared to be committed to wide-ranging economic reform at the microeconomic level whereas scepticism about rapid privatization and micro reform was a major driving force for the leading proponents of an independent Slovakia.

So, was the initial pessimism justified? The answer is clearly that it was not justified and that, so far at least, the Slovak Republic's economic performance in terms of growth, inflation and unemployment has exceeded expectations.

Table 1 below sets out some key economic indicators for the two Republics which show that the Slovak Republic appears to have performed well not only in absolute terms, but also relative to the Czech Republic.

The table shows that, after an initially difficult first year in 1993, the Slovak Republic performed well on these macro indicators in 1994 and 1995, particularly in 1995 when it clearly out-performed the Czech Republic, even on inflation. For 1997, EBRD and most other forecasters are projecting that GDP growth in the Slovak Republic will be 0.5–1 per cent higher than in the Czech Republic but that the inflation rate will be around 1.5 per cent lower in the Slovak Republic.

However, Slovak exports in the first 4 months of 1996 were lower than in the equivalent period of 1995 and a surge in imports has led to a rapid deterioration in the trade deficit, running at an annual rate of over $2 billion during this period. More worryingly, rapid growth in wages and slow growth in labour productivity are leading to substantial losses in competitiveness and rapid real appreciation of the Slovak koruna.

**Table 1.    Key Economic Indicators for the Czech and Slovak Republics 1993–96**

| Year | 1993 | | 1994 | | 1995 | | 1996 (Projected) | |
|---|---|---|---|---|---|---|---|---|
| | Cz | Sl | Cz | Sl | Cz | Sl | Cz | Sl |
| GDP growth (%) | −0.9 | −4.1 | 2.6 | 4.9 | 4.8 | 7.4 | 5.1 | 5.5 |
| Consumer prices % increase (end-year) | 18.2 | 25.1 | 10.2 | 11.7 | 7.9 | 7.2 | 9.2 | 5.9 |
| Export growth (%) | 9.8 | −16.9 | 9.2 | 25.0 | 19.3 | 26.8 | na | na |
| Trade balance ($bn) | 0.3 | −0.9 | −0.4 | 0.1 | −3.8 | 0.0 | −5.2 | −1.6 |
| Current account balance ($bn) | 0.1 | −0.6 | −0.1 | 0.7 | −1.9 | 0.6 | −3.3 | −1.2 |

*Source*:    EBRD Transition Report, November 1996.

Table 2 below reports data on wages growth, labour productivity growth and unit labour costs for the Czech and Slovak Republics for 1995 which clearly demonstrate the emerging concerns in both countries, but particularly in the Slovak Republic.

The rapid growth in earnings and unit labour costs in the Czech Republic is unsurprising given an unemployment rate of under three per cent and there was also a strong productivity performance. However, the poor productivity performance in the Slovak Republic together with the rapid growth of wages, and all of this occurring with an unemployment rate of 13 per cent, raises serious questions about the sustainability of recent economic growth performance.

**Table 2.    Productivity and Trade Competitiveness in the Czech and Slovak Republics 1995**

| | 1995 | |
|---|---|---|
| | Cz | Sl |
| Growth in manufacturing wages (local currency) | 18.7 | 15.2 |
| Growth in manufacturing wages (in $US) | 28.8 | 24.1 |
| Growth in labour productivity in industry | 20.5 | 4.0 |
| Growth in unit labour costs (in $US) | 6.9 | 19.3 |

*Source*:    EBRD Transition Report, November 1996.

Preliminary data for 1996 suggest that these problems have been continuing. These trends provide some indication that microeconomic policy and performance may not be strong enough to sustain recent aggregate growth and inflation experience in the Slovak Republic in the medium term.

Finally, it should also be noted that much of the good inflation performance results from the Slovak government strongly holding down energy and other utility prices. This is a factor that is common in other CEE economies, including the Czech Republic, but Slovakia has been particularly stringent over energy prices which, until August 1996, had not been raised to households since 1991. That implied a real reduction in (already very low) household energy prices of over 40 per cent. The August 1996 increase of 10 per cent for industrial consumers and 5 per cent for residential consumers does not represent any increase in real terms and, in addition, increases the cross-subsidy from industrial to residential consumers. This is not sustainable beyond the short run for energy or for the other utility prices that have similarly been held down. The inevitable catch-up will at some stage come through and be reflected in the overall inflation rate.

The discussions on both competitiveness and utility pricing and inflation above are particular instances of the relationship between microeconomic reform and aggregate economic performance (e.g., on growth, unemployment and inflation). Beyond a certain point, the absence of microeconomic reform can be seriously destabilizing for economic performance.

Considering the energy pricing issue, the classic example is in Bulgaria, where the massive declines in real ($-price) energy prices and in energy enterprise revenues have been a major factor in the growing inter-enterprise and government indebtedness which led to a full-blown banking, exchange rate and fiscal crisis in late 1996. Thus, on 1 July 1996, Vuglishta, the Bulgarian coal holding company, announced that it had incurred losses of lev 3.57 million in the first half of 1996 because of the delayed introduction of new coal prices, delayed to avoid increased losses by the power sector and other major coal users. In addition, they announced that the accumulated debt to Vuglishta from NEK (the national electricity company) and the heat companies had reached lev 4 billion or about $40 million at mid-1996 exchange rates.[1]

Given the shortage of tax revenue, it has become standard practice in Bulgaria in the 1990s for a substantial part of the losses of the electricity, heat and coal companies to be met by state guarantees of new bank loans to the enterprises rather than by direct subsidies. This provides the mechanism for transmitting the lack of reform in the energy sector to undermining the banking sector and provoking macroeconomic crisis. (Similar chains have occurred in the Ukraine and some other newly independent states (NIS), including Russia.)

The energy and other utility pricing issues have to date been nowhere near as acute in the Slovak Republic as in Bulgaria. Nevertheless, the inflationary benefits purchased from an absence of utility restructuring and price rebalancing can only be temporary. There will inevitably be damaging consequences for government finances, for investment and productivity growth if the government attempts to persist with them in the medium to long term. There are a number of other similar issues which we will discuss in subsequent sections of this chapter.

The general view is that the Slovak Republic has been the least keen of the Visegrad countries to actively pursue microeconomic reform. By microeconomic reform we mean items such as: the closure of loss-making enterprises; reductions in sector-specific and company-specific subsidies and cross-subsidies (overt and covert); the enhancement of open and competitive product and capital markets; and the encouragement of market-based industry and enterprise restructuring. Indeed, there are some suggestions that the Slovak Republic might be tempted to move backwards with the re-involvement of government in commercial economic life. We will appraise the evidence for this in the next section of this chapter. The key question, however, is whether or not the reform go-slow in the Slovak Republic after the break-up of the CSFR in 1992 matters in terms of current or future aggregate economic performance, e.g., on GDP growth rates and their sustainability.

The question of the relationship between the strength of microeconomic reform and aggregate economic performance and its sustainability will be discussed in later sections, taking the recent paper by Sachs and Warner (1995) as the starting point. The Sachs and Warner paper argues strongly that it is openness to trade and the absence of major trade distortions that is the single key determinant of economic performance. As the Brookings panel discussion showed, this argument is far from uncontroversial and Sachs admitted that 'trade liberalization alone would not be sufficient and should be interpreted as a proxy for the more far-reaching programmes of economic reform that come with it', but added that, in his view, trade openness was the key driving force behind the other reforms. Nevertheless, the simple Sachs-Warner thesis is a particularly useful framework for considering the recent history and potential future performance of the Slovak economy as it allows us to explore what are the essential elements of microeconomic reform for sustained growth in transitional economies.

The plan of the rest of the chapter is as follows. In the second section, we will briefly outline the history of economic reform (particularly microeconomic reform) in the Slovak Republic and highlight the issues that are most relevant for future sustained growth prospects. In the third section, we will appraise this position in the light of the Sachs-Warner hypothesis that trade openness is the critical condition for economic success and the chapter will end with a short concluding section.

## ECONOMIC REFORM IN THE SLOVAK REPUBLIC

### The Political Background

Many observers were relatively pessimistic about the outlook for the Slovak Republic when it became an independent republic in January 1993. This was partly because it was perceived as having an unpromising industrial structure relative to the Czech Republic, with much greater dependence on heavy industry and very little of its more glamorous neighbour's non-industrial attractions, e.g., for tourism. Perhaps the major concern was the political legacy and the expected economic policy outlook of the government of the new Republic.

It is worth remembering that the idea of 'Czechoslovakia' as a single country bringing together Czechs and Slovaks is a relatively recent one dating from the end of the nineteenth century and Tomas Masaryk's political campaigns. For generations before, the Czechs had been part of the German-speaking world and the Austrian part of the Austro-Hungarian Empire, while the Slovaks had been part of the Magyar world and the Hungarian part of the Austro-Hungarian Empire. The Slovaks only agreed to join in with the Czechs and Masaryk's provisional government in the summer of 1918 and the first Czechoslovak Republic was only formally established in 1920 under the Treaty of Trianon, after the defeat of an invasion of Slovakia in 1918–19 by the Hungarian Red Army under Béla Kun.

The inter-War Republic was a very centralized state and the Slovaks found themselves effectively ruled from Prague, with very little autonomy. This was clearly one of the factors behind the establishment of a notionally independent Slovak Republic under Nazi German tutelage and ruled by the Slovak Peoples' Party under Jozef Tiso. After 1945, the position in the eyes of many Slovaks reverted to rule from Prague and by the Czechs, e.g., with Czech school-teachers and policemen throughout Slovakia (as has been related to me by moderate Slovak nationalists).

In 1989, there emerged the Slovak Civic Forum party which was an active part of the Velvet Revolution and which did very well in the 1990 elections. However, from that point on it was the Slovak nationalists who made increasing headway and it was Vladimir Meciar, and his party (the HZDS), who won the June 1992 elections on a platform of Slovak independence. Long-standing political and ethnic nationalist aspirations clearly loomed large in that election victory but so did fears of the implications for Slovakia of the Czech economic programme as directed by Vaclav Klaus, with its emphasis on rapid privatization.

The key Slovak concern was unemployment. At the end of 1991, the unemployed were only 4.1 per cent of the labour force in the Czech Republic, as opposed to 11.8 per cent in the Slovak Republic.[2] Moreover, although the unemployment rate was (and remains) similar to the Czech level in Bratislava, it rises steadily as one looks eastwards towards the Ukraine. The HZDS and other Slovak nationalist political support comes much more from central and eastern Slovakia than from the western part of the country. Similarly, trade, cultural and other links for Slovakia, particularly in eastern areas, were much closer with Ukraine and other countries of the former Soviet Union relative to western Europe than for the Czech lands. In addition, in the 1990–92 period, the CSFR Federal Government and the Czechs took a very tough line on arms exports and to whom it was appropriate to sell arms. That seemed to seriously threaten the prospects for output and jobs not just in the Martin tank factory and other major Slovak arms producers (who had been selling primarily to USSR-supported countries such as Iraq) but also in the supplying companies.

In the event, the collapse of Comecon and the sharp economic declines in the former USSR (particularly the Ukraine and Belarus) made an alternative eastward-looking trade strategy for Slovakia infeasible. Similarly, the prospects for Russian-supported Slovak arms sales also disappeared. Nevertheless, the political economy of the new Slovak Republic was dominated by concerns that the Czech programme of rapid privatization combined with the apparent renunciation of an activist industrial policy would devastate Slovak industry and lead to rapidly escalating unemployment. For industrial towns, particularly in central and eastern Slovakia, this was a major fear. Hence, much of the economic rhetoric of the Slovak nationalists emphasized the need for caution and expressed strong reservations about the costs of a rapid privatizing and liberalizing economic policy for Slovakia.

In the event, as shown in Table 1, the output growth performance of the Slovak Republic has been quite similar to that of the Czech Republic. Further, although aggregate Slovak unemployment rates have been consistently around four times higher than Czech unemployment rates, there has been no trend increase to date in the relative Slovak rate. Thus, in retrospect, the economic fears of the Slovak nationalists in the early 1990s have not been borne out in practice. Nevertheless, these fears are important for understanding the course of Slovak economic policy in general and of its privatization policy in particular.[3]

## Privatization and the Scope of Government Intervention

When Slovakia became an independent republic in January 1993, it inherited not only the successful macroeconomic stabilization achieved by the CSFR but also the considerable progress that had been made in microeconomic reform, including a variety of legal and other institution-building reforms. In particular, it inherited the large-scale and wide-ranging privatization from the first round of the CSFR voucher privatization programme.

The newly fledged Slovak Republic also inherited strong public finances, a favourable internal and external debt position and an effectively complete trade liberalization. Thus, at the start of independence in 1993, quantitative restrictions on imports had already been removed,[4] the average weighted import tariff was only 5.7 per cent and external debt (net of official reserves) was about 27 per cent of GDP.

Indeed, the critical first stage of the post-Communist economic reform process was accomplished before independence. Not only had macroeconomic balance been largely achieved, but, by end-1992, 50 per cent of GDP was produced by the private sector; small privatization had been completed with the sell-off of over 10,000 enterprises; 70 of the largest Slovak companies had been privatized in the CSFR voucher privatization; and almost 14,000 private enterprises were in operation. Similarly, the first stages of banking reform were in place before independence, including the establishment of the Consolidation Bank to handle non-performing loans.

However, although subsequent progress in deepening the reforms has been limited, there has so far been little in the way of reversal of the reform inheritance. Thus, although a 10 per cent import surcharge was imposed in March 1994, this was reduced to 7.5 per cent in July 1996 and was due to be abolished in early 1997. Similarly, privatization of the banks has been held up but the restrictions were due to be removed by end-March 1997.

It is also fair to note that other CEE countries have also made limited progress since 1993 in some of the areas, e.g., in privatization of state-owned enterprises (Poland), capital market and banking reform, establishment of effective corporate governance procedures, utility price rebalancing and reform, etc. Progress in the Czech Republic in some of these areas (particularly utility restructuring and reform) has not been that much greater than in the Slovak Republic.

Nevertheless, there are clear differences between the pace of reform in the Slovak Republic and its Central European neighbours. For instance, surveys by the European Bank for Reconstruction and Development (EBRD) in 1995 and 1996 suggest laws fostering investment are less extensive than in the other Visegrad countries and although 'not imposing major obstacles ... are in need of considerable improvement'. In addition, the EBRD surveys show that enforcement of investment laws seems to be more of a problem in the Slovak Republic than in the Czech Republic and, to a lesser extent, relative to Hungary and Poland, e.g., as shown in the comparison of administrative and judicial support.[5]

However, according to the 1996 World Development Report, the Slovak Republic did not liberalize significantly less in 1995 than the other Visegrad countries. Its share of private sector output in GDP was 70 per cent in early 1996, with the private sector accounting for 67 per cent of industrial output and 57 per cent of total employment. This is comparable to Hungary although less than the Czech Republic (75 per cent of GDP) and higher than Poland (about 60 per cent of GDP). Similarly, the 24 per cent share of employment in small and medium enterprises was the same as in Poland and Hungary, albeit again less than the Czech Republic (37 per cent). The number of enterprises has continued to grow strongly, reaching around 47,000 in May 1996, an increase of 33,000 relative to end-1992.[6]

All of the statistics above suggest that private sector enterprise creation and growth has been strong both in absolute and in relative terms. Thus far, slower deepening of microeconomic reform does not appear to be adversely affecting the development of a newly emerging private sector.

One possible exception to this is on foreign direct investment (FDI) flows, which have been very low in the Slovak Republic – under four per cent of GDP by end-1994 as against seven per cent for Poland, 13 per cent for the Czech Republic and over 30 per cent for Hungary. (The figure for Poland will have sharply increased since end-1994.) The low level of FDI inflows is typically ascribed in newspaper comment to the political environment. However, economic factors may well have played an important role in the weak FDI performance – e.g., the investment law weaknesses discussed above, together with the slow development of capital markets and banking reform and the way in which the privatization programme for large enterprises has proceeded.

Privatization demonstrates some of the key differences of the Slovak Republic relative to the other Visegrad countries.

The Slovak government allowed the first wave of CSFR privatization to continue to completion during the first half of 1993. However, it did not have a second wave in 1994–95, unlike the Czech Republic. Seven hundred and fifty firms were privatized in the first wave with 503 being involved in the voucher privatization. The balance of the assets in the privatized companies was sold by direct sales, public tender etc.

The anti-Meciar government of 1993–94 embarked on a second wave of voucher privatization, and distributed the voucher books. However, following the return to power by Meciar in the 1994 elections, this was first postponed and then cancelled. In mid-1995, amendments were made to the 1991 CSFR Privatization Law which cancelled voucher privatization and gave the 3.5 million voucher-holders 5-year bonds issued (and guaranteed) by the National Property Fund (NPF) in place of their vouchers. The bonds can be used as part-payment for property. They can also be sold, used to buy shares of companies in the NPF portfolio and to pay off debts to the NPF. Hence, companies have some incentive to buy these bonds.

Instead, the government has pursued a policy of privatization by direct sale, typically with preference given to existing management, who can purchase the assets cheaply and in instalments. The main aspects of the scheme (which was intended to be completed by end-1996) are described in EBRD reports as follows. Around 600 privatization proposals, with a book value of koruna 136 billion (about US\$4.5 billion) were submitted to the NPF by March 1996. They were sold by direct sale, including management and employee buy-outs, with preference being given to existing management. Firstly, a price is agreed between the purchaser and the NPF. Following that, the purchaser makes a down-payment (typically 10–20 per cent) and agrees: (a) a series of instalments over which the balance is paid; and, (b) the amount to be invested in the company. However, this agreed new investment can be treated by the NPF as a contribution to the loan repayments. In addition, the companies can claim tax relief against the corporate income tax on this investment.

As can be seen, the system allows existing managers to purchase the existing assets on extremely favourable terms. The process is slow and does little to introduce either new capital or effective corporate governance. Indeed, the power of insider managers is considerably enhanced. Perhaps not surprisingly, there have been continuous accusations of cronyism, doubtful practice and corruption about this process.

Of course, the Slovak Republic is far from unique in facing such accusations and we cannot judge the merits of the claims. They do, however, seem to be rather more frequent and perhaps more factually supported than in neighbouring CEE economies. What does seem clear is that the idea of privatization as a way of depoliticizing economic activity is not one that seems to carry weight in Slovakia.

Indeed, as we will show, much of the basis of Slovak economic policy is to retain a considerable political influence over economic activity, including widespread fall-back powers. The key question for future economic performance is, therefore, how far this influence will permeate and distort the activities of the 60 per cent of economic activity now in the private sector.

The main focus of active government involvement in corporate affairs has so far concerned 'strategic companies'. The 1995 Law Relating to State Interests identifies 29 companies which will not be privatized because they are of strategic importance; and a further 45, some already partially privatized, where the state will retain an ownership stake with special voting privileges (either a 33 per cent stake or a 'golden share'). The 29 companies on the not-to-be-privatized list include the obvious candidates (e.g., gas, electricity generation, telecommunications, armaments). The 45 companies on the secondary list include companies in the agricultural sector, mining, chemicals, construction and engineering. The three largest banks were added to this second list in June 1996, but they were only retained on it up to end-March 1997.

This list (particularly the secondary list) seems to embody a very wide definition of 'strategic' companies relative to commercial activities. It includes some of the main exporting sectors, but all of them are selling into competitive markets. In addition, there have been discussions of involving private capital in some of the companies on the former list, e.g., the sale of stakes to a strategic partner in the telecommunications industry.

It should be said that there are currently legal disputes over the Law on Strategic Enterprises. The section on the secondary list was declared unconstitutional by the Constitutional Court in April 1996 on the grounds that it was unfair to other shareholders. It is not known at the time of writing whether or how the position has been resolved.

A particular instance of the pressures that have arisen concerns the structure of the downstream oil industry. The World Bank's 1996 World Development Report favourably mentions the role of anti-monopoly offices in the Czech and Slovak Republics on dismantling monopolies before privatization. It is therefore somewhat ironic that the Chairman of the Anti-Monopoly Office was dismissed and several other senior staff resigned in 1995 after having criticized the Slovak government's decision to sell the 200 petrol stations owned by Benzinol to Slovnaft a.s., the largest oil refiner in Slovakia. The government insisted on selling all 51 per cent of its stock *en bloc* and refused bids from Agip of Italy and OMV of Austria.[7]

The Slovak government preferred to retain a single, unbundled Slovak oil company that would own most petrol stations (80 per cent) in the Slovak Republic. This represented a clear victory for 'national champions' over competition policy.

However, in general, the Slovak Competition Law of 1994 appears to be closely modelled on EU Law, although it allows a defence against both restrictive agreements and market dominance on the grounds of economic benefits that is wider than either EU law or the equivalent Czech law.[8] Nevertheless, the Slovak Competition Office has also had some significant victories, e.g., against price-fixing cartels in the cement and fuel distribution businesses and it has clearly been active and effective at encouraging competition in a range of cases with a low political profile.

## Price Regulation and the Private Sector

Clearly, the current Slovak government has chosen to be politically interventionist in industrial policy and particularly in privatization policy. It has never made any secret of this nor of its intentions to do so. However, by and large, there has not been such intervention in the commercial operations of the firms in the 60 per cent of the economy in the private sector. There is now, however, a definite cloud on the horizon. That cloud is the new Prices Law passed in November 1995.[9]

Typically, CEE transition economies have adopted prices laws that allow for the regulation of a small number of prices by the Ministry of Finance, usually utility prices, rents and a few others. All other prices of goods sold on competitive markets are deemed to be unregulated and subject only to monitoring by the competition agency on conventional anti-competitive behaviour grounds.

The new Slovak Prices Law appears to blur this distinction and allows the Ministry of Finance (including its district and area offices) the powers to intervene if prices appear unreasonably high or there is *prima facie* evidence of undue profits. This is my interpretation of Paragraph 4 of the Law. Price regulation of natural monopolies is discussed separately in Paragraph 5.

The key definitions in the Law are 'economically justified costs' and 'appropriate profit'. The latter refers to the 'usual share of profit on domestic goods' and 'usual risks'. The Ministry of Finance is clearly given the power to specify a maximum acceptable rate of profit in Paragraph 2 of the Law but is provided with no criteria to determine how, when or why.

To enforce these (vaguely worded) provisions would require a considerable bureaucratic infrastructure which does not seem to have been created. In addition, government spokesmen have strongly claimed that they have no intention of using the Law in this way. Under their interpretation, it merely provides some residual fallback powers against potential gross abuses. But, even if this were the case (and there is no guarantee that some future government might not take a different view of how the law can be used), there is still a contingent threat of intervention comparable to contingent protection measures like anti-dumping and safeguards to trade policy.

The evidence is that contingent protection threats do affect the volume and composition of international trade. Thus the 'reserve powers' justification for the new Slovak Prices Law does not mean that the behaviour of firms will be unaffected. Indeed, the Slovak authorities would probably claim it as a benefit if firms refrained from raising prices as a result of this law being on the statute book, even if the proposed price rise could be defended fully on the grounds of market forces. That must have effects on potential supply, on investment and the cost of capital. Further, the mere existence of the law on the statute book must further reduce the authority of the Anti-Monopoly Office whether or not these provisions are used.

If this law were used to re-introduce widespread price controls (and so far there is no evidence that it has been or will be so used), it would clearly represent a major step backwards from a market economy.

## International Trade

The position on trade liberalization is good. The Slovak Republic became a member of the WTO in December 1994. The average weighted import tariff is 4.9 per cent and will fall to 3.8 per cent on implementation of the Uruguay Round. Quantitative trade restrictions were phased out by the CSFR in 1991 and there has been no move to re-introduce them. Export licences are only required for certain natural resource exports. Current account convertibility for all Slovaks was introduced in October 1995, following approval of a new foreign exchange law by the Slovak Parliament.

Not only has Slovak trade grown rapidly, but the geographical distribution of its trade has radically changed in line with other central European countries, but, as yet, its commodity composition has not much changed.

In 1995, according to the Direction of Trade Statistics Yearbook, Slovak identified exports were US$7,902 million, of which 46 per cent were sold to the EU. The Czech Republic still took 36 per cent of exports, but this share has been declining since 1993. Within Western Europe, the major export recipients in 1995 were Germany (25 per cent), Italy (6 per cent) and Austria (5 per cent). No previous Comecon partner (other than the Czech Republic) accounted for more than 4 per cent of Slovak exports. The picture is very similar for 1995 imports, with 31 per cent from the Czech Republic (and declining), 24 per cent from Germany, 6 per cent from Italy and 5 per cent from Austria. However, 13 per cent of imports came from Russia, mainly oil and gas.

In terms of commodity composition, exports to the EU are highly concentrated. In 1995, 43 per cent of Slovak exports were in five two-digit commodity groups: iron and steel, clothing, textiles, non-metal mineral manufactures and vehicles. In several of these, the Slovak contribution seems to be primarily in processing and re-exporting semi-finished imported goods, hence the balance in exports with Italy as well as neighbouring Austria and Germany. At the single-digit level, machinery and chemicals respectively accounted for 18 per cent and 13 per cent of exports as against 28 per cent and 24 per cent of imports. This suggests growing intra-industry trade in chemicals (e.g., exports of bulk chemicals and imports of pharmaceuticals) but imports of machinery to re-equip Slovak industry.[10]

A major force for sustaining trade liberalization is the Association Agreement with the European Union (EU). The fully-fledged EU Association Agreement came into force in February 1995. This not only specifies requirements on trade policy for Slovakia to have ready access to EU markets but also imposes various obligations (at least in the traded goods sector), e.g., on competition policy, on the use of subsidies and state aid, etc. As with competition policy, the EU Agreement, and the stated intention of the Slovak government to apply to join the EU, must be important in restraining pressures for protection.

The only offset to this rosy picture is the 10 per cent import surcharge imposed on all imports of consumer goods and foodstuffs in March 1994. However, at least it is a reasonably 'across-the-board', single-rate subsidy rather than a multiple-rate surcharge designed to maximize the degree of protection faced by particular industries.

The trade policy reform aspect is therefore much more encouraging for the development of a market economy. Since the Slovak Republic is a classic example of a small, open economy, this must have wide implications for the prospects of strong economic performance, e.g., on the degree of effective market competition faced by Slovak companies.

A further point about the trade policy reform is that it allows the Slovak Republic to import the benefits of other countries' stronger competition policies. The fact that, for instance, a high proportion of car parts used in the Slovak car manufacturing plant are imported from Germany and other countries means that the prices of these imports reflect the pressures of competition (and competition policy) in Germany and the other supplying countries. This helps hold down the costs of the Slovakian car manufacturer. In addition, the ready availability of imported cars (particularly used cars) produced in Germany and other countries with strong competition and strong competition policy holds down the price of the Slovakian-made cars. Hence, trade openness limits the degree to which foreign investors can limit competition in the local market by negotiating exclusive local production rights.

The impact of the Slovakian trade policy picture is reflected in the fact that the share of Slovak exports sold to EU countries now exceeds that of exports to the Czech Republic. Slovak companies also appear to be doing more than most CEE countries to maintain trading links with countries in the former Soviet Union.

## Bank and Capital Market Issues

The Slovak Republic has set up an independent central bank, the National Bank of Slovakia (NBS). The central bank and its governor appear to have achieved a real degree of independence. On a recent visit, we were told that there was no evidence of any government use of the NBS for directed credits although that did still appear to happen to a limited extent with the development banks.

The rest of the banking sector has been developing reasonably well and foreign banks have a significant presence, although, as discussed above, privatization of the Slovak banks has been delayed. There are concerns over non-performing loans, but this is not surprising. At end-1995, 'classified claims' (i.e., those with overdue payments of at least 90 days) amounted to koruna 132 billion – 29 per cent of total claims. This had fallen to koruna 121 billion by mid 1996. At end-1995, all but two Slovak banks met the interim capital ratio guideline of 7.25 per cent.

In general, the NBS has been strengthening supervision of the banks, e.g., through a 1996 amendment to the 1993 Banking Law which obliges banks to inform the NBS of any loan over koruna 1 million.[11]

The main issue of note is the weak development of non-bank financial intermediaries. Unlike in the Czech Republic, there is no major development of investment funds. Indeed, the Slovak government has taken a number of steps (e.g., *via* amendments to the Investment Funds Act) to actively discourage the emergence of powerful investment funds with the ability to enforce outsider corporate control. These actions have been legally challenged, but so far the government appears to have prevented the development of effective investment funds.

Similarly, again unlike the Czech Republic, there appears to have been little or no development of contributory pension funds.

An interesting issue for the development of capital markets will be what institutional responses take place (and are allowed to take place) as and when individuals can actively trade in the 5-year bonds they were given in return for the privatization vouchers they had purchased in the aborted second round of voucher privatization.

All of these responses appear to reflect a government policy of not allowing any effective intervention or outside control of company management other than by itself. The government may or may not use its powers, but it does not seem prepared to allow for any weakening of its powers to intervene from the emergence of powerful privately-owned financial intermediaries.

It is an interesting question whether and for how long this position is sustainable. Whether this policy will adversely affect the ability of companies and their incentive to make efficient investments remains to be seen. In the longer term, one must have doubts as to whether it is consistent with continued rapid growth.

## THE SACHS AND WARNER HYPOTHESIS ON NECESSARY CONDITIONS FOR SUSTAINED GROWTH

Sachs and Warner argue in their 1995 Brookings paper:

- that open economies (i.e., open to international trade) grow significantly faster than closed economies (4.5 per cent *per* year as opposed to 0.7 per cent *per* year over the period 1970–89);
- that open economies display a strong tendency to convergence and that convergence can be achieved by all economies, including those with low initial skill levels;
- that open economies have faster growth rates of investment and are less likely to have macroeconomic crises.

As stated in the introduction, the authors also emphasized that trade openness also played a significant role in encouraging economic policies conducive to a well-functioning market economy and providing earlier signals of the costs of poor policies.

In discussion, it was suggested that the very strong openness results might have been generated by using a 0/1 dummy variable for trade openness rather than a continuous variable. The standard endogeneity problems with the Barro growth model were also cause for doubt as to the strength of any causal relationship.

All of these reservations are well-made. Nevertheless, the hypothesis provides what may be a useful framework for considering the unexpectedly good economic performance of the Slovak Republic since 1993. In Slovakia, we observe:

(i)     a sustained sound monetary and fiscal policy;
(ii)    a well-functioning central bank;
(iii)   an open trading regime and currency convertibility;

but we also observe:

(iv)    a largely politically determined industry restructuring and privatization policy;
(v)     low weight given to the value of competition policy;
(vi)    an unwillingness to reform utilities and raise utility (and related) prices to economic levels;
(vii)   a reluctance to allow the significant development of private sector financial intermediaries;
(viii)  threats of wider government involvement in commercial activities, e.g., from the 1995 Prices Law.

In the narrower interpretation of the Sachs and Warner view, the relative success of the Slovak economy is not only unsurprising but can be expected to continue with continuing sustained growth rates of 5 per cent per year or more into the foreseeable future. So long as the good factors (i)–(iii) are present, so should be the favourable growth and trade expectations. On this view, items (iv)–(vii) may marginally reduce the expected growth rate (and can certainly be expected to adversely affect the level of consumer welfare corresponding to the *per capita* GDP levels) but should not have any significant effect on GDP growth – at least provided that the threats from the 1995 Prices Law and any further initiatives along these lines do not become major concerns for the traded goods and services sector.

The counter view is that as the growth process proceeds so the relative importance of the impediments in (iv)–(viii) will grow and the performance of the Slovak economy would, on the continuation of these policies, lag behind that of their more reform-minded neighbours. In particular, it seems clearly possible that continued politically-determined industrial policies plus restricted capital market developments could increasingly constrict sustainable growth rates.

An additional point is that the Slovak reforms have not yet been tested in a recession. It remains to be seen whether the Slovak authorities would be prepared to sustain their macroeconomic rigour and trade openness under the pressures of a recession that threatened seriously to raise unemployment. The presence of the adverse factors (iv)–(viii) may well increase the fragility of the sound macro and trade policies in bad times. But here political factors intrude, not least in terms of the desired future relationship between the Slovak Republic, the EU, and EU member states which include some of its most important trading partners.

## CONCLUDING COMMENTS

This chapter has shown that the growth and trade performance of the Slovak economy has been good and much better than expected, in particular relative to the Czech economy. The only area in which the Czech economy has clearly done better is on unemployment. Ironically, of course, it was fears of high unemployment from rapid microeconomic reform which was one of the main driving forces of the pro-Slovak independence movement.

The chapter has also clearly demonstrated the relatively slow pace of microeconomic restructuring and the unwillingness of the current and previous Meciar governments to establish an economy based on competition. The degree to which market forces, combined with a clearly delineated competition policy, are allowed to determine the structure of the economy has been clearly limited. This particularly applies to capital markets as shown in the antipathy to voucher privatization, a privatization policy based on insider management control and the attempts to prevent the emergence of effective non-bank financial intermediaries which could create methods of outsider corporate supervision other than by the government.

Thus, so far, sound monetary and fiscal policies plus an open trading environment in an economy where the majority of economic activity is in private hands (particularly in the tradables sector) has been sufficient to result in a good growth and trade performance. This is what the Sachs and Warner hypothesis would predict. The key question is whether it will continue to be sufficient.

The answer is that the Slovak economy should be able to continue growing at a good rate if one takes literally the Sachs and Warner view that trade openness is the absolutely dominant determinant of growth performance. However, that is to place a great deal of weight on some particular and not unproblematic regression results.

The alternative view, to which I am more sympathetic, is that the constraints from the reluctance to trust markets and institute thorough-going microeconomic reform will become progressively more important. Thus, under current policies, one should expect a slowing-down of the growth rate and trade growth, although not necessarily in the next year or so.

However, one key point in the Sachs and Warner view is the power of open trade policies to affect other areas of policy. It does seem to me reasonable to argue that a longer period of good growth performance could well have important knock-on effects. For instance, the reserve power clauses in the 1995 Prices Law would not be used, growing *per capita* incomes should allow utility reform and price rebalancing, and so on. In particular, the entrenchment of a strong export sector would significantly raise the costs of a backsliding that threatened trade opportunities and good economic relations with the EU. Finally, some years of such growth might well engender sufficiently robust private sector institutions as to effectively weaken the powers of the government to intervene in a damaging way on industrial policy and in capital markets.

The opposite is also true. The Slovak reforms are not yet as well entrenched as in neighbouring countries. The main risk is therefore that an early or serious downturn would trigger a series of market-unfriendly government interventions, including a loose fiscal policy and/or action against the independence of the central bank and/or trade restrictions. This would signal a clear move away from a market economy and back to a managed economy. One would then expect more extensive use of the government's potential powers of micro intervention and further developments as in the 1995 Price Law.

Currently, the risks of a Slovak return to a state-managed economy may be no bigger than the shadow cast by a man's hand. The key question, and the answer to the question posed in the title of this chapter, seems to me to rest in whether the period of strong growth in real incomes and trade will persist long enough to alleviate the fears of serious microeconomic reform. If so, market-led developments and pressures are highly likely to bring further reform, e.g., by encouraging the government to follow the next round of institution-building and other changes on which its Visegrad neighbours are already well-embarked.

This is the favourable outcome and one in which the power of trade openness can play a major role. It is, though, difficult to believe (*pace* Sachs and Warner) that trade openness is a sufficient condition for sustained economic performance and that microeconomic reforms have little or no influence in the longer run.

## NOTES

1. See FT East European Energy Newsletter, August 1996, p. 21.
2. United Nations Economic Commission for Europe Report for 1993 and subsequent years.
3. At least under the two Meciar-headed governments. Meciar has been Prime Minister since 1993 apart from a period in 1993–94.
4. Apart from import restrictions on some agricultural products, textiles, clothing, steel and coal plus import licences for oil, gas and weapons. See EBRD Transition Report, October 1994.
5. EBRD Transition Report, November 1995 and 1996.
6. EBRD Transition Report, 1995 and 1996.
7. See Fingleton *et al.*, (1996), p.138.
8. See Fingleton *et al.*, (1996), p. 80.

9. The discussion of the 1995 Prices Law is based on my interpretation of an unofficial translation of the Law obtained on a visit to Bratislava in April 1996.
10. Data on the commodity composition of trade is taken from the 1995–96 ECE Survey of Europe.
11. EBRD Transition Report, 1996.

# REFERENCES

EBRD, *Transition Report*, October 1994, November 1995 and 1996.

Financial Times *East European Energy Newsletter*, August 1996.

Fingleton, J., E. Fox, D. Neven and P. Seabright (1996), *Competition Policy and the Transformation of Central Europe*, London: CEPR.

Sachs, J.D. and A. Warner (1995), 'Economic Reform and the Process of Global Integration', *Brookings Papers on Economic Activity*, 1995:1.

United Nations Economic Commission for Europe (UN-ECE), *Report* for 1993 and subsequent years.

United Nations Economic Commission for Europe (UN-ECE), *Economic Survey of Europe*, 1995–96.

# 9
# Economic Competition in the Transitional Slovak Economy: Creation, Promotion or Protection?

*Eugen Jurzyca*[1]

## INTRODUCTION

The function of the Antimonopoly Office of the Slovak Republic (hereinafter referred to as the Office, or AOSR[2]) should be seen within the broader framework of dismantling socialism and building a market-oriented society. Each element of the economic transition has been very much linked to competition policy. In the broader sense, the AOSR's aim of creating a competitive environment is identical with escaping from a centrally planned economy and maximizing social welfare through the optimization of resource allocation. The AOSR, therefore, has not only been deeply involved in so-called standard areas of competition protection, namely monitoring concentrations, preventing dominant firms from abusing their economic power and dealing with agreements restricting competition. From its inception, the Office devoted a large portion of its capacity to influencing the privatization process, promoting the adoption of new laws, undertaking educational activities and requesting administrative bodies to remove measures negatively influencing the competitive environment. These circumstances have been mirrored in the portfolio of the Office's activities dealing with anti-competitive practices, influencing the legislative processes in Slovakia, influencing the industrial structure though privatization as well as in its personnel policy, in the relevant legislation prepared by AOSR, in the system of gathering information, and in public relations and international co-operation.

In this chapter, I describe the main philosophy, developments, special features and practical experience linked to particular areas in which the AOSR has been involved. Based on this description, I will try to formulate some recommendation for the proper functioning of competition policies in transitional countries as a contribution to the discussion concerning this topic. I hope that some of these ideas may also be relevant for developed economies.

## AOSR ACTIVITIES

The description of AOSR activities covers the period of time from 1991 to 1995 and is based on the annual reports of the Office as well as the personal experience of the author and his former colleagues. The end of 1990 and the first half of 1996 are not described in official reports, and are thus not analysed in detail. The data covering the year 1995 are taken from newspapers, journals and the relevant AOSR report. The respective statistics are also taken from annual reports. However, some numbers had to be estimated or adjusted either because they were not explicitly mentioned in the reports, or because the statistical methodology has been changed during the period of time covered by this chapter. To a certain extent, the statistics reflect the following features:

- Some cases had separate procedures opened against each party involved (for example the case against 40 co-operatives in 1992).
- Some papers, studies and reports do not distinguish between, on the one hand, cases conducted according to the Procedural Code of the Slovak Republic, which describes all rights and duties of all the parties involved and requires a relatively sophisticated approach and intensive work, and those cases involving basically the exchange of a couple of letters between the Office and entrepreneurs, on the other.
- There is dramatic difference between the time spent on a case which, for example, is initiated by the party harmed by a dominant firm or an agreement restricting competition, and those cases which are initiated by AOSR officers and aim, for example, at analysing the dominance of an enterprise. The weight of particular cases can hardly be measured and the best picture of the trends in particular AOSR activities can only be obtained by reading the description of all of them, which would require a much longer study than the present one.

### Agreements Restricting Competition

The Competition Protection Act prohibits agreements and concerted practices between entrepreneurs, as well as decisions of their associations, whose object or effect is or may be the restriction of competition, unless the law states otherwise. The scope of the law includes agreements among entrepreneurs active in the same relevant market (competitors) as well as those who undertake business in markets which are vertically connected. The AOSR philosophy towards vertical links has been more liberal because of their relatively limited harmful effect on competition. Statements covering horizontal and vertical agreements respectively in the Slovak Competition Protection Act were changed in 1994. Mandatory notification of all of them (including even trivial agreements) was replaced by a less dogmatic approach. The ban on such agreements is no longer absolute; instead, the balance between restrictions of economic competition and contributions to the consumer welfare is tested. The analysis involves four steps:

1. finding out if the agreement improves production or distribution, or contributes to technical and economic progress;
2. looking at the share of the benefit obtained by consumers;
3. ascertaining whether any restrictions of competition exceed those which are necessary to achieve the aims mentioned above;
4. checking whether competition would be limited in a substantial part of the relevant market.

The aforementioned change in the law was brought about by the fact that the efficiency of the original system was very poor. According to AOSR experience, many agreements significantly restricting economic competition were not filed with the Office. At the same time, a number of notifications lead to an increase in the administrative activities required at both the Office and the entrepreneurial subjects involved. The number of cases has been increasing and therefore the effort devoted to this area by AOSR and the entrepreneurs should be used as effectively as possible.

During the period of time covered by this chapter, mostly horizontal agreements prevailed. These involved particularly price fixing, division of a market and the prevention of potential entrepreneurs from entering a market. The majority of such agreements appeared in markets with oligopolistic structures.

**Table 1.   Agreements Restricting Competition**

|  | 1991 | 1992 | 1993 | 1994 | 1995 |
|---|---|---|---|---|---|
| Number of cases[a] of agreements restricting competition | 6 | 48 | 12 | 17 | 28[b] |

*Notes:*   a. Cases concluded with a decision taken in accordance with the Procedural Code of the Slovak Republic. b. Slovak Economic Journal, *Trend.*

If the analysis shows that the agreement's contribution to customer welfare is likely to be higher than the losses due to the restriction of economic competition, then it does not need to be notified to the AOSR. However, if entrepreneurs are not sure about the consequences of their agreements, they may ask the Office for a statement of its opinion. The burden of proof lies with the entrepreneurs.

During the initial period of the transition process in Slovakia, agreements restricting competition were mainly concluded because of the lack of experience with a market economy, because of the experience inherited from socialism, or even because of government policy. Such was the case, for example, of brick producers in 1991, who set prices centrally as they were used to doing when all of them belonged to the same legal entity. Such agreements, if they were discovered, were not punished severely. After the first years of 'naivety', entrepreneurs have become more sophisticated and, being partially aware of the harmful effects of their agreements, they have been trying to hide them. As an example of this development we can mention the case of cement producers. Initially, they tried to argue that the restriction of economic competition by price fixing was helpful for the whole industry, but by the end of the case (after two years), they did everything to avert suspicions of dividing up the market and price fixing.

In 1991, the AOSR issued a decision banning part of the agreement signed by eight Slovak brick producers and their former directorate in Brno. According to this agreement the former headquarters was responsible for preparing the system of price setting for the products in question, for comparisons of domestic prices, for direct setting of prices for individual firms and for elaborating the price list of materials used for the production of bricks. This case did not end with the imposition of a fine on the entrepreneurs involved, since awareness of the competition law at that time was very low. The decision was used rather for educational purposes, because such behaviour was relatively frequent.

A case illustrating the government's involvement in concluding agreements restricting competition took place in 1993. In this case Slovakia's two main gasoline station owners, Slovnaft and Benzinol, whose total share of the relevant market was approximately 90 per cent, fixed their product prices. It was proved that representatives of both firms met to discuss pricing policy. The result of this meeting was the application of uniform prices for gasoline in Slovakia. Both companies argued that this agreement was initiated by government officials; nevertheless, the sole responsibility was borne by them. The Office imposed relatively high fines equal to SK 2 million (70,000 USD) for each firm.

Another case, representing more sophisticated and also more classic behaviour, involved all the cement producers in Slovakia. The first evidence of the possible existence of a cartel agreement appeared as early as 1992. From that time on, the AOSR monitored the situation in the relevant market very carefully. The suspicion of concluding an agreement limiting competition also grew following discussions with representatives of western European competition authorities who had described the activities of cement producers in their own countries. The main proof was found in 1993 – the sheet of paper indicating the division of the market among cement producers in Slovakia was discovered at the table of one of the Cement Association officials during a visit by AOSR experts. Based on written documents and interviews with experts it was proved that the entrepreneurs in question had implemented agreements restricting competition over a period of at least two years.

In 1991, the parties agreed regularly to exchange basic economic data about their firms (outputs, costs, exports, inventories, profit, number of employees and average wages and salaries). This information was exchanged monthly and directors of particular firms then received aggregated tables. At about the same time, a consulting firm prepared documents about the geographical division of the market amongst individual cement producers. Quantity quotas for individual cement producers were suggested by this firm as well. The documents also contained statements such as: 'The particular region shall be supplied exclusively by the producer located there. If there is no producer in a region, a major supplier shall be designated'.

In 1994 the AOSR prohibited all cement producers from dividing up the market and setting cement sale quotas, as well as mutual exchange of basic economic data which could lead to co-ordination in setting cement prices. At the same time the Office imposed on the entrepreneurs concerned total fines equal to SK 19.96 million (USD 0.7 million). This represents the highest penalty imposed by the Office in its history. The parties appealed against this decision to the Supreme Court of the Slovak Republic. The original decision was fully upheld.

At the present time the behaviour of entrepreneurs is becoming more similar to the activities of their 'colleagues' in western countries. That requires a more sophisticated approach from the AOSR. Therefore, the Office has to use more advanced practices as well, as far as the methodology of investigation is concerned. The Office must use not only personal contacts with entrepreneurs and representatives of their associations, but information provided by consulting firms, specialized databases, etc. It is worth noting that the latter resources are still underdeveloped in Slovakia. A very important source of information is the domestic press. Therefore, AOSR monitors all domestic newspapers and journals, where it is possible to find, for example, news releases of various associations, articles written by journalists, relevant interviews with business persons, etc. The domestic and foreign press has been monitored very carefully at the AOSR and some of the information related to the agreements restricting competition was discovered this way. Each newspaper or magazine is being monitored by an expert who then gives the extract and key words of important articles to the library of the Office. Then the information is transferred to the internal computer network and is accessible to the whole staff.

To economise on its limited capacity the Office has developed basic 'guidelines' for deciding whether there is serious likelihood of the appearance of an agreement restricting competition. Therefore, the experts responsible for investigation firstly assess whether the market is sensitive in terms of concluding such agreements, how many subjects are active in the market, whether the price changes are suspicious, whether the entrepreneurs meet frequently, etc. Provided the full procedure has started, the Office checks the mutual correspondence of the entrepreneurs involved in the case and also interviews all the employees possibly connected with the agreement. This work is very time consuming; however, it is relatively successful.

## Concentration

According to the law, a concentration is subject to AOSR control if the combined turnover of its participants is equal to at least SK 300 million (USD 10 million) and at least two of the participants achieved a turnover of at least SK 100 million (USD 3.3 million) each. Concentrations are also reviewed by the AOSR in cases where the market-share of the participants exceeds 20 per cent of the total turnover of the goods in the market of the Slovak Republic that could be regarded as substitutes for the given products. As a consequence, the AOSR does not control small local mergers. The parties to the concentration are obliged to notify the AOSR within 15 days of the conclusion of the agreement or acquisition of control. Finalization of any concentration remains suspended for 30 days after the date of its notification.[3] The procedure at the Office is subject to provisions of the Procedural Code. Amendments to the law in 1994 brought a more liberal approach towards this area and initiated the use of the term 'concentration' instead of the more traditional 'merger'. The new word covers mergers, acquisitions of control, including establishment of joint ventures.

For the evaluation of concentrations, internal guidelines were elaborated by AOSR experts. These are aimed at ascertaining whether the concentration would have a harmful impact on the competitive environment to an extent which is not outweighed by the contribution to consumer welfare. They also involve criteria for selecting which notifications may be approved and which require to be moved on to the next stage of investigation.

During the period of time in question, the AOSR evaluated 158 projects relating to concentrations. Forty-four cases were concluded by the issuing of a decision. Two cases were not approved, while four cases were conditionally approved. In a decisive majority of the cases considered the Office agreed with the concentration. This means that its approach has been rather liberal, mainly because of the size of the Slovak economy, its openness, and the rapid pace of world trade liberalization.

Table 2.   Concentrations

|                                       | 1991 | 1992 | 1993 | 1994 | 1995 |
|---------------------------------------|------|------|------|------|------|
| Number of cases of concentrations     | 11   | 8    | 10   | 6    | 19[a] |

*Note*:   a. Slovak Economic Journal, *Trend*.

The evaluation procedure of the Office involves an assessment of whether the respective operation should be considered as a concentration, an assessment of whether the limit mentioned above has been reached and an analysis of whether the restriction of competition is compensated for by economic benefits.

Some problems in the area of concentration have been linked to the privatization process. Because the change of ownership is carried out in accordance with political rather than economic criteria, the likelihood that many cases of concentration are not notified to the AOSR is relatively high. It is hard to prove this on the basis of the available facts; some idea can nevertheless be gained if one compares the portion of property sold to foreigners in 1995 – which was roughly 2 per cent – with the fact that almost ten times as many concentrations were notified to the AOSR by foreign subjects since 1991. It is worth mentioning that this may also have been caused by the small size of domestic buyers, who simply do not meet the criteria for notification.

The main information on concentrations gathered by the Office comes from obligatory notification, which includes, among other things:

- Written agreement on concentration or the description of other procedures leading to concentration;
- Identification of the parties involved in the concentration, as applied for the Registration Court;
- Information on ownership and the personal inter-connections of the participants in the proposed concentration;
- Shares on the relevant markets, audits, balance sheets;
- Reasons for the concentration and its likely impact on competition;
- A list of main suppliers, customers and competitors.

The Office also usually requires other information. For this, it uses a special questionnaire. The AOSR also addresses other entrepreneurs acting in the same market, competitors, etc., in order to check the information provided by the parties to the concentration.

The following are examples of two cases where the Office took a positive and negative attitude respectively towards concentration.

In 1991, two state firms active in the same relevant market announced their intention to merge. The two firms in question were Slovnaft Bratislava and Benzinol Bratislava, both state-owned enterprises. The former owned approximately 30 per cent of the gasoline stations in Slovakia, while the latter owned two times as many – roughly 60 per cent. Based on the analysis evaluating the possible harmful effects of this concentration as against its contribution to the welfare of the whole society, the Office issued a negative opinion.

In 1995 the same two firms announced their concentration. Their intention to merge was publicly well known. The concentration was approved subject to certain conditions: Slovnaft is obliged to manage the construction of new gas stations in such a way as to ensure that its market share will not be higher than 50 per cent by December 31, 2000. This means that, by this date, Slovnaft will have to own 50 per cent or less of all gas stations serving the Slovak market. In addition, construction of Slovnaft's new stations should be done in such a way as to ensure that its market share is not increasing. Moreover, when supplying the market with gasoline, Slovnaft is obliged to apply the same set of trade conditions both to its own gas stations (and stations directly controlled by it) and to the gas stations of its competitors.

Among the arguments supporting this concentration, the following were particularly significant: several neighbouring refineries are located very close to Slovnaft, which means that Slovnaft operates in a rather tough competitive environment. If this concentration were not approved, Slovnaft might face serious problems, e.g., decrease in employment, worsening environmental protection, and budgetary troubles. Moreover, the number of gasoline stations has been growing rapidly for the last few years. It can thus be predicted that a number of new competitors will enter the market.

Only the future will show which of the two decisions was better.

A very interesting case illustrating the sensitive issue of balancing any harmful effects on competition ensuing from concentration against the benefits to society was the creation of a joint-venture, Eurotel. This entity was created by Slovak Telecommunications[4] and Atlantic West, B.V., Amsterdam. Eurotel was given the only licence for wireless (mobile) phone operation and was therefore supposed to be the only competitor for Slovak Telecommunications. If the concentration had not been approved, however, the operation of wireless phones in Slovakia would have been significantly postponed. Thus, the AOSR approved the concentration on the condition that in the future, if more licences were granted, Telecommunications should provide equal conditions while securing services for competitors – in the field of wireless phone operation. On the one hand, therefore, the positive effect was represented by the early presence of cellular phones in Slovakia, while on the other, Slovakia is still one of a few European countries where the progressive GSM system does not operate.[5]

## Abuses of Dominant Position

Dominant position in a relevant market is not legally prohibited in Slovakia; only its abuse is forbidden. The Competition Protection Act gives examples of such behaviour, e.g., enforcing inappropriate conditions in contracts; restricting production to the detriment of consumers; applying different conditions to individual entrepreneurs (discrimination); making the conclusion of the contract conditional upon another party accepting additional conditions, unrelated to the object of the contract.

It is presumed that an entity is in a dominant position if its share of the domestic supply or purchases in the relevant market (defined to include close substitute products) is at least 40 per cent; if it is not proved otherwise, dominance is defined as a position in which the entrepreneur is not subject to substantial competition.

As opposed to the original law on competition, the new Act no longer includes obligatory notification in the event of the internal growth of the firm bringing it up to 30 per cent of the market share. The wording of the new Act also changed. It no longer makes a distinction between dominant and monopoly positions; only the term 'dominant' is used.

As far as practical experience is concerned, it should be mentioned that the so-called 'reasonable deconcentration' managed by the AOSR in the early 90s brought significant changes in the industrial structure of the Slovak economy. Moreover, Slovakia is, in economic terminology, a 'small country' with relatively liberal foreign trade: the weighted average tariff rate amounts to approximately 2 per cent.[6] Therefore, the number of monopolies and dominant positions has decreased dramatically. Currently, this phenomenon, as well as abuses of dominance, have appeared mainly in the area of natural monopolies (heating,[7] postal services, telecommunications and the energy sector, i.e., electricity and gas). Of course, here the Office faces serious problems resulting from lack of capacity. While in some western countries there are special regulators for each such monopoly, in Slovakia regulation is divided between the so-called founding ministry (in fact the owner), the Ministry of Finance, which controls prices, and the Antimonopoly Office, which is responsible for acting against abuses of power generally.

According to another observation, it is clear that the cases are increasingly being initiated as a result of complaints, as opposed to the Office's own initiatives as was the prevailing tendency in the early stages of competition protection in Slovakia.

Among the most common anti-competitive practices we should mention are the application of unreasonable conditions in contracts, excessive pricing[8] and discrimination. Only a few cases have referred to tying and limiting supplies to customers.

### Table 3.   Abuse of Dominant Position

|                               | 1991 | 1992 | 1993 | 1994 | 1995 |
|-------------------------------|------|------|------|------|------|
| Number of cases               | 44   | 18   | 30   | 32   | 43[a] |
| Decisions prohibiting abuse   | 9    | 4    | 2    | 3    | 5    |

*Note*:   a. Slovak Economic Journal, *Trend*.

Forcing the application of unreasonable conditions can be illustrated by a case from 1994. In this case, an electric power supplier (SSE) made the signing of a contract for electric power supply with company KLF conditional upon the settlement of the loans of the joint-stock company ZVL equal to SK 13 million (USD 0.5 million). The management of ZVL decided to identify efficient parts of ZVL's assets and move them to a new company – KLF. The company looked unchanged and the management was almost the same. Therefore SSE required the fulfilment of obligations due to the original firm. The Office prohibited this abuse of dominant power and imposed a fine on SSE equal to SK 250,000 (USD 8,300). The sum looks relatively small, but the Office took into account the moral aspect of the case.

After starting a case, the Office usually proceeds according to the following steps:

- First, the relevant market is defined in terms of substitutability, time and geographical area;
- Second, the position of the subject in question in the relevant market is analysed;

- Third, the AOSR decides if the dominant firm's behaviour amounts to a violation of the Competition Protection Act.

## Measures of the Central and Local Administrative Bodies Restricting Competition

In the early stages of transition in the former Czechoslovakia, it was important to push the principles of economic competition through in all parts of the economy including those fully or partially subordinated to administrative bodies. The main reason for this was that knowledge of market economy principles and awareness of the appropriate legal framework was very limited even among central and local government officials. The other reason was that these entities adopted measures undermining competition due to the influence of interest groups. While the former incentive is gradually losing its importance, the latter is now more frequent. Of course, if the restriction of competition is lead by the interests of a strong industrial lobby, the issue is very sensitive politically and the AOSR's role is more complicated than if the case happens because of a lack of knowledge. Nevertheless, the Office has been relatively successful in this area. It is worth mentioning that taking action against measures restricting competition is not covered by the Procedural Code as is the case where the so-called standard activities of the Office are concerned. If the AOSR receives information on allegedly economically harmful behaviour on the part of an administrative body, it asks for detailed information and justification of why such a measure was adopted. It may then request remedial action. Surprisingly for many, the entities in question usually comply with such a request from the AOSR. The main reason for this seems to be the fear that information on their violation of the law on competition will be revealed, and this is risky especially for those who serve in elected positions.

To a certain extent, administrative measures restricting competition are similar to state aid matters. However, because of the lack of public money in Slovakia, such measures are mainly linked to the limitation of entrepreneurial activities, for example granting exclusive licences for particular firms. Very often a municipality restricts competition in order to benefit from a monopoly rent from their own firm, as is the case with funeral services or the collection and disposal of waste.

**Table 4.   Cases where State Administrative Bodies Restricted Competition**

|                 | 1991 | 1992 | 1993 | 1994 | 1995 |
|-----------------|------|------|------|------|------|
| Number of cases | 16   | 4    | 39   | 54   | 37   |

As an example of remedial action requested by the AOSR of a central administrative body we can mention the following case. In 1993, the AOSR analysed the behaviour of the Ministry of Interior of the Slovak Republic in regard to the agreement it concluded on co-operation with the company RIMI-EURO. The subject of the agreement was the supply of equipment for the transmission of secret digital signals by wireless, to secure safety in protected buildings. The agreement stated that the Ministry of the Interior, during the course of co-operation with the company named, would not conclude an agreement for setting up a similar or the same system with other entities. This implied that fulfilment of the agreement would restrict competition. At the request of the Office, both contracting parties modified the agreement.

The investigation procedure in this area is complicated not only because of the political sensitivity mentioned above, but also because of the lack of foreign experience to draw on, and the geographical location. Visiting remote villages can be expensive and also time-consuming. Nevertheless, it is worth focusing on the behaviour of central and local governments, since in a small country this can represent the main threat for misallocation of resources.

## Privatization

According to the Competition Protection Act, state organizations and state administrative bodies are required to secure an appropriate deconcentration of privatized firms. The Office is obliged to advance its view on privatization projects within a period of eight days. If the founding ministry or the Ministry of Privatization does not agree with the AOSR statement, the case is submitted to the government (Cabinet of Ministers). A similar statement also covers any change of ownership managed by municipalities. The latter are required to ensure the creation of a competitive environment in local markets.

Within the process of privatization, the Office issues viewpoints on privatization projects, viewpoints on public tenders for sales of enterprises, viewpoints on direct sales of enterprises or parts of enterprises. If the AOSR has enough information on the impact of a given privatization project on the competitive environment it either states that no concentration will take place, that no negative impact as regards competition will ensue from the privatization project, or that the economic advantages of concentration prevail over the restriction of competition. If the Office does not posses enough information it states that in the event of fulfilment of the criteria related to concentration set out in the Competition Protection Act, the operation would be subject to the approval of the AOSR.

The criteria used by the Office in assessing privatization projects include the current position in the relevant market, contestability of the market, import barriers, current and potential position of the firm in foreign markets, geographical location of the particular state firm's units, effectiveness of the division in terms of domestic and foreign comparisons, technological and economic links, etc.

The AOSR philosophy towards deconcentration was based on the idea of influencing industrial structures before privatization rather than afterwards. It also preferred the splitting of firms into more entities rather then fewer. It is very difficult to determine the optimal level of concentration in a relevant market; however, if there are more than the optimal number of private competitors, they can merge, and market forces would soon lead them to do so. On the other hand, if a firm was privatized into a number of subjects which was below the number deemed optimal, then it would be extremely complicated to divide up these private enterprises again (though new entry or import pressures could change the situation).

The Office also required the organization of public tenders instead of selling property to subjects chosen in a 'closed procedure'. The rationale for this was that the tender should help identify the best owners and also to maximize the income to society from privatization which could be used to counteract the economic and social problems inherited from socialism. By selling state property at a price close to zero, the group of privatized firms possess significant advantages compared to those who must start their businesses *ab initio*.

Generally, one can say that the dismantling of a centrally planned economy, including privatization, is as artificial as a centrally planned economy itself. Therefore, one should not require the creation of a perfect competitive environment within this process. What should be done is to create a situation where, once market principles are in force, the barriers to their effective operation are minimal.

As an example of AOSR policy towards privatization one can mention its lengthy discussions with the Ministry of Economy over the structure of the energy sector. The current structure of the electric energy complex involves the company SEP owning the transmission grid as well as almost all power plants and three separate distribution companies. On the one hand there are strong pressures to create one single entity, while on the other the AOSR has advocated the split-up of SEP into the subject operating the grid – representing the only natural monopoly in the whole sector – and power plants. A similar situation can be seen in the gas industry, where the Office has required a split between ownership of the pipeline crossing Slovakia and the pipelines supplying the country.

Another AOSR activity linked to the transfer of ownership concerned investment funds. Because of the importance of the voucher scheme in the first wave of privatization, the Office analyses the positions of the funds. There were 234 of them in the Slovak Republic owning 60 per cent of all shares issued at the time in question. In some companies the funds acquired the position of decisive stakeholders; moreover, there were companies in their portfolios functioning in the same markets. It should be mentioned that the current government has taken measures which weakened the position of investment funds in Slovakia significantly. The threat that they can negatively influence the competitive environment is currently very low.

The power of the Office used to be significant and the majority of privatization projects were influenced by it.[9] However, in Autumn 1994 the National Property Fund (NPF) became legally the most powerful entity in the process of privatization. The legal status of this organization is not completely clear, since the laws covering privatization have been brought before the Constitutional Court many times. Thus, in fact, the NPF decides how a firm is privatized. The only public control over NPF is that its representatives are appointed by the National Council of the Slovak Republic and that some of the transactions may be covered by those provisions of the competition law which are connected with concentrations. If the latter happened and the case was not notified to the Office there would be serious danger that such a concentration would be not valid.

In the first half of 1996 the Office issued 135 statements on privatization projects. Of these, in 68 cases the AOSR agreed with the projects in question, in 17 cases it mentioned that concentration may result. In 46 cases the Office proposed a different system of privatization; in three cases no opinion was expressed because of lack of information and in one case the Office disagreed with the project proposal.[10] Since 1991 the Office has reviewed more than 2,000 privatization projects, which occupied a significant portion of its capacity.

## Public Relations

Taking into account the stage of the transition process in Slovakia it was clear that public relations activities needed to be very intensive. Knowledge of the principles of economic competition was very limited, not only among the general public, but also among entrepreneurs, government officials and journalists. This observation can be illustrated by the fact that during the period of time monitored by this chapter only a few cases representing abuse of dominant position culminated with a decision forbidding particular behaviour. Taking into account the fact that the vast majority of cases were initiated by external entities, it has been apparent that they have not understood the competition law properly. Another fact showing the lack of knowledge of competition principles was that during the period of time when notification of agreements restricting competition was obligatory, the number of notified contracts was very low. The same refers to the mandatory notification of acquiring dominant position in a market. It is also worth mentioning that in the period 1991–92 the AOSR issued 69 preliminary decisions on concentrations. Only a very small portion of these were notified to the Office for final approval.[11] Some of the economic articles published in the Slovak press, as well as some of the economic laws adopted by the Parliament[12] and measures taken by administrative bodies during the early 1990s in Slovakia also demonstrate that the past 40 years influenced not only the economic performance of the country but also the way of thinking of the nation.

A pro-active educational policy in the field of competition is important in all economies, and particularly in transitional ones. Any law is useless if it is 'unknown'. Without being familiar with the Competition Protection Act, entrepreneurs may conclude so many cartel agreements that they would be beyond the possibility of proper regulation by the Office; they also may not know what abuses of dominant power consist of and what are their rights in this respect. Government officials may seriously harm the competitive environment by preparing and issuing pieces of legislation limiting competition. Journalists may negatively influence the market culture. There are many examples of countries with similar laws, structure of ownership, geographical location, and access to raw materials. Nevertheless, some of them are poor and others are rich. This difference in some cases seems to be caused by different business cultures. Another positive consequence of intensive education is that the AOSR's role would be much easier if it had more allies within the economy. All this would lead ultimately to maximization of the society's welfare.

Being aware of the necessity to inform the public about the principles of competition protection as well as about the AOSR's activities, the Office tried to increase the number of articles published in the Slovak press.

**Table 5.    Press Publicity Relating to Competition**

| Number of Articles Published in Press | 1991 | 1992 | 1993 | 1994 | 1995 |
|---|---|---|---|---|---|
| Total | 81 | 63 | 63 | 217 | a |
| AOSR authors | 17 | 1 | 23 | 62 | a |

*Note*:    a. Not publicly available at the time of writing.

AOSR representatives have appeared regularly on TV and radio. They have also given lectures for entrepreneurs throughout the country as well as at universities. Another tool of educational policy was publishing the majority of decisions issued by the Office, including commentary, and publishing annual reports in both Slovak and English languages. This has helped to promote better understanding of the development of the competitive environment and of the AOSR's approach towards protection of competition with respect to Slovak as well as foreign entrepreneurs. Inviting external experts to the Appeal Committee also contributed to increasing transparency. Among them were people from ministries, business associations, research institutes, universities and the press. The newest element of public relations at the Office is the introduction of access to the relevant information *via* the Internet.

## International Relations

The end of the 20th century and the beginning of the next one can be characterized by a process of globalization. In the broadest sense this trend involves the removal of barriers to trade, exchange of information, labour force mobility, free movement of capital (both influx and outflow), and breaking down social differences among countries, etc. History illustrates that isolation and refusal to participate in the process of international integration can lead to disastrous consequences. An integral part and leading force of the globalization process is competition policy. Therefore, the Office has emphasized the need for co-operation with foreign competition authorities as well as with the international organizations involved in competition protection.

As examples illustrating co-operation with the respective foreign authorities, one can point to the exchange of information, books, articles and other materials, as well as of experts, between AOSR and its partners. As specific examples one can cite the following:

- Harmonization of Slovak competition law with EU[13] legislation will create the conditions for deeper integration of Slovakia into the Union;
- AOSR experts attending training courses in Brussels helps them to learn more about the relevant experience in case handling at DG IV;
- a number of seminars organized by OECD[14] where particular cases and general policies are discussed with leading world experts are extremely beneficial for building the proper philosophy and legislation of the AOSR;
- long-term advisors from the Federal Trade Commission of the USA and the Antitrust Division of the Department of Justice in the early 1990s not only brought 'competition culture' to the Office but also created important personal links useful for further co-operation;
- Good contacts are maintained also with authorities in many other countries such as the UK, France, Germany and, of course, the Czech Republic, Hungary and Poland.

The scope of co-operation has been relatively broad and besides the areas mentioned above it has covered almost all fields related to competition: foreign trade liberalization, regulation of natural monopolies, health care reform, transportation, banking, insuring systems, pension reform, etc. It can be said that the AOSR's involvement in international co-operation has been very helpful not only for the protection of economic competition in the narrow sense representing standard areas of competition protection, but it also helped to make the AOSR one of the leading forces of the transition process in Slovakia in the early 1990s.

## Legislation

Of course, the main legislative activity of the Office was the preparation of the new Competition Protection Act that was adopted by the National Council of the Slovak Republic in 1994 with some amendments to the AOSR proposal. The main changes implemented in this Act are described in other sections of this chapter.

One of the main tools for managing the transition process in Slovakia has been to influence the legislative process in the country. In this activity, the AOSR has been involved both actively and passively. The former refers to bills elaborated by the Office itself; the latter has been represented by comments on various drafts of legislation pieces prepared by other government bodies or parliamentary deputies. Since almost every economic act is linked at least to a certain extent to economic competition, this work has occupied a significant portion of the AOSR's capacity.

Among the legislative measures prepared by the Office we can mention the Government Decree on Public Procurement adopted in 1991, which covered all areas of business activities (including services, works and goods) provided they were purchased by an entity using public money.[15] The Decree was very successful: the first few tenders saved several millions of USD. Later on, the Act on Public Procurement was adopted, with the Office still playing a role in the whole process. Unlike some other transitional countries, Slovakia adopted the public procurement rules relatively early on, only a couple of months after price liberalization took place; under tough price regulation it is not, of course, necessary to organize tenders. For the time being the system is not being used ideally; however, the basic conditions are set.

Another piece of legislation elaborated by the Office was the Act Abolishing the State Monopoly on Tobacco and Salt Enterprises. The old act had been valid since 1950 and limited economic competition in tobacco production and in the processing of salt.

A partial success was a bill on the regulation of natural monopolies prepared by the AOSR in 1993. The law was not approved by the government; a number of its elements have, however, appeared in other pieces of legislation. The main idea was to create 'umbrella rules' covering the most important principles for regulation of the energy sector, heating, drinking water distribution, sewage and telecommunications. These areas were basically chosen according to the following principle: a natural monopoly may be defined, semi-technically, as a firm that employs a given technology for which the output demanded can be produced most cheaply by a single firm (Ordover, Pittman and Clyde, 1994).

If the law were adopted, the proper conditions for privatization of the respective firms would be created. The main principles of the bill were:

- Public utilities must maintain a profitable service;
- Public utilities shall render safe and adequate service;
- All customers must be served on equal terms (if reasonable, the regulatory body can permit classification of customers);
- Public utilities may charge 'reasonable prices;
- Public utilities are protected from competition by licences;
- The owner of the public utility and the regulator must be different persons;
- The act should create conditions for further development of economic competition (e.g., new entrants, third-party access).

The AOSR's approach toward the individual sectors to be covered by the act in question was the following:[16]

**Electricity:**   The Slovak electricity company, Slovensky Energeticky Podnik (SEP) should be divided up. Power plants should be excluded to create a competitive environment in electric power production. Because of the structure of the whole industry, the split would not necessarily strengthen economic competition directly. However, it would encourage imports from other countries which are either already connected with Slovakia or will be connected in the near future. The necessity of such an approach can be illustrated by the fact that Slovakia imports a negligible amount of electric power from Ukraine despite the low prices.

**Gas:** Each of the pipelines should be owned by a different company. This would encourage competition in the distribution of natural gas and could create better conditions for third-party access.

**Drinking water:** State-owned companies should either be privatized or given to the local authorities, which should encourage competition by increasing the number of potential competitors.

**Telecommunications:** To introduce competition, it is necessary to create an economic and legal environment encouraging the telecommunications industry to function in a self-developing manner. Thus, the following principles should be taken into account: the process of regulation should be more transparent, based on relatively stable rules and implemented by a well-equipped and efficiently operating authority with minimal political interference; if price changes are postponed for political reasons and price cap regulation starts out with implicitly inherited distortions, misallocation of resources would occur; society's aims should be secured by public authority and financed by public money (coming from taxes); price differentiation among different time zones, regions and customers (in terms of their size) should be created or strengthened; the legal and economic environment should be gradually prepared for the Government to take a 'hands off' approach to controlling telecommunications operators; strengthening of the competitive environment is an unavoidable process leading to an increase in the variety of services and improvement in their quality (the sooner the main players – government, operators, regulator and customers – adjust to this trend, the better off they will be once the market opens); all kinds of subsidy should be abolished (including intra-institutional).

The government is currently reconsidering its stance – hitherto one of reluctance – towards the privatization of Slovak Telecommunications and the law concerning this sector is being changed accordingly.

One of the most recent efforts of the Office in the field of active legislation has been the preparation of a draft act on selling licences *via* auction. The aim of the bill has been to create equal conditions for all parties interested in acquiring a licence in the areas of casino services, mining of raw materials, broadcasting, foreign trade, environmental pollution, transport and telecommunications services. In such a way the monopoly rent usually ensuing from the holding of such a licence would be allocated more efficiently than under the non-transparent rules for granting exclusive rights for undertaking business.

As far as passive legislation is concerned (AOSR comments on the laws prepared by other entities), the Office expressed a negative opinion, for example, on the bill on prices, the law adjusting the activities of accident insurance companies, the laws regulating the activities of professional associations and chambers, the law on energy, etc.

The Office also commented publicly on other government measures. As an example we can mention the articles on the introduction of an import surcharge equal to 10 per cent on the import of manufactured goods. The idea behind the AOSR's legislative activities was that optimizing the allocation of scarce resources is possible through securing equality of opportunities. The former rule of a regulated economy with free market islands should be replaced by a deregulated system with economically justified exceptions.

## STRUCTURE OF THE AOSR AND LEGAL PROCEEDINGS

Since the inception of the AOSR, the internal structure of the Office has been tailored to the industrial structure of the Slovak economy. Except for some recent changes, for example the creation of the unit responsible for international co-operation, the Office was divided into the following sections/departments:

- *Department for Information and Administration*, responsible for securing any information related to the Office activities, maintaining the library, managing the Office's accounts, managing the computer network, etc.
- *Department of Legislation and Law* deals with methodological issues, prepares comments on the legislative proposals of other entities as well as bills elaborated by the Office. It also helps the Appeal Commission of the Office and helps to prepare materials for cases brought before the Supreme Court.
- *The First Executive Department's* portfolio is represented for example by crude oil products, the textile and clothing industry, leather and shoe-making industry, machinery for agriculture, the chemical industry, livestock production, etc.
- *The Second Executive Department* is responsible for the protection of economic competition in the areas of fuel, heating, the energy sector, metallurgy, electromechanical products, machinery, etc.
- *The Third Executive Department* handles cases connected to forestry, water, the construction industry, paper and cellulose production, the printing industry, furniture production, the glass industry, etc.
- *The Fourth Executive Department* is responsible for the fields of transportation, telecommunications, financial market, insurance, services, media, health care, culture, education, trade.
- *The Secretariat* of the Office serves the Chairman, deals with some international activities, and activities connected with public relations. Its

activities are probably the most flexible and depend very much on the tasks imposed on the Office by the government.

- *Local Branches* of the Office are currently located in Banská Bystrica and Košice. They are responsible for investigations and decision-making in cases related to their geographical areas. In the early 1990s the number of local branches was higher, but they were vested with fewer powers. Later the budgetary constraints of the Office, as well as the growing expertise of the experts located in the cities mentioned above lead to the abolition of some branches and delegation of increased powers to the rest. The branches are linked electronically to the Bratislava headquarters and their representatives visit the capital regularly. Thus, the consistency of the AOSR policy is secured.
- *The Vice-Chairperson* is responsible for deputizing for the head of the Office, chairing the Appeals Commission, some international co-operation, etc. He/she also oversees local branches and the Methodological Unit.

This office structure has proven useful, especially at the beginning of the transitional process in Slovakia. At that time, the creation of a competitive environment was more important than its protection and that required a very good knowledge of the structure of particular industries. The negative feature of such a structure is that, over time, the number of cases and other activities in the portfolio of particular departments may change. Thus, on the one hand some departments might have some free capacity, while the other departments might be overloaded. This would, of course, decrease the efficiency of the whole Office's functioning. Moreover, the longer the process of transition continues, the more the Office's activities will require lawyers and economists rather than experts familiar with the technical details of concrete production. However, the structure of the Office described above will probably survive for a relatively long time, but with more flexibility involved. Even in the history of the Office to date some cases have already been handled by inter-divisional task forces. This might be the solution for the future.

Proceedings before the AOSR may begin either on the initiative of the Office itself or on the basis of a complaint made to the Office by an external entity. Any such proceedings are covered by the general regulations of the Procedural Code, unless stated otherwise by the Competition Protection Act No. 188/1994 Coll. Proceedings are started the very day a complaint is notified to the Office, if the initiation is external. A proceeding ends with the issuing of a decision, within the period of time specified in the law, by the relevant Executive Department Director. It is possible to appeal against this first step decision. The chairperson decides the first step appeal on the basis of a proposal by the Appeals Commission, which consists of five members. Appeal decisions can then be brought before the Supreme Court of the Slovak Republic. So far, all AOSR decisions were upheld by this authority. The reason for this result seems to be not only the soundness of the AOSR's expertise but also the lack of expertise of the appealing parties.

## CONCLUSIONS

Any report or analysis can only be useful if it creates the basis for some predictions or viable recommendations. Below, I would like to summarize the conclusions that can be derived from the experience of the activities connected to the creation, promotion and protection of economic competition in Slovakia during the period of transition.

From the very beginning of the transition process greater emphasis should have been put on intensive *education about the principles of economic competition*. It was shown in this chapter that the awareness of the public, government officials and business-persons of this phenomenon in Slovakia has been relatively limited. It is possible to observe significant differences between transitional and developed economies not only in their legal framework, distribution of ownership, and structure of government, but also in the culture of the people. Nations recognizing the importance of unrestricted competition are doing better economically than those which accept its distortions. The most difficult part of market economics to implement in some post-socialist countries would appear to be the way of thinking.

In Slovakia the Antimonopoly Office is indirectly but seriously dependent on the central government. The reason for this is that the Chairman appoints all the decision-making officials at the Office and, at the same time he/she is appointed by the government and may be dismissed at any meeting of the cabinet. Thus all the strategic decisions, as well as the daily life of the Office, may to a large extent be determined by the Cabinet of Ministers, which in turn represents particular interest groups. A more *independent and therefore stronger office* would create better conditions for the development of a competitive environment in the country. This does not necessarily mean that all the activities of the Office should be isolated from political pressures. But some of them, if influenced politically, may complicate the process of transition. In transition countries where there is no tradition of protecting economic competition, the importance of having a strong entity dedicated to the promotion of market forces is even greater than in the developed countries.

A competition authority as described above is not the main engine for the promotion and protection of economic competition, neither in transition countries, nor in developed ones. The stage of equality of opportunities in a market seems to be determined rather by the balance of powers of different competitors and their lobbies (for example, the balance between incumbents and newcomers). However, leaving the battle over allocation of scarce resources solely to the competition of interest groups (i.e., without interference by a competition office or other similar body) may lead in extreme cases to the ultimate total victory of one econo-political entity in a country. In the 20th century, we can observe the results of the absence of 'artificial' protection of 'natural' economic competition in many countries. Winners of absolutely free competition accumulate power at the expense of the whole society in these countries, regardless of the way they reached their positions (concentration of ownership, revolution, free election, etc.). *The risk of such a concen-*

*tration of power seems to be much higher in transition countries*, than in more settled societies.

Moreover, one should remember that in many transitional economies, we face the task of dismantling the monopolistic structure of societies rather than that of preventing its appearance. Therefore, the creation and promotion of economic competition here deserves deep interest. It should be mentioned that total monopoly, in the sense described above, is very rare in the real world. However, the less an economy is free, the lower is its output. This means that even partial deviation from the optimal structures may cause sub-optimal allocation of resources. According to Freedom House's survey, 17 per cent of the world's population, working in free market economies, produces 81 per cent of total world output, while 36 per cent of people living in economically unfree countries produce only 5 per cent of the output.[17]

Another conclusion we can reach, based on the evidence of this chapter, and which at the same time supports the idea of *strong protection of economic competition* in transitional countries is the fact that the *main restrictions to competition there are not linked to the standard areas* like mergers, abuse of dominant position, agreements restricting competition, *which are very much influenced by globalization*. In other words, one may reasonably assume that if the integration of Europe continues, dominance will almost disappear in small economies, the importance of cartel agreements will decrease dramatically, etc. But it should be said that a greater danger, in terms of the distortion of economic competition, seems to be posed by the outputs of executive and legislative branches as a result of a lack of knowledge and experience of a market economy, or as the consequence of a balance of power biased in favour of particular interest groups. Here we can mention non-transparent privatization, granting licences and concessions according to unpublished rules, open government subsidies, the 'invisible hand' of central government reaching every business through the state ownership of so-called strategic enterprises (large banks, energy sector, telecommunications, etc.), and such legislation as the new act on prices, which allows government representatives to control basically any price and impose fines under vaguely defined circumstances.

Generally, we may predict that the more Slovakia moves towards a market economy, the more stress will be placed on the protection of economic competition rather than its creation. In the initial stages of dismantling the centrally planned economy it was necessary principally to *create competition* by privatizing 'easy-to-privatize' firms, allowing private entities to do business, opening the borders to international trade, adopting a basic legal framework for business (price liberalization), etc. Then, in the second phase, the main accent has been on *promotion of competition*, represented by the adoption of specific laws designed to strengthen competition in those areas where it already existed, by requiring administrative bodies to remove any measures limiting competition, by privatization of 'hard-to-privatize' firms (natural monopolies), by intensive education of business persons, government officials, and the general public, by further liberalization of foreign trade, etc. In the last stage of transition, *protection of economic competition* will be of prime importance. The main activities will be dealing with state aids, refining the legal framework, restructuring government, and the standard activities familiar in developed market economies. Of course, the aforementioned three categories for improving social welfare creation are not totally separated. All of them exist in each stage of the transition process; their respective roles are of different importance, however, at different stages of transition. For example, there will be always room for creation of competition in the areas traditionally reserved for natural monopolies.

*Economic competition should be created, promoted and protected intensively in transitional countries.* First, for the benefit of these countries, where optimal allocation of resources will directly lead to maximization of welfare. Second, for the benefit of developed countries, since increasing globalization leads gradually to the creation of a single economy, a single 'body'. In other words, despite the small size of the majority of transitional economies, their problems may influence to a large extent the situation in the rest of the world. Remember the 'entertainment' that can be caused to the whole organism by one small tooth. Of course, we cannot consider the activities of antimonopoly offices as the main engines for the creation of economic competition. Their proper functioning is rather comparable to driving a car with a steering wheel on the right side in a left-hand drive environment; small transition economies may work without strong, effective protection of economic competition. But both the risk of accidents and the effort required by the driver is higher.

## NOTES

1. The author is President of the Centre for Economic Development. He worked at the Antimonopoly Office of the Slovak Republic from January 1, 1991 to May 31, 1995. His experience from this period creates the basis for this chapter. The author is grateful to Mrs. Mária Krošláková and Mrs. Daniela Zemanovièová for their advice and comments. However, sole responsibility for mistakes rests with the author.
2. Before the split-up of Czechoslovakia, the official name of the Office was Slovak Antimonopoly Office.
3. Exceptions are special cases such as, for example, purchase on a stock exchange.
4. At that time it was part of the Administration of Post and Telecommunications, Bratislava, a state enterprise.
5. GSM licences were granted only in 1996. The holder was to start operation in the second half of that year.
6. *Pravda*, 4.6.1996.
7. Because of the housing system in Slovakia, with neighbourhoods of high concentration, district central heating can be viewed as a natural monopoly in some cases.
8. The Office has never taken a decision against excessive prices.
9. So far the Office has reviewed more than 2,000 privatization projects.

10. Národná obroda, 13.8.1996.
11. Lucia•itòanská: Presentation at the discussion club at M.E.S.A. 10.
12. National Council of the Slovak Republic.
13. Part of this activity is legally covered by the Euro-Agreement signed between EU member countries and Slovakia.
14. The OECD has created room for co-operation through various other programmes: 'Partners in Transition' and meetings within the 'Liaison Committee' may be mentioned in this context.
15. The main principles of EU Public Procurement rules were used here in simplified manner.
16. This approach refers to the period of time when the author worked at AOSR.
17. Freedom House (1995–96).

# REFERENCES

*Freedom House World Survey of Economic Freedom 1995–96*, published by Transaction Books.

Ordover, J.A., R.W. Pittman and P. Clyde (1994), 'Competition Policies for Natural Monopolies in a Developing Market Economy', *Economics of Transition*, 2(3), pp. 317–343.

**Part III**

**The Baltics**

# 10
# The Political Economy of
# Privatization in Estonia

*Alari Purju*

## INTRODUCTION

Estonia regained its independence from the former Soviet Union in August 1991. Some of the necessary legislation to start privatization was adopted prior to this event. However, the main institutional framework and conditions for the realization of the whole process were created afterwards. An important prerequisite of privatization was Estonian currency reform, which completed the separation of Estonia from the rouble zone and was accompanied by the introduction of the Estonian kroon (EEK). The monetary stabilization achieved after this step made a more business-oriented approach to privatization possible and encouraged foreign investors to participate in the process.

These vital political and economic events influenced discussions on the actual steps related to developing privatization programmes by different interest groups and political parties. Estonia's preconditions for ownership reform should be considered as the main reason why some aspects of the ownership reform in Estonia differed from similar programmes applied in other east European countries.

This chapter surveys preconditions for privatization in Estonia and the respective concepts of different governments. Also, the most important features of the different pieces of legislation which have determined the path of privatization in Estonia are characterized. The methods and results of small-scale privatization, large-scale privatization, restitution and land reform are also discussed. A special section is dedicated to an analysis of the Estonian voucher scheme and the privatization of dwellings. The conclusion will discuss the main results achieved and the main problems which had emerged during the process of privatization by the end of 1996.


## PRECONDITIONS FOR PRIVATIZATION

The dominant role of state ownership was more overwhelming in Estonia than in most other eastern European countries. Land belonged to the state and all economic agents rented this land from the state. Private homes made up 30 per cent of the living space; as there was no private ownership of land, however, this land would have to be privatized or restituted to the house owners. The share of condominiums (housing co-operatives) was relatively small (10 per cent). Approximately 60 per cent of the housing stock belonged to the state and municipalities. This is a greater share than in other eastern European countries, where condominiums predominated.

In rural areas, the dominant economic power resided with state and collective farms (semi-state institutions which received a large share of investments from the state budget). Rural inhabitants had a very limited amount of land (0.15 hectares per household) for personal use. In the 1980s the rural inhabitants were given the right to rent an additional plot of land from collective farms for vegetable growing. A substantial share of agricultural production was grown on these small plots (for example 30–40 per cent of vegetable production).

The productive assets in manufacturing, the service sector, and transportation also belonged to the state. Individuals were only allowed to own portable property. There existed semi-state-owned co-operatives in trade and construction. Only a limited number of persons were allowed to work on the basis of individual contracts (e.g., photographers, watchmakers, tailors and some other professionals).

This overwhelming state-ownership was created through: the nationalization of land, banks and large-scale industry in 1940, and land reform and collectivization in 1944–45 and 1947–50, respectively. As most of the population suffered in these violent changes, restitution of unlawfully expropriated property became a vital issue in the ownership reforms of the 1990s.

The state began to lose its dominating role in 1987 when the so-called small enterprises began to be founded. Estonian ministries, state enterprises, and other bodies were given the right to establish enterprises employing up to fifty persons by a special set of regulations established in resolutions of the Soviet Council of Ministers' Commission (from late 1986 and 1987). These enterprises were given special status. This status entitled them to tax allowances and greater control over profits, prices and salaries. By the beginning of 1991, 700 such enterprises had been established in Estonia.[1] In the later process of privatization a substantial proportion of these enterprises were transformed into firms in the private ownership of their managers. Furthemore, the production and assets of the parent state-owned companies from which these units were created, were transformed to and through these small enterprises.

Another preliminary step for the creation of a private sector was the introduction of so-called entrepreneurial co-operatives alongside the former large pseudo-co-operative sector (which first existed in agriculture and trade). A legal framework for these new co-operatives was created by the Soviet 'Law on Co-operatives' (1988, amended in 1989 and 1990). These co-operatives were set up mainly in the trade and service sector, though a rather large number of them were active also in manufacturing. Most of these co-operatives were later reorganized into private firms. A new legal regime for the co-operative sector was established by the 'Law on Co-operatives', passed by the Estonian parliament in August 1992. The number of non-agricultural co-operatives listed in the Estonian Register of Enterprises was 4288 in August 1992.[2]

The first joint ventures were established in Estonia in 1987. This form of mixed ownership between a domestic state-owned enterprise or co-operative and a foreign company increased rapidly during the following years. There were 11 joint ventures in 1988 and 320 by the end of 1992.

Leased enterprises were also established in Estonia on the basis of Soviet laws from 1989. These were brought into conformity with Estonian legislation by the Estonian government's 'Resolution on Lease Relationships' of 1991. Although the assets of a state enterprise may be leased to all kinds of physical and legal persons, a special legal form of lease enterprise was also introduced. A lease relationship is established by a petition of the employees, who must approve the proposed leasing contract with two-thirds of the votes at a special general meeting. The lease enterprise has full proprietary rights over all items produced by the enterprise, as well as all income derived from the enterprise. The amount of rent is stipulated by the lessor, taking into account previous profits and depreciation of the leased property. There were approximately 300 leased enterprises and structural units in Estonia in summer 1994.[3] As Estonia experienced high inflation during the years 1991–92 (inflation was 953 per cent in 1992) and a large number of leasing contracts were signed without any indexation of rental payments, these contracts turned out to be rather profitable for lessees. The introduction of these enterprises into the privatization process has also raised several legal complications. On the other hand, leasing contracts were a big stimulus for managers and employees of these enterprises during the pre-privatization stage, to raise the efficiency of production and look for potential foreign partners.

## PRIVATIZATION CONCEPTS OF DIFFERENT GOVERNMENTS

Discussion regarding privatization began to play a central role on the Estonian political and economic scene at the beginning of 1990. The central issues in these debates were the extent of restitution, the use of vouchers in privatization and the sale for cash of enterprises to economic agents whose sources of finance were unknown.[4] The fact that at the time Estonia belonged to the rouble zone and the Estonian community was afraid of becoming a money-laundry for the other regions of the Soviet Union aggravated the problems.

## Edgar Savisaar's Government (March 1990–January 1992)

The government formed after the Popular Front won the elections to the Estonian Supreme Council in March 1990, stated that its goal was Estonia's transition to a market economy. In comparison to Estonia's later governments, Savisaar's government was more centre-oriented, favouring a more step-by-step approach to economic changes and moderate protectionism (Savisaar later formed the Centrist Party). The first important law approved by the parliament during this period was the 'Law on Ownership' (approved in June 1990). The government formulated its privatization proposal in September of the same year. In the first stage, the legal basis for privatization was to be created, problems related to reprivatization were to be solved so as not to hinder the whole privatization process. An experimental sale of a limited number of large state-owned enterprises was designed. Small privatization in the trade, service and catering sector was a central issue for this stage of the programme. The privatization of state-owned dwellings (the initial idea was to sell them cheaply to the residents who were currently renting these dwellings), and the use of intermediate forms of privatization like leasing, was also planned to start.

The second stage was intended to expand privatization to small and medium-size enterprises in other sectors of the economy. The third stage should have involved large-scale privatization through selling enterprises to foreign and domestic capital (including payment by instalments), and the limited use of vouchers.[5] Savisaar later declared that preference should have been given to fast privatization for cash, which should not have excluded the restitution of nationalized property to former owners or their heirs. The initial position, however, was that the restored Republic of Estonia was not under any obligation to physical and legal persons for losses incurred during Estonia's occupation by foreign states.[6]

By the end of 1990, the parliament passed 'The Law on Small-Scale Privatization' prepared by the government.[7] In October 1990 the Department of State Property was founded. The main task of the new institution was the organization of small-scale privatization and supervision of the restitution process. Auctions of small-scale units started in March 1991. In February 1991 leasing programmes and the corporatization of state enterprises had already started. The municipalization of state property and the submission of applications for restitution began in the second half of 1991 (as both these activities were realized at the local government level, the start of these activities depended upon the speed with which these administrations were capable of fulfilling their tasks, including making the necessary preparations).

On June 13th, 1991 the Supreme Council adopted the 'Law on the Basis of Property Reform', which stipulated restitution and the use of vouchers as the main tools for privatization. This was motivated by a fear that selling off state-owned property might transfer it into the hands of foreigners, or of those who had accumulated money through speculation or Mafia-related activities. It was also a reaction against the ongoing 'spontaneous privatization' by managers of state-owned enterprises, who transformed state-owned assets into newly formed private entities, where the same people played a leading role in both.

In October 1991, the 'Law on Land Reform' was passed by the parliament. The law regulated the transformation of land from state ownership to private ownership. The main principle of this process was the restitution of property rights and the protection of the legal rights of the present users of land. The law envisaged that a rather wide circle of heirs of the former owner would be eligible to submit a claim for land. The law also fixed compensation for the full amount of land at June 1940 values.

The adoption of laws which were in conflict with the privatization programme of the government, showed that the political basis of the government in parliament was eroding. The reason was in part that the Popular Front was a rather loose coalition of different political groups, and lacked a common ideology and the discipline of a political party. The Savisaar government's attempt to continue sales-based privatization and its rejection by the Supreme Council, together with disputes over the citizenship status of most non-Estonians, were among the main factors that led to the fall of the government in January 1992.

## Tiit Vähi's Provisional Government (January–September 1992)

It was announced that this government would continue until the next elections in September 1992. The government was formed partially on the basis of the former government, and expressed its intentions to implement a programme reflecting the decisions of the parliament. Agricultural reform began after the adoption of necessary legal acts during spring 1992.[8] The 'Law on Privatization of Dwellings' was adopted in April 1992. The law also envisaged the introduction of national capital bonds in the process of privatization of dwellings. Small-scale privatization continued during the whole of 1992, but its legal basis was reorganized by the new law.[9] In several respects, Vähi's government largely continued the privatization process of the former government. Monetary reform and the introduction of the Estonian kroon in June 1992 substantially changed the general economic environment. This encouraged Vähi's government to acquire a clear direction in large-scale privatization policy: the emphasis was shifted towards sales, especially to foreign investors. An expression of this was the founding of a Treuhand-type Estonian Privatization Enterprise in September 1992, which also used know-how, consultants and financial support from the German Treuhandanstalt. This new institution was established to deal with large-scale privatization.

## Mart Laar's Government (October 1992–August 1994)

The politicians and political parties which later formed the 'Isamaa' (Fatherland) alliance, and which won the parliamentary elections of the restored Republic of Estonia in September 1992, were already represented in the Supreme Council of the former republic of the Soviet Union. Their programme stressed the need for fast ownership reform. The first step of privatization was to be restitution and compensation for unlawfully expropriated property. The need for extensive privatization was also mentioned.[10]

Compensation for nationalized property and its return to its former owners was the most important issue in the election campaign of the Estonian National Independence Party, another member of the ruling coalition in parliament following the 1992 elections.

The idea of using privatization securities (vouchers), in the form of national capital bonds, was first proposed by the Rural Centrist Party in 1990. The number of years employed during the Soviet occupation was proposed as a basis for calculating the value of the bonds. This approach was justified by the need to compensate for the poorly-paid work during those years. Furthermore, 'Isamaa' was considering the fast privatization of housing through privatization securities, whilst mentioning at the same time that it was necessary to take into account the interests of the owners of private homes and condominiums.

After parliamentary elections, a new government was formed by the coalition of 'Isamaa', the Moderates (the Social-Democratic Party and the Rural Centrist Party) and the Estonian National Independence Party. The coalition declared rapid privatization as its main goal for economic reform. An obvious contradiction existed between this goal and the emphasis on restitution and compensation, which are the most time-consuming methods of privatization. The new parliament began by adopting a special law to extend the circle of people eligible to claim the return of, or compensation for, unlawfully expropriated property to include the descendants of the sisters and brothers of the former owner.

The ruling coalition began extensive preparation of laws and other legal acts, several of which were passed by parliament or approved by the government. From the conceptual point of view, the most important were: the 'Concept for Using Privatization Securities' adopted by the government in February 1993; the 'Law on the Privatization of Dwelling Rooms', adopted by the parliament and promulgated by the President in June 1993 (which also specified the method for calculating national capital bonds)[11]; and the 'Law on Privatization', which set out conditions for the privatization of state-owned or municipal enterprises, and was adopted in June 1993. The latter law also cancelled the 'Law on the Privatization of State and Municipal Enterprises', and other laws and decrees specifying regulations provided by that law. The main goal of the 'Law on Privatization' was to give a general legal and institutional framework for small- and large-scale privatization, which had previously been treated separately. The law allowed the formation of the Estonian

Privatization Agency, which took over the functions of the Estonian Privatization Enterprise (so far responsible only for large-scale privatization) and the Department of State Property (which had so far supervised small-scale privatization and dealt with problems of restitution). The law also established the procedures for privatization, such as preparation for privatization, including the requirements for the privatization programme, and the conditions for the implementation of the process.

Another important event related to the principles of privatization was the amendment to the 'Law on the Basis of Ownership Reform' stating that 'the primary method of privatization shall be the sale of property for money, for securities issued to compensate for unlawfully alienated property, and for national capital bonds'.[12] This change abolished the leading role of restitution and vouchers previously established in law and equalized the different methods of privatization. Nevertheless, this formulation gave the government more space to manoeuvre, since the pro-restitution camp was calmed by a commitment that 50 per cent of the revenues accrued from selling state-owned or municipal property would go to the Compensation Fund. The 'Law on Privatization' also determined how privatization securities could be used in privatizing enterprises on the basis of the Concept for Using Privatization Securities, earlier approved by the government. It is only since 1993 that the real process of restitution in kind, land reform and privatization of dwellings (mainly for vouchers) has begun. Large-scale privatization was also speeded up.

Laar's government was supported until June 1994 by a solid majority in parliament. This made it possible to pursue a rather uniform privatization policy. The government created a post of Minister for Economic Reforms (without portfolio), who was responsible for the co-ordination of the ownership reform. Mrs. Liia Hänni filled this position from the elections and the formation of the government in October 1992 until the next elections in March 1995, when a new coalition formed the government.

## Andres Tarand's Provisional Government (August 1994–March 1995)

Mart Laar had to leave the post of Prime Minister in August 1994 because of several government scandals (disguised aspects of an arms purchasing contract with Israel, realization of cash-roubles gathered during monetary reform, disagreement about political allies in the opposition and business), because of which some parts of the coalition in the parliament stopped supporting the Prime Minister. The new prime minister came from the same government, where he had filled the post of Minister of Environmental Affairs. The whole government continued under the new Prime Minister with some small changes.

The privatization policy of the government had been under attack ever since it came to office, but, surprisingly, it did not become a very important political issue during this crisis and the Minister for Economic Reforms continued in the new provisional government. This government continued until the legally assigned term of parliamentary elections in March 1995.

## Tiit Vähi's Several Governments (March 1995–February 1997)

Privatization was an important issue during the elections in March 1995. The former government had continued the reform process and activated several fields of privatization, yet most of the goals it had stated were not achieved. Privatization in general has not been a simple task for post-socialist governments in eastern European countries. The Estonian reform was more complex than the reforms in many other countries, being oriented towards restitution and a voucher scheme which included complicated formulae for calculating the values of the vouchers that every resident received. This, together with the privatization of dwellings, land, and shares of enterprises, created a complicated system. Thus, privatization did not succeed in the way that most citizens had expected. On the other hand, if we compare the results of privatization in Estonia (which will be described in more detail in the following sections of this chapter and in Table 2), it is possible to see that Estonia looks rather successful in comparison with most other eastern European countries. Anyway, the former coalition was heavily defeated in the elections and the former opposition formed a new government.

Tiit Vähi is the leader of the Coalition Party and Rural Union (KMÜ) which consists of a number of parties, making it quite difficult to define its political profile. The strongest of the KMÜ partners, the Coalition Party, is really right- rather than left-wing in its programme. A large proportion of the members of the party are enterprise directors from the socialist period, but the party also includes prominent representatives of small private businesses. The rural parties tend to support protection of agricultural markets and propagate self-reliance with regard to agricultural produce. The other coalition partner initially, after the elections, was the Centre Party, whose leader Edgar Savisaar was Prime Minister when Estonia regained its independence. The Coalition Party and the Centre Party have not been extreme right-wing parties and relied on the social market economy slogan. On the other hand, the parties have been unanimous in their support for continued privatization.[13]

However, in the field of privatization, there is also a need for change as underlined by the new government. The previous government's plan to begin the rapid privatization of infrastructure had not been regarded as a serious programme. The least complicated enterprises should be privatized first and infrastructure enterprises should be restructured before determining which should be privatized. The Privatization Agency should be forced to make its decisions more public. Ownership reform has been obstructed by delays in land reform and necessary methods to simplify several procedures of land transformation have been proposed by the new leadership. An important point, as mentioned by the government, was the amendment of laws so that enterprises may be sold together with the land they occupy.

The coalition government was in office for a short period. After a scandal, the Centre Party was forced to leave the coalition in October 1995. The main issue was related to the methods used by the leader of the Centre Party, in his capacity as Minister of Internal Affairs in that government, for gathering information about the members of the political opposition and about the partners in the coalition.

A new partner in the coalition was the Reform Party. During the whole period this coalition was in office, problems and conflicts between the partners were common. The Reform Party, representing liberal views, and the Rural Party had an especially complicated relationship. The main problems were related to agrarian policy and customs tariffs, but other contradictions also emerged. The Reform Party left the coalition in October 1996.

During the period between November 1996 and February 1997, Prime Minister Vähi lead a minority government which included ministers from the Coalition Party, the Rural Union, the Development Party (a very small party with five seats in parliament) and some specialists who officially did not belong to any political party (Minister of Economic Affairs, Minister of Transportation). The political situation was therefore not very stable. The privatization programme was, nevertheless, implemented without any major changes. One reason for this was that the Privatization Agency was relatively independent and the government did not have a chance to influence its regular activities very much. A very important achievement during this period was starting the privatization of infrastructure. However, it is a paradox that under these circumstances Vähi came to be the first prime minister who had to resign office directly over a privatization issue.[14]

## Mart Siimann's Government (March 1997– )

A government with the same political support and with only very limited changes has continued under Prime Minister Mart Siimann from the Coalition Party since March 1997.

## SMALL-SCALE PRIVATIZATION

According to the 'Law on the Privatization of State-Owned Service, Retail and Catering Enterprises' (adopted in December 1990) providing for the initial regulation of small-scale privatization, entities with a book value of up to 0.5 million roubles were to be transferred to private ownership. The right to purchase property was given to adult residents of Estonia or to legal persons set up by Estonian residents, or to persons legally registered in Estonia.

The Department of State Property organized small-scale privatization on the basis of one of the following methods: (i) auctions; (ii) selling of shares; (iii) competition of business ideas (tender). However, at the request of the local government, insiders, local residents or current leaseholders could be given pre-emptive rights in the auction process. One reason for awarding pre-emptive rights was the desire to avoid drastic changes in the existing structure of services (especially in small towns and villages). The granting of pre-emptive rights was accompanied by a requirement not to change the usage of the property for at least five years.

As the law also provided a possibility of guaranteeing for these groups of people the right to buy the property at the initial price, in practice such guarantees became widespread. The initial price was based on an expert assessment. However, given the inflationary situation, these assessments were very problematic and property was often sold at a very low price. This resulted in severe criticism.

According to Department of State Property estimates, before the legal regulation of small-scale privatization was changed in May 1992, 80 per cent of the entities were sold at the initial price; in 10 per cent of the cases a real auction took place, 9 per cent of the entities were sold on the basis of business ideas and only four larger enterprises (1 per cent of the total number privatized), whose assets did not reach the limit of 0.5 billion roubles, were privatized by the sale of shares.

From May 21, 1992, essential changes were introduced into the legal regulation of small-scale privatization.[15] The scope of small-scale privatization was increased to include all other branches in addition to the service, trade and catering industries. The upper limit of the book value of entities included in the programme was increased from 0.5 million to 6 million roubles (one reason for this was the overestimation of assets devalued through inflation). A month later, during the monetary reform, this limit automatically changed to 600,000 kroons.[16] Competitive tender on the basis of business ideas was excluded from the methods of privatization. Also, the circle of participants was widened to include foreigners.

The preferential right to buy at the initial price was abolished. The workers and management of the unit to be privatized still enjoyed the pre-emptive right to buy the property, but they had to pay the price offered last at open auction. The same right was also offered to former employees of the enterprise who had retired on a pension from it, or the lessee of this property; however, in both cases it was necessary to pay the last price offered at auction. The requirement of maintaining the existing activity was also abolished as a general rule, but the organizer of a privatization had the right to put the property up for auction with additional conditions (for example, to maintain a former field of activity for some period). There also existed the problem of capital. To overcome this, purchasers were allowed to pay by instalments if the price exceeded 10,000 kroons until October 1993, after which the sum was increased to 250,000 kroons. The initial payment had to amount to at least 20 per cent of the total price.

At the beginning of 1991 the total number of privatized small-scale units was estimated at 1,200 service facilities, 500 shops, 350 kiosks and 800 catering facilities.[17] Later, during the time real privatization took place, this number decreased due to the liquidation of several entities, bankruptcies etc.

By the end of 1992, the list of enterprises to be privatized totalled 1,212 entities. Of this, 211 entities with a total purchasing price of 18.2 million roubles were sold in 1991 and 556 entities with an estimated total purchasing price of 41.9 million kroons (during the first half of 1992 enterprises were sold for roubles, during the second half of 1992 for Estonian kroons) in 1992. Thus, 767 entities with an estimated price of 43.6 million kroons were sold by the end of 1992.

During the first half of 1993, 193 entities were sold for a price of 104.2 million kroons. Altogether 960 entities from the initial small privatization list were sold by June 1993. After this date, the small privatization programme underwent major changes. Some of the unsold entities were transferred to municipal ownership, but several entities were also sold in 1993 and 1994.

The 'Privatization Law' adopted by parliament in June 1993 legally equalized small-scale and large-scale privatization. Since the middle of 1993, when one speaks of small-scale privatization, it is generally in the sense that for smaller enterprises the auction method was used for ownership transformation. On the other hand, any quantitative ceiling for including enterprises in the list for privatization by this method was abolished. Besides service, trade and catering enterprises, several small manufacturing and transportation enterprises were also privatized using the auction method. During the second half of 1993 an additional 50 entities were sold, taking the total number of small entities sold in 1993 to 243, with a purchasing price of 124.7 million kroons. In 1994, 126 entities were sold with a purchasing price of 68.2 million kroons. In 1995, these numbers were 120 and 79.8 million kroons, respectively, and in 1996, 84 and 148.7 million kroons.[18]

Small-scale privatization was thus relatively successful in Estonia, despite several changes in its legal regulation. In 1996 the private sector offered 89 per cent of real estate, renting and business services and 84 per cent of other services. The private sector's share in wholesaling was 98 per cent in 1996, while in retail sales it was 96 per cent.[19] More than 90 per cent of enterprises now active in the trade and service sectors belonged to the state and municipalities in 1991. Competition has emerged and these formerly neglected and under-developed sectors are the fastest-growing area of the Estonian economy.

## LARGE-SCALE PRIVATIZATION

The so-called pilot privatization of seven large enterprises by sale from summer 1991 till April 1992 was the prelude to large-scale privatization in Estonia. This programme was based on the legal regulation of small-scale privatization and was launched to give privatizers some experience in using different forms and procedures of privatization. One of the reasons for such a limited programme was the negative attitude of the public and politicians toward selling large-scale enterprises for inflating roubles.

The large-scale privatization programme *per se* was introduced in August 1992, when two acts regulating the privatization of entities with a book value of over 600,000 kroons were passed by parliament. In addition, the Treuhand-type Estonian Privatization Enterprise (EPE) was founded in September 1992. As previously noted, the EPE used know-how, consultants and financial support from the German Treuhandanstalt.

The 'Law on Privatization' passed on June 17, 1993, made the privatization of enterprises uniform, specified more clearly the methods of privatization and also introduced organizational changes. The Estonian Privatization Agency was founded on the basis of the Department of State Property and the EPE. The Privatization Agency and its Board acquired more independence in the process of managing the privatization process. The Minister for Economic Reforms filled the post of chairman on the board. The law only regulates the privatization of enterprises; agricultural reform and privatization of dwellings are regulated by other legislation.

The law guaranteed equal rights to all domestic and foreign physical and legal persons who wished to participate in the privatization process. However, legal persons, of which the Estonian state and municipalities make up more than one-third, are not entitled to participate in privatization. Nonetheless, some favourable conditions have been introduced for domestic economic agents. Estonian residents or legal persons, among whom the Estonian share is over 50 per cent, have an opportunity to pay the purchasing price in instalments over a period of up to 10 years, with an initial payment of at least 20 per cent of the price. The interest rate for these instalment payments was determined by the Board of the Privatization Agency. For example, for 1994 payments the interest rate was 15 per cent (inflation, in comparison, was 41.7 per cent in 1994, while the interest rates for loans from commercial banks were 20–30 per cent). For 1995 and 1996 this interest rate was reduced to 10 per cent.

Since June 1994, domestic economic agents may pay half of the price with vouchers. Initially this facility was given to enterprises privatized after that date. In summer 1994 vouchers became legally tradable and their price was far below their face value (see also the section below on vouchers). A government resolution allowing the payment of half of the price with vouchers also in enterprises whose contracts had been signed before June 1994, was adopted in November 1995.

While the opportunity to use vouchers for paying half of the price of privatized enterprises made financial conditions easier for new owners, the government decree of June 1996 shortened the period for payment by instalments from ten to three years (for sales realized after June 1996) and stipulated an initial payment of at least 50 per cent. The requirement that no more vouchers could be accepted than had been paid in cash was abolished in September 1996. Now the owners of newly privatized companies can pay the voucher part of the purchasing price at once. This helps diminish interest payments. The poor solvency of privatized enterprises (especially of those sold through the management buy-out scheme) was the main reason for all these changes.

In the case of selling agricultural processing industries, or entities serving the producers of agricultural goods, the law allows the Privatization Agency to grant pre-emptive rights for local agricultural producers' co-operatives.

The 'Privatization Law' envisages the following methods of privatization:

## The Sale of Shares of an Enterprise or its Structural Units by Way of Tender with Preliminary Negotiation

This method is used in cases where the organizer of a privatization sets additional conditions alongside the price. These additional conditions cover employment guarantees, creation of new jobs, investment guarantees, environmental issues, and other conditions relating to the activity of the enterprise or its structural units. The Privatization Agency sets no initial price for assets or shares; the bidders have to provide a three-year business plan for the enterprise they are applying to buy and a bank guarantee of five per cent of the value of the bid.

The tender procedure has been used mainly for the privatization of larger enterprises. The law stipulates that every potential buyer must be supplied with the necessary information and a possibility to visit any enterprise on the tender list. The Board of the Privatization Agency makes the final decision about accepting bids. The Board has the right to select a bid that does not offer the highest price. Negotiations with bidders take place in two stages. First, the selection of short-listed bidders is made on the basis of preliminary negotiations. Bidders included on this list (the main condition for this is the fulfilment of the formal conditions set out in the law) are invited to make a final bid on the basis of which the Board makes its decision. Altogether, 15 tenders were offered from November 1992 until December 1996. The first tenders included on average 30–50 enterprises; towards the end of privatization, the number of enterprises included in one tender decreased.

## The Sale of Property or Shares of Enterprises or their Structural Units at a Public or Restricted Auction

For an auction, no specific conditions are set. The auction lists are only published locally. The organizer of the auction sets an initial price for the object to be privatized, based on the book value and the experts' estimate. All participants must pay the participation fee and guarantee, usually 10 per cent of the initial price. Objects are sold to the highest bidder.

Auctioned enterprises are usually small. This method is only used if the assets of the enterprise are sold, or the primary value of the company is its trademark. This method was used to continue small-scale privatization which started under other laws and was expanded to involve other areas (e.g., manufacturing, transportation, etc.).

## Public Offering of Shares

Minority stakes in privatized enterprises are sold through public offering of shares. The sale of stakes averaging 25 per cent in 33 companies was realized by the Privatization Agency during 1995–96. The most important characteristic of the public offering in Estonia is that shares can be bought only for vouchers (details of this method are discussed below in the section on use of vouchers).

## Asset Sales where no Purchaser was found using the other Methods

In this case there is no deadline for submission of the bid. The Board of the Privatization Agency can make a decision whether or not to sell when the first suitable bid is received. This method has been rather popular among purchasers because the price of assets or shares has been relatively low.

The proceeds from the privatization of state-owned enterprises are allocated in the following way: 50 per cent goes to the Compensation Fund; 30 per cent to the government Reserve Fund (to cover the expenses of ownership reform); 10 per cent to the special pension fund account; and 10 per cent to the Labour Education Fund. These proportions are followed after subtracting the costs related to organizing privatization (to cover loans of privatized enterprises if it was impossible to include the transfer of these loans to the new owner) from privatization receipts. The regular activities of the Privatization Agency are financed from the state budget.

## Results of the Programme

The first international tender for the sale of 38 enterprises was announced on November 17, 1992. During 1993, two international and one local tender for a total of 117 enterprises were announced. The local tender was only advertised in Estonia and it included enterprises from the food processing and building material industries. From different tenders, 54 contracts were signed for a total purchase price of 353.2 million kroons. The amount of guaranteed investments was 236.8 million kroons and the new owners promised to maintain 9,099 employees.

Two international and two local tenders of 161 enterprises were announced in 1994 and 213 contracts were signed for a total purchase price of 1.3 billion kroons. The total value of guaranteed investments was 855.5 million kroons and the new owners promised to maintain 25,483 jobs.

During 1995, three tenders were announced. Altogether 142 contracts were signed from different tenders, with a total purchase price of 874.9 million kroons. The amount of guaranteed investment was 906.2 million kroons, with employment maintained for 16,031 persons.

During 1996 four tenders of 12 enterprises were announced. Altogether 43 contracts were signed for a total purchase price of 473.6 million kroons. The amount of guaranteed investment was 1,274 million kroons.

Altogether 410 enterprises were offered in 15 tenders and 452 purchasing contracts were made for the total sum of 3.0 billion kroons (approximately 250 million USD). However, the figures for enterprises offered and sold are not directly comparable, because in several cases units of the same enterprise were sold to different buyers and separate contracts were concluded for every unit. From the enterprises listed before January 1st, 1997 at least one contract has been made for 337 of them. Additionally, some contracts were signed for enterprises that were not included in the list of 15 tenders. The state sold mainly the minority stake that it still held in several private enterprises. It is possible to say that approximately 80 per cent of the enterprises included in the list of tenders were sold completely. Enterprises which were not sold during the first tenders were again offered in the later tender lists (for example, Keila Terko, a grain processing company, was offered in the third and sixth tenders, but was finally sold only in the eighth tender). Starting from the sixth tender, another method – the so-called 'leftovers' method – is used in the event of failure of sale through tender. Such enterprises and their units are sold to the first buyer without any deadline for bidding.

Approximately 16 per cent of the total purchasing price was paid by foreign buyers. Although some tenders were announced only locally, there were no restrictions on foreigners' participation.

It should be noted that the purchase price is not the same as the proceeds from privatization. As mentioned previously, the Privatization Agency subtracts from the purchasing price the costs related to the organization of the process. Another important point here is that in the majority of cases the purchaser paid only 20 per cent of the price immediately and another 80 per cent in instalments over a period of up to ten years after the contract is signed. In June 1996, together with the introduction by government decree of a possibility to pay 50 per cent of the purchase price with vouchers, the share of compulsory initial payment was increased from 20 to 50 per cent of the price. The total results of 15 sale tenders up to December 31, 1996, are presented in Table 1 below.

It is interesting to note that in the last tenders the total sum of guaranteed investments was relatively large in comparison with the purchasing price. There are several interrelated reasons for this. First, the quality of enterprises sold in the last tenders was on average somewhat lower than that of the enterprises sold at the beginning. Second, government institutions seem to have overestimated the readiness of foreign investors to participate in the privatization of Estonian enterprises.

Third, the financial situation of most enterprises worsened during their time on the list of privatizable enterprises. Furthermore, managers did not invest in the enterprises' capital stock due to the uncertain situation. Now the new owner has an additional investment requirement and very often there was a trade-off situation between the higher price and the investment guarantees. Although in some earlier contracts investment guarantees were fixed, the Privatization Agency has had problems in several cases over 'persuading' the new owner to make these promised investments.

### Table 1.   Privatization Tenders in Estonia

| Tender | Deadline for application | Number of enterprises listed | Number of bids received | Number of enterprises sold[1] | Number of contracts[2] |
|---|---|---|---|---|---|
| I | 22.12.1992 | 38 | 103 | 35 | 74 |
| II | 08.07.1993 | 52 | 180 | 48 | 73 |
| III | 23.11.1993 | 25 | 48 | 24 | 31 |
| IV | 16.12.1993 | 40 | 109 | 34 | 45 |
| V | 26.05.1994 | 49 | 142 | 36 | 38 |
| VI | 22.06.1994 | 56 | 108 | 47 | 60 |
| VII | 18.08.1994 | 14 | 26 | 13 | 16 |
| VIII | 22.12.1994 | 42 | 115 | 31 | 40 |
| IX | 09.02.1995 | 49 | 100 | 36 | 39 |
| X | 01.06.1995 | 13 | 50 | 12 | 14 |
| XI | 09.11.1995 | 20 | 49 | 14 | 14 |
| XII | 28.03.1996 | 4 | 4 | 4 | 5 |
| XIII | 30.05.1996 | 3 | 14 | 2 | 2 |
| XIV | 10.10.1996 | 2 | 2 | 1 | 1 |
| XV | 17.10.1996 | 3 | 8 | 0 | 0 |

*Notes*:
1. The number of enterprises sold takes into account all enterprises from which at least one unit has been sold in the process of tender.
2. The number of contracts adds up all contracts which have been made upon the units of enterprises sold in this tender.
*Source*:   Privatization Agency.

Another important factor which has influenced the purchase price has been the liabilities taken over by a new owner. All discussions about these issues have been rather complicated. One reason for this is that individual enterprises' financial obligations are quite varied in structure. Tax arrears account for a large share of them. If the new owner agreed to take over a substantial part of the enterprise's liabilities, it was possible to apply for a lower price in the bidding process. There were ten cases, out of 452 contracts, where the purchase price of an enterprise was

1 kroon. The new owner took over a substantial amount of liabilities and gave investment guarantees.

Table 2 describes the proportions of these parameters from the point of view of investors. The total purchasing price, liabilities and investment guarantees are compared with a share of each component.

Another important aspect is related to the role of foreign investors in the privatization process. Although the respective figures do not give a complete picture of foreign participation in the process, they make it possible to estimate some general features.

**Table 2.    Purchasing Prices, Investment Guarantees and Liabilities in Estonian Privatization**

| Year | Purchasing price | | Liabilities | | Investment guarantees | | Total | |
|------|------|------|------|------|------|------|------|------|
|      | mn kr. | % | mn kr. | % | mn kr. | % | mn kr. | % |
| 1993 | 353.2 | 45.0 | 195.6 | 24.9 | 236.8 | 30.1 | 785.6 | 100.0 |
| 1994 | 1333.8 | 46.3 | 689.2 | 24.0 | 855.5 | 29.7 | 2878.5 | 100.0 |
| 1995 | 874.9 | 37.7 | 538.9 | 23.2 | 906.2 | 39.1 | 2320.0 | 100.0 |
| 1996 | 473.6 | 40.9 | 230.3 | 19.9 | 453.6 | 39.2 | 1157.5 | 100.0 |
| Total | 3035.5 | 42.5 | 1654.0 | 23.2 | 2452.1 | 34.3 | 7141.6 | 100.0 |

*Source*:    Author's calculations.

Table 3 describes the role of foreign investments in the total purchasing price, investment guarantees and employment guarantees. It is necessary to mention here

**Table 3.    Role of Foreign Investors in Estonian Privatization**

| Year | Purchasing price | | | Investment guarantees | | | Employment | | |
|------|------|------|------|------|------|------|------|------|------|
|      | Total (mn kroon) | Foreign investment (mn kroon) | Share of for.inv. (per cent) | Total (mn kroon) | Foreign investment (mn kroon) | Share of for.inv. (per cent) | Total (mn kroon) | Foreign investment (mn kroon) | Share of for.inv. (per cent) |
| 1993 | 353.2 | 91.0 | 25.8 | 236.8 | 87.1 | 36.8 | 9099 | 1939 | 21.3 |
| 1994 | 1333.8 | 108.1 | 8.1 | 855.5 | 130.7 | 15.3 | 25483 | 2917 | 11.4 |
| 1995 | 874.9 | 76.7 | 8.8 | 906.2 | 193.4 | 21.3 | 7950 | 1460 | 18.4 |
| 1996 | 473.6 | 208.4 | 44.0 | 453.6 | 338.0 | 74.5 | 1274 | 50 | 4.2 |
| Total | 3035.5 | 484.2 | 16.0 | 2452.1 | 749.2 | 30.6 | 43776 | 6370 | 14.6 |

*Source*:    Author's calculations.

that in most cases investment and employment guarantees were compulsory for a three-year period after the privatization contract was signed. The last row sums up the respective parameters during the period 1993–96, and the average shares of purchasing price, investment and employment guarantees fixed in contracts with the foreign investor are also presented.

The figures in Tables 2 and 3 confirm that at the end of the period investment guarantees began to be more important than the purchasing price of enterprises. This aspect was considered to be especially important in the case of contracts signed with foreign investors. On the other hand, employment guarantees were less important in deals with foreign participation. There are two reasons which explain this phenomenon: (1) it would have been exceedingly difficult to force foreign investors to keep excess labour in privatized enterprises; (2) very often the most important advantage of the foreign offer was the investment guarantee together with the transformation of know-how, which enhanced the future development perspectives of the enterprise. In such cases it was not reasonable to introduce obstacles for the foreign investor.

The figures in Table 3 clearly underestimate the role of foreign investors in Estonian privatization. One reason for this is that Estonian legislation gave domestic investors one rather important advantage: they were obliged to pay only part of the purchasing price at the outset, with the opportunity to pay the outstanding amount by instalments. Several foreign participants preferred first to create a joint venture in which, formally, ownership was predominantly in the hands of Estonians registered in Estonia. Such a company then participated in privatization as an Estonian company.

A portion of the shares in several enterprises was reserved for public sale or, since the fifth tender, for vouchers. The shares of 33 enterprises were sold by public auction for vouchers between December 1994 and December 1996. The shares of the first two enterprises (49 per cent of the shares of the Tallinn Department Store in December 1994 and 20 per cent of the shares of the Saku Brewery in April and May 1995) were sold at a fixed price in voucher kroons. Although the price was in both cases substantially higher than the face value of the shares sold, the shares of both enterprises were significantly oversubscribed. Small investors were preferred, and the maximum amount for each subscriber was set at only 200 shares with a face value of 10 kroons. As the demand for shares was over four times higher than the number of shares offered, each investor got a quarter of the shares he had subscribed to in the case of Saku Brewery (to be precise, if the investor had applied for 200 shares, he or she received 46) for the same fixed price of 26 voucher kroons per share with a face value of 10 kroons.

On June 24, 1995, the Privatization Agency announced the sale of minority stakes in 6 enterprises for vouchers. In this case, and later, a different system was used for bidding and for determining the price of shares. The public could use two methods of applying for the shares. In the case of method 1, the subscriber determines the value of the vouchers he or she reserves for buying shares of an enterprise. The number of shares he or she really gets is determined by the equilibrium price and the value of reserved voucher kroons. By method 2, the investor also shows the maximum price he or she is ready to pay for an enterprise share. If the equilibrium price is higher than that accepted by the investor, the investor will get his/her voucher kroons back.

A maximum of 49 per cent of shares in a joint-stock company were sold for vouchers (in 8 cases out of the total of 33). Usually 20–25 per cent of the shares were sold for vouchers, with a majority stake having already been sold to a core investor. The lowest price was fixed at the level of 3 kroons for a share with a face value of 10 kroons. Only in four cases was the equilibrium price lower than the face value of the respective share. The highest price was 235 times higher than the face value of the respective share of the well-known confectionery factory Kalev (*Eesti erastamisagentuuri 1996 aasta tegevusaruanne*, 1997). However, here it should be mentioned that we are speaking about voucher kroons, whose market value was at that time approximately one-fifth of the cash kroon. Details of the Estonian voucher scheme are described in section 7 below.

## RESTITUTION OF UNLAWFULLY EXPROPRIATED PROPERTY AND PRIVATIZATION OF LAND

The objects of restitution are unlawfully expropriated land, buildings, ships, agricultural inventory, factory fittings. Property is not subject to restitution in cases where: it no longer exists in its original unitary form; if the property is in a person's *bona fide* possession; or in the case of shares. In these cases and also where the property has perished or if the claimants so request, compensation will be made in respect of the property. Property expropriated in the course of unlawful repression and property abandoned due to a genuine fear of repression during the period from June 16, 1940 to June 1, 1981, is subject to restitution.

The first deadline for applications for restitution of property was January 17, 1992. This deadline was extended until March 31, 1993, for those claimants who had a serious reason for not presenting the claim before the date fixed earlier. Here it is important to remember that the government in office from October 1992 was formed by political parties which, during the election campaign, had presented restitution as the most important, or at least the first phase of privatization. Yet, the extension of the deadline for claiming restitution also delayed other phases of privatization.

The list of people entitled to claim restitution of property included former owners, if they lived permanently on the territory of Estonia in June 1991 or if they were citizens of the Republic of Estonia on June 16, 1940; heirs of the former owner; public and religious organizations that operated until June 16, 1940 and whose statutory activity has not been terminated. The law also made it possible for foreigners, as heirs of the former owner, but who do not have citizenship of the 'old' or the 'new' Republic of Estonia, to claim property.[20]

By August 1, 1994, 206,275 applications for the restitution of 157,959 properties had been submitted to the County Restitution Commissions. In 75 per cent of the cases the restitution or compensation of farms and/or land was demanded.[21] This is a very large number considering that the Estonian population is only 1.5 million.

The restitution process started in August 1992, but for several reasons it proceeded slowly. One reason for this was the complicated order of introducing private ownership of land. The process was further complicated by the fact that it was carried out in parallel with the introduction of a new legal system and registers of real estate, measurement of land, etc. Approximately 80 per cent of claims had received an answer by December 1996. At the same time only 5,600 real estates had been legally registered and formed as of January 1st, 1997. New proposals for restitution were discussed in parliament in September 1995. The main idea of these proposals, put forward to speed up the restitution process, was first to complete the process of geographical mapping, and to complete all other necessary procedures later or when a particular piece of land was prepared for sale. This solution simplified the procedures, but it also created additional problems if, for example, the exact size of the plot was not certain or the land use had changed during the last fifty years. The final deadline for compensation and restitution in kind is July 1, 1998.

The value of unlawfully expropriated property was initially estimated at 29 billion kroons (1992 value). The value of nationalized agricultural land was estimated at 12.8 billion kroons, that of building lots (land) in towns at 7.0 billion kroons, that of forests at 0.6 billion kroons, that of assets in agriculture (excluding land and buildings) at 2.2 billion kroons, and the value of buildings in towns and in the countryside was set at 2.5 billion kroons.[22] The 'Law on the Evaluation of Land' (adopted on February 9, 1994) states that the forest will be compensated in accordance with the value of compensated land, at an additional 30 per cent of the value of the land in question. This decision increased the value of forests in the balance of expropriated property from 0.6 to 5.1 billion kroons.[23]

Restitution, especially if it concerns large buildings which are occupied by tenants other than the former owner, is a potential source of tensions. In order to soften these tensions the law requires the former owner or inheritor to continue the rental contract with the present tenant for at least three years following a positive decision about the restitution claim.

The privatization of land is regulated by the 'Law on Land Reform' and the 'Government Resolution On the Order of Privatization of Land by Public Offering and the Establishment of the Right to Cover Land With Buildings', adopted on April 13, 1994. The Privatization Agency, in co-operation with the local governments, is the organizer of any privatization of land, if the purpose of the process is to transform the ownership of land for business or production use.

There was no unified order of privatization of land to foreigners and legal persons; the government's decision served as the basis for such transformations until 1995. The long-term lease of land and buildings on it has been the solution in numerous cases. The Government decree of September 1995 stipulated that the Privatization Agency should settle the privatization of land necessary to serve a privatized company. At the same time, all transactions involving land and the sale of land from state ownership to private ownership are heavily dependent on the process of restitution.

## PRIVATIZATION SECURITIES (VOUCHERS)

### National Capital Bonds and Compensation Securities

Two types of privatization securities are used in Estonia. The basis for calculating the value of national capital bonds (NCB) is given in the 'Law on Privatization of Dwellings' (adopted in June 1993). Every permanent resident of the Republic of Estonia as of January 1, 1992, who is at least 18 years old may apply for NCBs. The basis for calculating the value of the NCB is the employment period (working years) in Estonia between January 1, 1945 and January 1, 1992. Persons with an employment period of less than ten years are given a so-called citizen's NCB equivalent to ten years' employment. Five years are added to one parent for every child and also to orphans. For unlawfully repressed persons, every year in prison or exile is calculated as three years of employment.

NCBs were initially designed for use in privatizing dwellings. For this reason, the basis for all calculations of the value of NCBs was the amount and book value of the housing to be privatized. On the basis of this value and the estimated total sum of employment years, the price of one year was fixed at 300 kroon.

The card (so-called 'yellow card') for calculating the length of employment was issued to residents who applied for it. Family members could add up their years and have one card for the whole family. A tenant could buy out the flat he/she is living in using the card. If, however, the owner of the card wanted to use the calculated value of his/her employment for buying some other privatizable object, a privatization securities account would be opened in his/her name in a bank registered to participate in transactions with privatization securities. The value of the object bought by him/her is deducted from his/her securities account.

### Securities Issued to Compensate for Unlawfully Expropriated Property

These are regulated by the 'Law on Determination of and Compensation for the Value of Unlawfully Expropriated Property' (adopted by the parliament on May 19, 1993), by the 'Order on Determination of Compensation for Unlawfully Expropriated Property' (Government decree of July 13, 1993) and by the 'Law on the Price of Land' (adopted by the parliament on July 9, 1992). Compensation Securities (CS) are issued to former owners and their heirs in cases where it is impossible to return the nationalized property in its physical form, or where they do not want to get it back. The value of the property in 1940 (when Estonia was incorporated into the Soviet Union and land, banks and large enterprises were nationalized) is first determined. It is then recalculated from EEK of 1940 to EEK of 1992, generally using the multiplier of 1:10, or 1:40 for land. The laws fix the procedures for cases where it is impossible to determine the value of the expropriated property.

Decisions regarding applications for the return of or compensation for property, the completion of cards for NCBs and privatization of flats to tenants are also made at the level of the local municipality. The central registers and the system of privatization accounts are designed to control the activity of the whole system. The applications for the return of or compensation for property, are received by the Register of Owners and Property. Information on the issue of CS and NCBs is sent to the Central Register of Privatization Securities.

Residents may open special privatization securities accounts in the branches of the seven banks which are involved in the system. Transactions with privatization securities are fixed in the Central Register, which has electronic mail communication with the banks. The Central Register of Privatization Securities is connected with the Register of Population and the Register of Enterprises.

Privatization securities are only recorded in electronic form, and not as security papers. The owner of privatization securities may receive from the bank a statement about the transactions and balance of the account. The system includes banks which have a network of subsidiaries throughout Estonia. There are thus at least 50 points where residents can open their accounts and carry out transactions.

## The Utilization of Privatization Securities

The same rules are valid for the utilization of NCBs and CS, making it possible to discuss the functions of privatization securities in general. The government has adopted the 'Fundamentals for Using Privatization Securities', as the general framework of the scheme. Dwellings, land, shares and assets of enterprises, the Compensation Fund bonds and securities of investment funds are all available in exchange for privatization securities.

The price of dwellings for privatization to the incumbent tenants is based on the book value of one square metre in a standard nine-storey tenement house. The actual price of a flat is calculated on the basis of coefficients fixed in the government's 'Decree on the Privatization of Dwellings'. The coefficients take into account the age, type and location of the building and the number and condition of auxiliary rooms. The value coefficient of one square metre of the flat could range between 0.1 and 3.0 (from 30 to 900 EEK). Until December 1, 1994, the tenant could buy the flat in which he/she lived at this calculated price, using the NCB card. The 'Order of the Privatization of Dwellings' also fixes the conditions for payments in cash (and payment by instalments). After January 1, 1995 the local municipalities were permitted to sell dwellings at the market price for cash or privatization securities, either to persons or to real estate companies.

The users of agricultural land or the plot upon which a house is built can purchase this land for privatization securities. The price to be paid in securities or cash is based on the price used for land taxation. One idea was to simplify land substitution by using privatization securities. If the former owner or his/her heirs are using another plot of land, they can receive compensation in securities and can use these securities to pay for the land they are actually using. The problems of return of and compensation for land are regulated in the 'Law on Land Reform' and other legal acts.

Shares in privatized enterprises are sold for cash or privatization securities. The Privatization Programme for 1994 prepared by the Estonian Privatization Agency and adopted by the government proposed an average of 25 per cent of shares to be sold for vouchers. The sale of shares was to be organized in auctions where private persons and investment funds could bid. However, there were delays in implementing the programme and 49 per cent of the shares of the first enterprise privatized in this manner, the Tallinn Department Store, were sold only in December 1994. In 1995, minority stakes in a total of 16 enterprises were sold for vouchers.

The sale of minority stakes in 16 further enterprises was announced in 1996. Since the fifth tender, a portion of shares has been reserved by the organizer of privatization for sale for vouchers and the core investor has been able to buy for cash the majority – but not all – of the shares in most cases where the financial situation of the enterprise is healthy.

One of the main features of the Estonian system is that it has to make possible the simultaneous sale of all shares (without postponing the transaction to the next round), while the participants should be given a chance to withdraw if the price is unacceptable.

In the Estonian scheme, it is also possible to buy property of enterprises for privatization securities, if the Privatization Agency decides to sell an enterprise in this way. Privatization securities can be used for buying dwellings, land, shares and other assets until December 31, 1998.

Until summer 1994, only relatives were allowed to put their working years together and use them to pay for some asset. Since 1994, however, vouchers have been freely tradable. In spring 1997 the introduction of vouchers onto the list of securities traded in the Tallinn Stock Exchange was discussed and from the end of May 1997, the vouchers were traded there for the first time. This required some organizational changes related to the registration of vouchers in the Central Register of Securities. Since March 1996, the official price of privatization securities has been calculated by the Ministry of Finance on the basis of market transactions. That price fluctuated during the whole of 1996 at around 16–18 per cent of the face value. In February 1997, information about the new possibilities for using vouchers (especially important were, e.g., the opportunity to use vouchers for paying by instalments in the privatization of enterprises; flotation on the market of minority shares in Estonian Gas within the framework of the voucher scheme; and a new regulation making it possible to use vouchers to cover mortgage payments to the Fund for Dwellings), led the price to increase to 25–30 per cent of the face value in just one week.

An owner of privatization securities can also invest through institutional intermediaries such as investment funds. Their main goal is to diminish investor risk by compiling portfolios of shares in different enterprises and other securities. As in mid-1995, five privatization investment funds were operating in Estonia in May 1997. However, two mergers of funds occurred during this period and two new funds came on the market. Another possibility to diminish investor risk is to use the opportunities offered by the Compensation Fund.

## The Compensation Fund

The Compensation Fund was intended to have the role of balancing the demand, expressed in privatization securities, and the supply covered by different privatized assets. The Fund was to issue bonds of different maturities and interest rates, which should be tradable on the secondary market.

The Compensation Fund was financed through the transfer of 50 per cent of the money earned from privatization for cash. In 1996, this share was diminished to 45 per cent when state-owned assets are sold and to 25 per cent when municipal property is sold.[24] The Compensation Fund buys the privatization securities for bonds and invests the money received from privatization for cash into other financial institutions, which then lend out the money. This money is intended to be invested in Estonian enterprises, in the construction of dwellings or reconstruction of infrastructure. The sum of money received by the Compensation Fund has already diminished due to privatization costs. The bonds issued will be repurchased by the Compensation Fund after January 1, 2000. The total value of the Fund's assets was 496 million kroons on September 11, 1995.[25] By the end of March 1997, the amount of assets had increased to 1,220 million kroons.[26]

During 1994, 1995, and 1996 the Fund had eight series of emissions of bonds worth a total of 360 million kroons. On May 7, 1997, the Compensation Fund announced a ninth emission of bonds. The Fund sells its bonds, with a nominal value of 100 kroons for voucher kroons, at a price that is equal to the price of vouchers in the open market. As the value of vouchers has been far below their nominal value (vouchers were traded at a price of 16–18 per cent of their nominal value at the end of September 1995, which means that if one working year was made equal to 300 kroons then the equivalent of it is traded for 48 to 54 kroons), the bonds are sold for a price that is close to 400 voucher kroons.

The Compensation Fund also paid interest on bonds twice a year. There was a fixed 7 per cent base interest rate per annum. An extra interest rate was paid on top of the basic rate depending on the financial results of the Fund. Altogether, the interest rate paid by the Compensation Fund bonds was 16.85 per cent in 1994 and for the first half of 1995, 15.6 per cent calculated for the whole year. For the second half of 1996 the interest rate was 12 per cent. In 1997 a new system was introduced, according to which the interest rate is based on the interbank interest rate of the money market of Estonia (Talibor) plus 1.5 per cent (the interest rate could thus be approximately 6–8 per cent). The maturity time of the ninth emission was shortened from six to five years. The Compensation Fund will be closed when all of its obligations are fulfilled.

## Some Results of the Voucher Programme

As described above, there are two types of privatization securities. As regards NCB, the sum of 8.5 billion kroons represents the final total because the issue of cards has now been completed.[27]

The total value of CS depends on the number of claims, as well as on the relationship between physical return and compensation. The smaller the amount of physically returned property, the greater the value of CS issued, and *vice versa*. This factor has a direct effect on the vouchers side and assets side of the balance, but does not influence equilibrium. Until September 1995, CSs with a value of 3.2 billion kroons were issued, but as only a small proportion of restitution claims have been resolved, this figure could increase significantly. The Ministry of Finance estimated that this figure could increase to 11.5 billion kroons. In May 1997 the value of the CSs issued was 5.5 billion kroons and the forecast of the eventual total amount was lowered to 8.5 billion kroons.[28] Thus, the total value of vouchers could be 17 billion kroons. As people could buy their flats using a card which was issued on the basis of the length of their employment (voucher kroons with a value of 2.1 billion kroons were utilized for buying flats), the expected value of vouchers would be 14.9 billion kroons. On March 10, 1997, there were 7 billion kroons in privatization accounts, while the value of assets sold for vouchers was 6.2 billion kroons (to which should be added dwellings sold for 'yellow cards', with an estimated value of 2.1 billion kroons).

The value of privatized property can only be roughly estimated. It will also depend on political decisions concerning the amount of assets to be privatized, and the behaviour of persons involved in the privatization process. The land, dwelling rooms, shares and other assets of enterprises are in an economic sense very different and their estimation in the framework of a single scheme is fraught with difficulty. Also, the mechanisms for evaluation and sale are very important for determining how vouchers are matched with assets. Some assets are privatized to their users for the calculated nominal value (flats, land). Other types of property are sold through auction-type mechanisms for cash or for vouchers. Selling a greater share of property through the auction-type mechanism should help absorb more privatization securities.

Land has the most important role in the balance of assets. According to Ministry of Finance estimates, the value of land privatized for vouchers could be 3.0 billion kroons (this includes both the value of agricultural land and that of plots of land in cities, and it is assumed that another part of the land will be returned in kind). The value of property and shares privatized for vouchers is estimated at around 4.6 billion kroons, and the value of dwellings at 2.1 billion kroons (excluding the value of dwellings already privatized for yellow cards); the value of other privatized properties in the housing sector (especially properties which could be used for different types of business activities) is put at 1 billion kroons, and bonds of the Compensation Fund at 4.5 billion kroons (see Table 4). Therefore, the balance of vouchers and privatized assets depends heavily on the speed of the administrative processes which make the transformation of land ownership possible.

**Table 4.   The Value of Privatization Securities and Privatized Assets
(Billion Kroons, March 10, 1997)**

|  | Potential value | Value of issued securities or sold assets |
|---|---|---|
| National Capital Bonds (NCB) in the form of yellow cards | 8.5 | 8.5 |
| Compensation Securities (CS) | 8.5 | 5.7 |
| Total value of privatization securities issued | 17.0 | 14.2 |
| NCBs used in the form of a yellow card directly for the privatization of dwellings (without registration in the Central Register) | 2.1 | 2.1 |
| NCBs registered and in use for privatization of assets other than dwellings | 6.4 | 6.1 |
| Total value of privatization securities registered in Central Register and usable for privatization | 14.9 | 11.8 |
| Total value of assets sold for privatization securities | 14.9 | 4.75 |
| Public sale of shares | 3.0 | 1.37 |
| Fixed assets of industrial enterprises | 1.6 | 0.96 |
| Enterprises' dwellings | 2.1 | 1.06 |
| Properties other than dwellings in the housing sector (workshops) | 1.0 | 0 |
| Land | 3.0 | 0.29 |
| Bonds of the Compensation Fund | 4.2 | 1.07 |

*Source*:   Ministry of Finance of the Republic of Estonia.

The balance should not be looked upon in static terms only. The timing of different privatization procedures is extremely important. For example, 200,000 restitution claims need time to be processed. The whole privatization process should not be stopped totally for that period. Some assets should also be available, e.g., for CS which are allocated only after lengthy investigation of the claim.

Popular expectations of privatization are another important part of the process. If procedures are badly organized and/or time-consuming, the interest of residents in participating will diminish. In a formal sense, this could help equilibrate the privatization balance, but in the long run it will very much complicate the process. In an atmosphere of suspicion and confusion, the whole privatization process could grind to a halt, while the basis for protracted legal cases could be created by several changes of privatization strategy, which would leave no time for real privatization. Furthermore, the adjustment of the demand and supply sides of the voucher scheme over a longer period is very important for creating appropriate expectations. The steep decline of the price of vouchers below their nominal value has caused heated political debate. At the same time, the interest of private economic agents in vouchers has rapidly increased. Although the speed of privatization has been much slower than different political parties have claimed, especially during election campaigns, the investment funds and real estate firms realized that through this scheme a large amount of property is transformed and it is possible to do very good business there. Large amounts of shares which were bought for vouchers but are now tradable for cash, have been introduced for trading on the tiny Estonian securities market through this scheme.

## Privatization of Infrastructure

A step-by-step approach was to prevail in the privatization of infrastructure, oil shale mines and power stations, as the government and the Privatization Agency state (*Erastamisprogramm valitsusse*, 1995). The basic principles governing infrastructure privatization may be outlined as follows. First, all state-owned companies in this field were to be reorganized into joint-stock holding companies. Second, several units serving mainly supportive functions to the main activity in the respective field, were to be privatized separately. Third, the way was opened for the main activities to be privatized. The predominant part of the shares could be sold to some core investor or to several foreign partners, with the Estonian state remaining a minority share-holder. The Estonian state could diminish its participation by selling shares for vouchers to those resident in Estonia.

At the end of 1995 the Privatization Agency established a special working group to draw up privatization plans for infrastructure enterprises. Financial support provided by the EU's PHARE programme was used for this purpose. Initial privatization plans were presented to the government in June 1996. Further, the respective ministries, the Privatization Agency and PHARE consultants had to prepare more detailed privatization schedules for Eesti Energia (a power engineering company) and Eesti Põlevkivi (an oil shale mining company) by November 1, 1996 and for other infrastructure enterprises by January 1, 1997. A special department was set up in the Privatization Agency to deal with the privatization of infrastructure.

In May 1996, 66 per cent of the shares of the national airline, Estonian Air, had already been sold. Also 100 per cent of the shares of the state-owned insurance company Eesti Kindlustus, had been sold. In August 1996 a two-stage tender of 70 per cent of Eesti Merelaevandus (a marine transportation company) was announced. This process reached its second stage in May 1997. The master plan for the privatization of Eesti Energia is being prepared. However, several legal and administrative problems must be solved before privatization can begin in this field. For example, for the privatization of power stations, it has been considered necessary first to pass a legal act regulating the supply of electricity and to establish an institution supervizing the process. Also, the price of electricity is regulated by the state and is still relatively low. The same is true in the case of railway transportation, where the tickets for passengers are several times lower than costs. For these reasons there seems to be some social need for a time-lag in preparing privatization in these fields. The draft of the law regulating the energy market is still being discussed in the relevant government institutions.

## THE OWNERSHIP STRUCTURE OF ECONOMY AND THE REMAINING STEPS OF PRIVATIZATION

### Structure of the Economy

The private sector was predominant in most branches of the Estonian economy by the end of 1996. Over 90 per cent of the turnover in retail sales, wholesale and catering and over 80 per cent of services and output in industry was produced by the private sector in 1996 (see Table 5). One explanation for the especially large share of private enterprises in retail sales, wholesale, services and catering is the fast progress of the small-scale privatization. Another reason is linked to the emergence of a large number of private firms not directly linked to privatization. However, it is very difficult to estimate the exact share of the firms created as a result of privatization and the share of other types of firm.[29] It is estimated that one-third of small companies and two-thirds of medium-sized and large companies in the private sector emerged as a result of privatization.

The development of the securities market is also a precondition for the privatization of infrastructure, especially in cases where small investors are involved in privatization. In fact, the voucher scheme and the sale of a portion of the shares of privatized enterprises for vouchers have been a good impulse for creating a secondary market for these shares. Estonia introduced a central (electronic) register of securities in spring 1995. The central register of privatization securities had been put into operation earlier, in 1993. The stock exchange was opened in spring 1996. Approximately 20 shares were traded by banks and investment companies as of spring 1997.

### Interest Groups and the Political Process

The initial concept of privatization gave clear preference to the former owners of nationalized property and their heirs. The predominant role of restitution is an expression of this preference. National capital bonds were introduced as a counterweight and the idea of diminishing the role and costs of the state and municipalities in the housing sector supported this approach. The Estonian scheme did not offer any preferences for the employees of privatized enterprises. This could be one reason why the share of new private firms is so high. The state did not manage to keep the amount of privatized assets at a level which could clear demand at the level of the nominal price of vouchers, so the market price of vouchers was at a level of 16–18 per cent of their nominal value from September 1995 till January 1997, and a little higher, at 25–30 per cent, since February 1997. This has caused a situation where the declared and planned preferences could not be implemented and thus the ownership reform has given more advantages to entrepreneurs. This result might be better for future economic growth, but it could also be a source of social tension and disappointment for those who suffered during the Soviet occupation.

## Evaluation of the Methods of Privatization

Privatization affects the economic activities of enterprises in several ways. An important question connected with the different methods of privatization is who the new owners are. The possible alternatives are: the working collective or managers of the privatized company; an Estonian investment group; a foreign company active in the same field; or a foreign investment group. In addition there is a possibility that a part of the shares are sold for vouchers, but as these are a minority of shares and there is always a core investor in such cases, this alternative will not be analysed separately.

This problem requires special examination, but the information based on several articles could be a basis for a preliminary investigation (Niitra, 1995; Sarnet tahab Silvetist vabaneda, 1995). Most companies privatized to managers or working collectives complained about a lack of working capital and problems with payments by contract to the Privatization Agency. There is strong political pressure to ease the conditions of such payments and this pressure has already succeeded in forcing parliament to introduce the relevant legislation and amendments which also allow those companies which were sold before June 1994, i.e., before vouchers were made tradable for cash, to pay part of the price in vouchers. In such cases, the face value of the vouchers is taken into account. Note that in October 1995 the nominal value of vouchers was more than five times higher than their cash value on the market (i.e., to pay, for example a price of 1000 kroons, the company could buy on the market vouchers with a nominal value of 1000 kroons but pay only 200 in cash for them). Such companies have mentioned that they do not have the necessary finances for investments and purchases, or the know-how necessary to gain access to the markets of developed countries. These problems have been more acute in the case of medium-sized and large enterprises. For small firms privatized through auctions, the payments problem has not been so critical, because the required investments are smaller and the turnover time is shorter.

There are several successful cases where the purchaser was a foreign company with a similar production profile. In such cases the Estonian partner very often became a link in the technological circle involving a wider group of partners. However, in most cases a preliminary condition for such a linkage was to change from being a producer of finished goods to a producer of semi-finished goods or a subcontractor undertaking certain operations. There are also some examples in the food industry where the foreign investor was very interested in protecting its own market.

As mentioned above, the emergence of Estonian financial groups only started in 1995, when they began to participate actively in privatization. There are some examples where an investment group has hired new management after purchasing a company and succeeded in restructuring a firm (e.g., the Tallinn Department Store).

There are also some examples where the core investor is a foreign investment group, but in most cases such a group was co-operating with a firm active in the same field and the management was offered by a foreign firm. Then structural changes in the firm began, in most cases, if the partners had a prepared and agreed strategy and contract on the implementation of an appropriate scheme. In fact, it is probably too soon to examine effectively the opportunities and risks of such co-operation.

## The Influence of Privatization on Employment

Most privatized enterprises reduced the number of people they employed by one-third on average. At the same time, the number of guaranteed jobs is one condition of the privatization deal (the conditon is valid for three years in most cases) and the new owners have not been free in their decision-making with regard to terms of employment. The official rate of unemployment in Estonia was 2.3 per cent in December 1996. However, this figure takes into account only those people who receive unemployment benefit. If we add to this figure the people registered as unemployed but who do not receive these benefits, the rate could be 5 per cent. This result is rather paradoxical because the cumulative decline in GDP was 37 per cent during 1991–94.

One explanation of this phenomenon is related to the behaviour of enterprises. Even those firms where the output declined by two to three times retained most of their workers, paying them the minimum wage (the minimum wage was 680 kroons per month until December 1996, but was increased to 845 kroons in February 1997) or less. For enterprises such a solution was acceptable because when making people redundant enterprises have to pay them up to the average wage for eight months (the actual sum depends on the time the person had been employed). The workers have not been interested in leaving enterprises because unemployment benefit is much lower than the minimum wage. Another reason is that the official and unofficial private sector absorbed rather a large share of the people who left the state-owned companies. As these enterprises have an interest in declaring their turnover and revenues as being lower than they really are, the decline of the economy could also be overestimated. There are other factors which could increase future unemployment (termination of employment guarantees, increases in wages which make labour more expensive, possible increase in unemployment benefits). On the other hand, positive structural changes and the growth of the economy could ease this problem.

## CONCLUSIONS

Privatization in Estonia has many features which are similar to the same process in other eastern European countries. However, there are also some preconditions for ownership reform specific to Estonia. These include extensive migration from other republics of the former Soviet Union; only regaining independence from the former Soviet Union in August 1991; an initial commitment to the rouble zone (the national currency, the Estonian kroon, was only introduced in 1992); and the predominant role of state ownership in housing. There was a very strong readiness to embark on the transition to a market economy and the concomitant economic reforms, because the goals of these reforms were identified with that of achieving political independence for Estonia. Therefore, the population was prepared to suffer the difficulties created by the reform.

All the Estonian governments since 1990 have declared privatization to be the central issue of the continuing reforms. Differences have occurred between the political parties about privatization methods and which interest groups should be preferred in the process. Two approaches may be distinguished: 1) the so-called restitution approach, which gave priority to restitution and also distribution by vouchers; and 2) the entrepreneurial approach, which stresses the role of core investors and management in the process of privatization. During the period 1990–96, seven governments preferring one or other of these approaches have been in office. However, though some changes of emphasis on different methods have occurred, the privatization process has continued along basically the same path.

Restitution has played a more important role in Estonian ownership reform than in most other eastern European countries. This is reflected in the eligibility of a wider circle of heirs of former owners, in compensation for destroyed property, in the evaluation methods, etc., which have made the amount of compensation enormously large (in nominal terms). On the other hand, there are political and social preconditions that promoted such developments in the transformation of ownership.

Restitution is connected first of all with land reform. A wide circle of subjects, combined with complicated administrative and legal issues, have made the restitution of land a very slow and expensive process. This in turn makes privatization of land to other economic agents who would like to use it for production purposes virtually impossible. Small-scale privatization has been successful in Estonia. Although during the period 1991–96 different methods were used, the process was virtually completed in the trade, services and catering sectors by the end of 1994. The private sector now dominates in these sectors of the economy (see Table 5).

Table 5.   Share of Private Sector in Turnover (per cent)

|  | 1990 | 1991 | 1992 | 1993 | 1994 | 1995 | 1996 |
|---|---|---|---|---|---|---|---|
| Retail sales | 10 | 35 | 81 | 87 | 94 | 96 | 96 |
| Wholesale | 10 | 30 | 54 | 90 | 90 | 92 | 98 |
| Catering | 10 | 40 | 86 | 86 | 94 | 95 | 95 |
| Services | 10 | 30 | 55 | 73 | 83 | 87 | 89 |
| Industry | 5 | 10 | 35 | 52 | 58 | 64 | 82 |
| Housing | 30 | 30 | 30 | 35 | 58 | 65 | 70 |
| Commercial banks (share capital) |  |  |  |  |  | 86 |  |

*Sources*:   The Privatization Agency; the Bank of Estonia; Eesti Tööstus 1993, 1994, 1995; Statistical Yearbook 1995, 1996.

Large-scale privatization started with the so-called experimental privatization of seven enteprises during 1991–92. Beginning with the first tender of 38 enterprises in November 1992, this process acquired a central place in the privatization process. Altogether, 410 enterprises were offered in 15 tenders and 452 purchasing contracts were made for the total sum of 3.0 billion kroons. Approximately 90 per cent of the enterprises were privatized by January 1997 (taking into account state-owned enterprises and infrastructure enterprises like Eesti Energia etc.).

Two types of privatization securities are used in Estonia. The NCBs are issued on the basis of a person's period of employment. Every employment year is considered to be worth 300 kroons. Compensation securities (CS) are issued to the former owners of unlawfully expropriated property and their heirs, if they do not want this property back, or if the return of this property is not possible. First the value of the property in 1940 is determined and then recalculated into 1992 EEK by multiplying by 10 (by 40 for land). In privatization the NCBs and the CSs are used in a similar way.

A specific feature of the Estonian scheme is that vouchers can be used for buying flats, land and shares of enterprises. On the one hand, an opportunity has thus been created to promote privatization in different areas of the economy. On the other hand, this brings about many difficulties, as it is necessary to compare the value of very different assets.

Political decisions have been important in the creation of the necessary preconditions for the privatization concept. The Estonian voucher scheme is one of the most complicated schemes in the eastern European countries. This is partly the result of the specific preconditions of the economic reform in Estonia. The political debate has forced different political parties and interest groups to argue strongly for their respective interests, without taking into account real opportunities and the value of available assets in the privatization process.

The activity of the Compensation Fund is very important for balancing the whole system. Bonds issued by the Compensation Fund will be an investment possibility, both afterwards and until the end of the privatization process, as there is not enough property available to cover demand in vouchers. Bonds are also tradable for cash from the beginning of the issue.

Although a very complex privatization scheme has been created, the process has continued in Estonia during the period of 1991–96 without major setbacks. The private sector has achieved a dominant role in the economy, partly thanks to privatization, and partly thanks to the emergence of a set of new private firms.

## NOTES

1. Frydman *et al.*, 1993: 147.
2. Frydman *et al.*, 1993: 154.
3. Klein and Tali, 1995: 156.

4. In discussions on privatization, the following dilemmas have been mentioned as being most important: (i) should ownership reform be comprehensive and rapid or should firms be sold off gradually after the new rules of economic behaviour emerge; (ii) should state property be sold or given away (possibly using vouchers); (iii) should restitution play a major part in ownership reform, or is it necessary to take into account other considerations and restrict the scope of restitution; (iv) should the employees of privatized enterprises have a special claim, or should there be no preferences for them as state assets were created through an unfair redistribution of resources from one sector to another; (v) is it especially important to support domestic firms, or do we need to encourage foreign investors to participate in privatization? In Estonia, during the first three years of privatization, the debate revolved principally around the second and third of the aforementioned dilemmas.

5. Eesti Vabariigi Valitsuse erastamiskontseptsioon (1990).

6. Savisaar (1993).

7. The 'Law On the Privatization of State-Owned Service, Retail and Catering Enterprises' (December 13, 1990).

8. 'Law on Agricultural Reform' ( March 11, 1992), 'Law on the Price of the Land' (July 9, 1992), the government Decrees on the 'Application of the Law on Agricultural Reform' (March 12, 1992) and on the 'Order of Reception of Claims for Compensation, Purchase and Lease of Land' (May 8, 1992).

9. The 'Law on Privatization of State and Municipal Enterprises' (May 21, 1992), which amended the 'Law on Privatization of State-Owned Service, Trade and Catering Enterprises' (December 13, 1990).

10. 'Isamaa' valimisprogramm, 1993: 9–10.

11. Eluruumide erastamise seadus (1993).

12. Erastamisseadus (1993).

13. Estonia does not seem to fit the 'left-turn' model discussed in an analysis of the results of elections in several eastern European countries in 1993–94, when left-wing parties, descendants of the communist parties of the region, tended to return to power. In Estonia, in contrast, none of the parties that came to power after the elections was a successor of the Communist Party. The former Estonian Communist Party, now part of the Justice electoral bloc, failed to clear the five per cent threshold required for representation in parliament. On the other hand, a fear has been expressed that the corporate interests of members of the Coalition Party could dominate the reform. See Lahe (1995).

14. A very critical problem emerged in connection with the voucher scheme (the concept itself is described below). Vouchers have been used in Estonia for the privatization of different types of state-owned property (shares, land, and dwellings). Incumbent tenants had a preferential right to use vouchers for buying the flat they were living in. At the same time, restitution also had an imortant role in privatization and a very acute problem emerged in connection with flats or houses which were given back to former owners or their relatives. Though limits on rental payments until summer 1998 were introduced by the government, and new owners could terminate the contract with tenants only in certain cases specified in the law, the number of people having to leave their flat is increasing. Under these circumstances it was also set out in the legal provisions, that people living in flats returned to their former owners have a preferential right to participate in auctions of flats organized exclusively for them, which are not subject to voucher applications and are free (e.g., flats of Russian officers and other people who have

emigrated from Estonia). On the other hand, there was a right to buy for vouchers not only flats which belonged to state, but also flats which belonged to certain enterprises (so-called employer's dwellings). The formal difference between these two groups of flats was lacking, because these were basically state-owned enterprises. On the other hand, this difference was very important, as it determined the circle of people who could participate in the privatization of such flats. While Vähi was a chairman of the Tallinn City Council (before becoming Prime Minister for the second time), a scheme was devised whereby approximately two hundred flats in central Tallinn were first transferred to the category of employer's dwelling rooms of Tallinn Municipality and then privatized to a limited group of people. People buying these flats for vouchers in some cases payed 10–20 times less than their market price. It was argued that most of these flats were in very bad condition and people buying the flats for vouchers had to invest a lot of money in them.

15. The Law 'On Making Alterations and Amendments to the Law of the Republic of Estonia On Privatization of State-Owned Service, Retail and Catering Enterprises' (May 21, 1992).

16. The exchange rate used in the introduction of the Estonian currency was 1 kroon=10 roubles. The Estonian kroon was pegged to the Deutschmark in relation 1 DEM=8 EEK. This fixed exchange rate has remained at the same level in March 1997.

17. Klein and Tali , 1995: 146.

18. The source of this data is the Estonian Privatization Agency.

19. See figures in Table 3.

20. Here the expressions 'new' and 'old' are used very loosely because the present Republic of Estonia is the direct successor of the Republic of Estonia of the period between the two World Wars.

21. Kein and Tali, 1995: 164.

22. Hänni (1993a).

23. Kuidas väärtustada EVP-sid? (1995).

24. When state-owned assets are sold for cash, 45 per cent of the received sum will go to the Compensation Fund, 25 per cent to the governments's Reserve Fund for Ownership Reform, 25 per cent to the Dwellings Fund and 5 per cent to the Environmental Fund. When municipal property is sold, then 25 per cent will go the Compensation Fund, 50 per cent to the Local government Fund for Dwellings, 25 per cent to the Local Government Fund for Ownership Reform. When land is sold, 45 per cent of the earnings will go to the Compensation Fund, 25 per cent to the Local Government Fund for Ownership Reform, 25 per cent to the the Local government's Dwellings Fund and 5 per cent to the Environmental Fund.

25. Müüki tuleb uus kogus Hüvitusfondi obligatsioone (1995).

26. Hüvitusfond loobub lisaintresside maksmisest (1997).

27. Hänni (1993a).

28. Erastamisväärtpaberite väljaandmine ja kasutamine (1997).

29. One source of information is the Register of Enterprises of the Statistical Office of Estonia. Unfortunately it is impossible to evaluate on the basis of these figures the share of private firms created as a result of privatization and the share of such firms which were created separately from the privatization process. In the Register of Enterprises, there were 6,223 state-owned enterprises, 2,692 municipal enterprises and 81,736 different types of private enterprises as of July 1, 1995. If we compare these figures with the

number of privatized enterprises before that date (1,380 in the small privatization and 244 in the large privatization), the difference in favour of private enterprises emerging separately from privatization seems to be huge. However, according to estimates of the Statistical Office, approximately 30,000 enterprises are active. This figure includes 11,000 farms. Rather a large number of private enterprises were created separately, but the main reason for their creation was to participate in the privatization process. For example, managers or some of the workers in a state-owned company could create a private joint-stock company to participate in the process of the privatization of the state-owned company for which they worked. From one state-owned company several private units could emerge, which compete with each other and with outsiders in privatization. Also several private firms created without any linkage to the privatization of an enterprise could later participate in the auction of equipment or buildings of a privatized company.

Another possible way of comparing the amount of privatization is to evaluate the total purchasing price of privatized enterprises with the value of assets and other types of investments. Altogether, the total book value of the assets of state-owned enterprises was 3.1 billion kroons (excluding infrastructure) at the beginning of 1993. The total purchasing price of privatized enterprises from the same set was 2.1 billion kroons in the middle of 1995. Though some of the enterprises were sold for a symbolic 1 kroon and in other cases the purchasing price was up to 15 times higher than the book value of the enterprise, on average, according to estimates of Uku Hänni, a specialist of the Department of the Ownership Reform of the Ministry of Finance, the difference between these two parameters was not more than 20 per cent in favour of the total purchasing price in 1994.

The total sum of direct investments was 3.5 billion kroons in 1993 (including 1.7 billion kroons or 48.6 per cent into state-owned and municipal companies, mainly in the field of infrastructure and communal services, and 1.8 billion kroons or 51.4 per cent into the private sector); the amount was the same in 1994 (1.64 billion kroons or 47.0 per cent into state-owned and municipal companies and 1.86 or 53.0 per cent into private companies). The total amount of investment guarantees offered in the process of privatization was worth 237 million kroons in 1993, 855 million kroons in 1994 and 906 million kroons in 1995. When we compare these figures it could be said that guaranteed direct investments into privatized firms accounted for approximately 30 per cent of total direct investments in the private sector in 1993, 1994 and 1995. Among foreign direct investments 6.5 per cent were related to privatization in 1993 and 1.1 per cent in 1994, according to balance of payments figures (Eesti maksebilanss 1994, 1995). However, these figures do not reflect the real situation correctly either. There are several reasons for this. As the purchasing price of privatized enterprises could be paid in instalments only by Estonian enterprises (owning at least 51 per cent of the share capital of the company which makes the tender), several foreign partners preferred to form such a private company with an Estonian partner before privatization. In addition, some Estonian companies bought privatized firms with investment and payment guarantees given by foreign partners. The most famous such case is the privatization of the largest Estonian hotel, Viru, in Tallinn when a company with a share capital of 600 kroons (USD 50) bought the hotel for 145 million kroons presenting all necessary payment and investment guarantees with the backing of a Finnish investment group.

# REFERENCES

Eesti Erastamsiagentuuri 1996.a. tegevusaruanne (The Report of the Estonian Privatization Agency 1996), Tallinn, 1997.

Eesti maksebilanss 1994. aastal (1995) (The Balance of Payments of Estonia in 1994) *Eesti Panga bülletään*, No. 3, p. 22.

Eesti Statistika (1993) (Estonian Statistics 1993), *Kuukiri*, No. 8, pp. 32–34.

Eesti Vabariigi Rahandusministeerium (1997), 'Erastamisväärtpaberite väljaandmine ja kasutamine' (Ministry of Finance of the Republic of Estonia (1997), 'Emission and usage of privatization securities').

Eesti Vabariigi Valitsuse erastamiskontseptsioon (1990) Tallinn. (The Privatization Concept of the Republic of Estonia 1990).

'Eesti Vabariigi Valitsuse erastamisprogramm 1995. aastaks (1994) Projekt' (The Privatization Programme of the government of the Republic of Estonia for 1995. A Project).

Eluruumide erastamise seadus (1993), (Law on Privatization of Housing), *Riigi Teataja*.

'Erastamisprogramm valitsusse. Küsimustele vastab majandusminister Andres Lipstok' (1995), (The Privatization Programme in government. Interview with the Minister of Economic Affairs), *Äripäev*, December 13.

Erastamisseadus (1993) (The Law on Privatization 1993), *Riigi Teataja*, Nr.45, lk.1179–1193.

Erastamisväärtpaberite kasutamise alused (1993), (The Concept for Using Privatization Securities 1993), *Rahva Hääl*, April 5.

Frydman, R., Andrzej R., J. Earle *et al.*, (eds) (1993), 'Estonia', in *The Privatization Process in Russia, Ukraine and the Baltic States*, London: Central European University Press, pp. 130–193.

Hänni, L. (1993a) 'Erastamisväärtpaberite kasutamise alused. Seletuskiri' (The Concept for Using Privatization Securities. An Explanatory Letter), *Rahva Hääl*, April 5.

Hüvitusfondi seadus (1993), (Law on the Compensation Fund, 1993), *Riigi Teataja*, Nr.35, lk.902–903.

'Hüvitusfond loobub lisaintresside maksmisest' (1997) (The Compensation Fund is giving up paying extra interest rates), *Äripäev*, April 30.

'Isamaa' valimisprogramm (1993) (The Election Programme of 'Isamaa' 1992), Tallinn: Vaba Maa.

Klein, A., and V. Tali (1995), 'The Process of Ownership Reform and Privatization', in Lugus, Olev, (ed.), *Transforming the Estonian Economy*, Tallinn, Institute of Economics pp.140–168.

'Kuidas väärtustada EVP–sid?' Intervjuu Uku Hänni ja Veiko Taliga (1995) (How to give value to vouchers? Interview with Uku Hänni ja Veiko Tali from the Ministry of Finance), *Maaleht*, September 21.

Lahe, K. (1995) 'Estonia After the Elections', *The Baltic Review*, Vol.7, Spring/Summer, pp. 30–33.

'Müüki tuleb uus kogus Hüvitusfondi obligatsioone' (1995).

Niitra, S. (1995) 'Erastatud ettevõtted on raskustes' (The Privatized Enterprises have problems), *Päevaleht*, September 9.

Omandireformi aluste seadus (1991), 'Maareform täna.Õigusaktid ja kommentaarid' (Law on Basis of Property Reform (1991), Agricultural Reform Today. Legal Acts and Comments), Tallinn: Kinnisvaraekspert, pp. 9–24.

Póllumajandusreformi seadus (1992) (Law on Agricultural Reform, 1992), *Riigi Teataja*, Nr.10, pp.143–150.

'Sarnet tahab Silvetist vabaneda. Intervjuu Eesti Erastamisagentuuri peadirektori Väino Sarnetiga' (1995). (Interview with the General Director of the Privatization Agency), *Äripäev*, December 11.

Savisaar, E. (1993), 'Raha eest erastamisest ja poliitilisest vóitlusest selle úmber 1990. aastal' (On the Privatization for Cash and the Political Battle Around It In 1990), *Postimees*, May 10–12.

Statistical Yearbook 1995 (1995), Statistical Office of Estonia, Tallinn, pp. 257, 265.

# 11
# Privatization and Regulation of
# Public Utilities in Latvia

*Junior R. Davis*

## INTRODUCTION

In Latvia, public energy and telecommunications utilities and transport services are natural monopolies which operate within a complex infrastructure where competition is limited. These large monopolies have a dominant position in the domestic market and operate in a loosely regulated environment. There are relatively few regulatory and legislative control mechanisms governing Latvia's energy and public utilities. Whereas in the UK, regulatory authorities like Oftel, Ofgas and Ofwat operate effectively within a clear legal framework and with the power of legal and financial sanctions available to them, in Latvia there is no comparably comprehensive system of supervision over the business activities of the utilities. The Latvian Cabinet of Ministers has assigned the tasks of regulation (especially of the politically sensitive issue of price and tariff setting) to several public institutions which, due to a lack of resources and ineffective co-ordination, spasmodically analyse the activities of these monopolies based mainly on information provided by the firms themselves. These regulatory functions have been organized in an ineffective manner, and are largely impotent because they are executed by several public institutions which do not co-ordinate their activities. Although some action has been taken to split up conglomerates, the recently established agency for prices and competition has no effective powers to break up monopoly enterprises. Profit margins of many distribution networks remain very high. Competitive pressures come mainly from the liberal trade regime and tight monetary and fiscal policies.

The privatization and regulation of public utilities in the Baltic States generally, and Latvia in particular, have occupied centre stage in the political and economic debates concerning the development of the region. In Latvia, political and economic considerations concerning especially public utility regulation, but also privatization, have coalesced around both interest and political groups with their own agendas. The most contentious issues regarding the effective regulation and privatization of public utilities in Latvia concern: (i) the appropriate ownership of the utilities; (ii) the nature of the regulatory structure, in particular whether regulation should be conducted by an independent agency, a branch of the Ministry of Economy, Finance or Transport, or the enterprise itself; (iii) the desirability of allowing entry and competition; and (iv) the choice of procedures for the control and setting of prices.

An analysis of these issues within the prevailing political economy environment is the subject of this paper.[1] It is argued that the problems which have constrained progress in both developing and introducing effective public utility regulation and privatization in Latvia are due to: (i) a lack of policy consistency on the part of the government; (ii) the recent banking crisis and economic recession; (iii) inadequate anti-trust (competition law) and legal environment; (iv) the *ad hoc* development of complex and non-independent public utility regulatory structures; and (v) effective political resistance by particular interest groups both within the Saeima (Latvian parliament) and among public utility managers.

The privatization of large state monopolies in Latvia is only just beginning. For example, the Latvian Privatization Agency (LPA) has recently received four applications from potential strategic investors to privatize the Latvian Gas company.[2] The government intends to carry out the privatization of monopolies as soon as possible, which has attracted great public interest and a lot of political debate. The pro-market reform Latvian Way coalition government of Andris Skele has been widely criticized in the Saeima and the press for seeking to privatize the government oil enterprise Ventspils Nafta and the power utility Latvenergo. Although these utilities are, in some quarters, seen as being vital to national security, a related factor concerns the political issue of domestic ownership *vis-à-vis* the foreign ownership of national assets, an issue which, for example in the agricultural sector, has had a discernible influence on the type of privatization policies introduced (see Davis, 1996). This chapter will review and discuss the main political economy and competition policy issues associated with the regulation and privatization of public utilities through a case study of the telecommunications (Lattelekom) and energy utilities (Latvenergo, Latvia Gas) in Latvia during transition.

## POLITICAL INDEPENDENCE AND FOUNDATIONS FOR ECONOMIC CHANGE

Latvia, along with the other two Baltic States, developed mass popular movements during the Gorbachev era of the late 1980s. Initially, these movements characterized themselves as favouring liberalization within the Soviet system. Later, as they gained momentum, they evolved into organizations aimed at regaining full independence. In Latvia, The People's Front became a significant political force, electing a majority of the Latvian Soviet Socialist Republic (SSR) Supreme Soviet (parliament) in the republic's 1990 elections. At the same time, the Latvian Communist Party was splitting into national and pro-Moscow wings, weakening its hold on power in the country.

The general decentralization of the economic system begun by the Soviet authorities in 1988 reinforced political demands for an end to Soviet domination. Concurrently, Latvian scholars and activists advocated a restoration of independence based on a variety of conventions and precedents in international law. These factors led to the Latvian SSR Supreme Soviet's formal declaration of the restoration of Latvian independence, and the re-establishment of the Republic of Latvia on May 4th, 1990. The undoing of the 1940 Soviet annexation of Latvia continued until the failed August 1991 coup attempt against Gorbachev in Moscow. On August 21st, 1991, Latvia's parliament declared full independence and sovereignty, as well as the restoration of the 1922 Satversme (Constitution).

In accordance with the idea of the restoration of an independent Latvian Republic, the parliament proclaimed the sanctity of private property and ownership rights, providing a legal basis for the restoration of property rights to former owners whose property had been seized under Soviet rule. Thus the concept of property restitution, or compensation for it, was a basis for Latvia's renewed claim to national sovereignty and independence. A variety of legal acts governing restitution were subsequently adopted.

However, the transition from a command economy to a market-oriented one had its roots in a different privatization process. The effective privatization of some state property had begun before the USSR collapsed. The Soviet system was frequently abused by enterprise managers, who had the ability to control state property for their own benefit, treating it as though it were their own. Some of the economic reforms introduced in the late 1980s, particularly the introduction of procedures for leasing assets to labour collectives with subsequent right of purchase, and the legalization of co-operatives, intensified this tendency. Managers transferred assets and revenues from their state-owned enterprises (SOEs) to new private co-operatives they controlled.

An additional factor of significant importance in the transition process was the introduction of an independent budget based on tax revenues. In May 1990, the Latvian SSR Supreme Soviet adopted a new national budget system and initiated tax reform. Prior to this, all taxation had been implemented according to the Soviet Union's system. Parliament accepted a completely new tax package which included: personal income tax; profit tax (taxation of legal entities); social security tax; turnover tax; land use tax; and property tax. This tax package was implemented through procedures outlined in umbrella legislation covering all taxes and duties (see Shteinbuka and Kazaks, (1996) for a fuller discussion of these matters).

## Monetary and Financial Sector Developments

Beginning with the first budget of post-Soviet independent Latvia, adopted for 1991, the financial policy of the government may be characterized as a policy of fiscal prudence. In order to achieve macroeconomic stability, the Latvian government has implemented controls over budget expenditures, which have included the suspension of the indexing of salaries and social security payments, with the result that residents have fully borne the effects of inflation.

**Table 1.   Latvia: Basic Indicators of Economic Development 1993–96**

|  | 1993 | 1994 | 1995 | 1996 forecast |
|---|---|---|---|---|
|  | (growth rates in %) | | | |
| GDP at constant prices | −15.0 | 0.6 | −1.6 | 1.0 |
| Consumer prices | 109.1 | 35.9 | 25.0 | 17.8 |
|  | (in % of GDP, unless otherwise indicated) | | | |
| Deficit of state budget | 1.0 | −1.9 | −4.0 | −1.6 |
| External debt | 8.9 | 9.2 | 9.2 | 11.0 |
| Foreign trade balance |  | −6.9 | −11.5 | −13.0 |
| Current account |  | 5.5 | 0.7 | −0.5 |
| Unemployment (% end of period) | 5.3 | 6.5 | 6.6 | 7.2 |

*Source*:   Central Statistical Bureau, forecasts of Ministry of Economy, 1996. European Economy, Economic Reform Monitor No.1. Supplement C., May 1996.

Since 1993, Latvia has introduced a reasonably successful programme of economic stabilization and structural reforms. In 1994 GDP rose by 0.6 per cent, with most growth originating in the services, construction and forestry sectors. Whilst output has declined in agriculture and industry, services now account for 60 per cent of GDP, which is up from 39 per cent in 1991. Despite consumption and investment growth during the first quarter of 1995, demand contracted sharply during the latter half of the year following the April/May 1995 banking crisis. Real GDP declined 1.6 per cent in 1995, making Latvia the only Central and Eastern European country with negative economic growth in 1995 (see Table 1). Despite the monetary contraction which followed the banking crisis, further progress in controlling inflation has been limited. Although the government's inflationary target of 15 per cent has been exceeded, at 20.2 per cent in March 1996 Latvian inflation is the lowest among the Baltic States.

In July 1992, the Latvian rouble was made the sole legal tender for payment within Latvia. This was a necessary precondition for implementing an independent monetary policy. Successful financial and monetary policies made it possible to curtail the decline in GDP between 1992 and 1994, and to reduce inflation. Nevertheless, in the middle of 1995 a new financial and economic crisis ensued in

Latvia. One of the most telling signs of this crisis was the suspension of activities of a number of banks and their subsequent liquidation.

An analysis of the reasons behind the crisis reveals essential drawbacks in the economic structure of Latvia. Two principally different, parallel spheres of the national economy were illuminated. One was the 'old system' which was created under the socialist conditions of the command economy, with inefficient state-owned assets and outdated technology. The other, based on principles of private business, is still in the initial stages of development, even though it noticeably influences economic processes in the country. The 'old' economic system is predominantly industry-based and partly linked with agriculture and transport; whereas the 'new' system predominates in the sphere of trade, banking, finance and services. Obviously, this division should only be regarded as a convenient generalization with numerous exceptions. However, it does help to clarify a number of national economy processes which are so far insufficiently understood, including the financial and banking crisis of 1995.

The two spheres of the national economy have been moving in different directions. Since 1992, the state enterprise sector, with few exceptions, has been sinking into a deep economic crisis as its share of GDP continues to diminish. The indebtedness of state-owned enterprises, including large outstanding tax liabilities, is also growing at an increasing rate. Large amounts of raw materials and finished products remain unsold, with their total value unchanged over the past few years, amounting to approximately LVL 65–75 million (US$ 120–140 million). Furthermore, municipal public utility companies are also in a very difficult financial situation. Land reform is making slow but steady progress although there remains no official real estate market. In practice there are various distorted and disguised forms of this market, such as lease, rights of use, etc. (Davis, 1996).

Until recently, the crisis in the 'old' state enterprise sector was to a certain extent counterbalanced by the rapidly growing private sector. This largely explains the relatively low level of unemployment (6–7 per cent) and stability of the lat. If this were to have continued into the future, perhaps the private sector would have become the dominant part of the national economy, state-owned enterprises would be privatized and gradually cope with their problems, with all of this leading to accelerated economic growth. In fact the situation worsened, becoming more dramatic, complicated and resulting in an unexpected financial and banking crisis.

One of the reasons for this crisis was the clash between the rapid development of the private sector, and stagnation in the state and municipal sector. The increasing number of banks, the growth of their capital and assets, the increasing numbers of new firms and expansion of trade, was all gradually slowed down by the sluggish pace of privatization and land reform. Thus, it could be argued that whilst the 'old' sector of the national economy was decaying, the 'new' overheated. This situation may be illustrated by examining the relationships between companies and banks. Different categories of enterprises have contrasting relations with banks. Private businesses remain the main customers of banks and obtain the largest share of total loans, whilst the SOEs used hardly any credits. Their main means of survival becomes clear when examining the state budget.

In 1995, the forecast budget deficit of LVL 40 million, actually approached LVL 90 million (US$ 180 million), –4 per cent of GDP. Ministry of Economy (1996) data show that the major tax debtors were SOEs and other firms. Thus, the SOEs were credited by the state, and not the banks. The total amount of their tax debt exceeded the total amount of the budget deficit (Ministry of Economy, 1996).[3] Therefore, a deformed national financial structure has developed, where every week at treasury bill auctions the government drains the nation's credit resources in order to finance the budget deficit. Banks extend the remaining credit resources to private sector businesses at high interest rates. These businesses in turn evade taxes in order to survive and avoid bankruptcy. The lack of effective bankcruptcy legislation has enabled a number of enterprises to escape strict financial discipline. This lack of financial control has been partly responsible for the problem of inter-enterprise arrears and has resulted in major budgetary difficulties. The situation is particularly severe in the Latvian energy sector. This situation led to a halt in the growth and development of the private sector in Latvia at the end of 1995.

As a result, the state may have become a financial intermediary between banks and other investors. It borrows money at high interest rates and subsidizes SOEs in a covert way. Moreover, the debts incurred by SOEs are growing. An examination of this situation suggests that the recent financial crisis was not solely caused by banking or budget difficulties *per se*, but was also due to a crisis in the existing structure of the national economy, where a large, inert and inefficient state sector still plays a major role.[4] This chapter will return to some of these issues within the context of energy sector privatization and regulation (with particular reference to Latvenergo) in Latvia. The most important aspects of competition law and the main regulatory bodies regarding the public utilities and their functions in Latvia, are now discussed below.

## PUBLIC UTILITY REFORM AND REGULATION IN LATVIA: OVERVIEW OF COMPETITION POLICY AND UTILITY REGULATORY SYSTEM

Most prices for goods and services in Latvia have been liberalized for almost five years. Price liberalization was virtually completed at the end of 1992 and only a few administered prices remain, most importantly in the transport and energy sectors, but also as rents in public sector housing. Utility prices are administered by several different agencies. For example, heating prices are set by local governments and transport prices by the Ministry of Economy. Decisions on price increases are mainly based on cost calculations of the enterprise, consumers' ability to pay, and the profit margins of the enterprise. In cases where a proposed price increase is above 5 per cent, approval from the State Anti-Monopoly Committee (SAMC) must be obtained. There is some evidence of SOE price inflation based on unjustified price rises. The current approach is based on CPI + X (where the evaluation of X is not generally publicized) and may encourage cost-plus pricing behaviour of an inefficient sort; administratively entrenching an internal disincentive for cost reduction and introducing a system which, once established, is often difficult to dismantle.

It is in the area of energy supply, utilities and transport services, however, where natural monopolies operate within a complex infrastructure and competition is rather limited. These large monopolies have a dominant position in the domestic market and operate in a loosely regulated environment. As previously noted, there are relatively few regulatory and legislative control mechanisms governing Latvia's energy and public utilities. The most important aspects of competition law and the main regulatory bodies and their functions are discussed below.

## The Legal Framework

In Latvia, the 'Law of the Republic of Latvia on Competition and Restriction of Monopolies' (the so-called existing Law), passed in December 1991 and amended in 1993, provides the basic concepts of competition legislation and describes the rights and responsibilities of the major competition regulatory authority, the State Anti-Monopoly Committee. Currently, the 'New Draft Law on Competition and Restriction of Monopolies' and the law 'On the State Committees for Protection of Competition' are being prepared. These new drafts refer to market participants and any of their associations, as well as to state and municipal institutional activities subject to regulation as entrepreneurial activities. The so-called draft Law also refers to those natural and state monopolies which are currently not regulated by other laws. This law also includes foreign companies which are active in or could influence the Latvian market.

Both the exisiting and new draft Laws on competition cover all goods, services and sectors of the economy, with the exception of militiary production and intellectual property law. The laws have been drafted in accordance with the principles of Article 90(2) of the EC Treaty. Both the existing and new draft Laws on competition include a general prohibition of restrictive agreements among entrepreneurs, including vertical and horizontal agreements, if they distort competition. Both laws provide for the right of a competition institution to issue an order for those involved in competition law violation to stop this practice (special authority in the case of illegal mergers is not provided). In the event of failure to comply with the order, the State competition protection authority is allowed to impose a penalty on the institutions. The fined institutions have a right of appeal to the Latvian courts.

The draft Law includes provisions which correspond to Article 85(3) of the EC Treaty, e.g., it contains a general prohibition of abuse of dominance; it defines (with regard to mergers which cover the establishment of control and joint ventures) and provides for prior notification within a merger process, or if participants have a turnover which exceeds the stated minimum amount. The existing Law provides for notification if the merger has resulted in control over at least 25 per cent of a particular market. The draft Law provides the criterion that the total previous annual turnover of the participants of a merger should be at least LVL 1 million. Both the existing Law and the draft Law state that a merger may only be implemented if the State competition authority has given it the go-ahead. In all other cases, the Latvian Register of Enterprises is prohibited from registering the new market entrant.

Furthermore, the draft Law provides for the prohibition of mergers which may result in the dominant position of any market participant or in the prevention, restriction or distortion of competition in a particular market. It does not provide for any exemptions.

## General Competition Policy Procedures

As previously noted, in Latvia competition legislation is controlled by the State Anti-Monopoly Committee (SAMC), which is supervised by the Ministry of Economy. The SAMC and its chairperson were nominated by Resolution of the Council of Ministers in November 1992. The new draft Law provides for the reorganization of the existing SAMC to form the State Committee of Competition Protection, within which a Competition Board will act. The Competition Board will make all decisions regarding violations of competition law; and its decisions may be overruled only by the Latvian Appeal Court. The draft Law also provides that the members of the Competition Board be nominated by the Saeima for five-year terms.

Both the existing and draft Laws provide for the following rights of the SAMC:

- to require and request from enterprises the necessary information for effective competition control (including commercially secret information);
- to require written explanations from an enterprise's management related to any inspection or query; and
- to require 'economic grounds' for cases where a monopoly increases the price of an essential good.

According to the Law, enterprise officials, state and municipal institutions are responsible for submitting the required information within 5–10 working days and for allowing the SAMC's officials to familiarize themselves with the enterprise's documentation.

The existing Law allows the SAMC the right to impose a penalty (fine) on the guilty party of up to 10 per cent of its total income, if the order to cease monopoly or unfair practice is ignored. The draft Law extends this right to include cases of prohibited mergers, abuse of dominance and failure to comply with SAMC orders and allows penalties of up to 10 per cent of the net turnover of the previous financial year. Neither of the laws contains prescription or interim periods or provides for business secrecy, outside of the Law On Civil Service, which applies to the public sector. The European Bank for Reconstruction and Development's *Transition Report* (EBRD, 1995), in assessing the state of legal reforms in transition economies, has assigned Latvia 2 points on a scale of 1–4 where 4 is both the highest standard and score. According to the EBRD's assessment, Latvia's progress in promoting the extensiveness and effectiveness of legal rules on investment is unclear; legal advice difficult to obtain and this imposes constraints on creating investment vehicles. Furthermore, judicial and administrative support of the law is rudimentary and its administration deficient (EBRD, 1995).

## State Aid, Competition Policy and Regulation

The situation with respect to existing state aid was briefly alluded to above. However, with the exception of the agricultural sector, priority is given to free market forces. Although some small amounts of agricultural support are provided, these do not contravene Latvia's Free Trade Agreement with the EU, as agriculture is exempt from this. Future state aid will be constrained by the current budget crisis and Latvia's obligations under the EU Free Trade Agreement and later by the Europe Agreement and World Trade Organization (WTO) conventions. The Ministry of Finance, which is responsible for state aid matters, has recently set-up a State Aid Surveillance Commission to monitor developments.

Overall, the activities of the local authorities to promote greater competition as required under Decision No.314 of the Council of Ministers of 5th August 1992 on the 'Functions of Competition Promotion and Restriction of Monopolies to Be Delegated to Local Authorities' have also been poorly implemented and are generally ineffective. Practically nothing has changed since 1990 concerning the promotion of competition (e.g., in terms of encouraging a competitive tendering scheme for certain services or inputs), or the quality of work and services provided, whilst utility prices have in general risen faster than the rate of inflation. Competition is further impeded by duties imposed by local authorities, tax or payment privileges, order of distribution of state subsidies for agriculture, and the granting of government-guaranteed loans, etc. The lack of transparency in allocating contracts for public works has also impeded the development of competition in the public utility sector.

## THE POLITICAL ECONOMY OF TELECOMMUNICATIONS SECTOR REFORM AND REGULATION

The 'Law on Telecommunications' (10.05.1993) and the law 'On Regulation of Entrepreneurial Activity in the Power Sector' envisage that price, tariff and service quality considerations should be regulated by the Council of Telecommunications Tariffs (TTC). The main tasks of these institutions are the elaboration of tariff calculation methods in accordance with EU requirements, and to ensure transparency in tariff formation. In the telecommunications field, the regulating functions of the TTC are supervised by the Ministry of Transport. Commercial activities are carried out by Lattelekom. Lattelekom is a joint venture between the Republic of Latvia (Ministry of Transport) which owns 51 per cent of the company's equity and a joint venture group called Tilts Communication which holds a 49 per cent share. Tilts Communication's share is distributed among the group as follows: Cable and Wireless (63 per cent), Telecom Finland (27 per cent) and the International Finance Corporation (10 per cent).

Under the so-called 'Umbrella Agreement' of January 1994 between the Republic of Latvia and Tilts Communication and within the existing competition law framework, Lattelekom has been granted exclusive rights, in accordance with the Law on Telecommunications, to develop, administer and operate the public telecommunications network for twenty years, in order to provide Latvia with a modern, new communications network.[5] The 'Umbrella Agreement' requires Tilts Communication to provide organizational modernization, managerial expertise, buying power and technical assistance to upgrade the physical network and restructure the corporate organization of Lattelekom. A new corporate structure has been introduced and substantial investment has been made in the network infrastructure. Tilts Communication committed itself to invest US$ 160 million in Lattelekom over a three-year period in return for an equity stake of 49 per cent. Between January 1994 and 1995, Tilts invested US$ 89 million and owned 30 per cent of the equity in Lattelekom.

The telecommunications terminal equipment market is completely liberalized and telephone, telegraph, data transmission equipment, faxes and private networks are provided in the free market. All terminal equipment requires compulsory certification from Lattelekom to ensure they meet the Latvian public network safety standards. Although Lattelekom has been granted some exclusive rights to provide basic telecommunications services, all other types of services, e.g., the establishment of a special state network and a public mobile radio telecommunications network, usage of satellites etc., are legally only possible after receiving a licence from the department of Communication of the Ministry of Transport. However, Lattelekom itself set the regulations controlling the acquisition of a licence, e.g., to create a public mobile network or connections to it. Any enterprise with a licence issued by the Ministry of Transport is allowed to install and use combined satellite systems. This obviously places Lattelekom in a strong market position *vis-à-vis* new market entrants.

The exclusive right granted to Lattelekom to provide basic telecommunications services until 2013 appears very generous compared to the policies proposed by the European Union. EU rules do not permit basic monopolies after 2003 and if Latvia expects to join the EU prior to 2013, it will have to adjust its legislation accordingly. In any case, pursuing a protracted period of monopoly control may in the long run be detrimental to customers. Throughout Europe, there are plenty of examples where liberalization through the introduction of competition and technical change has delivered greater benefits to consumers.

## Regulation of the Telecommunications Industry

The Law on Telecommunications, which became effective on 10th May, 1993, established the TTC. The TTC is an independent body of seven people appointed for a period of five years. The TTC operates in the context of a Tariff Policy which, whilst regulating prices, also secures a commercially reasonable rate of return for Lattelekom. The regulatory responsibilities of the TTC are to:

- set tariffs and rates for basic telecommunications services;
- review complaints from telecommunications users on the application of tariffs and their rates for basic telecommunications services; and
- submit recommendations to Lattelekom on the application of tariffs for basic telecommunications services.

The Law on Telecommunications defines the rights, obligations and responsibilities of telecommunications users, network operators and State institutions which are associated with the administration and exploitation of telecommunications networks, connection to the public telecommunications services, as well as State control and supervision of the use and allocation of radio frequencies. Furthermore, the law states that Lattelekom will operate under conditions of natural monopoly as defined by the Law 'On Restriction of Competition and Monopolies' (03.12.1991), whereby the tariffs of the basic telecommunications services that it provides are regulated by the TTC.

## Regulation of the Network (interconnection)

As previously noted, Lattelekom is allowed to propose interconnection policies subject to the approval of the TTC. However, the notion of applying a 'commercially viable rate' (see 'Law on Telecommunications') for interconnection is ambiguous as no methodology is prescribed in either the Umbrella Agreement of 1994 or the revised Phase 1 Tariff Agreement of July 1996. The Open Network Provision (ONP) Directive of the EU clearly intends that national regulators adopt a cost-oriented system for interconnection, based on the principle of a cost-related access element together with a capacity-based component to account for the cost to the operator of having the interconnecting traffic coursing through its system. Latvian telecoms policy could move towards an 'equal access' basis utilizing specified essential interfaces by the date at which Lattelekom's monopoly ends. The specification of essential interfaces avoids the problem of interconnection points by side-stepping the virtual and co-location issues, and often improves the quality of the incumbent network as the connecting network is usually digital and more up-to-date. These interconnecting agreements should be transparent and contracted between competing parties on a non-discriminatory basis. As will become clear, this, unfortunately, is probably not always the case in Latvia.

Provided that all laws concerning land ownership and lease, etc., are observed, state institutions and the telecommunications organization have the right, where necessary, to install telecommunications lines and distribution equipment within the boundaries of state, local government and private property. However, the Law on Telecommunications does not provide the right for individuals to set up private networks which may compete with Lattelekom. Private telecommunications networks may only be used by the individuals themselves, and must not contravene the exclusive rights of Lattelekom. However, as previously noted, according to the Law on Telecommunications, Lattelekom has the authority to provide interconnection services to other licenced public telecommunications operators at a so-called 'commercially viable' rate. Key issues which remain unresolved in Latvia concerning any such interconnection agreement include the following:

- whether interconnecting parties would need to bear the costs associated with full direct costs, consequential costs and overheads of interconnection; furthermore, whether the capital employed would be regarded at the rate of the overall cost of capital;
- whether competitors would be required to contribute to Lattelekom's universal service obligations by additional interconnection fees; and
- interconnection points would probably be offered at appropriate geographical locations and network architectural points subject to availability, network integrity and national security. Such interconnection points may be either co-located with the basic network or remote. Probably competitors will have to bear the cost of bringing their network to interconnection points.

The commercial negotiations concerning interconnection are conducted between Lattelekom and its competitors. Although according to the 'Law on Telecommunications' these should be non-discriminatory between competitors, this situation significantly strengthens the bargaining power of Lattelekom in such negotiations. The Ministry of Transport does have the right to intervene if, after 60 days, agreement is not reached between negotiating parties. However, this power does not amount to effective regulation of interconnection, transparency and open network access along the lines of the EU's ONP Directive.

The 1994 Umbrella Agreement proposed a tiered system of discounts for all customers switching to digital services. Residential users received additional benefits of free local charges during the first year. It is only possible to confirm the relative success of this policy in terms of either encouraging digital migration or promoting new connections through the subsequent experience of recent net connections to the network. The data services branch of Lattelekom (supported by Telekom Finland) has recently installed an optical fibre data transmission network with a capacity of 155 megabytes per second. The optical fibre network connects Riga, Tallinn, Helsinki and Stockholm, although only the Helsinki–Stockholm connections were operating to full capacity at the time of writing. The introduction of such a high-speed network in Latvia could open new co-operation and communication opportunities for foreign business and entrepreneurs in Latvia.

## Regulation of Prices

The development of Lattelekom represents the largest investment project in the history of Latvia. New digital switches have been installed in Riga, Cesis and Ventspils and the digital network's capacity has expanded (connecting around 100,000 customers). The waiting list for a telephone line fell by 28 per cent (37,278) and Latvia's telephone density rate of 28 lines per 100 people is one of the highest in Central and Eastern Europe (CEE) (Lattelekom, 1995). The fibre-optic network has been expanded and the number of new payphones has increased rapidly, generating revenues above those forecast. Capital expenditure on the oldest parts of the analogue system has also grown, amounting to LVL 3 million in 1995. Tariffs since 1994 have been rising steadily in the telecommunications sector. Although tariffs were raised for users of the digital system, the number of outgoing calls in the public network during 1995 grew by 17.6 per cent (domestically by 22.4 per cent and on international lines by 3.7 per cent) (Ministry of Economy, 1996). These figures are based on Lattelekom submissions and recommendations to the TTC. Table 2 shows tariffs for basic telephone services as of July 1996 as part of Lattelekom and the TTC's Phase 1 Tariff Agreement, reached in May 1996 and later revised in July 1996 (Phase 2 of the Tariff Agreement was scheduled to begin on 01.01.1997 and end on 30.06.1997).

Rural residents and some pensioners receive a discount of 25 per cent and 40 per cent respectively on basic subscription charges from Lattelekom. There is no explicit reference in either the Umbrella Agreement of 1994 or the revised Phase 1 Tariff Agreement as to whether these discounts form part of a general policy of universal service. The implied reasoning appears to be the promotion of the needs of low users, whilst widening access to the network, or both. The top line comparisons of tariffs presented in Table 2 suggest that business users are paying too much and residential users too little for basic telephone services. The proposed rural resident and pensioner discounts which reduce the monthly subscription charges, will probably exacerbate this divergence.

The likely effects of the 'time of day' discounts during peak call periods will be to increase the volume of calls in those periods. This may encourage the low value users' calls to occupy more of the Latvian network in peak periods, to the detriment of higher value business users. More generally, and as a means of promoting a more transparent policy of universal service, the introduction of a 'light user scheme' would allow provision for reasonable and affordable access to the network as well as affordable usage. Table 3 illustrates the extent to which business rates are more expensive than residential rates for comparable access services. These ratios demonstrate the degree of residential subsidy by business connections.

**Table 2.   Phase 1 Tariffs for Basic Telephone Services from 1st July 1996**

| Subscription Charge | LVL | Period |
|---|---|---|
| Residential | 1,00 (discounts as offered by Lattelekom may be applied) | Per month, per line |
| Business | 6.00 | Per month, per line |
| Local Call Charges All customers:- if Lattelekom charge on a usage basis | 0.012 | Per minute |
| if Lattelekom do not charge according to usage | 1.00 | Per month, for each subscriber number |
| | This fixed monthly charge for local calls will have the following staged introduction: | |
| 01/07/98–31/12/96 | LVL 0.50 per month for every subscriber number | |
| 01/01/97–31/12/97 | LVL 0.75 per month for every subscriber number | |
| 01/01/98– | LVL 1.00 per month for every subscriber number | |
| National Call Charge All customers: | 0.08 | Per minute |
| Calls to mobile phone All customers: | 0.33 | Per minute |
| International Call Charges All customers: | | |
| Zone 1 | 0.20 | Per minute |
| Zone 2 | 0.58 | Per minute |
| Zone 3 | 0.60 | Per minute |
| Zone 4 | 0.83 | Per minute |
| Zone 5 | 0.90 | Per minute |
| Zone 6 | 1.00 | Per minute |
| Zone 7 | 1.10 | Per minute |

*Source*:   Lattelekom reports, 1996.

**Table 3.   Ratio of Business and Residential Telephone Tariffs**

| | 1994 | 1995 | 1996 |
|---|---|---|---|
| Connections | 7 | 7 | 7 |
| Connections over 40 per cent discounted residential rates | 11 | 11 | 11 |
| Rentals | 7 | 7 | 7 |
| Rentals over 25 per cent discounted residential rates | 10 | 10 | 10 |
| Rentals over 25 per cent discounted residential rates | 12 | 12 | 12 |

*Source*:   Calculated from Lattelekom Annual Reports, 1994, 1995, 1996.

In nominal terms, the residential access market appears relatively inexpensive when tariffs are expressed in US$ terms. Furthermore, per minute usage tariff rates are low, ranging from 2 to 4 US cents for local calls and 4 to 15 US cents for trunk calls. However, the overall structure of the new tariffs as part of the Phase 1 Tariff Agreement raises doubts as to whether the former can recover its directly attributed costs of access and usage. This observation may only be substantiated in respect of the tariff data provided; without access to the financial accounts of Lattelekom this is more difficult to place in an overall context. If Lattelekom's residential customers are generating insufficient revenue to cover the costs of providing residential access and usage, the problem will be further compounded by the real reductions in tariffs brought about by the domestic rate of inflation during the price policy period. Between 1997 and 1999 the price cap formula ensures that tariffs falling within the basket are to increase by no more than the rate of price inflation.

Regarding Phase 2 (1997 till end-1999) of the Tariff Agreement, each regulated monopoly item will be limited in terms of price cap increases (between 01.01.1997 and 30.06.1997) by the following formula:

$$Pt = Et*I$$

where

$Pt$ = Proposed tariff (Lats) for service;
$Et$ = Existing tariff (US$) for service; and
$I$ = Change in the Consumer Price Index (per cent) during previous December to December period.

The price cap formula sets the overall weighted maximum increase in an identified basket of basic service tariff items. If Lattelekom proposes to increase the tariff for any item by more than the above formula allows, then additional documentation will be required as justification. The TTC will consider a Lattelekom proposal in the light of the additional documentation, the Latvian economic environment, progress in telecoms modernization and the Telecommunications Tariff Policy. At the time of writing, it was impossible to validate the scope of the price cap in terms of which services fall within the tariff basket, as Appendix 1 of the Tariff Agreement outlining these matters was not generally available.

Lattelekom and the TTC have agreed that, as of 1st July 1997, a price cap control based on a Tariff Basket concept will be introduced. This is quite common in Europe because it encourages the operator to improve efficiency, is relatively straightforward to calculate, (in theory) removes political interference from tariff setting and focuses regulatory control on those services of highest public concern. The Tariff Agreement is intended to provide enough flexibility for Lattelekom to respond to changing market conditions and to enable continued investment within the framework of a price cap mechanism of tariff regulatory control. Perhaps most importantly, it is intended to begin the process of removing cross-subsidy between services, although this is not an explicit function of the price cap.

The price cap formula sets out the overall weighted maximum increase in an identified basket of basic service items. Tariffs for the individual items within the basket may be altered by any percentage with the proviso that the weighted average percentage increase is no more than that calculated from the formula above. The weighting coefficients of the individual items are calculated from the respective revenue contribution from the basket items in the previous year's audited accounts. The formula for determining the weighted average increase is as follows:

$$I > \sum \left[ \frac{AR(i)}{TR(b)} \times \frac{PT(i) - ET(i)}{ET(i)} \times 100 \right]$$

where

$I$     = Changes in CPI in the previous period from December to December;
$AR(i)$  = Revenue in previous year's accounts for basket item $i$;
$TR(b)$  = Total revenue of all basket items in previous year's audited accounts;
$PT(i)$  = Proposed new tariff of basket item $I$; and
$ET(i)$  = Existing tariff of basket item $i$.

Although it is difficult to assess the efficacy of the proposed price cap formula, it is unlikely to stimulate efficiency improvements in the network *vis-à-vis* the transference of costs to retail customers brought about by the effects of general price inflation alone. Allowing regulated tariffs to rise by the rate of inflation may encourage cost pass-through over efficiency gains. Thus, cost-plus pricing behaviour by Lattelekom could continue, avoiding the necessary efficiency and restructuring adjustment costs that might have been required in a more competitive domestic market. Moreover, in the context of Lattelekom's network, infrastructural and service modernization programme, the impact of currency devaluation on the costs of imported expertise and technology are likely to be unsystematically higher for Lattelekom, compared to the economy as a whole.

## A Review of the Telecommunications Regulatory System

In common with other CEE countries, implementing effective regulation and competition-enhancing policies in the telecommunications sector appears to be a very difficult balance to achieve. In Latvia, the telecommunications network strategy has been: (i) to maximize the role of the state telephone company, Lattelekom, as the primary vehicle for telecoms development; and (ii) to encourage additional investment and development through competition in other parts of the sector where potential returns are sufficient to support more than one player. However, too much competition may inhibit the effectiveness of Lattelekom, whilst too little may fail to stimulate the desired acceleration of development. In the case of Latvia, in terms of the existing regulatory framework the balance is tipped more in favour of Lattelekom than new entrants. This is also true of Poland and Hungary, where alternative investors have been wary and thus a far smaller investment impact than was expected has taken place in the sector.[6] This is all the more acute in the case of Lattelekom, where Tilts Communication has insisted upon exclusive rights as a condition of investment and where the problem of achieving the right balance between monopoly rights and competitive concessions becomes crucially important. The next section moves on to consider the political economy of energy utility privatization and regulation in Latvia during transition.

## THE POLITICAL ECONOMY OF ENERGY SECTOR REFORM AND REGULATION

### The Structure of the Energy Sector in Latvia

The Latvian Ministry of Economy operates in co-operation with the state and municipal institutions. The state minister of energy in the Ministry of Economy is politically accountable to the Saeima on state policy performance in the energy sector and has the right, without any special approval, to represent the ministry and give direction within this area of competency to any employee or institution of the ministry, as well as to the managers under the Ministry's control. The Ministry of Economy has the following main responsibilities to the energy sector: (i) to develop the economic regulation mechanisms necessary for the rational use of energy resources, including domestic fuels and renewables; (ii) to introduce a methodology for price and tariff setting to be approved within the specific area of competence; (iii) to propose draft laws and legislative acts that regulate the activities of energy producers under conditions of natural mono-poly; and (iv) to consider proposals to create state reserves for fuel and oil products.

To achieve these aims, the Ministry of Economy created the Department of Energy. Some of the ministry's functions have been delegated to the Latvian Energy Agency (LEA), which is both supervised by and works with the Ministry of Economy. The main function of the LEA is the development and implementation of energy strategy and policy in Latvia. The Anti-Monopoly Committee has no direct influence on the energy companies, but it is responsible for ensuring company compliance with the 'Law of the Republic of Latvia on Competition and Restriction of Monopoly'. One of the main tasks of this committee is to supervise business relations among different monopoly enterprises within the energy sector.

Most of the enterprises within the energy sector are organized as joint-stock companies (JSC) and enjoy a monopoly in their area of business. The most important of these energy enterprises are:

- 'Latvenergo', a 100 per cent state-owned monopoly supplying electric power and largely under the direct control of the Latvian Privatization Agency. Latvenergo's activities include fuel and material reserve provision, power importations, export and transit and a district heating supply monopoly in Riga and some of the largest Latvian cities (around 25 per cent of total heat supply). Distribution to final consumers is provided through seven regional enterprises (also under ministerial control). Latvia Siltums provides supply to smaller conurbations from heat-only boilers. Several small municipalities now have their own heating utility. Since 1990, Latvenergo has undergone several transformations until it acquired its current form of a state-owned joint-stock company (JSC).

- 'Latvia Gas' is a gas supply monopoly which provides the regional distribution and delivery of natural and liquefied gas to customers, as well as operating the main gas pipelines and the underground storage facility 'Incukalns',[7] unique in the Baltic States.
- 'Ventspils Nafta', which is Latvia's largest trans-ship terminal to the Baltic sea coast for oil and oil products.
- 'Latvia Oil' is one of the largest companies which, together with a number of private structures, supplies oil products to Latvia for domestic use.

All shares in the JSCs belong to the state, with the main shareholder being the State Property Fund. In 1995, 32.5 per cent of the shares in Latvia Gas were privatized. In February 1996, Latvenergo and Ventspils Nafta were also included in the the Latvian government's general list of enterprises to be privatized.

Due to the slow progress with privatization and doubts as to the safety of some energy installations in Latvia, foreign investment in the energy sector has been limited.[8] Most financial assistance has come from western European governments and international financial institutions offering funds for the restructuring of the sector. At the time of writing, there exists no national energy programme in Latvia and all of the Saeima political parties have simply developed a position, rather than an energy policy or programme of their own. Although in 1989 an energy programme was being developed, it was abandoned by 1990. There has been very little institutional and overall management change in the energy sector; merely a series of re-evaluations of the existing organization and the execution of new versions.

To date, the development of energy policies in Latvia has acquired the character of sectoral programmes, in that they focus narrowly on increasing total consumption and regional changes that are conducted on the basis of the often limited information available and necessary to the particular sector. Presently, most energy sector planning takes place at the state level, using low- or medium-quality data. However, planning is done at the consumer and distributor levels which are partially privatized. Nonetheless, this does not adequately compensate for the lack of a national energy strategy, since their activities are based on other basic statistical data and experience. The implementation of existing sector-specific legislation, for example the Energy Supply Regulation Board, has also been greatly delayed. All of the aforementioned factors have combined to delay the development of the energy sector in Latvia.

## Latvenergo and the Electric Power Sector

As previously noted, the main electricity producer and supplier in Latvia is the state joint-stock company Latvenergo, which supplies (produces and imports when necessary) more than 99 per cent of Latvia's electricity (with an output of 3890 million kWh in 1995). Latvenergo is also the main producer and supplier of heat energy in the cities of Riga, Liepaja, Salaspils and Olaine, where 4.95 million Gcal were delivered to consumers in 1995. Most of the power generation is provided by two medium-sized thermal plants and three hydroelectric stations on the Daugava River. Since 1965, the Latvian power system has operated as part of an integrated network with the power systems of the neighbouring countries. The power grid of the Baltic States is now controlled by a dispatch centre located in Riga.

Private sector involvement in energy supply has been limited to the development of local and regional heat boiler houses, energy sector service companies and small hydro and wind stations. Latvia Gas is the main supplier of gas to Latvenergo (and is in the process of privatizing 32.5 per cent of its shares). Approximately 50 per cent of Latvia's power supply is provided by renewable hydro resources, and is thus comparatively 'green'; but hydroelectric expansion is still politically unpopular.[9]

In 1995 electric power consumption declined 0.5 per cent from the previous year to 6,228 million kWh (of which 4,780 million kWh were delivered to end-users, with the balance accounted for by losses and production requirements). In order to satisfy this demand, 36 per cent of Latvia's electric power requirements in 1995 were purchased from neighbouring countries (868 million kWh from Lithuania – the Ignalina nuclear power plant; 861 million kWh from Russia, and 528 million from Estonia – the oil shale power plants) and 1 per cent from other domestic producers. 1995 purchases from neighbouring countries were substantially higher than in the previous year, as the result of a significant decrease in the Daugava River. Latvia's pattern of final energy demand is similar to that of Estonia and Lithuania. Around 40 per cent of the power supplied to end-users is consumed by industry, 31 per cent by commercial and government institutions, 24 per cent by households and 5 per cent by the agricultural sector. In describing the structure of electric power consumption in Latvia in the 1990s, it should be noted that there was a significant decline in the agricultural sector's power consumption. Its relative share has decreased from 16.5 per cent in 1990 to the current level of 5 per cent. The main reason for this is the restructuring taking place in the agricultural sector (the transition from collective farms to a private family farming structure) (see Davis, 1996). Whilst in most cases the aforementioned consumers' share of electric power consumption has declined, it has significantly increased in the service sector.

As previously noted, the problem of inter-enterprise arrears is particularly severe in the energy sector. As energy suppliers have been unable to obtain payments from their customers, they have incurred arrears to their suppliers (mainly Gazprom in Russia). The Latvian government has had to intervene by making payments on behalf of importers in order to guarantee the continuation of energy supply for the country. Six of the seven large power and heat stations belonging to Latvenergo may be fuelled by both natural gas and heavy oil (mazut). However, due to the rapid increase in the price of natural gas, Latvenergo has shifted its fuel structure for power generation towards the increased consumption of heavy oil.[10]

## Energy Price Regulation

In accordance with Regulations No.185 of the Cabinet of Ministers (21.11.95) energy prices and tariffs are determined as follows:

- electric power purchase and sales prices – by the Cabinet of Ministers;
- thermal energy and hot water tariffs – by municipalities; and
- natural gas and liquefied gas prices – by the Ministry of Economy.

Other energy resource prices are determined by the market. An Energy Regulation Board is in the process of being established to determine the prices and tariffs of electrical power, thermal power and natural gas. It is thus too early to assess its functions and performance in energy price regulation. With the increase in the price of electrical energy purchased from other countries (on average from LVL 0.0116/kWh in 1995 to 0.0131/kWh in March 1996), as well as with increased capital and production costs, electrical energy sales prices have grown. In conformity with Regulations No.299 of the Cabinet of Ministers of October 10th, 1995 'On Electrical Energy Sales Prices', a levelling of electrical power tariffs has been approved (see Table 4).

**Table 4.   Power Tariffs in Latvia from July 1st, 1996 (exc. VAT)**

| | Time independent | Night | | Day | | |
|---|---|---|---|---|---|---|
| Household | 0.0285[1] | | 0.019[1] | | 0.031[1] | |
| Other, load< 60 kW | 0.028[1] | 0.023[2] | 0.019[1] | 0.015[2] | 0.0331[1] | 0.029[2] |
| Other, load 60–400 kW | 0.025[1] | 0.022[2] | 0.019[1] | 0.015[2] | 0.029[1] | 0.025[2] |
| Other, load> 400 kW | 0.020[1] | 0.016[3] | 0.015[1] | 0.014[3] | 0.024[1] | 0.0195[3] |

*Source*:   HBS, Oko-Institut, FFU (1996).
*Notes*:
[1]  Tariff, connection with 0.4 kV line;
[2]  Tariff, connection with 6; 10; 20 kV line; and
[3]  Tariff, connection with 110 kV and more kV line.

As part of its overall energy sector objectives, the government introduced (1st July, 1996) ten new electricity power tariffs to cover the costs of Latvenergo's operations and including a reasonable profit from invested capital, whilst making the tariff setting and pricing procedures more transparent (see Table 4). Large consumers, mainly industrial complexes using more than 60 kW, pay a stepped tariff which is load-dependent. Fuel prices (particularly oil imports) are established at market (border price) rates. The retail price of electrical energy has increased on average by 40 per cent over the period 1995 to 1996.

In the industrialized market economies of the EU and the USA, industrial electricity tariff rates are between 45 and 55 per cent of those for households. For example, in the EU, electricity tariffs average 7 US cents per kWh for large industrial users and 15 US cents per kWh for households (both including indirect taxes). In Latvia, although tariff charges are not inverted (i.e., charges to industrial users are not above those to households), they are very close to parity (see Table 4). Thus, as households are usually more expensive to supply than industrial consumers per unit of electrical energy (due to the higher distribution costs to households and the fact that they contribute much of the peak-load demand, which is normally supplied by generation capacity with the highest marginal costs), it is reasonable to conclude that electricity tariffs in Latvia do not reflect the true economic costs of generation and that distribution is inefficient.

During the 1995/1996 heating season, thermal energy tariffs fluctuated from LVL 4.24 to LVL 28.74 per Gcal (3.66 to 24.78 LVL/MWh, including 18 per cent VAT). However, during the 1994/1995 heating season, tariffs ranged from 6.18 to 18.73 LVL per Gcal (5.33 to 16.15 LVL/KWh). These tariff fluctuations are the result of some regional municipalities setting thermal energy tariffs that were lower than those calculated, and covering the difference using other income resources.

The price of natural gas is determined by contracts between the state joint-stock company Latvia Gas and the Russian natural gas supplier Gazprom, which is the only supplier of natural gas to Latvia. These natural gas supply contracts are signed annually. The sales price for natural gas is currently around LVL 58.80 per thousand n.m$^3$ (excluding VAT) with the exception of households and cars. The price of natural gas sales to inhabitants is LVL 85 per thousand n.m$^3$ or LVL 0.68 per person per month where a gas meter is not installed. In Latvia, the market prices for all kinds of oil products are not regulated. Until June 1st, 1996, petrol sales prices ranged between LVL 0.18 to LVL 0.21 per litre (including an excise tax of LVL 0.04 per litre). Since then, Amendments to the 'Law On The Excise Tax' have been introduced (01.06.1996), the result of which has been a significant increase in the retail price of oil products, excluding mazut. The price of solid fuel (coal, peat and firewood) is regulated by the market. Table 5 shows the costs of the main energy resources and sales prices determined by the monopolies in 1995.

**Table 5.    Costs of the Main Energy Resources and Sales Prices Determined
by the Monopolies in 1995**

| Producer | Energy resource | Measure | Costs | Price | Difference in LVLs |
|---|---|---|---|---|---|
| 'Latvia Gas' | Natural gas | LVL/ 1,000 m$^3$ | 51.38 | 58.64 | + 7.26 |
| | Liquefied Natural Gas | LVL/ ton | 275.70 | 251.36 | −25.34 |
| 'Latvenergo' | Electricity | LVL/ kWh | 0.0173 | 0.0174 | + 0.0001 |
| | Heat | LVL/ Gcal | 12.94 | 12.18 | − 0.76 |
| | | LVL/ MWh | 11.16 | 10.50 | −0.66 |

In Latvia, all costs are included in the energy prices, including investment for the renovation of equipment. However, Table 5 shows that the sales prices of LPG and heating in 1995 did not cover costs. During 1995, LPG was subsidized by natural gas, although this did not correspond with official government policy in the energy sector.

## A Review of Energy Sector Regulation

As in most formerly centrally planned economies, electricity tariffs in Latvia were very heavily subsidized and thus are politically much more difficult to raise. Therefore, although some progress has been made in raising tariffs, further price and tariff rationalization will be difficult to introduce in Latvia whilst a coalition of consumers, politicians and trades unions opposed to price increases remains strong and influential. However, establishing electricity and gas tariffs which reflect the true economic costs remains one of the government's chief energy policy goals. Electricity consumers must, in the future, make current consumption decisions based on the knowledge that prevailing tariffs reflect the true economic costs of energy production. Nonetheless, Latvia's energy utilities remain relatively attractive to domestic and especially foreign investors.

More generally, the government should facilitate private and local initiatives in the development of energy generation and distribution services (e.g., by encouraging competitive tendering, contracting out for service provision); by enforcing transparent pricing rules, the publication and dissemination of public utility data; by tackling the divergence between the drafting and implementation of legislation (i.e., tougher anti-monopoly laws are needed); and improve the economic environment so as to address the lack of investor confidence in the energy utilities' privatization process.

As previously noted, the national power utility Latvenergo, Ventspils Nafta and the state electro-technical enterprise VEF have also been transferred for privatization. There has been a lot of controversy concerning the wisdom of privatizing Latvenergo and Ventspils Nafta, as both are considered to be extremely profitable for the state. It has been argued that if these companies were sold at their true value, any domestic bidder would be priced out of the bidding process (EIU, 1996). These political considerations, together with the lack of confidence in the Riga Stock Market following the banking crisis, will probably delay the privatization of the energy utilities.

To discuss these issues in more depth, a case study of the political economy considerations concerning the privatization and regulation of Latvia's energy utilities is presented below.

## POLITICAL ECONOMY AND FINANCIAL CONSTRAINTS ON ENERGY SECTOR PRIVATIZATION

### Political Economy Constraints on Energy Sector Privatization

The roots of the politically pervasive, post-independence Russo-phobia in Latvia are deep. Latvia has the smallest proportion of ethnic residents among the Baltic States; around 53 per cent of the population is ethnically Latvian, the rest is made up of Russians and other former Soviet Union (FSU) nationals. The issue of citizenship in Latvia has assumed the greatest political significance among the Baltic States. For example, in October 1991, just two months after achieving independence, the Latvian Supreme Council declared a need for citizenship to take a form that would 'eliminate the consequences of occupation and annexation of Latvia by the Soviet Union' by distinguishing 'the community of citizens of the (interwar) Republic of Latvia from the great number of Soviet citizens' who had taken up residence in Latvia (Dmitriev, 1996).[11] Although the post-independence years in Latvia may be characterized by reasonably peaceful political change, by 1993 the Latvian Popular Front government led by Ivars Godmanis was weakened due to a number of ministerial resignations, economic recession and deep unpopularity at home. It split into two increasingly xenophobic political factions: Constitution (Satversme) and Homeland (Teversme). The current government is a coalition between the Latvian Way (a right-of-centre party with a strong free market orientation) and a centre-left party, the National Union of Economists (formerly part of Harmony, a group of left-wing parties) led by Andris Skele.

As previously noted, the government intends to carry out the privatization of large state monopolies as soon as possible. This process is at an early stage and has led to much political conflict and debate. For example, the government is being widely criticized in Parliament and through the press for seeking to privatize the government oil enterprise, Ventspils Nafta, and the power utility Latvenergo, because they are seen as being vital to national security and economic independence. Furthermore, the LPA has recently received four applications from potential strategic investors to privatize the Latvian Gas company. As previously noted, the applicants included the Russian Gazprom consortium, Ruhrgas of Germany,

Gaz de France, and the Latvia-based Parekss Banka. The Russian Gas company Gazprom and German consortium Ruhrgas, and Preusen Electra have been successful in the bid for the right to acquire shares (each being allowed to purchase up to 16.25 per cent of the shares) in Latvia Gas. However, the state will still retain a 66 per cent stake in the enterprise. In the context of privatization, it may be argued (as is the convention in the UK) that a firm with up to 49 per cent state ownership is considered to be privately owned (and its output should thus be considered private), Latvia Gas therefore remains essentially state-owned. This calls into question the government's degree of commitment to further privatization. The competitive gains which should be realized through privatization – for example, better corporate governance, strong demonstration effects, an improved market-oriented business culture, a more efficient utilization of resources and the attraction of more foreign investors – may be retarded.

Government policy in the energy sector is also influenced by public organizations such as: the Association of Heat Companies; the Latvian Society of Electric Engineers; the Small Energy Foundation (an organization supporting the development of small and alternative energy producers); and a number of non-governmental organizations (NGOs) mainly working in the field of education.

The LPA is considering plans to divide the state-run Latvenergo energy company into two enterprises when it is privatized. Latvenergo could be divided into a generating and supply company, and an administrative enterprise. The LPA also envisages a similar ownership structure as that introduced for Latvia Gas, where the state retains a stake of around 75 per cent, whilst 25 per cent would be sold to private companies. This raises the question of who the potential investors in Latvenergo might be. There is still some debate about this in Latvia, with different positions being taken by the LPA and the Economics Ministry. The latter places emphasis on strategic partners (particularly energy companies) assisting the SOE to improve its operations and corporate governance structures; whereas the LPA has also placed emphasis on attracting western financial investors.

There has, however, also been some pronounced opposition to the privatization of Latvenergo. In March 1996, Latvia's social democratic parties launched a campaign and petition to protest against the privatization of what they see as the strategically important monopoly utility enterprises: Latvenergo, the Latvian Gas company, the Latvian Shipping Company, the Ventspils Nafta oil company and the Latvian Savings Bank. The Latvian Social Democratic Workers Party's (LSDSP) deputy chairman Egils Baldzens maintained that the campaign would go on for a month. The parliamentarians' signatures were gathered by three parties: LSDSP, the Latvian Social Democratic Party and the Political Union of the Disadvantaged. The social democrats maintain that the privatization of strategically important enterprises would result in increased service charges. Baldzens argued that, if the ruling parties do not change their stance, then over 50 per cent of the Saeima would vote against the privatization of these enterprises, the parties would even organize a national referendum on the issue (BNS, 1996).

On the other hand, the former State Minister for the Energy Industry, presently Councillor of the Minister of Economy, Mr Ozolins, considers the privatization of Latvenergo to have been greatly politicized. A recent article by the leader of the Democratic Party, Mr Saimnieks Ziedonis Cevers, in Neatkariga Rita Avize (June 26th, 1996) tried to show that the division of Latvenergo into several independent institutions would be impractical. Ozolins (and others) have argued that the origin of these reports is Latvenergo's senior management. However, the President of Latvenergo has refuted these accusations. Ozolins maintains (as does the Latvian Economics Minister Guntars Krasts) that Latvenergo's shares should not be sold by public auction to investment funds or banks and that instead a strategic investor should be sought.

In response to these developments, Guntars Krasts announced in June 1996 that he was ready to resign if the state-run energy utility Latvenergo was privatized subject to political influence rather than economic considerations (BNS, 1996). The minister stated that economically grounded Latvenergo privatization rules would be drafted in 1997 (BNS, 1996). Krasts maintains that approximately LVL 1.2 billion are to be invested in the development of Latvenergo. An additional LVL 37 million is expected to be attracted to the enterprise over the next five years (however, given the government's high fiscal deficit, it is difficult to envisage a means by which this extra money might cost-effectively be raised without further privatization). Nonetheless, Krasts maintains that any potential Latvenergo investors should be energy companies, not banks and other financial institutions, and that when privatizing Latvenergo, approximately 5 per cent of the company's capital could be sold in a public offering for privatization vouchers.

## Financial Market Constraints on Energy Sector Privatization

As previously noted, it could be argued that the recent banking crisis in Latvia was not solely caused by banking or budget difficulties *per se*; but was also due to a crisis in the existing structure of the national economy, where a large, inert and inefficient state sector still plays a major role. It borrows money at high interest rates and subsidizes SOEs in a covert way. If the share of domestic cash of a suitable monetary aggregate is taken as a rough measure of banking system trustworthiness, this point may be further emphasized. For example, Korhonen (1996) shows that the share of domestic currency of M1+Lat time deposits has been surprisingly stable between 1993 and May 1995. The banking crisis during the first half of 1995 did not encourage the population to convert their Lats from bank deposits to currency (the currency in circulation did not increase), but because a large proportion of other components of M2 disappeared, the share of currency in M2 grew. This may be interpreted as a sign of confidence in at least some of the Latvian banks and the Lat as a currency. In this context, therefore, the privatization of SOEs is a central factor in the future development of the Latvian economy.

Although banking deregulation in Latvia has successfully created a functioning and reasonably stable two-tier banking system, with a growing propensity to provide long-term financing to the economy, the recent crisis has affected confidence. Moreover, the further privatization of Latvian enterprises will, in all probability, create demand for some debt financing. Some Latvian banks are already in a position to provide such funding, so long as the companies are creditworthy. Demand for credit may also be considered quite important for the banks as a source of revenue.[12] The securities markets in Latvia are still so underdeveloped that they will probably not have much impact on the results of the banks. The share market is still at an embryonic stage of development, owing to the slow progress in the privatization process, and although the treasury bill market functions reasonably well, the volume is so small that its impact on the whole banking sector is negligible. Thus, on the one hand, it will be difficult to finance new investment and restructuring of the privatized energy utilities domestically. On the other hand, given the nascent stage of development of the financial markets and the lack of investor confidence both on the domestic front (although this is returning) and abroad, it seems difficult to envisage the financial system being in a position to exert control over firms and their managers, or the adoption of a relationship between the financial system and enterprises based on the German or Japanese insider model of close involvement by banks and major shareholders as described by Corbett and Mayer (1991). It is also difficult to imagine, at least in the short to medium term, either an insider model, or the Anglo-American outsider framework, based on dispersed ownership exercised through the stock market, being implemented without more effective and legally enforceable regulation of the Latvian energy and banking sectors (assuming the state eventually privatizes its majority share holding in Latvenergo, Latvia Gas and Ventspils Nafta).

## CONCLUSIONS

The development of the Latvian energy sector may be promoted by privatization, restructuring and the modernization of energy companies and the settlement of legislation in the power sector. The privatization of the energy sector is necessary to increase the efficiency of energy generation, develop competition, reduce political influence in awarding service and management contracts, and to save limited public resources by replacing them with private capital. A major step in this process has been the politically necessary, but difficult step of privatizing the largest energy utilities. Although the partial privatization of Latvia Gas has been reasonably successful in attracting foreign investors, it still raises doubts concerning: (i) the regulatory environment within which the firm will operate; (ii) corporate governance; and (iii) the intentions and commitment to privatization of the government *vis-à-vis* the future sale of its stake. An advisory working group under the auspices of the Ministry of Economy is currently developing a series of conceptual provisions for the privatization of the SOE Latvenergo. Although the government has repeatedly asserted its intention both to improve and to monitor corporate governance in the sector, little has been achieved in this regard, with the exception of the removal of political appointees on the boards of the state-owned enterprises earlier this year (BNS, 1996).

To increase and encourage domestic and foreign confidence in energy utility privatization, the process needs to be more transparent and de-politicized. Furthermore, an improvement in the flow of available information regarding the possibilities of privatization and the SOEs to be privatized to the public would also be a positive development. Where possible, the proceeds from privatization should be used to restructure the market and the enterprise, rather than as an additional source of state treasury revenue, easing public sector financial difficulties.

With regard to the telecommunications sector, the role of Lattelekom in developing the network's infrastructure and financial performance over the last two years has been good. However, the TTC needs greater regulatory powers concerning the issues of tariff setting and new market entry into the telecommunications market. Although the quality of telecommunications services has improved, the spending power of the population (including businesses) has not matched the growth in digital system telephone subscription tariffs (Ministry of Economy, 1996). In the short term this will require a change in the domestic use of telephones, i.e., increased personal rationing.

The Saeima should provide more adequate legislation regarding the regulation of the public utilities sector and mechanisms to ensure compliance with the aforementioned legislation. If, as the government maintains, it is committed to the promotion of greater competition and market-oriented improvements among the public utilities, it will need to consider the following: (a) the lack of transparency in utility service price setting and control (the privatization or externalization of tariff collection should also be considered); (b) the lack of transparency in awarding service contracts for public utility works; (c) the lack of effective competitive tendering procedures for the provision of public utility management, inputs and services; and (d) the need to establish a clear distinction between municipality control and its role in providing central heating plant (CHP), local generation and ancillary services. Some of the private firms providing CHP maintenance and cleaning services were previously part of the municipal authority. Thus, given that in general the financial resources of the public utilities, particularly in the energy sector, are limited, established business networks are preferred over widening market access and greater competition. Moreover, taxes and duties levied at the municipal level often have the effect of discouraging private entry in providing public utility input, maintenance or other ancillary services.

More generally, the government should facilitate private and local initiatives in the development of services (e.g., by encouraging competitive tendering, contracting out for service provision); by enforcing transparent pricing rules, the publication and dissemination of public utility data; by tackling the divergence between the drafting and implementation of legislation (i.e., tougher anti-monopoly laws are needed); and improving the economic environment so as to address the lack of investor confidence in the privatization process. As noted by Major (1992), the main principles of regulation should be to:

- facilitate private and local initiatives in the development of services;
- to set the general framework but not the operational objectives for individual service businesses;
- to let the effective demand for services initiate the emergence of different forms of supply;
- to enforce pricing rules for services but avoid 'petty tutelage' of service companies;
- to set central priorities for the utilization of centralized resources without constraining the freedom of private investors in service development; and
- to implement a sensible regional policy in the development of nationwide infrastructural networks, but using market-conforming measures to channel resources instead of appeasing one or another form of political pressure by distributing gifts in the form of service investments.

Latvia has to date failed to satisfy most of the above principles in the privatization and regulation of its energy and public utilities. This must be the key focus of future telecommunications and energy sector reform developments, if privatization remains one of the government's chief goals.

## NOTES

1. A further point (outside the scope of this paper) concerns the urgent need for a suitable investment programme in Latvia's energy utilities to overcome pressing short-term difficulties in the energy sector. This would improve the reliability and security of energy supplies, and initiate energy efficiency and conservation measures in industry and households.
2. The applicants included the Russian *Gazprom* consortium, *Ruhrgas* of Germany, *Gaz de France*, and the Latvia-based *Parekss Banka*. The *Gazprom* and German consortium *Ruhrgas*, and *Preussen Electra* have been successful in the bid for the right to acquire shares in Latvian Gas.
3. Profit and company tax income declined by 38 per cent during the period 1994 to 1995. This was also linked to the banking crisis and the introduction of a new unified tax rate of 25 per cent in 1995 by lowering it for SOEs, trading companies and the banking sector (Ministry of Economy, 1996).
4. It should be noted that the above is only one of many factors which led to the banking crisis in Latvia during 1995. Poor bank management, the *excessive* influence of shareholders and poor bank regulation were also important contributory causes.

5. Exclusive rights were also granted to ED & F Man (subsidiary Baltic Sugar Company) to ensure the purchase of all domestically produced sugar-beets between 1993 and 1996.

6. In Latvia, the licensing and growth in GSM systems and the cellular mobile network is steadily growing in response to increased competition and deregulation. For example, Latvian Mobile Telecoms, which was launched in January 1995, has achieved 53 per cent coverage and 9,440 subscribers, and a new competitor, LatGSM, was launched in the fall of 1996.

7. At *Incukalns*, Latvia has unique geological conditions which favour gas storage. There are about 150 domed structures made of sandstone at 600–800m depth within a 20ha area. Above the structures is clay, within them is artesian water; the gas, at 100 to 105 (max) bars, displaces the water. The station acts as the main distribution facility for all three of the Baltic States receiving gas at 30–45 bars along two pipelines from Russia. The facility lies under the umbrella company Latvia Gas. The plant is soundly designed but of obsolete technical standards.

8. For example, a 1994 assessment of the operational efficiency and safety of the Daugava River cascade hydro power plants and the design of measures for tightening such criteria, was criticized by the NORPLAN company with the financial support of the EBRD (HBS, 1996).

9. Generally, the use of hydroelectric power is a politically sensitive issue in Latvia because the population finds the risk of losing agricultural land that they have only just re-acquired unacceptable.

10. The consumer (creditor) debts of Latvenergo declined from LVL 68.9 million in April 1993 to LVL 29.6 million as of July 1994; however, this had increased to 44.9 million LVL as of January 1996. The largest short-term debts of Latvenergo as of January 1994 are to Latvia 1Gas (LVL 6.4 million). Its long-term debts (mainly loans) totalled LVL 10.3 million. Creditor debt of Latvia Gas declined from LVL 96.2 million as of January 1993 to LVL 28.6 million in 1994; however, this amounted to LVL 51.5 million by January 1996. The largest creditors' debts of Latvia Gas as of January 1996 were (i) loans from credit institutions, LVL 28.4 million; (ii) to the central budget, LVL 10.8 million; and (iii) suppliers, LVL 6 million. Latvenergo's after-tax profit was LVL 9.03 million in 1995, and net turnover equalled LVL 135.03 million.

11. Although adoption of this 'Citizenship Law' was postponed, an interim policy reserved citizenship rights for citizens of interwar Latvia and their descendants, such that 34 per cent of Latvian residents were ineligible to vote in the June 1993 Saeima elections and non-Latvians have been effectively marginalized in terms of certificate eligibility in the privatization process. This law maintained the interwar definition of citizenship, as well as enforcing a 10 year residency and Latvian language fluency requirement to acquire naturalization; which in any case the government instituted on a quota basis. Recent estimates suggest that approximately 700,000 people (out of a population of 2 million) are non-citizens (without official status) in Latvia (Dmitriev, 1996). Partly in response to pressure from the EU (which Latvia aspires to join) and Russia, the Latvian government has relaxed some of these policies and its stance on certain issues, e.g., the operation of annual quotas on naturalization which were suspended in July 1994. However, the unclear legal status of ethnic minorities in Latvia is a continuing source of political tension with Russia.

12. The remaining Latvian banks need relatively high interest rate margins to maintain profitability, as the quality of the failed banks' loan portfolios has without exception

been very low. Thus, a large share of the loan portfolios of operating banks are in practice non-performing. The loss provisions banks have so far accumulated will probably be insufficient to cover their losses (Korhonen, 1996).

## REFERENCES

Baltic News Service (1996), various issues.

Corbett, J. and C. Mayer (1991), 'Financial Reform in Eastern Europe: Progress with the wrong model', *Oxford Review of Economic Policy*, Vol. 7(4), pp. 57, Oxford University Press and the Oxford Review of Economic Policy Ltd.

Davis, J.R. (1996), 'The Political Economy and Institutional Aspects of the Process of Privatizing Farming and Land Ownership in the Baltic States', Discussion Paper No. 96/7, CERT, Heriot-Watt University.

Dmitriev, C. (1996), 'Hostages of the (Former) Soviet Empire', *Transition*, Vol. 2(1), 12 January 1996.

EBRD (1995), *Transition Report*, London: The European Bank for Reconstruction and Development, 1995.

Economist Intelligence Unit (1996), *Estonia, Latvia, Lithuania: Business Report*, 2nd Quarter 1996, London.

HBS, Öko-Institut, FFU (1996), 'Electricity in Eastern Europe: Latvia', mimeo.

Korhonen, L. (1996), 'Banking Sectors in Baltic Countries', *Review of Economies in Transition*, 3, 1996, Bank of Finland.

Lattelekom, Annual Reports 1996, 1995 and 1994.

Major, I. (1992), 'Private and Public Infrastructure in Eastern Europe', *Oxford Review of Economic Policy*, Vol. 7(4).

Ministry of Economy (1995/96), 'Economic Development of Latvia', Report, Riga, Latvia.

Shteinbuka, I. and M. Kazaks (1996), 'Fiscal Adjustment in Latvia under Transition', Discussion Paper No. 96/1, CERT, Heriot-Watt University.

# 12
# Concentration of Capital in the Process of Voucher Privatization in Lithuania

*Rasa Morkûnaitë*

## INTRODUCTION

The process of privatization was considered in Lithuania as the main sphere of the economic reforms. All political parties and social groups in Lithuania supported this approach. The major dispute concerned issues relating to the method (or methods) of privatization, i.e., whether to implement a commercial or distributional privatization model.

A compromise solution – to use investment vouchers for privatization only in selected sectors, e.g., in the privatization of housing, and in small-scale privatization – was proposed as well. In such cases investment vouchers are a really suitable instrument. It was proposed to implement large-scale privatization using cash (commercial privatization model). The main argument of the supporters of commercial privatization was that it is the only scheme which can provide an appropriate corporate governance system.

The Parliament of Lithuania unanimously approved the model of distributional privatization. All political parties supported this populist decision, declaring that the distributional model of privatization ensures 'social equity and justice', allowing the creation of a capitalist class, and arguing that it would reduce social tension in society as well. Political reasons were also of importance; it was stated that using the vouchers would keep out the influence of Russian capital. The distributional approach received wide support from the public in Lithuania, especially as the expectations of the public were strengthened by propaganda promising high dividend rates, high profitability of the shares and higher living standards.

In 1991 an ambitious privatization programme was proposed which envisaged divesting two-thirds of all state assets through a mass privatization programme for domestic purchasers (through auction sales of small entities and share subscriptions for larger enterprises) complemented by 'hard currency' sales open to all purchasers.

The initial privatization programme was to take place between September 1991 and June 1994 (later extended to mid-1995) and originally set out to privatize the majority of housing and more than 3,000 enterprises. A separate programme for land restitution and agricultural privatization was also launched.

The voucher privatization programme has been rather successful in removing a large number of enterprises and housing from formal ownership by the state. From the beginning of the voucher privatization process until October, 1995 (i.e., to the end of the initial privatization programme) there were 5,706 enterprises privatized out of the 6,500 slated for privatization.

Table 1.   Privatization of State-Owned Enterprises as of October 1995, per cent

| Sector of economy | By number of privatized enterprises | By the share of privatized state capital |
|---|---|---|
| Total | 86 | 83 |
| Industry | 88 | 91 |
| Transport | 86 | 31 |
| Construction | 91 | 98 |
| Trade | 82 | 72 |
| Public utilities | 77 | 30 |
| Services provided for households | 94 | 97 |
| Other | 83 | 96 |

*Source*:   Ministry of Economy, 1995.

Only 42 enterprises, or 0.6 per cent of all state assets, were sold for cash and only in half of these was there any foreign investment.

Compared to other eastern and central European countries, the privatization programme in Lithuania achieved good results in transferring ownership into private hands (see Table 2).

Nevertheless, the results fell short of initial targets, and other, less transparent privatization transactions also contributed to the surprisingly significant changes in ownership. Official estimates indicate that approximately 35 per cent of all state-owned assets were privatized as a result of this voucher privatization programme, while estimates of assets privatized outside of this programme (e.g., *via* management and employee buy-outs using retained earnings) range from 15–30 per cent of all assets.

**Table 2.  Privatization of Large-Scale Enterprises, per cent**

| | |
|---|---|
| Czech Republic | 82 |
| Hungary | 75 |
| Estonia | 74 |
| Lithuania | 57 |
| Russia | 55 |
| Latvia | 46 |
| Slovakia | 44 |
| Mongolia | 41 |
| Poland | 33 |

*Source*:   OECD, 1995.

On the whole, the privatization programme in Lithuania has resulted in too little corporate governance by strategic owners with the necessary skills and financing to bring about enterprise recovery. As it was supposed that insider-owned firms would perform better than outsider-owned firms, the vast majority of all voucher-privatized assets ended up in the hands of employees and management. The third major ownership group emerging from privatization in Lithuania comprised investment companies.

## INVESTMENT COMPANIES (ICs)

Though the introduction of investment funds and their participation in the privatization process is common to most countries in transition, investment companies (ICs) in Lithuania can be treated as a specific feature of the privatization process.

The introduction of investment companies allowed the accumulation of investment vouchers legally, as well as more efficiently and provided some guarantees for small investors. It also created the possibility of introducing core-investor principles into the privatization process. Investment companies became major players in the privatization process.

Investment companies were legalized on 30th October, 1991, by government decree. However, they were treated as a means of privatization but not as a financial institution. Only the most basic principles of their activities and requirements relating to their operations were determined. The strategy for the further development of ICs was not clear: should they operate as mutual funds or as holding companies, actively participating in the management of the companies? Neither the status nor the functions of investment companies were precisely defined. The normal requirements for financial institutions, such as prospectuses, diversification and management qualification requirements, were not adopted.

This attitude towards ICs was caused by a lack of institutional supervision and enforcement. The Lithuanian Securities Commission was only established by government decree in September 1992.

On the other hand, it was mistakenly concluded that the stock market would automatically cure the problems. This mistake arose from a failure to distinguish between buying stocks and buying the company. People optimistically assumed that the equity market would serve as the market of corporate control, that is, as an instrument for corporate governance and, hence, as an effective mechanism for raising external finance much needed by privatized enterprises for their restructuring projects.

ICs were formed by Lithuanians with a variety of backgrounds: academics, former managers of state-owned enterprises (SOEs), public officials, banks, groups with common business interests. Frequently, a controlling interest was held by a small number of founding members. ICs had little liquid capital, the majority of their capital being in the form of vouchers, company shares or physical assets.

Nevertheless, several restrictions were applied to ICs:

- the accumulated authorized capital was limited to 8 million litas. This limit was clearly too low for some structures; and groups of ICs owned by the same persons emerged;
- any investments by an IC in other investment companies could not exceed more than 10 per cent of its authorized capital;
- investments in enterprises being privatized by public subscription could not exceed 30 per cent of the authorized capital of those enterprises. This restriction gave rise to opposition on the part of ICs, strengthening of competition and informal agreements between ICs;
- no less than 80 per cent of investments had to be used to acquire the shares of privatized enterprises (this limited the participation of investment companies in auctions); and
- investment companies, having acquired the shares of privatized enterprises, could sell them only at the Stock Exchange. This restriction froze legal trading between ICs, because the National Stock Exchange began operations only in September 1993.

About 400 investment stock companies were registered. The most active period in terms of IC establishment was at the end of 1992. In 1993 the assets acquired by ICs comprised one-third of the privatized state assets, though the share of actual firms was considerably smaller. This could be explained by the fact that the ICs joined the privatization process later and participated mostly in the privatization of large-scale industrial enterprises.

In 1994 the situation changed slightly, since most of the ICs were not very active in the process of privatization. Most of the investments were made in 1992–93. As the process of privatization continued, the share of the assets acquired by ICs decreased to 21 per cent.

On average, capital of 100–300 thousand litas was accumulated per IC, though a few were able to increase their capital to 1–8 million litas. Nevertheless, most ICs comprise informal groups with large amounts of capital. Regarding IC activities, two main groups of ICs may be distinguished:

- *ICs or groups of ICs participating actively in the process of privatization.* These acquired control of enterprises and were involved in the management of the enterprises. Usually, the founders of these ICs are representatives of other entities (banks, insurance companies, other enterprises). They form conglomerates or groups, diversifying their activities. Some of them are active throughout the country, some only in the regions where they were established.
- *ICs participating in privatization, but not acquiring control of an enterprise.* They had no possibility to influence the activities of the enterprises; their only option is to trade on the securities market.

## ACTIVITIES OF ICs

Looking at the prospectuses of the ICs, it becomes evident that ICs up to now have not been prepared to act as mutual funds. Indeed, the main goal of ICs was primarily the accumulation of property. Most ICs lacked an investment strategy, and their investment portfolios were formed accidentally.

The main spheres of investment were those where a quick and permanent return was possible and/or those not requiring major investments. Such spheres include, first and foremost, the trade and catering sectors. Although the largest number of privatized entities belong to this sector, the other major sphere is industry, and the privatized assets of industrial enterprises comprise almost 70 per cent of all privatized assets.

Major investments in the industrial sphere were channelled towards profitable (or potentially profitable) sectors. Ownership by ICs across sectors is fairly even, except in three industrial branches – chemicals, forestry/wood/paper, and building materials – where in each case ICs together own approximately 40 per cent of privatized assets. Buildings and land belonging to enterprises, as well as enterprises' social assets, served as other incentives for the privatization of certain entities.

As a result of ICs' participation in the process of privatization, some 6–8 financial-industrial groups have emerged. They have participated in the process of privatization, commerce, manufacturing, and provided insurance and credit services. These major groups of ICs control more than half of the assets acquired by all ICs, though the number of entities acquired by their groups comprise only 45 per cent of all privatized entities. Taking into account their control over a majority of the enterprises (e.g., by participation in the board of directors), it could be stated that in reality they control a much greater amount of assets. It should be remembered that there was no real evaluation of enterprises' assets at the beginning of privatization and their market value could be much higher. Groups of ICs control such sectors as electronics, building materials, and the wood and food processing industries. Comprising a strong lobbying group, they can ensure a more favourable legislative framework.

So far, ICs have been engaged in the activity of accumulating investment vouchers and exchanging them for shares in privatized enterprises. However, managers of ICs understand the problems that need to be faced, which are as follows:

- insolvency in the majority of the industrial sector;
- the ongoing restructuring process;
- a lack of capital on the part of the ICs ;
- underdeveloped securities market;
- changes in the legal and regulatory environment; and
- a lack of portfolio management skills.

A large number of ICs were not able to survive. ICs were not able to accumulate financial resources for enterprise restructuring and actively monitor the management of enterprises. On the other hand, the formal transformation of ownership is not the only prerequisite for the effective performance of the enterprises. The most essential precondition is a competitive environment in which the enterprises can function. Ownership effects on restructuring are hardly discernible, due to the fact that the mass privatization scheme of Lithuania was not able to provide a competitive environment.

As the credo of privatization was 'as fast as possible', no time was foreseen for the preparation of the enterprises. The problem of inter-enterprise indebtedness was not solved, and the issue of the multi-functionality of the enterprises was not addressed. Social assets, such as sports and catering facilities, summer houses, kindergartens, etc., as well as supplementary departments (transport, construction, repair, and instrument shops), were part of the enterprise structure and were privatized together with the main production departments. Most of them were financially not viable, and it is not surprising that the debts of the privatized enterprises have continued to grow up until now.

The privatized enterprises operate in the same environment as newly-established private entities. In most cases, the position of the former is worse due to the unresolved debt issue. The huge amount of indebtedness to the state budget and social security fund has caused the insolvency of many potentially viable enterprises.

The establishment of conglomerates during the process of privatization, methods of their formation and operation as well as the problems they faced can be illustrated by the example of the EBSW conglomerate (see Box 1 below).

---

**Box 1.    The EBSW Conglomerate**

The EBSW conglomerate included closed joint-stock commercial companies, banks, insurance companies, mass media, etc. At the beginning of the privatization process nine investment companies were established. About 30 large-scale as well as smaller enterprises were privatized by them. However, the main goal was to buy shares cheaply and to sell them at a much higher price, while no estimates were made concerning the investment required. The strategy chosen for privatization was to acquire what was possible, but not what could be really profitable. However, it later became evident that it was impossible to efficiently manage a large number of companies belonging to different sectors, and that the former managers were not able to work in the new market conditions. It was difficult to fire such managers, due to the fact that the enterprises were acquired cheaply, and sometimes semi-legal methods of acquisition were used. However, the restructuring of such enterprises required large amounts of investment impossible to raise at short notice. So the group founded a credit institution working on the 'pyramid' principle, and borrowed from the banking sector as well as other companies. The financial resources of the privatized enterprises were used for the privatization of others, thus building a large-scale insolvent pyramid. Often property was pledged as security to the banks in return for loans that were ultimately used for different purposes. The credits were occasionally guaranteed by companies going bankrupt, and the funds received were paid to off-shore companies or 'lost' in other ways. The crisis of the credit institutions and the banking sector in 1994–95 significantly influenced the activities and financial position of the EBSW conglomerate.

The consequences of these processes are rather complex. The financial groups comprise a new political bloc, although their political doctrine or ideology is not very clear. A concentration of property and financial resources creates strong monopolistic effects in the local market, hampers competition, constricts the establishment and the activities of smaller companies and influences price levels. As no formal ownership relations between the structures of the financial-industrial groups can be observed, control of such structures by the anti-monopoly institutions is hardly possible.

## CONCLUSIONS

The concentration of capital affects the social structure of Lithuanian society. The representatives of the new elite are closely connected with the state bureaucracy, forming the new strata of society, and producing a negative impact on the security and stability of society as a whole.

Minor shareholders of major investment companies as well as financial groups have the potential for gain in the long run, though a negative tendency towards their elimination in semi-legal or illegal ways can be observed.

Most Lithuanian citizens who are shareholders of the ICs have encountered a lot of problems:

- insufficient information on the activities of ICs;
- no possibility of participation in the management or decision-making of an IC;
- low rate of dividends (or none at all);
- low liquidity of IC shares; impossibility of selling them on the stock exchange; and
- a lack of legal protection for investors in the event of bankruptcy or liquidation of ICs, and possibilities for founders or managers to manipulate the privatization process.

It can be stated that the expectations of this group of citizens were not satisfied. They did not acquire capital or improve their living standards due to the privatization process.

# Part IV

# The CIS

# 13
# Privatization and Restructuring in Russia: A Review and Micro Evidence from St. Petersburg

*Derek C. Jones*

## INTRODUCTION

The main purpose of this chapter is to present evidence drawn from recent surveys in Russia in two areas – corporate governance and the new trade unions. The pivotal importance of issues concerning corporate governance has been stressed by many transition scholars (e.g., Aghion and Blanchard, 1994; Boycko *et al.*, 1996). The theoretical issues raised concerning new forms of enterprise ownership and control are all the more salient because, unexpectedly, employee ownership has proven to be a widespread feature of the privatization process in several transition economies (Nuti, 1995). This development has been generally unwelcomed by most economists. Also during the last couple of years there have been some informative attempts both to describe (e.g., Blasi, 1995) as well as to assess the economic effects of new structures of ownership and control in Russia (e.g., some of the essays in Frydman, Gray and Rapaczyski, 1996). Equally, for diverse reasons including the rapid pace of change, it is clear that existing empirical work leaves many questions unresolved and that additional empirical work is needed.[1] We make a modest step in that direction in the main part of this chapter, in which we draw on our survey data to report new findings for both privatized and non-privatized firms on the nature and effects of different structures of ownership and control. There does not appear to be much support for the claim that either state-owned firms or employee-owned firms are worker-controlled. Our findings suggest that in transition economies privatization does not produce fundamental changes in inherited patterns of corporate governance but rather has served to strengthen managerial control. There is no strong evidence that the key obstacle to enhanced performance is employee ownership.

A related set of issues concerns the nature and the role of trade unions (and, more generally, the preferred form of industrial relations). No matter what forms of ownership ultimately emerge in Russia (and other transition economies), there is much disagreement on the role to be played by trade unions within firms (and possibly more generally). (Compare, for example, Freeman, 1993 and Silverman *et al.*, 1993.) Central to many discussions is the issue of which trade unions are to be encouraged. Here some argue (e.g., AFL-CIO, 1993) that the unions that have succeeded the old official unions (in Russia, the FNPR unions), are incapable of reform. Acceptance of this position implies that a genuine independent labour movement must be based on unions without precursors. To date much of the empirical work that has appeared on such topics is quite limited and mainly based on case studies (e.g., Clarke *et al.*, 1993). In Section 3 we report findings based on new survey data for trade union leaders in St. Petersburg on the nature of successor unions.[2] In the main we find that successor unions are capable of reform.

While ours is not a theoretical contribution, implicitly we argue that the issues we address (as well as many other related matters), are most fruitfully investigated by economists undertaking research in transition economies as processes of institutional and organizational change. Hence conceptual frameworks that are inter-disciplinary and also based on an evolutionary paradigm (e.g., Murrell, 1992) often may be most appropriate. From this perspective, we draw on work about western firms to present a typology of firms which may be helpful in understanding organizational change in firms in transition economies. In a similar vein, in the final section we develop the implications of our findings, and offer some conjectures on strategies which may help to facilitate restructuring in some firms and which typically have not been advanced. We argue that in some circumstances it may be appropriate to strengthen the role of employees as owners within firms *vis-à-vis* managers. Moreover, since there is much evidence that trade unions have often been part of the portfolio of institutions that have distinguished successful market economies, in the Russian context (and perhaps in other transitional economies too) in some cases consideration might be given to measures which encourage trade unions to better equip themselves to play the role of an effective employee representative alongside management.

It must be emphasized that some of the findings in this chapter constitute the first stage in what will be a longer-term, cross-national, collaborative project whose eventual aim is to make progress over existing studies in investigating these complex issues. The process of data collection is ongoing; this chapter, based on findings from only one city in Russia, should be viewed as a report of work in progress.[3] In addition, the author is aware that insufficient attention is given to other issues in the structure-conduct-performance area, including the role of competition and market structure in facilitating restructuring.

# CONCEPTUAL AND INSTITUTIONAL FRAMEWORKS

## The Conventional Wisdom and the Expected Effects of Ownership on Performance

In considering the effects of new forms of ownership on enterprise performance and enterprise adjustments, the dominant approach in the corporate governance literature is based on classifying firms by ownership. An open joint-stock company issues publicly traded ownership shares; the company's assets are owned by individuals in proportion to their shareholdings, and the firm is controlled by those who own a controlling packet of shares. A closely-held firm is owned and operated by a person or group closely attached to the firm as owner(s) and/or manager(s). In the case of open joint-stock companies, two alternative possibilities with respect to the exercise of effective control over enterprise operations may be distinguished: predominant ownership by insiders or by outsiders (Bim, Jones and Weisskopf, 1994). Insiders include all the people working in the enterprise. An insider-controlled firm may be effectively controlled by its managers, by its workers (either directly or indirectly, e.g., *via* a workers' council), or by some combination of the two. Outsiders include those whose attachment to the enterprise is based on an ownership stake rather than on work within the enterprise. Outsiders may be individual owners or shareholders, or they may be institutional shareholders (i.e., financial intermediaries such as investment trusts).

The case for open joint-stock companies – and an active capital market in company shares – rests mainly on the putative advantages of such a system in raising capital funds, in allocating those funds flexibly among competing enterprises and in disciplining managers. Outsider control means that agency problems will be minimized and enterprise decisions will be guided primarily by the objective of maximizing returns on investors' capital. The justification for this approach is that only outsiders can be expected to proceed rapidly with enterprise restructuring, not hesitating to liquidate unprofitable assets and to dismiss redundant workers; moreover, outsiders are more likely to be able to mobilize new resources to invest in the enterprise and less likely to be able to evoke and to rely on soft government budget constraints. Critics question whether stock markets actually perform their intended functions effectively, especially in the context of formerly centrally planned economies with very underdeveloped capital market institutions. Advocates of closely held firms argue that such firms are more likely to be characterized by a focused, tightly-knit, flesh-and-blood ownership group with a strong stake in enterprise performance – as compared with the alternative of external ownership of joint-stock companies.

The outsider-control model has several variants depending on the locus of effective control and the terms on which shares are made available to buyers. On the one hand, there could be open sale of shares in corporatized state enterprises in the hope that a 'strategic (core) investor' (domestic or foreign) will turn up and take over control, or in the expectation that an active stock market will discipline management even in a context where share ownership is widely dispersed among many small investors. On the other hand, there could be established strong financial intermediary institutions (holding companies, mutual funds, etc.) which are expected to buy controlling packets of shares in companies and proceed to restructure and monitor them. There also exists, however, the possibility of a different outcome in the event that no external strategic investor takes over control (because shares are diffused among many small investors, or because the bulk of the shares cannot be sold and remain in the hands of state property agencies), and no appropriate financial intermediary institutions emerge, and no well-functioning capital market develops. This default outcome is that the locus of effective control over the 'privatized' state enterprises really does not change – it continues to be run by previous managers, influenced by workers, with government authorities continuing to take a strong interest in the enterprise.

In insider-controlled firms, the security and stability of the enterprise and its workforce will weigh more heavily in decision-making. Many economists believe that insider ownership in general, and worker ownership in particular, will result in economic performance inferior to that of externally owned and controlled firms (e.g., Hinds, 1990; Boycko *et al.*, 1996). It is argued that the perceived interests of enterprise workers are likely to conflict in important respects with the long-run interests of their enterprise. In particular it is held that in firms in which non-managerial workers dominate, that there will be under-investment in capital equipment, that productivity will be low as worker-owners expend little effort and that layoffs will be resisted. The conventional wisdom is that significant employee ownership will have detrimental effects on enterprise performance and undermine the ability of newly-privatized firms to undertake meaningful restructuring (e.g., Frydman *et al.*, 1993b).[4] For reasons including allegedly superior solutions to agency problems, it is argued that when insiders dominate, the most efficient form of insider ownership is manager (rather than worker) ownership (e.g., Boycko *et al.*, 1996).

## An Alternative Conceptual Framework with Examples from the West

There are several reasons why the framework outlined above may not always be most appropriate for transition economies such as Russia. For example, Aoki and Kim (1995) note that much of the traditional analysis assumes an idealized view of advanced market economies and that the argument for the promotion of outside ownership and efficient securities markets ignores crucial matters such as inherited factors and assumes competitive product and labour markets. Especially in the context of transition economies, Earle and Estrin (1996) argue that the effects of employee ownership may be dependent on a host of factors such as market conditions and that, in particular cases, some forms of employee ownership may be the best feasible solution to the choice of ownership structure.

**Table 1.   Typology of Employee Ownership according to Control and Return rights**

| Return rights held by employees | Control rights held by employees | | | |
|---|---|---|---|---|
| | **None** | **Participation in control** | **Sharing of control** | **Dominant control** |
| None | $OA_1$ Conventional firms | $OA_2$ Quality circles involving majority of workers | $OA_3$ Employee representation on board of directors | $OA_4$ British Industrial Common Ownership: e.g.Scott Bader |
| Small | $OA_5$ Profit-sharing: ESOPS: e.g. Occidental Petroleum; Kimberly Clark | $OA_6$ Profit-sharing with participation programmes | $OA_7$ Co-determina-tion with another programme; e.g. in Sweden co-determination sometimes exists with convertibles | $OA_8$ British Retail Coops1 |
| Moderate | $OA_9$ ESOPs[2]; e.g. Proctor and Gamble; Corning; Rucker Plans; | $OA_{10}$ Scanlon Plans; John Lewis; Lincoln Electronics; Polaroid; Japanese Mfg. | $OA_{11}$ Producer co-operatives[3]: e.g. UK Clothing Denmark | $OA_{12}$ Producer co-operatives;[4] e.g. UK footwear |
| Majority | $OA_{13}$ ESOPS; e.g. Vermont Asbestos; Harcourt, Brace and Ivanovich; Lincoln S & L | $OA_{14}$ ESOPS: e.g. Brooks Camera; Hyatt Clark; Ruddick | $OA_{15}$ ESOPS: e.g. Weirton Steel; Rath; French building PCs | $OA_{16}$ Producer co-operatives; e.g. Mondragon, Italy; French Consulting; US Plywood |

*Notes*:
1. In some cases workers constitute a majority of the decision-making board and employees have tiny amounts of profit sharing and ownership.
2. Information on ESOP is largely derived from Blasi and Kruse (1991: 14–20 and chapter 4).
3. Workers share control with other organizations, such as labour unions and consumer co-operatives.
4. Workers have majority control of decision-making bodies, but modest amounts of profit-sharing and/or individual ownership.

While we are in agreement with most of these observations, we wish to emphasize what we believe is a particular shortcoming of the mainstream, specifically the use of a conceptual framework that in its conception of organizational processes is quite narrow. In particular there is a tendency to identify ownership with control and to take an overly static view. To illustrate these points we draw on a typology of ownership arrangements developed in several papers by Ben-Ner and Jones (e.g., 1995) to investigate firms in the west. They note that ownership of an asset consists of two central rights – the right to control its use and to enjoy its returns. Diverse allocations of control and return rights between two major groups in organizations, employees and owners of capital who are not employees, are identified. A typology of ownership arrangements is developed and examples associated with them are offered. In Table 1 we reproduce that typology, where the cells define 16 types of ownership arrangements, denoted by OAi (i =1,..,16). Rather than explain all of the cells, by focusing on selected cases, we endeavour to illustrate the key ideas. The first ownership arrangement, OA1, represents the benchmark 'conventional' firm, where employees have no ownership rights at all: they neither share formally in profits or revenue or hold stock, nor do they have decision-making rights (beyond any assigned to them due to their organizational position).[5]

The other arrangements in the cells in the top row describe situations where provision exists for employees to have some degree of participation in control without any arrangement for participation in economic returns. Thus OA2 describes firms with arrangements ranging from consultation by management with employees, to teamwork, to participatory schemes on issues selected by management. Firms with consultative participation arrangements include US firms with quality control circles. OA3 ownership arrangements include, for example, German and Swedish firms with statutory co-determination schemes, implemented through elected workers' councils, various work teams, where employees make their own work assignments, and GM's Saturn plant, where employees elect their own supervisor – schemes whereby employees share control over non-strategic issues affecting their immediate work environment.

Excepting OA1, the arrangements in the cells in the first column describe situations where provision exists for employees to have some degree of participation in economic returns, without any arrangement for participation in control. Thus OA5 represents firms that practice limited forms of profit- or revenue-sharing, such as Sears and ICI and many firms with limited employee stock ownership plans (ESOPs). In OA9 firms employees have moderate rights to returns but do not share in control as in many gainsharing plans. OA13 includes firms with ESOPs where employees constitute the largest shareholder block (enjoy majority return rights) but do not have *de facto* dominant control rights. This was the case in the (now defunct) Vermont Asbestos and Lincoln Savings and Loan (Blasi and Kruse, 1991).

In all other cells, employees have some combination of return and control rights. Thus OA6 firms combine small degrees of employee shares in both control and returns, typically by combining schemes that allow workers some say in decisions related to their immediate work with profit or revenue sharing. OA7 firms resemble OA3 ownership arrangements with the addition of small employee return rights, such as German and Swedish firms with co-determination and a profit-sharing or an employee stock ownership scheme (e.g., ASEA and Volvo). Examples of OA10, where participation in control coexists with moderate rights to returns, include Scanlon plans, the chain of the John Lewis Partnership and most of the core Japanese manufacturing firms (Jones and Kato, 1995) and some of the mainly profit-sharing companies covered in the large survey by Kruse (1993: Tables A2.1 & A3.7).

Finally, there are firms where employees enjoy dominant control rights and a majority of the returns (Bonin, Jones and Putterman, 1993). Examples of such firms (cell OA16) include the Mondragon producer co-operatives (Whyte and Whyte, 1988), Italian and French producer co-operatives (Estrin, Jones and Svejnar, 1987), US plywood producer co-operatives (Craig and Pencavel, 1992), and an increasing number of firms in the US where the management trust on behalf of an ESOP holding the majority of shares has ended and full control was transferred to employee-owners.

This alternative conceptual framework may also be used to examine the expected economic effects of different ownership structures. While the argument is developed more fully elsewhere (see, e.g., Ben-Ner and Jones, 1995), contrary to the conventional wisdom, it is argued that some types of insider-owned structures can be justified on several grounds (Ben-Ner, 1993). This is shown to be especially the case when insider-owned structures exist in combination with participatory human resource management policies. Insider ownership and control is arguably more conducive to enterprise stability and long-term employment relationships and thus may contribute to better economic performance in a number of ways. The closer alignment of the goals of the different economic agents within firms may better motivate workers to join in restructuring efforts and to better use their accumulated experience and firm-specific knowledge. In particular, if enterprise success is reflected in a higher stock price, ownership by non-managerial employees (as well as managers) will have a direct positive effect; the interest of the firm is then more aligned with the interest of its employees. For several reasons, these interest alignment effects can be expected to be more significant in firms in which the precise institutional arrangements enable broad participation by employees (not restricted to executives) and in which employee ownership constitutes a significant part of the average employees' wealth.[6]

Goal alignment effects of employee participation *via* information sharing (e.g., small group activities) are more subtle (but not necessarily weaker) than effects through ownership. Small group activities may provide valuable opportunities for both management and workers to learn about each other in a more co-operative atmosphere than traditional collective bargaining settings, and thus develop stronger trust. With stronger trust, sharing vital business information with workers will help convince them that it is in their interest to improve productivity and firm performance. Various forms of employee participation may play an important role in providing employees a voice in the firm and thus reduce the costs of exit from the firm, saving specific human capital. In the absence of unions, these arrangements may provide the sole voice mechanism, while in the presence of unions they may supplement the direct voice mechanism of unions. Also, greater enterprise stability may encourage more salvaging of still useful capital stock, and it may help to avoid a cascade of business failures due to the shutdown of one key enterprise in a productive structure still characterized by an inflexible network of input sources and output outlets.

At the same time, it is important to recognize that the relationship between alternative ownership arrangements and individual motivation, individual performance, organizational structural variables and ultimately organizational performance is expected to be quite complex. In particular, while in general we expect to see a strong and mainly positive interaction between control and return rights, the relationship between employee ownership with balanced control and return rights on the one hand and productivity on the other hand is not monotonic. Rather, a well-balanced employee ownership arrangement will initially induce a positive productivity effect; then, while combining moderate returns rights with comparable control rights, for reasons such as agency problems, the effect may become negative, and only when switching to dominant employee ownership does the effect becomes positive again, relative to the conventional firm.

## Ownership Arrangements: For the USSR and Russia

While the typology depicted in Table 1 was originally constructed to describe cases in advanced western economies, it may be usefully adapted to illustrate institutional structures concerning enterprise ownership and employee participation in the former USSR and the new Russia. Note in particular that, in the former USSR, for many years the standard employment contract was comparable to that prevailing in capitalist economies – employees had no formal ownership rights and most received what was effectively a fixed wage. Hence OA1 may also be viewed as the benchmark case, though now for a state-owned firm within a centrally administered command economy.

The typology is also useful because it points to the limited degree of participation in control that employees in some firms enjoyed in the USSR, especially during the attempts at reform during the 1980s. One of the channels through which this participation potentially took place was through membership in trade unions. Until about 1990, essentially all employees in St. Petersburg (as in the rest of the USSR) were members of the old, official unions. These official unions were postulated to have dual functions. First, trade unions were subservient to the Communist Party and, like many other institutions, were an integral part of the centrally administered system. At enterprise and industry level this meant that a key task of union officials was to ensure that plan targets were fulfilled.[7] The second function of unions, albeit within this framework, was to represent the interests of individual members. However, in practice, to the extent that union leaders (at branch and enterprise levels) directly served the separate interests of members, most believe this was done mainly by social and welfare activities, especially handling social security claims and disbursing holiday vouchers. In a system of central planning, union leaders were not involved in functions traditionally associated with western-style collective bargaining. Moreover, typical protest forms like strikes and slow-downs were completely prohibited.

However, even before the late 1980s there had been many partial attempts to reform unions, including efforts to promote improved member involvement in achieving production targets and in protecting members' interests. While most scholars have concluded that innovations did not produce basic changes (e.g., Slider, 1987), some scholars find evidence of change (e.g., Pravda and Ruble, 1986). Moreover, in tandem with the machinery of the old union, in former times diverse structures, for example production committees and brigades,[8] existed at the enterprise level. Potentially such bodies had meaningful implications for workers' interests (Grancelli, 1988; Gerchikov, 1992), and acted to move some firms modestly away from OA1 – mainly along the top row, to OA2.

Subsequently the fundamental changes in the new Russia have had potentially major implications for institutional arrangements in Russian enterprises. Concerning trade unions, the critical step in changing the 'transmission-belt' model took place in September 1989, when delegates at a congress of the old 'official' unions declared their independence from the Communist Party. A year later, the centralized structure of the old arrangements was overturned, at both national and regional levels. Thus, in the Leningrad (St. Petersburg) region, a new, decentralized federation emerged in March 1991 to serve successor unions. Accompanying these changes in trade unions, apparently important changes are also underway, though at varying rates, concerning the inherited, formally non-union bodies and their relation to successor union structures within enterprises. Thus, at the plant level, the labour collective (the body comprising the entire workforce) is a body whose importance has possibly grown recently. For example, for medium and large firms, the law on privatization provided that the labour collective played a key role in choosing the form of privatization (Bim, Jones and Weisskopf, 1993). The existence of these various bodies suggests the possibility of mechanisms for employee involvement and that at least some Russian firms (especially those which remain in the state sector), might be best described as belonging in the OA2 or OA3 cells. These developments also point to the potential for rivalries in the quest to represent workers' interests.

Of course, the effects of the legislation on privatization is potentially a much more important development for the location within the typology of those Russian firms formerly in the state sector. While Russian officials such as Chubais initially were strongly opposed to legislative provisions favouring insiders,[9] legislation that was in fact adopted allowed employees in medium-and large-scale Russian enterprises, voting as members of their worker collective, to choose from among three privatization options and all the options provided for insiders to purchase blocks of shares (although not always voting shares) at concessional rates.[10] But it was the option enabling workers and managers to buy as much as 51 per cent of company shares which was chosen overwhelmingly by the enterprises being privatized. Thus in privatized enterprises by April 1994 (shortly before the completion of voucher privatization in July 1994) it is estimated that insiders owned 62 per cent of shares (see Table 2). In terms of the typology, for the overwhelming bulk of cases where some measure of employee ownership was present, this means that the arrangements that best describe privatized Russian firms have nearly always shifted in a southerly direction. If participation in economic returns through ownership was accompanied by participation in control, then the typical movement after initial privatization would have been in a south-easterly direction.

Table 2.    Distribution of Ownership in Privatized Russian Firms

|  | | 4/94 | 12/94 | 6/95 | 7/96 |
|---|---|---|---|---|---|
| Insiders: | Total | 62 | 60 | 56 | 51 |
|  | Employees | 53 | 49 | 43 | 35 |
|  | Managers | 9 | 11 | 13 | 16 |
| Non State Outsiders | | 21 | 27 | 33 | 45 |
| State | | 17 | 13 | 11 | 4 |

*Source*:    Bogomolov, 1996.

However, it is believed that since then substantial additional changes have occurred in the structure of ownership in privatized Russian firms. The picture based on the official data for the middle of 1996 is shown in Table 2. While in some cases data for 1996 refer to firms that had been privatized in the post-voucher stage (and presumably include some firms privatized under the 'shares for loans' scheme), in the bulk of cases the data suggest that important changes in ownership have occurred in firms that were privatized *via* the voucher scheme. By the middle of 1996, and presumably reflecting the ability to trade shares freely, we see that nonstate outsiders were close to gaining parity ownership with insiders. Moreover, while in April 1994 managers held on average about one-seventh of insider equity (9/62), by July 1996 the share of managers in insider ownership was now almost one-third. Thus it does seem as though the pace at which non-managerial employees have been selling shares has quickened and that these shares are being purchased by both managers and outsiders.

In terms of the typology, these most recent changes suggest that the typical  movement during the last couple of years would probably have been in a northwesterly direction. At the same time, in such turbulent times and with pervasive agency problems it is quite possible that an enormous range of possible configurations has arisen in the institutional arrangements that lie behind these aggregate trends.

In turn, the turbulent context of transition economies (especially in Russia and the continuing dramatic changes in ownership in many firms), suggests that several of the conceptual considerations discussed earlier might be especially relevant. In particular, the instability of organizational components and the massive uncertainty within which firms operate produce changing incentives for individuals (especially managers) and key groups within organizations and provide additional reasons why, in this context, the links between changes in participation in control and in return rights may be expected to be non-linear. In other words, in a fast-changing context it may be impossible to expect clear-cut predictions for organizational performance from different structures of ownership and control which often are being subject to major changes.

# EVIDENCE ON THE NATURE AND EFFECTS OF OWNERSHIP

## A Brief Evaluation of Existing Work for Russia

As already noted, because of the variety of choices made with respect to privatization of Russian enterprises as well as the subsequent changes, we would expect very different patterns of ownership to be emerging within Russia.[11] The available evidence supports this view; but it also shows that in the majority of medium-and large-scale Russian enterprises, privatization has led to predominantly insider ownership, and this has typically facilitated managerial rather than worker control. Thus far, one of the largest bodies of evidence for Russian firms is survey data by Blasi (1995, 1996).[12] Using various measures for a non-random sample of enterprises, he finds that in 1993 worker ownership typically co-existed with managerial control and that this had not changed much a year later.

Other studies have also appeared which have begun to analyse in more detail diverse aspects of these changes in ownership, including relationships with enterprise performance. With one important exception (see below), the limited work to date has typically been undertaken for rather small samples of firms and employs methods that are predominantly qualitative and does not attempt to test hypotheses using statistical methods.[13] While these studies for Russian firms tend to find that the performance of newly privatized firms typically disappoints, in the main the evidence that is presented to account for this record tends to be largely anecdotal.

Perhaps the best known exceptions are the several studies which draw on a data collection exercise organized by the World Bank for a representative sample of 394 manufacturing firms. The most useful studies that draw on this data are by Earle *et al.*, (e.g., 1995).[14] This paper provided evidence relevant to the conventional wisdom, namely that for reasons including easier access to capital markets, firms with outside ownership are expected to be more efficient than firms with insider ownership (e.g., Boycko *et al.*, 1993). In addition, for reasons including allegedly superior solutions to agency problems, it is argued that the most efficient form of insider ownership is manager (rather than worker) ownership (e.g., Earle *et al.*, 1995; Boycko *et al.*, 1996). To provide evidence on these propositions the authors are able to categorize firms by dominant ownership and estimate a variety of regression models to examine relationships between indicators of restructuring (e.g., employment adjustment and capacity utilization) and ownership. However in the main the authors find at best only weak evidence of such links, especially for privatized firms with different dominant owners.[15]

There have also been some useful studies by the ILO, e.g., Standing (1995). In the latter paper, the ambitious aim is to identify, both in theory and in practice, firms that have '...exemplary labour and employment practices and mechanisms to ensure development in terms of skill, social equity, economic equity and democracy' (1995: 3). After operationalizing a measure of 'human development' in the enterprise, the impact of differences in human development (HD) for enterprise performance is then evaluated by using data for 384 Russian firms. Preliminary empirical work suggests an inverse association between measures of performance such as labour costs/total costs and values of HD.

Taken as a whole, these recent studies provide us with very good information on the nature of the new forms of ownership and control in privatized Russian firms but evidence on the effects of the new structures of ownership and control that is rather weaker. At the same time, an implication of the approach reviewed in the previous section is that even at the best of times it will be difficult to do good empirical work in this area; in a context of systemic change these difficulties are greatly magnified and must lead us to be quite cautious in evaluating the evidence to date. For example, when examining the effects of privatization upon enterprise performance and enterprise adjustment, most studies include variables only on financial participation (return rights) or participation in decision-making (control rights), but not both. This is extremely problematic because, as we have argued, there are strong theoretical reasons to believe that the two rights interact with each other and do so non-monotonically. The enormous difficulties of undertaking field work in Russia mean that studies must often be based on small samples, and that details on the often complex links between ownership and control are often very sketchy. As a result, there is not much systematic evidence concerning linkages between structures of ownership and formal mechanisms for control (e.g., board composition, joint labour management committees) and employee influence and the dynamics of ownership and formal control and employee influence. The omitted variables problem is severe, and the estimates on employee ownership variables that arise from such studies may have the wrong sign.

In addition, our alternative conceptual framework indicates that the degree of employee return rights (e.g., the per cent of ownership by employees or the per cent of profit allocated to employees), its nature (e.g., current *versus* delayed compensation) and the specific form of employee control rights (e.g., quality circles and self-managed teams) matter for performance. However, few studies (for the west, let alone transition economies) are able to include variables that capture the diversity in programmes of participation in returns and decision-making, and hence their findings are biased in an unknown direction. Also, currently there are few data available at enterprise level with which to gauge what is actually happening with respect to the distribution and the dynamics of ownership, (as well as the relations between ownership and control). Moreover, differences in employee control measured at different levels of control rights held by employees may differ not only in magnitude but also in sign.

Finally, essentially all studies adopt an economic approach and concentrate on the link between a particular structure of ownership and organizational performance. However, both individual factors and structural organization variables affect organizational performance, and may do so in opposite ways, and empirical studies should investigate both types of variables.

## Our Survey Data and Evidence on the Nature of Ownership and Control in Russia

To begin to provide additional information on some of these matters, we arranged for surveys to be administered to two samples of firms in the St. Petersburg region.[16] The first of these samples was administered in 1993 to 72 manufacturing firms in St. Petersburg. All of the firms in the sample had operated as state-owned enterprises during the Communist era, but some had been privatized and others not. 67 of the 72 firms provided information that was useable. The second sample was administered in 1994 to 60 manufacturing firms; in this sample most of the firms had already been privatized. This was a completely different and smaller sample than in the previous year; nearly all of the firms that were approached provided at least partial information.

The information we obtained on the structure of enterprise ownership is reported in Table 3. The data in Part A show that, on average, firms in our first sample had 36 per cent insider ownership, of which 4 per cent was managerial ownership. But when we restrict attention to firms that had been privatized, the corresponding figures are considerably higher – 63 per cent and 8 per cent.[17]

Among firms in the second sample (Table 3, Part B), we see that there is again evidence of substantial insider ownership in privatized (joint-stock) firms. In almost two-thirds of the cases (24/37) insiders owned a majority of shares. In all cases there was some insider ownership.

Table 4 details different dimensions of employee involvement; again our findings are based on the two samples previously discussed. From the first sample we have data on board composition for 41 privatized firms in 1993 (see Table 4, Part A). These show that, on average, insiders accounted for about 45 per cent of members of the board of directors – considerably less than the average share of insider ownership. In most cases (26/41) employee representation on the board amounted to 10-25 per cent of the total (compared to employee ownership levels that average more than 55 per cent). By contrast, about 1 in 6 members on the board was a manager – about twice as high as the average level of managerial ownership.

**Table 3.  Employee Ownership in St. Petersburg**

**Part A:  Share Ownership by Groups (first sample)**

| Group | | All Firms | | Privatized Firms |
|---|---|---|---|---|
| | | **% of total share owned** | | |
| Insiders | | 36.07 | | 62.83 |
| Employees | 31.62 | | 55.09 | |
| Managers | 4.45 | | 7.74 | |
| Outsiders | | 63.93 | | 37.15 |
| **Total** | | **100.00** | | **100.00** |

**Part B:  Distribution of Ownership (Joint-Stock firms) (second sample)**

| | Inside Share Ownership | |
|---|---|---|
| **% of ownership** | **No. of firms** | **% of firms** |
| 75.01–100 | 13 | 35.14 |
| 50.01–75 | 11 | 29.73 |
| 25.01–50 | 8 | 21.62 |
| 10.01–25 | 5 | 13.51 |
| 00.00–10 | 0 | 00.00 |
| **Total** | **37** | **100.00** |

| | Outside Share Ownership | |
|---|---|---|
| **% of ownership** | **No. of firms** | **% of firms** |
| 75.01–100 | 4 | 10.81 |
| 50.01–75 | 9 | 24.32 |
| 25.01–50 | 11 | 29.73 |
| 10.01–25 | 3 | 8.12 |
| 00.00–10 | 1 | 2.70 |
| 00.00 | 9 | 24.32 |
| **Total** | **37** | **100.00** |

**Table 4. Control and Employee Influence in St. Petersburg**

**Part A: Composition of the Board in Privatized Firms ($n = 41$) (first sample)**

| Group | | % of the Board |
|---|---|---|
| Insiders | | 45.24 |
| Workers | 28.78 | |
| Managers | 16.46 | |
| Outsiders | | 54.76 |
| **Total** | | **100.00** |

**Distribution of Worker Composition of the Board**

| % of the Board | No. of firms | % of firms |
|---|---|---|
| 50.01–100 | 6 | 14.63 |
| 25.01–50 | 9 | 21.95 |
| 10.01–25 | 26 | 63.42 |
| 00.00–10 | 0 | 00.00 |
| **Total** | **41** | **100.00** |

**Part B: Year 1993 (first sample)**

| Privatized Firms Employee Influence | Privatization | Supervisor | Wages | Employment |
|---|---|---|---|---|
| Admin. Decides | 21 | 10 | 36 | 29 |
| Tiny | 18 | 18 | 12 | 17 |
| Moderate | 9 | 28 | 8 | 10 |
| Co-determination | 2 | 0 | 0 | 0 |
| N | 50 | 56 | 56 | 56 |
| Mean | 1.84 | 2.32 | 1.50 | 1.66 |
| Std. Dev. | (0.93) | (0.77) | (0.74) | (0.77) |

| Non-Privatized Firms Employee Influence | Privatization | Supervisor | Wages | Employment |
|---|---|---|---|---|
| Admin. Decides | 7 | 5 | 14 | 11 |
| Tiny | 8 | 1 | 5 | 5 |
| Moderate | 3 | 1 | 3 | 6 |
| Co-determination | 0 | 0 | 0 | 0 |
| N | 18 | 22 | 22 | 22 |
| Mean | 1.78 | 2.50 | 1.50 | 1.77 |
| Std. Dev. | (0.73) | (0.86) | (0.74) | (0.87) |

Hyp. Tests:
Difference in means of Priv. in privatized and non-privatized firms; t-stat = 0.90

Table 4 (*contd.*)

Difference in means of Super in privatized and non-privatized firms; t-stat = 0.34
Difference in means of Wage in privatized and non-privatized firms; t-stat = 0.00
Difference in means of Policy in privatized and non-privatized firms; t-stat = 0.56

**Year 1991**

| Privatized Firms Employee Influence | Privatization | Supervisor | Wages | Employment |
|---|---|---|---|---|
| Admin. Decides | 12 | 4 | 27 | 21 |
| Tiny | 12 | 13 | 15 | 22 |
| Moderate | 25 | 28 | 14 | 11 |
| Co-determination | 5 | 0 | 0 | 0 |
| N | 54 | 55 | 56 | 54 |
| Mean | 2.42 | 2.62 | 1.77 | 1.82 |
| Std. Dev. | (1.01) | (0.62) | (0.83) | (0.75) |

| Non-Privatized Firms Employee Influence | Privatization | Supervisor | Wages | Employment |
|---|---|---|---|---|
| Admin. Decides | 6 | 2 | 10 | 7 |
| Tiny | 5 | 5 | 4 | 7 |
| Moderate | 4 | 10 | 3 | 3 |
| Co-determination | 0 | 0 | 0 | 0 |
| N | 15 | 17 | 17 | 17 |
| Mean | 1.87 | 2.47 | 1.59 | 1.77 |
| Std. Dev. | (0.83) | (0.72) | (0.79) | (0.75) |

Hyp. Tests:
Difference in means of Priv. in privatized and non-privatized firms; t-stat = 2.07 (5 per cent sig.)
Difference in means of Super in privatized and non-privatized firms; t-stat = 0.82
Difference in means of Wage in privatized and non-privatized firms; t-stat = 0.71
Difference in means of Policy in privatized and non-privatized firms; t-stat = 0.24

**Year 1994 (second sample)**

| Employee Influence | Privatization | Supervisor | Wages | Employment |
|---|---|---|---|---|
| Admin. Decides | 2 | 24 | 19 | 25 |
| Tiny | 6 | 23 | 32 | 22 |
| Moderate | 5 | 6 | 2 | 6 |
| Co-determination | 0 | 0 | 0 | 0 |
| N | 13 | 53 | 53 | 53 |
| Mean | 2.2 | 1.7 | 1.7 | 1.6 |
| Std. Dev. | (0.7) | (0.7) | (0.5) | (0.7) |

**Year 1991**

| Employee Influence | Privatization | Supervisor | Wages | Employment |
|---|---|---|---|---|
| Admin. Decides | 3 | 23 | 14 | 21 |
| Tiny | 7 | 24 | 30 | 22 |
| Moderate | 12 | 6 | 9 | 10 |
| Co-determination | 1 | 0 | 0 | 0 |
| N | 23 | 53 | 53 | 53 |
| Mean | 2.5 | 1.7 | 1.9 | 1.8 |
| Std. Dev. | (0.7) | (0.7) | (0.7) | (0.7) |

Hyp. Test:
Difference in mean of wage 91 and wage 94; t-stat = 1.69
Difference in mean of LF91 and LF94; t-stat = 1.47

From both samples we gathered information on employee perceptions of influence on four key issues. In both cases information was solicited both at the time when the questionnaire was administered (i.e., 1993 for the first sample, and 1994 for the second sample) as well as for an earlier time (1991 in each case). Data were gathered from both privatized and non-privatized firms. In assessing employee participation, a five-point scale was used (with '1' representing a very low degree of employee influence, '2' & '3' reflecting moderate employee influence through mechanisms such as consultation and the provision of information, '4' indicating that management and workers jointly decided an issue and '5' reflecting employees perceiving that they alone make decisions on an issue). However, since there were no responses of '5', Table 4B contains only four categories.

From Table 4, Part B we see that, for firms in both samples, levels of employee influence were typically perceived as quite modest. Thus the bulk of respondents felt that in four issue areas – method of privatization, choice of supervisors, wage policy and employment policy – there was either no employee influence (administration decides) or a modest amount of employee influence (falling well short of management and workers jointly deciding). For example, this is the case in 1993 for the first sample in 39/50 responses concerning privatization and on 46/56 cases concerning employee influence on employment policy. For both samples, there is some evidence that employee influence was relatively weakest concerning issues of employment and wage determination and relatively strongest concerning choice of supervisors.[18]

It is interesting to note that the evidence from the first sample in both 1991 and 1993 suggests that the degree of employee participation is not substantially different for firms which have been privatized (and in which employees typically own many shares) and for firms which remain in the state sector. For example, in 1993 both the average levels of employee participation on particular issues as well as the distribution of responses is quite similar. Moreover, t tests typically[19] indicate that there are no statistically significant differences in the average level of perceived employee participation for privatized and non-privatized firms. To explore some of these relations further, we examined correlation coefficients between employee ownership and various measures of employee influence. Typically we found a negative relationship between employee ownership and employee participation – i.e., increases in employee ownership are associated with reductions in employee influence. So far as board composition is concerned, the correlation coefficient is only 0.07. A simple regression accepts the hypothesis that there is no correlation between employee ownership and employee membership on the board.

Finally, in both samples, there is evidence that in 1993 and 1994, compared to the situation that prevailed during the final days of the Communist era in 1991, there has been some slight fall in the perceived degree of employee influence on particular issues. This reduction in employee perceptions of influence is especially pronounced in firms that have been privatized. For example, comparisons of the average level of participation on an issue for 1993 and 1991 for privatized firms in the first sample always reveals a fall in employee influence. A similar picture prevails using data for the second sample of firms (which lumps together privatized and non-privatized firms).

## Effects of Ownership and Control on Economic Outcomes

We also undertook a variety of exercises both to examine adjustment paths for firms during early transition and also to isolate any possible effects of ownership and control on economic outcomes. Since we have more economic data for the firms in the first sample (in principle this comprises firm-level data for six reporting periods, for every six months from the end of 1991 to the start of 1994), that is the sample on which we focus attention. We use two approaches.

In some of these exercises we emulate what we might label a qualitative approach – for example as used by Estrin, Gelb and Singh (1995) in their cross-national study. In this one computes a key indicator, such as the ratio of labour costs to sales (LC/S), total costs to sales (TC/S), or liabilities to sales (L/S), and examines both how it changes over time and also whether it is associated with variables such as forms of ownership. In other exercises we follow some of the literature (e.g., Earle *et al.*, 1995) and attempt to test for statistical significance in patterns of evolution by estimating fairly simple cross-sectional regressions. In these the dependent variable is a selected measure of performance and the set of explanatory variables includes measures of ownership (and/or control or influence) and usually a lagged value of the dependent variable. At the outset we note that there are difficulties with both procedures in part because the sample size is small and also because there are many gaps (missing variables) in the data. We begin by discussing the qualitative evidence.

From the information we assembled on key indicators such as TC/S and LC/S at six-month intervals, it is clear that there is evidence of change during early transition. For example during early transition for sample firms typically the labour force fell drastically. To examine the hypothesis that ownership affects economic outcomes we also computed these key indicators for each 6-month period for groups of insider- and outsider-owned firms. In the vast majority of cases there were no statistically significant differences in adjustment at a given point in time for firms in different ownership classes. However there were exceptions and typically these reject the hypothesis that insider-owned firms are less efficient.

For example, for firms that are owned by insiders in early 1994 we find that the ratio of total costs to sales averaged 1.61 (n = 15) as compared with 4.97 (n = 31) in outsider-owned firms. The t value for the difference in means was 1.74 (significant at the 10 per cent level). When a similar exercise is undertaken, but using the ratio of labour costs/sales, we find that insider-owned firms had lower ratios in the first half of 1994 (32 per cent, n = 15) compared to 48 per cent (n = 34) for outsider-owned firms, though the difference in means is not statistically significant at customary levels of significance. Most conspicuously, whereas the liability/sales ratio for insider-owned firms was halved in late 1993 compared to early 1994, for outsider-owned firms the ratio almost doubled (statistically significant at 10 per cent level).

When we look at particular cases in the same sector with different ownership structures, the results are broadly supportive of what we find for the total sample. For example, for four firms in manufacturing that are insider-owned, all of our ratios involving total costs fell in 1994 (compared to 1993), while in a single outsider-owned firm the ratios increased.

Finally we consider results from the simple regressions. In the vast majority of cases we do not find statistically significant results. For example, in none of the regressions of the form, $TC/S_t = \text{cons.} + a_1.TC_{t-1} + a_2.INS$, were the coefficients on ownership structure (in this case INS) significant. Thus, based on the results of this small survey there is no support for the view that insider ownership has deleterious effects on economic performance or that it hinders restructuring. In turn these findings suggest that, in the dynamic context of transitional economies, the links between ownership and control may be more complex than originally suggested by many.

## THE NATURE AND ROLE OF TRADE UNIONS

Another potential avenue for employee involvement is through membership in trade unions. In transitional countries, where plural trade unions now exist, this potential might have been realized through employees joining either unions that have succeeded the former official unions or in new trade unions that are also independent of the state. But whereas in many transition countries a substantial number of employees have elected to join trade unions without precursors, in much of Russia it appears that, to date, employees have chosen overwhelmingly to affiliate instead with successor unions (Jones, 1995a). In addition, in many transitional economies, turbulent conditions can permit some employee participation which is not necessarily union-based and even without formal *de jure* changes. Thus, as we have noted, in Russia the worker collective often continues to be an important body; it played the key role in choosing options for medium- and large-scale firms that were privatized (Bim *et al.*, 1993).

To gather more systematic data on whether the latest reforms have produced actual changes in labour unions[20] and other mechanisms for employee involvement, a survey was administered[21] which was designed to capture information on several themes – membership, structure, functions, leadership, compensation and democracy. Key findings, which are reported more fully elsewhere (Jones, 1995), are summarized under a number of headings.

## Union Membership: Successor and Alternative Unions

Whereas union membership was almost automatic in the old unions, recently the decision to be a union member has become a matter of a choice. One might, therefore, expect membership rates in successor unions to have fallen significantly. However, aggregate data provided by the Confederation and estimates of union density in enterprises from the surveys show that union density in successor unions is typically very high with a median level of membership exceeding 90 per cent.

The new alternative unions (unions without precursors) have attracted much attention (e.g., Borisov *et al.*, 1994).[22] In view of the claim that the impetus for the new unions was especially strong in St. Petersburg (e.g., Temkina, 1992), it might be expected that there would have been significant switching by members from successor unions and that more than one union would have emerged to represent different groups of workers within enterprises. To provide information on this point, respondents were asked to estimate membership in unions other than their union (all of which were successor unions). Always this was reported to be tiny – never amounting to more than 2 per cent of the workforce, and often zero. While it is always hazardous to rely too heavily on estimates made by members of one union about membership in a rival union, based on this evidence for the St. Petersburg region it does not appear that membership in alternative unions or multiple unionism at the same plant were strong phenomena. In addition, the evidence indicates that union presence is very, very modest in the newly emerging private industries.

## Who are the Union Leaders?

In the old unions, the perception[23] is that the typical union leader was, first and foremost, a member of the communist Party. Leaders were apt to be male, well-educated, middle-aged and not to hail from a blue-collar background. In several respects the survey data show that this profile of leaders in successor unions had not changed much: the mean age for union leaders is 47; almost 90 per cent of union leaders are male; 78 per cent had attended or graduated from post-secondary schools; and most had considerable work experience – 68 per cent had worked at least 10 years in their previous job.

However, important changes appear to be underway. Whereas in the old unions, all the leaders had belonged to the technical/managerial end of the occupational spectrum, in successor unions, by contrast, almost three of every four union leaders surveyed had been a specialist of one sort or another before becoming a union officer. Moreover, in terms of their affiliation with the Communist Party, 22 per cent of today's leaders had never been members of that Party. Of the remainder, 52 per cent of the sample are former members and only 25 per cent continued to belong to the Communist Party (or its successor bodies). In addition, the data showing cross-tabulations on party membership and political beliefs strongly suggest that there is no relationship between a union leader's status concerning the Communist Party and political beliefs.

## Union Functions: What do Union Leaders Do?

The changes ushered in by the advent of *perestroika* mean that the framework within which unions function has dramatically changed. Fundamentally, both the monopoly power of the Communist Party and the system of central planning (including central wage fixing) have formally collapsed. However, in part because at the time of the survey there was no new labour code in place, exactly what these changes mean in practice for the former 'dual functions' of unions remains unclear, For example, the role of unions in determining wages and employment is uncertain. Also, successor unions have usually inherited substantial assets from the old unions, especially infrastructure such as kindergartens, houses and vacation centres. Along with ownership, however, comes potential obligations to serve their members by administering these assets (thus constraining how unions might otherwise allocate their scarce resources). To gather new data on the question of what successor unions actually do in this radically new but still evolving context, union leaders were asked to evaluate a variety of tasks in order of the priority they assigned when deciding how to allocate their time and other union resources. A five-point scale was used (1 = most important, to 5 = least important).

From Table 5 we see that, broadly speaking, respondents view issues as falling into three categories. Consistently ranked as most important (receiving a '1' in at least 50 per cent of cases) are: improving or protecting pay; helping members solve problems and grievances on the job; protecting job security; and improving safety and health at work. If top priority issues are defined by responses of '1' or '2' then in at least 65 per cent of cases, to this list must be added administering social security and keeping members informed. The issue which consistently ranks as being of lowest priority today is a task which, under the old system, consumed much of local leaders' time – arranging for holidays at union-owned facilities. (Fewer than 1 in 5 union leaders rank this as either 1 or 2, while 50 per cent rate the issue as a

4 or 5.) In the past, product distribution at 'firms' in the USSR was an important way for union leaders to serve members who lived in shortage economies. But today the survey evidence indicates that union leaders no longer spend much time on matters concerning distributing products and consumer goods. Issues usually accorded medium priority are: improving the way the union is run; improving or protecting benefits; and organizing non-members.

**Table 5.  Allocation of Time and Resources by Union Leaders in St. Petersburg in 1993**

| | Issue | | | | | | | | | | |
|---|---|---|---|---|---|---|---|---|---|---|---|
| **Priority** | **6** | **7** | **8** | **9** | **0** | **1** | **2** | **3** | **4** | **5** | **6** |
| 1 | 5 | 5 | 1 | 0 | 1 | 2 | 4 | 5 |   | 4 | 0 |
| 2 | 3 | 1 | 5 | 7 | 4 | 8 | 1 | 4 | 5 | 9 | 8 |
| 3 |   |   | 0 | 6 | 2 | 7 | 3 | 7 | 9 | 1 | 6 |
| 4 |   |   | 0 |   | 8 | 8 |   | 9 | 0 | 6 |   |
| 5 |   |   |   |   |   | 6 |   |   | 0 | 9 |   |

*Note*:   All entries are percentages of total responses: the median number of responses was 82.
76 =  helping members solve problems and grievances on the job.
77 =  improving of protecting pay.
78 =  improving safety and health at work.
79 =  keeping members informed.
80 =  improving the way the union is run.
81 =  distributing products or consumer
82 =  protecting job security.
83 =  improving or protecting benefits.
84 =  arranging for holidays at union-owned facilities.
85 =  organizing non-union workers.
86 =  administering social security.

# Union Structure

In the past, reflecting industrial organization under central planning, union members belonged to industrial (branch) unions and craft unions did not exist. Evidence on the formal structure of successor unions, including their relation to other bodies, is derived mainly from interviews and visits. This shows that the inherited structures still exercise a powerful influence – in 1992 the members of the new confederation were overwhelmingly branch unions. But in addition to 33 branch (industry) members, for the first time four unions that each represented workers at very large enterprises had joined the regional confederation. Presumably they believed that direct affiliation (rather than representation through a branch.) would better serve member interests.

Another important change concerns the process of de-emphasizing the role of the centre. This is indicated, for example, by personnel cuts. Staff at the Confederation has been reduced from 100 in 1992 to 30 in September 1993. Similar processes have occurred at the branch and, where appropriate, individual union levels. Finally, the existence of various institutions outside though alongside trade unions (e.g., the work collective) suggests the possibility of rivalries between different institutions which seek to represent workers' interests. However, the strong impression gained from enterprise visits was that this is not typical.

## Leaders' Compensation and Effort

The survey data show that both monetary rewards and hours worked varied considerably. Thus whereas about 4 per cent of union leaders worked fewer than 40 hours *per* month, in 12 per cent of cases officers spent more than 240 hours a month on union business. Another clear change that has occurred concerns the earnings of union leaders relative to previously important reference groups, such as the senior manager. In the past, reflecting the almost co-equal status of union presidents and senior managers, union leaders typically earned about 70–90 per cent of what a director earned. In 1993 the best estimates are that union leaders seldom earned more than one-third of a top manager. However, union leaders' wages continue to be linked to average worker earnings, receiving between 2.8 and 4 times the average wage in the enterprises visited. In other words, the fall in relative earnings of union leaders fundamentally reflects the improved position of managers relative to all other groups.

One key issue in the area of compensation concerns the belief that in the old unions membership in the Communist Party had a positive influence on a union leader's salary. To see if such differences persist we calculated mean compensation by Communist Party status. On average, individuals who had never been in the Party earned about 18 per cent less than those who have left the Party who, in turn, earned about 15 per cent less than those who remained in a communist organization. Moreover, when compensation equations are estimated to further explore factors that potentially account for variation in leaders' compensation, the results of such an exploratory exercise also indicate that members of the Communist Party are paid significantly more than never-communists and ex-communists and thus point to the apparent persistence of communist privilege in this regard.

## Union Democracy

The available accounts indicate that the old Russian unions fulfilled their dual functions through 'democratic centralist' structures and procedures. These were associated with significant bureaucratization with, for example, little turnover of personnel in leadership positions (Ruble, 1981: chapter 3).[24] Moreover, other bodies that existed alongside unions in the old structures were viewed in a similar light. Thus, formerly there was a limited level of employee autonomy in brigades

(Van Atta, 1989) and, again reflecting the influence of the Communist Party, a high level of formalism characterized elections of brigade leaders (Slider, 1987). Ruble (1981:33) observed that production conferences were also a failed institution insofar as they did not enhance employee participation.

Diverse evidence that attempts to gauge democracy in successor unions was collected.[25] Evidence on elections shows that most of the time there were multiple candidates for a position – in only 35 per cent of cases was there only one candidate competing for a post, while 34 per cent of the time the contest was a two-horse race.[26] From information on measures of incumbency, the median time that respondents had held their current position in the union was one-two years. But 15 per cent had held office for more than six years – i.e., well before the reform process began in earnest. Importantly, more than two in three union leaders reported that they were newly elected to their current position. And while data for current leaders on jobs held in unions sometimes indicate substantial turnover, the data also indicate potentially conflicting tendencies. They reveal tendencies both for many union officials to have risen through the ranks,[27] as well as for much new blood to have appeared recently in successor unions.

Table 6.    Determinants of Tenure and Whether Leaders are Newly Elected:
Union Leaders in St. Petersburg in 1993
(Standard Errors in Parentheses)

| | (1) | (2) | | (1) | (2) |
|---|---|---|---|---|---|
| Variable | Tenure | Newly Elected | Variable | Tenure | Newly Elected |
| Constant | 199.26 | 7.4459** | CPNEVER | −24.51 | 4.1609 |
| | (135.35) | (3.785) | | (14.62) | (43.38) |
| HIED | −30.385* | 0.2839 | EXCP | 0.275 | −0.0037 |
| | (18.00) | (0.7329) | | (14.31) | (0.0123) |
| ACE | −9.1082 | −0.1397** | STATE92 | 8.323 | 1.7365* |
| | (7.482) | (0.0678) | | (11.21) | (0.9226) |
| ACESQ | 0.1130 | | RIGHT | | −1.4072* |
| | (0.0811) | | | | (0.8291) |
| MALE | 54.554 | −2.0244 | LEFT | | 0.1293 |
| | (30.81) | (1.266) | | | (0.8534) |
| PROF | 46.615** | −0.9779 | $R^2$ | 0.37 | −15.945 |
| | (22.50) | (1.235) | Log-likelihood | | |
| PROFPA | 19.663 | | N | 61 | 60 |
| | (12.61) | | | | |
| PROFMA | −12.667 | | | | |
| | (12.59) | | | | |

*Notes:*    In column 1 are OLS estimates, where Tenure = the number of months in office. The estimates reported in column 2 are from a binomial probit in which the dependent variable is whether the union leader is newly elected.
\* Statistically significant at the .10 level; \*\*at the .05 level; \*\*\*at the .01 level (two-tailed tests).

To explore some of these issues further, two sets of exploratory multivariate exercises were undertaken. First, we estimate OLS regressions in which the dependent variable is the length of time (TENURE) the leader has been in office. From Table 6 we see that tenure in office (column 1) is related at conventional levels of statistical significance to some individual characteristics. Those who have a higher education are more likely to have assumed office more recently. Also those with a professional background are more likely to have longer tenure in office. At conventional levels of statistical significance, there is no relationship between tenure in union office and either age, parents' professions, or gender. While there is no statistically significant relationship between tenure and having quit the Communist Party (EXCP), individuals who were never in the Party are also more likely to have a relatively short tenure than others. No evidence is found that tenure is affected by legal form of ownership (STATE92).

Next we estimate binomial probit models in which the dependent variable is whether or not the union leader is newly elected to that position. The probit estimates suggest that women and younger individuals are more likely to be newly elected to union office. Perhaps surprisingly, firms which remain state-owned are also more likely to have new leaders. All other individual variables, including level of education, profession and professional background of parents are found not to be statistically significantly related to being newly elected. This equation also shows that there is no significant difference between the ability of communists, never-communists and ex-communists to be newly elected.

## CONCLUSIONS AND IMPLICATIONS

In the first main section we noted that the conventional wisdom concerning ownership structures in transition economies stresses the dangers attending any level of employee ownership. Next we used an alternative conceptual framework first to examine why, under certain conditions, combinations of employee participation in economic returns and in control might be expected to produce considerable improvements in enterprise performance in privatized firms and then to identify and locate the changes in enterprise organization in the former USSR and in mainly privatized enterprises in the new Russia. However, we noted (as have others, e.g., Nuti, 1996) that often such relationships are expected to be quite complex. In the context of the new Russia, where measures to facilitate and structures governing participation in control and in economic returns appear to be both unstable as well as often disconnected, and where factors other than these are arguably more important determinants of economic performance, it is unlikely that ownership changes as yet will have been expected to have led to systematic and pronounced economic effects. In the subsequent empirical sections we reviewed existing micro evidence on the nature and effects of changes in enterprise organization and control in privatized firms in Russia and also presented some fresh evidence on several issues relating to employee ownership, employee participation and trade unions. These findings are derived mainly from new enterprise-level data that are being collected from ongoing collaborative projects not only in Russia, but also in Bulgaria, Estonia, Latvia and Lithuania. It must be stressed that, for a variety of reasons, our results are only preliminary. Not only are our samples rather small, but we are able to examine only some of the ownership and participation variables which theory suggests are pertinent. Bearing in mind these important caveats, our findings are as follows.

The privatization processes in Russia, as in many transitional economies, have somewhat unexpectedly resulted in a substantial amount of employee ownership. In many firms, insiders are the predominant owners. However, there are substantial differences in ownership patterns. While in many respects these findings are not new, our findings on the nature and scope of employee participation are more novel. We find that (non-managerial) employee ownership typically has not been accompanied by much employee influence on enterprise decision-making (to the extent that this can be judged by employees' own perceptions). We find, similarly, that there is not much (non-managerial) employee influence in state firms yet to be privatized. There does not appear to be much support for the claim that either state-owned firms or employee-owned firms are worker-controlled. Our findings suggest that in transition economies privatization does not produce fundamental changes in inherited patterns of corporate governance but rather has served to strengthen managerial control.

Furthermore, in firms that have been privatized, during early transition there is mainly weak evidence that different structures of ownership and control have resulted in patterns of enterprise adjustment and performance that are basically different. There is no strong evidence that the key obstacle to enhanced performance is employee ownership.[28]

Our other set of findings concerns the nature of successor trade unions. By using new and unusual data for leaders of successor unions, aspects of 'actually existing' unionism in Russia during the early phases of transition to a market economy are studied. While there remains a clear need for additional data, especially for other unions in other regions of Russia, on the basis of the existing data some tentative conclusions can be drawn. In particular our findings indicate that in many ways successor unions differ from the old, official unions. As such, our findings differ from the views of many (e.g., Mikhalev and Bjorksten, 1995).

The characteristics of today's union leaders suggests movement away from the profile of leaders in the old unions. In particular, the role of membership in the Communist Party (and its successors) had diminished considerably. Many changes point to greater decentralization and democracy within the autonomous organizations that have succeeded the old Russian unions that were subordinate to the Communist Party. There is evidence that much new blood has appeared in leadership positions in successor unions and that the average tenure of union leaders has fallen. Past or present membership in the Communist Party is not related to the likelihood of a leader being newly elected. No evidence is found of a relationship between a union leader's status concerning the Communist Party and political beliefs. Furthermore, the picture that emerges concerning union functions and priorities clearly indicates movement away from the old, dual function model. In the past an emphasis on production was paramount; in serving the subsidiary function of members' interests, union leaders devoted much attention to social-welfare matters. But today, union leaders tend to have a pluralist view of economic interests and the concerns that loom largest concern wages and job protection. In terms of formal union structures, there is also evidence of considerable change. Particularly noticeable is the emergence of more decentralized structures. The survey data imply that unions without precursors do not appear to be a big factor at all in most plants in St. Petersburg. Relative to enterprise managers, there has been substantial erosion in union leaders' compensation. Equally, unlike the homogeneity that characterized the past, there is evidence of significant variation in compensation and effort among union leaders. In sum, these data suggest that the hypothesis that successor unions in Russia are incapable of reform is not supported.

However, there are also examples of 'institutional inertia'. In some ways (e.g., age and education) the typical leader in successor unions resembles his precursor. The branch (industrial)-based nature of formal union structures also indicates strong and enduring links with the past. But the fact that those who have never belonged to the Communist Party have lower levels of tenure in union office, and that individuals once or currently affiliated with the Communist Party have higher compensation, suggests the persistence to some degree of former patterns of privilege.

In sum, the findings on the extent of change are not uniform and the situation is quite complicated. On the one hand, even before the introduction of widespread privatization, there is evidence of substantial movement away from the old bureaucratized, transmission-belt model. Many leaders of successor unions are new and their chief concern is to represent their members' interests on 'bread-and-butter' issues. Such evidence suggests that many successor unions in St Petersburg appear to be genuine unions that are not dominated by leaders who emerged under the old regime. However, there is some inertia and communist entrenchment and the influence of the old guard on the policy-making process within successor unions in Russia probably cannot be ignored.[29]

Generally the early view that depoliticization would speedily and reasonably painlessly produce a 'transition to the market' has been replaced by a recognition that transition and privatization is a much more complicated business. Thus in many privatized Russian firms it seems that the astonishing changes in economic policies, including privatization, have produced a disappointingly slow degree of change in key areas such as managerial turnover. The extent of restructuring appears to have been quite limited and this has coincided with a dramatic consolidation of managerial powers.

To try to alleviate this situation, the transition literature (e.g., OECD, 1995) calls for several standard measures. To counter abuses of power by managers and to encourage managerial turnover there is an urgent need for a more transparent and enforceable legal and institutional framework to govern the operation of embryonic capital markets. Analogously measures to provide for more open and clearer managerial contracts would encourage managerial incentives (and lengthen the time horizon of managers). To reduce the opportunities for rent-seeking, more competition needs to be fostered, especially in those sectors where there is extensive monopolization (though these benefits need to be balanced against the potential erosion of network capital in a more competitive environment, as pointed out by Ickes and Ryterman, 1993). To help to fill the 'socialist red hole' (the virtual absence of small firms) in the size distribution of firms inherited from socialism, the process of encouraging the entry of new firms must also be fostered.

However our findings, and the conceptual framework from which they are drawn, may have implications for policy and additional strategies that in some cases are arguably part of the host of institutional changes that are required. Since privatized Russian firms are quite heterogeneous, in some circumstances restructuring might be better facilitated by measures designed to strengthen the role of employees as owners within firms.[30] Rather than always viewing employee ownership as a temporary phenomenon (with ownership quickly passing to outsiders or to managers), stabilizing employee ownership at reasonably high levels and making employee ownership productive may make much sense for selected companies which have yet to see substantial productivity gains. Trying to make employee ownership work better (and thus to reduce the present informational asymmetries between managers and employees) might make particular sense for those companies located in areas in which what one might call the cultural preconditions for collective decision-making remain strong, where the social costs of change have been especially acute and where there is evidence of co-operation between managers and employees. One measure that might be introduced in this respect is a requirement that employees hold shares for a minimum period. While such a policy would not fundamentally impede the development of capital markets it might help to begin to nurture an ownership culture in a country where an ownership mentality often conflicts with historical custom and practice. In addition, since there is some theoretical and empirical evidence for transition economies that employee ownership may be an efficient complement to other forms of ownership (Jones and Mygind, 1996, for the Baltics) fiscal incentives might be given to outsiders who invest in companies in which there is also some degree of employee ownership.

Furthermore, we note that successor unions in Russia have demonstrated their ability to reform. The evidence of progressive, evolutionary changes in actual practices and sustained member commitment to successor unions which appear to be genuine trade unions indicates that successor unions are adapting to a radically different environment, that real though gradual change is possible, although constraints serve to hamper the pace of change. In turn this implies that it may be neither socially nor economically optimal to clear away all vestiges of the old institutional arrangements. On the contrary, the St Petersburg experience and the evolutionary paradigm suggests that in facilitating the emergence of a new institutional arrangements it is perhaps more efficient to build gradually on parts of the old system (Stark, 1992). At minimum, successor unions are a good complement to the alternative unions. During times of economic uncertainty and political polarization, not to support institutions that have a measure of popular acceptance and which are struggling with problems posed by unfamiliar environments and the need to continue the processes of internal reform, and instead to attempt to shape policy in the direction of an 'institutional big bang', may not only be impossible but potentially destabilizing.

Indeed, when judged against a benchmark of limited managerial change, it seems that often there has been swifter and more extensive change in union personnel and practices. In these circumstances a cost-effective strategy in some cases might be to consider measures which encourage and enable trade unions to play a new role – perhaps to better equip them to play the role of an effective employee representative alongside management. his might be done through training which better enables trade unions to play a technical assistance role for employee shareholders – for example, offering advice on shareholder rights and responsibilities and on the relationship of shares to other forms of net worth. In this capacity, trade unions would also help to monitor managerial performance. In addition, to foster participation, consideration might be given to the state mandating employee participation, for example through statutory provision for works councils or board-level representation (co-determination).[31]

Finally we offer a more general observation and conjecture. While we sympathize with the view (e.g., Frydman *et al.*, 1996) that, based on western experience, there are limited portfolios of institutions that have been associated with success in many advanced economies in the past, we also note that most analyses which adopt a comparative institutional approach (e.g., Aoki and Kim, 1995) tend to emphasize only selected institutions – for example, banks. The role of key structures in the labour market is often neglected or relegated to a peripheral or abstract role in accounting for economic success. But we share the view of theorists who argue that labour has played a crucial role in capitalist development (e.g., Lazonick, 1991). Also we note that, in some economies, including Japan and the former West Germany, there is abundant evidence that trade unions were an important ingredient in the institutional set up that contributed to economic success (and including during their own postwar transitions). Moreover, we note that in today's global economy, effective human resource management practices (including employee ownership) often constitute an important part of the makeup of successful companies; frequently the new industrial relations also include trade unions playing a co-operative role.[32] Examination of the roles trade unions might play in firms in which there is extensive employee ownership may be particularly worthy of consideration in other transition economies, especially those CIS countries where successor trade unions appear to fit well with other aspects of the institutional environment and where there is evidence of the persistence and value of long-term relationships among key economic agents.

## APPENDIX – DEFINITIONS OF THE VARIABLES

STATE92 = Dummy variable for whether or not enterprise was state-owned in 1992.
PAYRATE = Earnings per hour (Roubles).
COMP = Average monthly compensation (roubles).
HIED = Dummy for whether of not the union leader had higher education.
AGE = Age of union leader.
AGESQ = AGE*AGE.
GENDER = 0=male; 1=female.
CPNEVER = Dummy for whether respondent was ever a member of the Communist Party.
CPCUR = Dummy for whether respondent is currently a member of the Communist Party (or a successor body).
EXCP = For those who were (are)in the Communist Party, a dummy for whether or not they have quit the party.
LEFT = Dummy for whether or not the respondent has political sympathies for parties on the left (socialists, labourists etc.).
RIGHT = Dummy for whether or not respondent has political sympathies for parties on the right (Democrats, radicals etc.).
CENTRE = Dummy for whether or not respondent has political sympathies for parties in the centre.
PROF = Dummy for whether or not individual has a professional background.
PROFMA = Dummy for whether or not individual's mother had a professional background.
PROFPA = Dummy for whether or not individual's father had a professional background.

## NOTES

1. Until quite recently the empirical evidence on the nature as well as the effects of corporate governance in transitional economies was quite slim. While recent studies do improve matters much, as recent surveys indicate (e.g., EBRD, 1995; World Bank, 1996) often these studies continue to suffer from diverse problems. Frequently these stem from the difficulty in obtaining data for large and representative samples of firms. Also empirical work on the effects of ownership structures usually needs to identify corporate governance with the main owner, and contains limited information on the dynamics of ownership and on the links between ownership and control. We review some of the literature for Russia in Section 2.

2. Most of these findings appear in Jones (1995).
3. Some of the work reported herein draws on other papers, notably Jones (1995) and Jones and Weisskopf (1996).
4. There are, of course, many other forces besides ownership structure that potentially affect enterprise performance. Historical factors and the institutional and regulatory framework may be especially important in firms in transitional economies (Clague and Rausser, eds, 1992. In an uncertain environment managers and workers may form strategic alliances and focus on short term survival and the scale of inter-enterprise debt is also clearly important (Ickes and Ryterman, 1993).
5. Of course, real-life ownership arrangements cannot be classified in a 4x4 table; some actual arrangements may span several cells, and arrangements represented by the same cell may differ in their details. In adducing examples, we emphasize the diversity of plans that constitute similar ownership arrangements. For example, a similar degree of employee control may be implemented by affecting the issues on which employees have influence, or the extent to which they share control over some issues along with management by varying the frequency of employee involvement, and so on. In this examination we cannot explore these trade-offs in detail. For more discussion see BenNer and Jones (1995).
6. Analogous arguments can be developed for profit sharing. While many argue that profit-sharing plans are subject to the 'free-rider' problem, arguably this will be alleviated when workers develop a strong long-term commitment to the company and/or when workers engage in active peer monitoring. Also, information sharing can be thought of as a mechanism to facilitate the development of a long-term commitment to a firm by its workers. It follows that the favourable productivity effects of financial participation are complemented by information sharing.
7. The fact that unions had no separate identities had several implications for the structure and functioning of the labour movement. For example these 'official' unions were the only unions, were organized along industry (branch) lines, and were strongly centralized. Top union leaders were likely to be members of the Communist Party and were believed to be almost as well paid as top administrators (directors) of enterprises.
8. Many of these bodies were set up during the 1980s as part of efforts to improve productivity and reduce alienation. For example, within firms, workers were organized into brigades, structures that provided for worker participation. Brigade leaders were elected by workers. (See Van Atta, 1989).
9. For references see Nuti (1996: 5).
10. For more detail on privatization in Russia, see Bim *et al.*, (1994); Boycko *et al.*, (1993). For general accounts of privatization in former communist countries see Frydman *et al.*, (1993a); EBRD (1994 ) and Estrin, ed. (1994).
11. There is also substantial diversity in patterns of ownership within and across other transition economies. For the Baltics, see Jones and Mygind (1996).
12. Some of these findings are similar to those reported earlier, e.g., by Ash and Hare (1994).
13. For example, some of the earlier World bank studies, e.g., Commander (1994).
14. These studies cover a range of issues and together constitute an impressive body of work. For a review see Alfrandi and Lee, *Transition*, 1995, Vol. 6(7–8), pp.11-12.
15. There are other studies of Russian firms that use multivariate analysis and which focus on issues other than links between corporate governance and economic performance.

For example, to examine the links between market structure and enterprise adjustment, Ickes and Ryterman (1993) use data for 150 firms in five regions. They find strong support for their view that market structure plays an important role in the decision to adjust.

16. Again, this is part of an on-going data collection process that *eventually* will include detailed data that will be comparable in coverage across several countries and which will be collected in co-operation with the relevant statistical authorities. These data will cover many areas, including information on the distribution and amounts of ownership amongst employees, managers, key groups of outsiders and the state. Concerning employee involvement, there will be detailed information on structures and patterns of control over time by key agents, though the different institutional arrangements will likely mean that such information will not be directly comparable. By comparison, the data discussed in this paper are much more limited and the samples are largely samples of convenience.

17. The outsider 63 per cent ownership includes private individuals, private firms and state agencies; in enterprises yet to be privatized, most if not all the shares are in the hands of state agencies.

18. To some degree this pattern reflects the structures that prevailed in the former USSR; while wages and employment were centrally determined, employees had considerable influence in other areas including election of supervisors. See Jones (1995).

19. The single exception is for the issue of privatization in 1991. At that time a variety of procedures for privatization (including the role of employees in choosing a privatization option) were being actively discussed.

20. To date there has been relatively little work (and mainly case studies) on the actual changes that have occurred in Russian trade unions and industrial relations. (See, for example, Gordon and Klopov, 1992; Borisov *et al.*, 1994; Temkina, 1992; Clarke *et al.*, 1993).

21. The survey was administered to a sample of union leaders in St Petersburg in 1993. For details see Jones (1995).

22. During this early phase of transition and embryonic collective bargaining, in principle more than one union may exist at an establishment. While specific details of actual practices are scarce, it is believed that unions without precursors are a significant force in certain industries such as coal where the Independent Trade Union of Miners (NPG) has a membership of about 400,000. See also Borisov *et al.*, (1994) for a study of independent Russian unions for pilots and air traffic controllers and the relationship of these bodies to successor unions.

23. Unfortunately, there do not seem to be precise data with which one can make comparisons. The impression of the profile of the average union leader comes from several sources, for example Rutland (1988).

24. For example, an auditing commission, which included members of the Communist Party, assembled nominations for leadership positions. In turn '...the system of auditing commissions combines with the unions' nomenklatura personnel structure to predetermine the outcome of any union election' (Ruble, 1981: 47). See also Rutland (1988).

25. In so doing we note that there is a long history of examining this theme for western trade unions (see, for example, (Edelstein and Warner, 1976; and Taft, 1962). Furthermore, these and other studies that attempt to measure democracy in other organizations, indicate that there is no single ideal indicator or measure and that there are

obvious problems in interpreting some of the evidence. For example, long tenure in office or few candidates for a position may imply either a strong and popular incumbent (whom no-one wants to challenge) or an entrenched incumbent with considerable resources.

26. Similar formal indicators of democracy have been used in evaluating unions elsewhere. In his classic study of American unions, Taft (1954) found that on average 23.4 per cent of offices were contested. See also Allen (1954) for British unions. If similar formal indicators are used in St. Petersburg, then contemporary Russian successor unions would probably be judged at least as democratic as were US and UK unions in these studies.

27. Evidence on some of these matters is also available from enterprise visits. At one large firm, union affairs were handled by a trade union committee of 45. More than half of the members of this body had changed during the last two years, including some through a recall provision. This body met monthly though individual members would meet with their constituents (e.g., in workshops) each week. On another occasion I was present at a meeting of the Trade Union Confederation during a visit by a delegate of the National Confederation from Moscow. This was quite a lively meeting with active participation by all present.

28. Other work for new private firms points to the crucial importance of other barriers such as human capital (Barberis *et al.,* 1996).

29. These findings for Russia, are consistent with the limited available data for other former communist countries in central and eastern Europe (e.g., Jones, 1992, 1995; Swiatowski, 1994). These studies suggest that everywhere there has been significant change in key aspects of industrial relations. In particular, there is evidence of transformation in successor unions in countries for which information are available. At the same time, while all countries began with a virtually identical system of industrial relations there is no evidence of convergence to a single new system of industrial relations.

30. There is also some evidence on the beneficial effects of employee ownership in former command economies (See Jones (1993) for the case of Poland). See also Bim *et al.,* (1993) for an evaluation of the performance of new co-operatives in Russia.

31. Furthermore, it seems that one reason for the ability of managerial power to persist is the isolation of individual firms and the absence of an effective external monitoring mechanism. One remedy that has been suggested for this problem is the development of an external institution – a lead bank – to play this role, with the bank owning equity in firms, though not necessarily a majority share (e.g., Aoki and Kim, 1995). It is interesting to note that, within a context of widespread employee ownership, a bank is already effectively serving this role of enterprise monitor – the Caja Laboral Popular in the Mondragon complex of production co-operatives (Whyte and Whyte, 1988). For clusters of firms with substantial employee ownership and which are located in the same region, the arrangements in the Mondragon complex, in particular the employee bank, as well as other components in the structures that have been devised to support individual firms, may warrant a closer look.

32. For reviews of the human resource practices of successful firms see the essays in Lewin, Mitchell and Zahidi (1996). See also Kleiner and Ay (1996) for evidence on the positive contribution made by unions and other mechanisms of employee representation to macroeconomic performance.

# REFERENCES

Aoki, Masahiko and Hyung-Ki Kim, (eds) (1995), *Corporate Governance in Transitional Economies,* Washington, D.C.:World Bank.

AFL-CIO (1993), Report to the Board of Directors, Free Trade Union Institute, 1991–92 Washington.

Aghion, P., O. Blanchard and S. Burgess (1994), 'The Behavior of Firms in Eastern Europe, pre-Privatization', *European Economic Review,* Vol. 38, pp. 1327–49.

Allen, V.L. (1954), *Power in Trade Unions,* N.Y.:Longmans.

Ash, Timothy N. and Paul G. Hare (1994), 'Privatization in the Russian Federation:changing enterprise behaviour in the transition period', *Cambridge Journal of Economics,* Vol. 18, pp. 619–634.

Ben-Ner, Avner (1993), 'Organizational Reform in Central and Eastern Europe: A Comparative perspective', *Annals of co-operative and Political Economy,* Vol. 64(3), pp. 329–365.

Ben-Ner, Avner and Derek C. Jones (1995), 'Employee Participation, Ownership and Productivity: A Theoretical Framework', *Industrial Relations,* October.

Bim, Alexander S., Derek C. Jones and Thomas E. Weisskopf (1993), 'Hybrid Forms of Enterprise Organization in the Former USSR and the Russian Federation', *Comparative Economic Studies,* Vol. 35(1), pp. 1–37.

Bim, Alexander S., Derek C. Jones and Thomas E. Weisskopf (1994), 'Privatization in the Former Soviet Union and the New Russia', in Estrin, Saul, (ed.), *Privatization in Central and Eastern Europe,* Longman.

Blasi, Joseph (1994), 'Russian Labor-Management Relations: Some Preliminary Lessons from Newly Privatized Enterprises', in Voos, Paula B., (ed.), proceedings of the Forty-Seventh Annual Meeting, Madison, WI: IRRA Series.

Blasi, Joseph (1995), 'Russian Enterprises after Privatization', mimeo, Rutgers University.

Blasi, Joseph and D. Kruse (1991), *Employee Ownership,* New York: Harper Business.

Blasi, J. R. (1996), 'Corporate Ownerships Corporate Governance in the Russian Federation', Research Report on the Federal Commission on the Capital Market, May 1996.

Bogomolov, Oleg (1996), 'Some Lessons of the Privatization in Russia', in Ostojic, N. and N. Scott, (eds), 'Privatization in the Economies in Transition', proceedings of the ECPD International Round Table, Beograd.

Bonin, John, Derek C. Jones and Louis Putterman (1993), 'Theoretical and Empirical Studies of Producer Co-operatives: Will the Twain Ever Meet?', *Journal of Economic Literature,* Vol. 31, September, pp. 1290–1320.

Borisov, Vadim, Peter Fairbrother and Simon Clarke (1994), 'Is there Room for an Independent Trade Unionism in Russia' Trade Unionism in the Russian Aviation Industry', *British Journal of Industrial Relations,* Vol. 32(3), September, pp. 359–78.

Boycko, M., A. Schleifer and R. Vishny (1993), 'Privatizing Russia' *Brookings Papers on Economic Activity, #2,* pp. 139–192.

Boycko, M. A. Schleifer and R. Vishny (1996), 'A Theory of Privatization', *Economic Journal,* Vol. 106, March, pp. 309–19.

Brown, E.C. (1966), *Soviet Trade Unions and Labor Relations,* Cambridge, Mass.: Harvard University Press.

Charup and Webster (1993), 'Private Manufacturing Firms in St. Petersburg', mimeo, World Bank.

Clague, C. and G. C. Rausser, (eds) (1992), *The Emergence of Market Economies in Eastern Europe*, Oxford: Blackwell.

Clarke, S., P. Fairbrother, M. Burawoy and P. Krotov (1993), *What about the Workers?*, London: Verso.

Clegg, Hugh (1976), *Trade Unionism Under Collective Bargaining*, Oxford: Blackwell.

Commander, S., S. Dhar and R. Yemtsov (1995), 'How Russian Firms make their Wage and Employment Decisions', mimeo, World Bank.

Craig and Pencavel (1992), 'Plywood Co-operatives', *American Economic Review*

Earle, J.S. and S. Estrin (1996), 'Employee Ownership in Transition', in Frydman, R. *et al.*, (1993a), Vol. 2., pp. 1–62.

Earle, J.S. and L. Leshchenko (1995), 'Ownership Structures, Patterns of Control and Enterprise Behavior in Russia', mimeo, Central European University.

EBRD (1994), *Transition Report for 1994*, October, London.

EBRD (1995), *Transition Report for 1995*, October, London.

Edelstein, J.David and Malcolm Warner (1976), *Comparative Union Democracy*, N.Y.: Wiley.

Estrin, Saul, (ed.) (1994), *Privatization in Central and Eastern Europe*, Longman.

Estrin, Saul, A. Gelb and I. Singh (1995), 'Shocks and Adjustment by Firms in Transition: A Comparative Study' *Journal of Comparative Economics*.

Estrin, Saul, D.C. Jones and Jan Svejnar (1987), 'Productivity Effects of Worker Participation: Producer Co-operatives in Western Economies', *Journal of Comparative Economics*, Vol. 11, pp. 40–61.

Fan, Q. and B. Fang (1995), 'Are Russian Enteprises Restructuring?', mimeo, World Bank.

Freeman, Richard (1993), 'What Direction for Labor Market Institutions in Eastern and Central Europe?', in Blanchard, O. *The Transition in Eastern Europe*, NBER.

Frydman, R. *et al.*, (1993a), *The Privatization Process in Russia, Ukraine and the Baltic States*, CEU Privatization Reports, Vol. 2, Budapest, London, New York: CEU Press.

Frydman, R. *et al.*, (1993b), 'Needed Mechanisms of Corporate Governance and Finance in Eastern Europe', *Economics of Transition*, Vol. 1 (2), pp. 171–207.

Frydman, Roman, K, Pistor and A. Rapaczynski (1996), 'Exit and Voice after Mass Privatization: The case of Russia', *European Economic Review*, 40, pp. 581–588.

Frydman, R., C. Gray and A. Rapaczynski, (eds) (1996), *Corporate Governance in Central Europe and Russia*, Budapest: CEU Press.

Gerchikov, Vladimir (1992), 'Business Democracy: Work Collective Councils and Trade Unions' in Szell,G., (ed.), *Labor Relations in Transition in Eastern Europe*, de Gruyter: Berlin.

Gordon, Leonid and E. Klopov (1992), 'The Workers' Movement in a Post Socialist Perspective', in Silverman *et al.*, (1992), pp. 27–52.

Grancelli, Bruno (1988), *Soviet Management and Labor Relations*, Boston: Allen and Unwin.

Hinds, M. (1990), 'Issues in the Introduction of Market Forces in Eastern and Central European Socialist Economies', March, Washington, D.C.: World Bank.

Ickes, B.W. and R. Ryterman (1993), 'From Enterprise to Firm: Notes for a Theory of the Enterprise in Transition', mimeo, Penn. State University.

Ickes, B.W. and S. Tenev (1995), 'On Your Marx, Get Set, Go: The Role of Competition in Enterprise Adjustment', mimeo, Penn. State University.

IMF (1993), 'Latvia – Recent Economic Developments', IMF, April.

Jones, Derek C. (1993), 'The Effects of Worker Participation on Productivity in Command Economies: Evidence for the case of Polish Producer Co-operatives', *Managerial and Decision Economics*, Vol. 14, 5, pp. 475–485.

Jones, Derek C. (1995), 'On Successor Unions in Transitional Economies: Evidence from St. Petersburg', *Industrial and Labor Relations Review,* October, Vol. 49(1), pp. 39–57.

Jones, Derek C. (1995a), 'On Successor Unions in Former Communist Countries: Evidence from Bulgaria, the Czech Republic, Estonia and Russia', mimeo, Hamilton College, and forthcoming in *Advances in Industrial and Labor Relations*, Vol. 7.

Jones, Derek C. and Takao Kato (1995), 'The Productivity Effects of Bonuses and Employee Ownership: Evidence Using Japanese Panel Data', *American Economic Review*, June, Vol. 85(3), pp. 391–414.

Jones, Derek C. and Niels Mygind (1996), 'The Effects of Employee Ownership on Productive Efficiency: Evidence from the Baltics', mimeo.

Jones, Derek C. and Tom Weisskopf (1996), 'Employee Ownership and Control: Evidence from Russia', mimeo, Hamilton College and forthcoming in Proceedings of the Forty-Eighth Meeting of the Industrial Relations Research Association.

Katz, Harry C., Sarosh Kuruvilla and Lowell Turner (1993), Trade Unions and Collective Bargaining: Suggestions for Emerging Democracies in Eastern Europe and the Former Soviet Europe', in Silverman *et al.*, 1993.

Kleiner, M. and C.R. Ay (1996), Employee Representation and Economic Growth: Theory and Evidence from Advanced Countries' in *Advances in Industrial and Labor Relations*, v.7.

Lazonick, W. (1991), *Business Organization and the Myth of a Market Economy,* Cambridge University Press.

Lewin, D., D. Mitchell and M. Zaidi, (eds) (1996), *Handbook of Human Resources*, Greenwich, Conn.: JAI.

Mikhalev, V. and N. Bjorksten (1995), 'Wage Formation During the Period of Economic Restructuring in the Russian Federation', mimeo, OECD, Paris.

Murrell, Peter (1992), 'Evolution in Economics and in the Economic Reform of the Centrally Planned Economies', in Clague, Christopher and Gordon C. Rausser, (eds), *The Emergence of Market Economies in Eastern Europe*, Cambridge Mass.: Blackwell.

Mygind, Niels (1994), 'Socialism in Transition', mimeo, University of Copenhagen.

Nuti, Mario (1995), 'Employeeism: Corporate Governance and Employee Ownership in Transitional Economies', mimeo, London Business School.

Nuti, Mario (1996), 'Employee Ownership in Polish Privatization' mimeo, London Business School.

OECD (1995), OECD Economic Surveys:The Russian Federation OECD, Paris.

Pravda, Alex and Blair Ruble (1986), *Trade Unions in Communist States*, London: Allen and Unwin.

Ruble, Blair (1981), *Soviet Trade Unions*, Cambridge University Press.

Rutland, Peter (1988), 'The Role of the Communist Party on the Soviet Shopfloor', *Studies in Comparative Communism*, XXI, 1, pp. 25–44.

Silverman, Bertram, Robert Vogt and Murray Yanowitch, (eds) (1992), *Labor and Democracy in the Transition to a Market System*, N.Y.: Sharpe.

Silverman, Bertram, Robert Vogt and Murray Yanowitch, (eds) (1993), *Double Shift*, Sharpe.

Slider, Darrell (1987), 'The Brigade System in Soviet Industry', *Soviet Studies*, Vol. 39(3), pp. 388–405.

Standing, Guy (1992), papers presented at the ILO Conference on Industrial Restructuring, Moscow and St. Petersburg, October 1992 (obtainable from ILO, CEET, Budapest).

Standing, Guy (1995), 'Promoting the 'Human Development Enterprise': Enterprise restructuring and Corporate Governance in Russian Industry', ILO, Labour Market Paper No. 8.

Stark, David (1992), 'Path Dependence and Privatization: Strategies for East and Central Europe', *East European Politics and Societies*, 6, pp.17–54.

Taft, P. (1962), *The Structure and Government of Trade Unions*, Harvard, Cambridge.

Temkina, Anna (1992), 'The Workers' Movement in Leningrad 1986–91', *Soviet Studies*, Vol. 42(2), pp. 209–236.

Van Atta, Don (1989), 'A Critical examination of Brigades in the USSR', *Economic and Industrial Democracy*, Vol. 10, pp. 329–340.

Whyte, W.F. and Whyte (1988), *Mondragon*, Cornell University: ILR Press; New York: Ithaca.

World Bank (1996), *World Development Report 1996*, Oxford.

# 14
# Privatization in Ukraine: Stages, Actors and Outcomes

*Larisa Leshchenko and Valeriy Revenko*

## INTRODUCTION

The Ukrainian privatization programme was initiated in a society characterized by overall dominance of the state sector in the economy, by the virtual absence of robust capital and financial markets, and by a lack of understanding of the essence of these both on the part of the population in general and policy-makers in particular. Whereas central and eastern Europe (CEE) had already witnessed an explosion of privatization activity in 1992, Ukraine since then has been making backwards and forwards movements, trying to overcome political opposition and the legislative vacuum, and implementing a variety of legal and illegal forms and methods. The initial plan of privatization in Ukraine, together with the numerous amendments and corrections launched at different stages by the Supreme Council of Ukraine or by the President, were rather ambiguous and complicated. Ukraine demonstrated substantial slowness in its implementation of privatization, against a general background of delay in executing all other components of market reform. Only in October 1994 did President Kuchma initiate a new phase of privatization in Ukraine, putting it on the more simple, transparent and straightforward track of mass privatization.

There are several periodicals in Ukraine, both newspapers and magazines, which reflect the current situation and the peculiarities of the privatization process. Among these are two official publications, namely, the *'State bulletin on privatization'* published since the end of 1992; the *'Investment newspaper'* published for more than two years, and *'Courier of Privatization'*, which reflect the official point

315

of view on privatization and report on the results of privatization and the roles of the different actors involved. Due to the strong support from USAID in the period 1991–94, a magazine entitled *'Privatization in Ukraine'* was issued by the Harvard Project on Economic Reform in Ukraine (PERU) which was established in Kiev in 1990 and, together with the first publication by R. Frydman, A. Rapazcynski and J. Earle (1993) contributed a great deal to policy-makers' understanding of the essence of the privatization process. *'Privatization in Ukraine'* was succeeded by the monthly *'The Ukrainian Economic Monitor'*, containing regular summaries and statistical data on privatization results, prepared by T. Voronkova and L. Verhovodova.

Ukrainian scholars represent a whole range of views on the concept and course of privatization in Ukraine. V. Lanovyi, for example, represents the camp of the architects and proponents of the Ukrainian choice of privatization path, while some others, e.g., V. Heets and M. Shvaika, have analysed the privatization process at different stages and expressed a great deal of criticism, both with respect to the design of the privatization programme, its methods of implementation and the capacity of the executive to implement it. D. Snelbecker, advisor from the PERU project, analysed the nature of the process, its speed, and the role of international organizations and has recommended improvements to Ukraine's privatization programme in the course of the mass privatization stage. The latest publications of two other Ukrainian scholars, V. Revenko and V. Cherniak, are more systematic in nature, attempting to analyse both the positive and negative outcomes of Ukrainian privatization both in its own right and in comparison with other countries of the region.

Based on all the previous evidence, this chapter will not only recount the privatization process in Ukraine with all its peculiar features, but will argue that in reality there have been three distinct phases in this fluctuating and ambiguous process and the resulting evolution of ownership from the perspective of the main actors, laws, and institutions involved, and the outcomes.

The first section of the paper discusses the initial legal framework and the peculiarities of the first stage of the privatization process, i.e., 1991–93, which may be described basically as a case-by-case phase. At that time the concept of privatization and the first laws were adopted, and the state bodies to conduct the process of privatization were established. However, the high level of uncertainty and lack of comprehension regarding the role of the various market actors and institutions and the limited capacity of the executive power in carrying out privatization led to serious challenges in elaborating a distinct strategy and well-designed plan, and substantially slowed down its implementation.

The year 1994, described in the second section of the paper, is treated by authors as the second phase of the privatization process in Ukraine since it stands apart in terms of new actors and institutions; it was the peak period for the use of non-competitive methods and at the same time saw a moratorium on all sale-purchase agreements. Ultimately, the 'rules of the game' were drastically changed and new ones imposed at the end of the year. This year could be considered as a transition period in the shift from a case-by-case approach to the mass privatization stage.

A revised mass privatization programme was launched at the very end of 1994 and characterizes the third, most probably the last phase of Ukrainian privatization. Initially, at the beginning of 1995, it was not very successful due to several serious flaws in the design of auction procedures for the sale of shares and to the fact that there were too few enterprises on the supply side; later on, however, one can see significant progress being attained, owing to the support of various international donors which enabled the bottlenecks to be overcome. Despite some side-effects, at the end of 1996 privatization in Ukraine resembled an assembly-line with around 400 enterprises supplied monthly and, as a result, in the ownership structure of almost 4000 companies a dominant stake is in private hands.

The last section of the paper presents a comparative study of all three stages of the Ukrainian privatization process and provides evidence of a substantial speeding up of the process at the third stage, with the clearer role of the various market actors and institutions and the shift towards competitive methods in the course of mass privatization. Among the major achievements of the latter phase are the following: the small privatization programme was completed in 1996; more than 4000 medium and large enterprises are privately owned; the list of companies not subject to privatization is being revised (shortened), and the process of ownership transformation has shifted towards cash transactions, which seems to be a more efficient allocation mechanism.

# OVERVIEW OF THE FIRST STAGE OF PRIVATIZATION IN UKRAINE, 1991–93

The first stage of privatization in Ukraine was characterized by the complexity of the social and economic problems following the acquisition of state independence and by the lack of qualified policy-makers able to make decisions and their short-sighted intention to minimize the costs of implementing a privatization programme, which resulted in even more cumbersome and expensive procedures. Unfortunately, the policy-makers responsible for the design of the privatization programme failed from the very beginning to demonstrate any profound knowledge of the basic principles, targets and challenges of privatization, and thus the process of de-statization and restructuring was substantially slowed down. Moreover, this created room for a variety of illicit transactions by those in society who were immediately ready to exploit all the advantages of economic reforms and in the course of the resulting 'spontaneous' privatization gained thousands of times more than their 1/52 millionth share[1] of state-owned assets, while others ultimately lost even this guaranteed minimum.

It is worthwhile mentioning that the first steps of the economic reforms were undertaken in 1988–91, while Ukraine was still part of the former Soviet Union, with the adoption by the Supreme Council of the laws 'On individual working activity', 'On co-operation' and 'On enterprise', which envisaged new types of companies, created room for competition and encouraged entrepreneurial behaviour, on the one hand, and were aimed at increasing the independence of economic agents and reducing the state's intervention in their activities, on the other.

Discussions about the necessity of privatization in Ukraine started in 1990 and took the form of the first 'Concept on De-statization and Privatization of State Enterprises, Land and Housing' (hereinafter 'Concept'), adopted by the Supreme Council on October 31, 1991. The Concept was the first legislative act which defined, albeit in rather general terms, the goals, methods, means, scale and rate of ownership transformations in Ukraine. The main dilemma of mass privatization in ex-communist societies – whether to grant insiders with privileges in acquiring shares in privatized companies or not – has been resolved in Ukraine in favour of the workers and managers. However, the implementation of this principle at different stages of an endless process of privatization led to distinct outcomes in terms of ownership structure. According to the Concept, insiders (enterprise working collectives[2]) received priority rights and privileges in acquiring enterprises and land, and citizens of Ukraine were granted the right of free choice with regard to the subject and method of privatization, or selecting a financial intermediary. It was envisaged that to acquire a slice of state property one could use cash, loans and privatization certificates. The process of intensive de-statization and privatization was supposed to last for 4–5 years and aimed at transferring 60–65 per cent of the state enterprises to private hands, although the notion of a privatized or privately-owned firm was not properly defined at that time.[3] The next step in the privatization process was marked by the adoption of three laws in Ukraine in March 1992: the Law on Privatization of the Property of State Enterprises, the Law on Privatization of Small State Enterprises and the Law on Privatization Certificates.[4]

Privatization, as the process of transferring productive assets from the public sector to private owners involving some type of a sale-purchase agreement, has been regarded as an effort to restructure the economic system, to accelerate economic growth by eliminating massive state intervention and promote competitive incentives to increase efficiency, both allocative and productive. Equally important, the government hoped to reduce budgetary pressures resulting from subsidies and transfer payments towards state enterprises, and thereby also to induce managers to shift from rent-seeking to profit-making behaviour. Revenue-raising through the sale of enterprises played a secondary role due both to the low value of assets in the post-communist economies and to the existence of the voucher scheme for mass privatization, which implied the transfer of productive assets to the citizens free of charge.

According to the initial design set out by the architects of the privatization programme, privatization certificates (vouchers) were supposed to be given to each citizen of Ukraine in the form of a personal 'special bank account' which was not tradable for cash and could be used only to pay for shares in privatized companies. The main objective of using this form of voucher was to ensure that every citizen would use it only as a means of payment for shares in privatized companies and in this way to guarantee participation in the privatization process. Another reason behind the 'special bank account' was to make the process of voucher issuing less expensive. However, the result was the opposite of that anticipated: it turned out to be the most inefficient and inconvenient approach. During the rather long period during which they existed – 1992–mid-1995 – only 8 million people (15 per cent of the population) opened their bank accounts and used them to acquire shares in privatized companies. 'Special bank accounts' were used mainly by insiders to buy shares in their companies since the procedure for their utilization by outsiders, especially individuals, was rather complicated and not very transparent.

The fact that the vouchers were non-tradable substantially slowed down their take-up. Another weak point in their design was their nominal value of 30,000 karbovanets[5] whose value was reduced to nothing due to the extremely high level of inflation in Ukraine in 1992–93; the face value of the voucher was multiplied by a factor of 35 in November 1993 to become 1,050,000 karbovanets. Indexation of the voucher was accompanied by indexation of the value of the assets of privatized enterprises based on their book value. Unfortunately, due to the absence of capital markets, the book value of productive assets was the only characteristic which could be used to appraise the market value of any enterprise to be privatized. This was one of the numerous reasons why some companies were sold for a trifling sum. Another reason was the prevalence of lease-buy-out among the methods of privatization during the first two phases of privatization, in 1992–94.

The first State Programme for Privatization of the Property of State-Owned Enterprises, which was adopted by a Resolution of the Supreme Council of Ukraine on July 7, 1992, envisaged that objects to be privatized should be classified into six groups according to the initial (book) value of their capital assets, as specified in the balance-sheet for the quarter preceding the date when the decision on privatization of the entity was made and taking into account a number of qualitative characteristics. There were several adjustments to the classification rules (due to inflation and hyperinflation, which affected the book value of enterprises). Ultimately, according to the Edict of the President of Ukraine of June 23, 1995, 'On measures of implementing privatization in 1995', all enterprises are classified in the following way:

- *Group A* – objects with a book value of less than Krb 33,600 mn at January, 1, 1995 prices[6] (except objects in group D);
- *Group B* – objects with a book value of between Krb 33,600 and 2,150,000 mn, where the share of the value of assets per employee does not exceed the nominal value of the property certificate by more than 1.5 times (except objects of group D);
- *Group C* – objects with a book value of between Krb 33,600 and 2,150,000 mn, where the share of the value of assets per employee exceeds the nominal value of the property certificate by more than 1.5 times (except objects of group D);

- *Group D* – enterprise-monopolies; enterprises belonging to the military-industrial complex which are under the programme of conversion; enterprises which are privatized with foreign capital involvement in accordance with international agreements; enterprises with a book value of more than Krb 2,150,000 mn;
- *Group E* – objects whose construction is unfinished; assets of liquidated enterprises;
- *Group F* – allocations (shares) which belong to the state in the property of enterprises with mixed ownership.

There are several methods of privatization of state-owned assets stipulated by the law:

- sale of the objects of privatization or unfinished construction by auction or by tender with exclusive right to use property certificates;
- sale of enterprise shares by auction, by tender, on the stock exchange or by other competitive method;
- lease-buy-out;
- purchase of the assets of a state enterprise using the alternative plan of privatization;
- purchase of a small-scale state enterprise by a 'buyers association' created by employees of the enterprise.

In the case of the majority of the above methods, cash or privatization certificates could be used. For each group of enterprises certain methods of privatization were envisaged (Table 1). Preferential rights to choose a method of privatization belong to the working collective, although suggestions could made by any executive body or any interested party.

Table 1.   Methods of privatization for different categories of enterprises

| No. Methods of privatization | Categories | | | | | |
|---|---|---|---|---|---|---|
| | A | B | C | D | E | F |
| 1.  buy-out by 'buyers' association' | + | | | | | |
| 2.  buy-out with alternative privatization plan | + | + | + | + | | + |
| 3.  Lease-buy-out | + | + | + | + | | + |
| 4.  Auction | + | + | + | | + | + |
| 5.  Commercial and non-commercial tender | + | + | + | + | + | + |
| 6.  Tender with payment delay | + | + | + | + | + | |
| 7.  Share sales of open JSC | | + | + | + | | |

In order to conduct the whole process of privatization in Ukraine a special institution – the State Property Fund (SPF) – was set up in accordance with a Resolution of the Cabinet of Ministers of Ukraine of August, 19, 1991. Since then it has played the first fiddle in a not very well-assembled orchestra which also incorporates the State Savings Bank, the Ministry of Finance, the Anti-monopoly Committee, the Securities Commission, independent auditors, property appraisers and local governments, and which has the role and responsibility of handling the privatization process in Ukraine. From the very beginning there were two main state bodies responsible for conducting privatization in Ukraine: namely the State Property Fund and the Ministry of De-statization. The ministry was then eliminated and all power was assumed by the SPF. It became responsible for drafting privatization laws and related normative acts regulating the privatization process, and for preparing annual privatization programmes, which are then submitted to parliament for approval. The SPF is also vested with the authority to execute the following functions:

* determination of patterns and procedures for the transformation of ownership;
* supervision of the efficiency of the utilization of Ukraine's state-owned assets and implementation of corporatization procedures.

Corporatization was treated as the first step in the privatization process and, in accordance with the famous Presidential Decree of June 1993, enterprises were transformed into joint-stock companies with 100 per cent of the shares retained by the SPF on behalf of the state and acting as its main agent in the privatization process. Corporatization remained the first stage of privatization for medium- and large-scale enterprises (mainly in group B); however, initially it was implemented in a rather disorganized way. It took two years before the process of corporatization was put on a more simple and straightforward track. In the subsequent stage of privatization the SPF undertook the sale of shares to various private buyers following rules stipulated by the law and clarified later in this chapter.

The protracted debate between those who advocated and those who opposed the granting of privileges to insiders in acquiring enterprises shares ended in a compromise; employees were given priority rights to buy shares in their own enterprise at book value, using privatization certificates and cash. Workers and managers may pay up to 50 per cent of the nominal value of the privatization certificate in cash in addition to vouchers in order to get more shares at a nominal value. In addition, managers can buy up to 5 per cent of the shares of a privatized company with payment deferred over the course of the year. The first step in the distribution of shares to employees on advantageous terms is called a 'closed subscription', in contrast to the 'open subscription' at the next stage, when outsiders may join in the marathon race of buying company shares on a competitive basis. It is worth noting that, due to these rules and to the low book value of capital assets, insiders were granted substantial privileges from the very beginning and quite often bought their enterprises for a mere token price. This was especially the case for lease-with-buy-out which was the most popular method of privatization in the period 1992–94.

There are a few, mainly 'technical' issues which distinguish the Ukrainian privatization process from others in the region. According to the law, the privatization of a state enterprise could be initiated by almost any interested party: workers and managers, the State Property Fund, local authorities, Ukrainian or foreign citizens and companies, and so-called 'buyers' associations', comprising a group of people intending to buy an enterprise jointly as common property. Although such associations could presumably have involved people simply on the basis of their common interest in buying a stake in the company, in practice they served as an instrument for workers and managers to gain certain privileges (deferred payment), since 'buyers' associations' were given such an advantage only in instances where they included working collectives. Another important feature relates to the 'share placement plan' which has to be set out at the very beginning of the privatization process by the privatization commission established for each privatized company and comprising representatives of the working collective, the State Property Fund, local authorities, potential buyers and sometimes the Anti-monopoly Committee expressing the diverse interests of their respective bodies. The Privatization Programme itself was framed in such a way that enterprises in Group B could theoretically be acquired in their entirety by insiders, while in Group C they could not be acquired entirely by workers even if the latter used all their vouchers and cash on preferential terms.

Leasing as a method of gaining control over the enterprise by workers (mainly managers) with subsequent buy-out, has a special position among all other methods of ownership transformation. The first leased companies appeared in the former Soviet Union before Ukraine became independent and their objective was to give companies more independence and more incentives for entrepreneurial activities. Ukrainian legislation on leasing was adopted in 1992 and since then has undergone numerous amendments. From the very beginning, leasing was a very attractive option for working collectives since they enjoyed priority rights to lease their enterprise and the rent they paid to the state was fairly low and was not adjusted even for high inflation.

Leased enterprises can be divided into two categories. In the first category the working collective of the enterprise had a strong incentive to privatize their enterprise and to convert it into some type of collective ownership (closed joint-stock company or collective enterprise) in order to avoid penetration of outsiders. The allocation mechanism of shares for a closed joint-stock company or collective enterprise was discretionary; employees could choose a way of distributing the shares of the company on the basis of a variety of different principles (e.g., taking into account the wages, tenure or other quantitative characteristics of workers). They also had the right to choose their own mechanism for reallocating shares (of those who quit) among the members of the working collective as well as distributing shares to newly hired employees. The other category of enterprises is characterized by reluctance towards any form of privatization since leasing permitted the enterprise insiders to gain working control over an enterprise for a negligible rent with the possibility of subsequent buy-out for a negligible sum. Typically, leasing, along with the relevant allocation mechanisms and forms of collective enterprise, frequently became a major hindrance to the privatization process and the subsequent restructuring of enterprises in Ukraine.

A presidential decree of May 1993 pushed such enterprises towards privatization, giving them the choice either to buy out their enterprise or the state could terminate the lease agreement and sell the enterprise to outsiders. Although from 1995 no new leasing agreements were permitted, lease-buy-out was one of the most popular privatization routes. There was some lack of understanding of the role of financial intermediaries in privatization and only in 1993 did work begin to introduce licensing of their activities as trust companies exercising proxy functions with privatization securities. Consequently, during 1992–93 not much progress was achieved either in the development of legislation with respect to ownership transformation in Ukraine, or in its implementation.

# OVERVIEW OF THE SECOND STAGE OF PRIVATIZATION IN UKRAINE, 1994

By the beginning of 1994 the demands for financial intermediaries to be established and for a legal framework to regulate their activities had become irrepressible. In February 1994 two major decrees were signed by the President: 'On investment funds and investment companies' and 'On the unified system of privatization bodies'. The former created room for new market actors and the latter simplified and unified the system of institutions responsible for conducting the process of ownership transformation both in the centre and in the regions. The priorities of the state in the area of privatization as well as quantitative objectives for 1994 were reflected in the State Programme of Privatization for 1994. The state intended to privatize 20,000 firms in group A, 8,000 in groups B, C, D and F, and 1,200 in group E. 2,030 enterprises were slated for corporatization. However, this plan turned out to be too ambitious and by the end of the year only around 30 per cent of the original target was achieved for small businesses in group A and 23 per cent for medium and large enterprises. Less than the half of the enterprises envisaged for corporatization were actually corporatized.

Regulations governing the investment funds and investment companies approved by the decree of the President allowed them to attract investments both in the form of cash and in the form of vouchers. Investment funds exchanged vouchers and cash for certificates issued by themselves. At the same time, numerous trust companies were established with the function of serving small investors. However, due to the weakness of the legal regulations governing their activities, and especially the absence of proper insurance provisions, in 1994 Ukraine witnessed an explosion of abusive behaviour by financial intermediaries and Ukrainian citizens were taught a lesson in risks and financial fraud.

A slight increase in privatization activity can be seen during the first half of the year. At the same time, the share of 'semi-legal' transactions became more substantial. The executive bodies lacked the capacity to proceed with case-by-case privatization. Finally, on July 29, 1994 the newly elected parliament passed a resolution 'On Improvement of the Privatization Mechanism in Ukraine and Intensifying Control over its Administration'. This resolution was widely called the 'privatization moratorium', although it prohibited only the privatization of medium and large enterprises by cash sales and called for proper legal regulation of that process, and it did not at all affect small privatization or the sale of shares in exchange for vouchers. Opponents of privatization at different levels within the state administration used this so-called moratorium to slow down the process in general. As a result, there was a significant drop in the number of companies privatized after the passing of the resolution and the necessity to undertake some steps to accelerate privatization process became unavoidable. Another outcome of the parliamentary resolution of July 29, 1994 was a list of enterprises to be excluded from privatization. This list totalled 6,300 enterprises and was submitted by the government in exchange for the lifting of the moratorium on December 7, 1994. Included in the list are enterprises designated strategically important[7] for Ukraine, as well as enterprises whose inclusion in the list has no conceivable rationale. This measure had a negative impact on the pace of privatization, on the one hand, but preserved some attractive enterprises for later privatization by cash sale to strategic investors, on the other.

In October 1994 President Kuchma undertook substantial steps in order to accelerate the transformation process in society and launched an ambitious, revised mass privatization programme. The presidential decree 'On Measures for Ensuring the Rights of Citizens to Use Their Privatization Certificates' outlined the key principles of the programme and was aimed at simplifying the procedures of privatization. The programme referred to enterprises in Groups B, C and D, and stipulated that, in order to be privatized, they had to be valued on the basis of their book value by January 1, 1995, and go through the new share allocation procedure. Privatization certificates (vouchers), an inherent part of most mass privatization programmes in the countries of the Central and Eastern Europe and the former Soviet Union, were again involved in Ukraine, but under an altered form and with different procedures for their use. From January 1995, in accordance with the decree of President Kuchma, privatization certificates were distributed in paper form instead of the old system of 'special bank accounts' and only those who had not used their 'special account' were eligible for the new voucher and the new scheme.

Together with the introduction of a new form of voucher, another type of privatization security was introduced by another Decree of the President on November 24 'On compensation of losses of the savings of the population in the Saving bank of Ukraine and State Insurance Company since 1991 due to inflation and hyperinflation'. Only those who had bank accounts prior to January 1, 1992, were eligible for so-called compensation certificates worth 2,200 times more than their savings by that time. Those who received compensation certificates did not lose their savings but were able to use the compensation certificate as a means of payment for shares in privatized companies. Compensation certificates turned out to be the first fully tradable privatization security.

## OVERVIEW OF THE THIRD STAGE OF PRIVATIZATION IN UKRAINE, 1995–96

## Legal Framework

These reform measures of the President, taking upon himself the legislative initiative at the end of 1994, later on affected the whole privatization environment in Ukraine; they introduced new actors and simplified the rules of the game; they altered the old, inefficient form of voucher and made allocation mechanisms more transparent and 'user-friendly; they, created more room for outsiders to participate in ownership transformation processes and substantially intensified the process itself. Both the form and the terms for submission of all the necessary documents – namely the privatization plan, share placement plan, etc. – were clearly defined. The old system of vouchers in the form of special bank accounts was replaced by paper privatization certificates, which simplified the procedures for using them, although they still remained untradable and thus created serious constraints for strategic investors to get access to stakes in enterprises. The Decrees of the President required that 100 per cent of the shares of enterprises in Group B, not less than 70 per cent of shares of Group C and up to 70 per cent of shares of Group D were supposed to be transferred to insiders and/or distributed to the citizens of Ukraine and financial intermediaries through a system of certificate auctions. The rest of the shares were to be commuted for compensation certificates issued in February 1996 to pay off the losses of population that had been incurred in their saving accounts due to inflation and hyperinflation since 1991. Last but by no means the least important type of privatization security, designated for the privatization of housing, is the so-called 'housing check'. Those who already had private housing or apartments privatized for cash were, however, eligible for housing checks which could be exchanged for shares in privatized companies.

One of the last initiatives of President Kuchma – the decree of March 19, 1996 – was aimed at improving the privatization process in the last stage of mass privatization. December 31, 1996, was envisaged as the deadline for the investment of property certificates, and, last but not least, included the incentive scheme that managers of enterprises who met the deadline for privatization specified under the legal documents would be allowed to purchase an additional 5 per cent of the shares on a preferential basis using their compensation certificates. All together this brings to a total of 10 per cent the shares available to managers and gives them a handsome incentive to meet deadlines.

## Allocation Mechanism and Certificate Auctions

According to the amended official procedure for privatization, the State Property Fund of Ukraine, through its regional branches and representatives in districts, cities and towns, is supposed to establish for each enterprise a commission responsible for preparing the privatization of that enterprise. Such a commission includes the general manager of the enterprise (who is also chairman of the commission), the chief accountant, a representative of the SPF and, in some cases, a representative of the Anti-monopoly committee. The commission submits a draft founding charter for the open joint-stock company, the asset valuation documents, a draft stock placement plan and a list of those people entitled to privileges in the acquisition of the privatized enterprise.

The allocation mechanism for the shares of an open joint-stock company is reflected in the draft stock placement plan, which has to be approved by the State Property Fund. There are tough rules regarding the allocation of the shares of any joint-stock company, depending on the category to which the enterprise belongs. For enterprises in group C, for example, all shares remaining after distribution to the employees and not sold through the certificate auction are to be sold for compensation certificates; for group D at least 50 per cent of the shares are to be sold to employees and through auctions, and at least 25 per cent sold for compensation certificates. For enterprises in the latter group the draft stock placement plan includes information on the number of shares which are supposed to be sold through competitive methods for cash, and the terms and methods of transaction to be applied.

A presidential decree 'On Measures to Support the Rights of Citizens to Use Their Property Certificates', together with the 'Provisions on the Procedures for Holding Certificate Auctions' and 'Provisions on the Certificate Auction Centres', approved by the Cabinet of Ministers of Ukraine in February-March 1995, replaced the old and inefficient system of 'deposit accounts' with paper privatization certificates (vouchers) and created a market for shares. 45 million vouchers with a nominal value of 1,050 mn karbovanets were printed and distributed among all the citizens of Ukraine except those who had already used their right to acquire a 1/52 millionth part of state-owned property and were not eligible to participate in the new procedure (such persons counted for almost 15 per cent of the population).

In order to ensure that all citizens of Ukraine enjoyed an equal right to acquire shares in the open joint-stock companies and other objects of privatization all over the country, a national network of Certificate Auction Centres, including a national Ukrainian Certificate Auction Centre and regional Centres, along with representative offices, was established. The regional centres were intended to provide people with the necessary information on the property being sold, to collect applications, together with privatization certificates, from Ukrainian citizens and financial intermediaries, and to maintain databases concerning the distribution of shares of privatized companies. The regional centres process the applications and submit the information to the Ukrainian Centre, where the privatization auctions held by the permanent commission established by the Centre take place.

There are different schemes for determining the blocks of shares to be sold by auction, representing the supply side of the transaction. Its demand side comprises legal entities, private individuals and financial intermediaries who are recognized as buyers. Those eligible to participate can bid using their property privatization certificates at their full face value, with the exception of the financial intermediaries, who have the right to bid with the reserve price on the condition that they have submitted at least 100 vouchers. After the auction value of the shares – which matches the demand and supply side of the transaction – is determined, all individuals and financial intermediaries who submitted bids without a reserve price are considered winners of the auction. Those who submitted bids with a reserve price become winners if and only if their reserve price is greater or equal to the auction price. Otherwise they are losers and their bids are not satisfied. Another limitation applied to financial intermediaries is that they may bid for no more than 5 per cent of the shares in each company, but they can bid for shares of more than one company in the course of one auction. It is worth mentioning that the auction price may not drop below the nominal (face) value of a share. Compensation certificates can be used as a means of payment at so-called compensation certificate auctions which are designed using the same principles, the only difference being that the auction price of the share can drop below the nominal value in the event of the quantity supplied exceeding quantity demanded.

The laws regulating the privatization process in Ukraine, as in the majority of CIS countries, have been openly criticized for being too vague and open to conflicting interpretations. However, with the voucher stage of the privatization process approaching completion, Ukraine made substantial progress in making its privatization procedures more streamlined, clear and transparent.

# THE PRIVATIZATION PROCESS: A COMPARATIVE ANALYSIS OF THE THREE PHASES

In July 1992, the Ukrainian parliament adopted the first State Programme for Privatization, aimed at denationalizing the property of state enterprises, creating a new social group of private owners, fostering competition and constraining monopolism. The programme set as its goal the privatization of 15 per cent of state-owned assets during 1992. However, these objectives turned out to be infeasible and were not achieved, due to lack of experience, legislative gaps, the inadequacy of the state administration system and even due to political controversy. 1992, however, did see the real beginning of the privatization process in Ukraine and permitted some useful lessons to be drawn, and paved the way for the creation of the legal and regulatory framework necessary to implement privatization targets in the future. In 1993 the process started to pick up speed (see Chart 1). The first phase of privatization was a period of trial-and-error, of first steps and drawing the first lessons. It was a time when the policy-makers made initial investments into the design of the legal and institutional framework for privatization in Ukraine. By the end of that period some bottlenecks needed to be overcome and the first attempts to extend and improve the programme were undertaken.

**Chart 1. Pace of privatization**

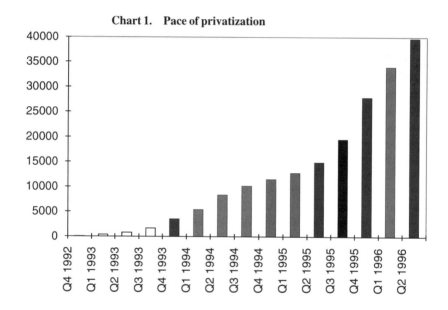

1994 may be regarded as a watershed year in Ukrainian privatization. New privatization priorities were reflected in the State Programme of Privatization for 1994 approved by the parliament. It was aimed at boosting the privatization of enterprises in groups A, expediting the privatization of entities in groups B, C, D and E and insuring wide participation by the citizens of Ukraine in the privatization process through the use of 'special bank accounts'. During the first half of the year, the privatization processes were implemented more dynamically than before, until the adoption of the parliamentary moratorium of July 29, 1994. From then the rate of privatization dropped substantially and the number of privatized companies in the second half of the year decreased by 1.5 times in comparison with the first half. Although by the end of the year only 28.4 per cent of the target set out under the State Privatization Programme had been fulfilled, the impetus of privatization in 1994 was higher than before.

Substantial progress has been made during the latest stage of privatization (1995–96) both in terms of creating organizational structures to support mass privatization (a complete system of privatization agencies, a Ukrainian centre for certificate auctions and an extended network of regional centres, and 2,000 centres for collecting applications from citizens of Ukraine for participation in auctions), as well as simplifying and unifying privatization procedures. As a result, in 1995 one-and-a-half times the number of entities were reported privatized by comparison with 1993–94 and twice the number of entities privatized in 1994.

**Table 2.   Pace of privatization for different groups of enterprises, 1994–96**

|                  | Group A | Group B, C, D, F | Group E | Total |
|------------------|---------|------------------|---------|-------|
| **1994**         | **6079** | **1824**        | **44**  | **7947** |
| 1 quarter        | 1481    | 350              | 10      | 1841  |
| 2 quarter        | 2279    | 669              | 12      | 2960  |
| 3 quarter        | 1372    | 431              | 9       | 1812  |
| 4 quarter        | 947     | 374              | 13      | 1334  |
| **1995**         | **13231** | **3113**       | **57**  | **16401** |
| 1 quarter        | 759     | 484              | 7       | 1250  |
| 2 quarter        | 1550    | 601              | 4       | 2155  |
| 3 quarter        | 3778    | 788              | 17      | 4853  |
| 4 quarter        | 7144    | 1240             | 29      | 8413  |
| **1996, first half** | **10915** | **1815**   | **55**  | **12785** |
| 1 quarter        | 5104    | 970              | 23      | 6097  |
| 2 quarter        | 5811    | 845              | 32      | 6688  |

Table 2 reflects a breakdown of privatized companies by their type (the group they belong to) quarterly since 1994. One can argue that the pace of small-scale privatization in 1994–95 has been relatively more rapid than that of the companies in groups B, C, D, and F. In 1996, however, one can see an equalization of the speed of small- and large-scale privatization while significant and sustainable progress was being achieved along both dimensions. Corporatization of medium and large enterprises carried out by selling the shares through certificate auctions resembled an assembly line, processing companies at a rate of around 400 each month. Moreover, the number of small businesses privatized during the first half of 1996 almost matched the number attained in the course of the whole previous period of implementation of the privatization programme.

The results of the latest stage of privatization in Ukraine are impressive. By the end of 1996 – the deadline for the collection of vouchers – about 84 per cent of the population of Ukraine had picked up their privatization certificates or opened 'special bank accounts'. The SPF began to take steps to thin out the list of enterprises excluded from privatization in order to increase the number of enterprises on the supply side and to meet the increased demand caused by the introduction of compensation certificates and the possibility of using housing certificates, which had initially been designated exclusively for the privatization of housing. As far as the collection of compensation certificates was concerned, the population became much more active by the end of the year (15 per cent of the total value of compensation certificates had been claimed by citizens) in comparison with the beginning of the year, due to the fact that the list of enterprises included in compensation certificate auctions was enriched with more attractive ones. The total number of small-scale businesses transferred into private hands accounted for 36,085 entities, including 29,221 privatized since January 1, 1995. In the area of large-scale privatization, a total of 8782 companies were transformed into joint-stock companies since 1992 with 3121 companies corporatized and then privatized in the course of 1995 and 3009 in 1996.

In 1992–93 the main method of large privatization was lease-buy-out, which allowed former *nomenklatura* and 'red directors' to acquire invaluable state property 'for a song', quite often violating the law. The majority of these buy-outs led to employee ownership or collective ownership in the form of closed joint-stock companies with top managers playing the 'first violin' in the corporate governance of firms thus privatized, and quite often imposing restrictions on the restructuring of the enterprises. But the highest number of various types of buy-outs occurred in 1994 – the year which represented the peak of non-competitive methods.

The following charts broadly reflect the shifts in the distribution of privatized companies by method of privatization towards the more competitive methods. The bias would become even more evident if one were to look separately at enterprises in different groups. There is a clear tendency towards the creation of joint-stock companies on the basis of medium and large enterprises in the last stage of privatization, and for small businesses the share of auctions increased. For instance, in 1995 – the year of drastic change – 46.0 per cent of small businesses were privatized through buy-outs by 'buyers associations' and 34 per cent through lease-buy-outs, which means an overall predominance of non-competitive methods. By the beginning of 1996 competitive methods start to replace buy-outs; hence, in the total number of privatized companies the percentage of joint-stock companies created *via* the further sale of the shares becomes equal to the percentage of lease-buy-outs.

Taken separately, for the different groups, the picture is even more striking. The former method became predominant for enterprises belonging to groups B, C, and D (78 per cent), while the share of the latter is around 2 per cent. The prevailing method of privatization for small companies is still buy-out by a 'buyers association' (53 per cent), followed by lease-buy-out (20 per cent). However, the share of auctions among the methods of small-scale privatization increased to almost 10 per cent. The following series of charts present all three phases of privatization from the point of view of the prevailing method of privatization in a very clear way. The first two charts closely resemble each other, while the last one reveals a predominant tendency to substitute non-competitive methods with competitive ones. In 1996 the corporatization of enterprises with further sale of shares to different interested parties became the dominant method of ownership transformation for medium and large enterprises.

**Chart 2.   Distribution of companies by method of privatization, 1992–93**

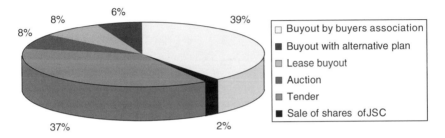

**Chart 3.   Distribution of companies by method of privatization, 1994**

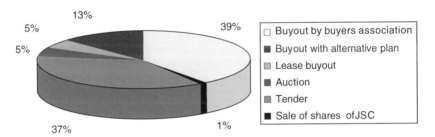

**Chart 4.   Distribution of companies by method of privatization, 1995**

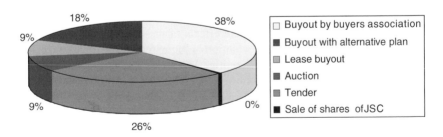

Official statistics on the number of privatized companies, provided by the State Property Fund, incorporate all the enterprises which underwent the process of privatization, irrespective of the subsequent ownership structure of the company, i.e., the size of the stake retained by the state. A major concern of the

SPF over the last year has therefore been to gauge the 'depth' of privatization, on the basis of companies with more than a 70 per cent stake transferred to private ownership. From this point of view 780 companies sold more than 70 per cent of their shares to private owners in 1992–94, while by the end of 1996 this number reached 4,662. The most recent results on the privatization of medium and large enterprises in Ukraine (groups B, C, D and E) provide even clearer evidence of a substantial shift towards competitive methods of privatization. In 1996 around 75 per cent of these companies were privatized through corporatization and further selling of shares *via* the system of certificate auctions.

**Chart 5**

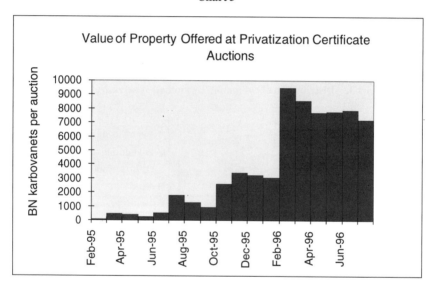

In order to understand the possible effects of the peculiarities of the privatization process in Ukraine on the evolution of future ownership one could analyse at least the results of the certificate auctions. From the beginning of 1995 and up to the end of 1996, 22 certificate auctions took place. The preliminary results of the first 19 auctions demonstrate that the most active participants in these auctions are financial intermediaries, with almost 90 per cent of the shares put up for auction in this manner being acquired by them. So far about 800 financial intermediaries, i.e., trust companies, investment funds, companies and banks collected more than 19 million property certificates; more than 14 million of these certificates have already been exchanged for shares in privatized companies through the system of auctions. The number of companies sold through these auctions became stable and the value of property offered at privatization certificate auctions substantially increased and also became stable (see Chart 5) despite a slight decrease in the number of shares offered.

During the mass privatization stage in Ukraine, competitive methods of distributing shares in companies, i.e., certificate auctions and the hitherto less popular allocation mechanisms such as compensation certificate auctions and the stock exchange, created room for outsiders to become the owners of privatized companies. It is useful to get a picture of the process from the point of view of the emerging ownership structures and to understand the role of auctions in this respect. The State Property Fund provides the most recent information for the aggregate structure of ownership emerging as a result of the privatization process in Ukraine reflected in Chart 6. It demonstrates that, despite all the efforts, three-quarters of the productive assets in the Ukrainian economy still belong to the state. However, the auction results provide an implicit estimate of the stock being acquired by some categories of buyers, namely, individuals – outsiders – and financial intermediaries, which is extremely useful in evaluating the future ownership transformations. The range of the volume of shares being traded varies significantly among enterprises, from 0.2 per cent to almost 90 per cent. The price of the shares for some companies rose 50 times while others remained at the nominal level – a fact which reflects the low level of attractiveness of some enterprises, on the one hand, and the great attractiveness of others, or lack of market information, on the other.

**Chart 6.  Distribution of JSC by the size of the stake retained by the state**

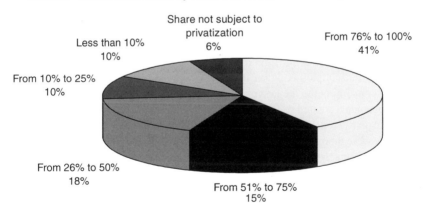

There is evidence from some case studies of privatized companies that since the launch of the mass privatization programme there has been much less room for insiders to acquire control of their companies, which is a good sign from the point of view of future restructuring prospects. So far one can see only a few cases of clear restructuring taking place in Ukrainian enterprises, albeit with different speeds for different dimensions of restructuring. For example, enterprises are more active in undertaking changes to their internal structures and altering their line of business, while at the same time they appear very reluctant to make changes involving any decrease in labour force participation; they are forced to look for new suppliers and customers intensively, but turn out to be rather indifferent to undertaking any investment. There is not much difference between the behaviour of state-owned and privatized companies in Ukraine. Both face hard budget constraints due to the lasting economic crisis, the substantial drop in production and the severe state budget deficit. Some enterprises reveal a much greater ability to overcome their transition problems while others face real troubles, and there appears to be no distinct correlation with their ownership type. There may be evidence of the long-run effects of privatization which will take shape in the next post-privatization stage when the secondary market will play an important redistributive role. However, such an analysis would require additional research and could be a subject for a future study. One may expect positive outcomes of the reform measures as a result of the macroeconomic stabilization and the significant reduction of the inflation achieved during the last year, as well as the commitment of the current government to the reform path.

## CONCLUSIONS

When analysing the history of Ukrainian privatization one can observe three distinct phases in its development, taking into consideration the legal and institutional framework, key actors and outcomes: first, the initial or case-by-case stage (1992–93); second, a transition period (1994), and third, the mass privatization stage (1995–96).

Among the main obstacles to the privatization process in Ukraine one can see the lack of political will, numerous adjustments to the legislative base and the methods of its implementation during the course of privatization, and endless debates concerning the 'negative' list of enterprises not subject to the privatization. These problems created serious restrictions to the restructuring of enterprises, both state and privatized, because they faced a situation which was too full of uncertainty and they were therefore not willing to undertake any investment.

Attempting several times to adjust legislation when the privatization process was underway had an effect akin to that of continuously changing horses in midstream. They were very costly both for firms which already started privatization and for the process as a whole. Even 'positive' corrections of the privatization path, such as replacing employee buy-outs by competitive methods of privatization, incurred costs and led to slowing down the pace of privatization at its various stages.

The current year – 1997 – is supposed to put a full stop to the story of voucher privatization and set the stage for the development of the secondary market and the capital market. We would argue that the mass privatization stage in Ukraine has established favourable conditions for further ownership transformations and the subsequent restructuring of enterprises.

# NOTES

1. The population of Ukraine is 51.9 million.
2. Working collectives at Ukrainian enterprises comprise *all* employees, both workers and managers.
3. There is no clarity with regard to the definition of privatized enterprises even now. In statistical reports one can see companies which went through the process of corporatization and started to sell shares to private owners being counted as privatized, irrespective of the size of the stake retained by the state.
4. Almost at the same time, the Supreme Council also adopted several other laws regulating property rights in Ukraine, including laws on ownership, on entrepreneurship, on leasehold of state enterprises, on foreign investment, on companies, on securities and the stock exchange, and on types of property rights with respect to land.
5. Temporary Ukrainian currency introduced in 1992 and replaced by the *hryvnia* in September 1996.
6. The previous adjustment of the book value of objects to be privatized was carried out in November 1993.
7. Mainly enterprises in the energy sector, and firms with unique production and output.

# REFERENCES

Cherniak, V.K. (1996), 'Ukrainska pryvatyzatsiia: na foni svitovoho dosvidu' (Ukrainian privatization: against the background of world experience), *Holos Ukrainy*, October 1996.

Frydman, R., A. Rapaczynski and J.S. Earle, (eds) (1993), *The Privatization Process in Russia, Ukraine and the Baltic Republics*, Budapest: CEU Press.

Heetz, V.M. (1994), 'Privatizatsiia v Ukraine' (Privatization in Ukraine), *Viche*, no. 3, 1994.

Lanovyi, V.T. (1993), 'Pro stan pryvatyzatsii v Ukraine' (On the situation with privatization in Ukraine), *Viche*, no. 8, 1993.

Leshchenko, L.L. (1994), 'Privatizing Ukraine: Will the Ukrainian People Become Richer?', East European Series, Working Paper no. 7, Institute for Advanced Studies, Vienna, Austria.

Revenko, V.L. (1997), 'Blesk i nishchenta ukrainskoi privatizatsii: metodologicheskie aspekty' (Brightness and poverty of Ukrainian privatization: methodological aspects), *Dilovyi visnyk*, no. 1, 1997.

Shvaika, M.A. (1995), 'Auktsiony po prodazhe aktsii' (Auctions for sale of shares), *Viche*, no. 1, 1995.

Snelbecker, D. (1995), *The political Economy of Privatization in Ukraine*, CASE Research Foundation, Warsaw.

# 15
# Should Competition Authorities be
# Concerned about Monopoly Pricing?
# The Example of Ukraine

*Marie Clark*

## EDITORS' NOTE

This chapter is very much a practitioner's 'view from the field', based on detailed work in Ukraine. As such it tries to deal with some very concrete, practical issues not normally covered or even encountered in academic studies of transition economies. Partly as a result of this, it side-steps a number of economic issues and principles that a more 'remote' economist would wish to see taken into account. It provides, in the editors' view, some fascinating insights into the evolution of economic policy in transition economies where the understanding of the market economy has still not penetrated very deeply.

## INTRODUCTION

The issue of monopoly pricing is a high priority for the Anti-Monopoly Committee of Ukraine (AMC) and in 1995 they requested assistance from the UK's Know How Fund. Coopers and Lybrand had been working with the AMC on a methodology for investigating allegations of excessive prices. A draft set of guidelines to be used by AMC officials was in preparation, and the next stage would be to test these on some real cases.

Monopoly pricing is not only a concem in Ukraine, but is also a major issue in other transition economies. In Russia, for example, the UK's Office of

Fair Trading worked with the Russian competition authorities on their guidelines.

This work raises a number of difficult theoretical, technical and political problems, some of which I shall discuss in this chapter, but first there is the key question of whether the AMC should be involved in detecting monopoly prices at all. Our view is that the AMC should be, but some advisers, mainly from the United States, have sought to discourage all anti-monopoly committees from investigating prices.

The first section provides some background information on the competition law in Ukraine and the Anti-Monopoly Committee of Ukraine. In the following sections I discuss our reasons for believing that the AMC should be involved in the investigation of prices, some of key problems that the AMC will need to face and our recommended approach.

# BACKGROUND ON THE SITUATION IN UKRAINE

The main responsibilities of the AMC are the demonopolization of the economy and the fostering of competition, and to protect the interests of consumers and businesses against the abuse of monopoly power and unfair competition.

Setting monopoly high prices is prohibited by the 'Law of Ukraine on Limiting Monopolism and Preventing Unfair Competition in Entrepreneurial Activities'. Under this law the AMC has the power to impose a fine of up to 5 per cent of turnover for violating the law.

The Price Inspectorate, which is part of the Ministry of Economy, and local government also has the right to investigate prices and to regulate the prices of enterprises that are registered by the AMC as 'monopolisers'. A monopolist is defined to be any entity with a 35 per cent share or more in the supply of a particular good or services. In 1994 this register included over 800 entities, but many of these would not have been considered monopolisers as we would understand the term. Considerable efforts have, however, been made by the AMC to reduce the size of the register and we understand that there are now less than 400 registered enterprises.

We have not yet been able to establish how many enterprises are subject to regulation given the number of regional offices involved, but we have the impression that there are a significant number. Investigations by the Price Inspectorate are carried out very quickly in a matter of a few days and focus on whether an enterprise has complied with taxation law which sets out what 'expenses' are 'allowable' in calculating the costs and so the profits of a firm. Price controls are also based on calculations of allowable costs and profit norms.

As with many things in the former Soviet Union, the division of responsibility between the AMC and Price Inspectorate is a little unclear, but the AMC seems to be under considerable political pressure to address the issue of monopoly pricing. To date, the AMC of Ukraine has been involved in only a few cases, but has put considerable effort into developing some initial guidelines that Coopers and

Lybrand have been working on with them. The regional anti-monopoly committees have been involved in more cases, but the approach seems to be similar to that adopted by the price inspectorate, being based on 'allowable' costs. Enterprises have been fined and ordered to reduce prices by the extent to which their reported costs have been overstated.

## THE ROLE OF COMPETITION AUTHORITIES

This raises the question whether the competition authorities should be involved in determining whether prices are reasonable?

In most countries the focus of competition law is on market structure, the behaviour of firms and the implications for competition. There are only a few countries where competition authorities are involved in determining whether prices are reasonable. United States anti-trust legislation focuses on creating conditions for effective competition. In other countries, such as Germany and France, the law covers excessive prices but I understand that there are few cases where a decision has been based on adverse findings about prices and profits.

In the US excessive prices are not regarded as an abuse of market power and US experts have advised the AMC that it is not the role of competition authorities to determine whether prices are reasonable. They argue that high prices are part of the competitive process as, in the absence of barriers to entry, these will attract new entrants. The market will therefore be self correcting and intervention by the competition authorities will distort this process. The role of the competition authority is to ensure that firms do not behave in a way that creates or raises barriers to entry. High profits might also be defended as a reward for greater efficiency, investment in new technology, and innovation.

We need to recognise that the situation in transition economies is very different from that in established market economies. In many industries competition is not effective and this situation might not be self correcting given institutional, regulatory, financial and cultural barriers to entry. The role of profitability as a signal to potential entrants is also less effective given the lack of transparency. For these reasons monopolistic markets could persist for some time. Even if the AMC takes steps to address some of the above in order to promote competition, there might still be seen to be a need for price regulation in the transition period.

Macro-economic arguments are also relevant. At a time of rapid inflation, monopolistic price increases can add to the adjustment cost of reducing inflation through monetary policy. Moreover, a widespread collapse in incomes has made price increases for basic essentials so politically sensitive that the AMC has to respond positively to complaints. In an economy unused to competition, it would be a brave AMC official who argued that he did not even need to look at prices as long as action was taken to get the market structure right.

Some economists would, I think, still argue that an ability to charge excessive prices is because of these barriers to entry and that the focus of any investigation should therefore still be on the barriers. Investigation of prices and profits can, however, provide valuable information about the scale of barriers to entry into a market. The argument can, therefore, become very circular. Investigation of prices can also help the AMC to identify priorities for action in a situation where barriers to entry are high in many industries.

Another problem with a more conventional, economic approach is that it seems to draw a distinction between barriers to entry that are created by the anti-competitive behaviour of a firm which would be regarded as an abuse and a firm that is able to charge high prices because of some 'natural' barriers to entry such as a first mover advantage which would not be regarded as an abuse. In both cases there is a market failure and therefore an efficiency loss. We should also remember that utilities are profit-regulated in the US. In many industries in Ukraine the barriers to entry are not a result of the behaviour of the enterprises but of the wider economic situation, including financial barriers and weak demand, and institutional arrangements.

Further, we need to recognise the political constraints on decisive action against entry barriers. Demonstrating that prices are excessive can strengthen the AMC's case for addressing institutional barriers to entry which might have been created by the government or by industry groups that have the support of sponsoring ministries. The AMC's role in this area is also closely linked to its role in the areas of demonopolization and privatization. The main objectives of the AMC are to promote competition which can very often put it at odds with other government organizations. To establish that an industry is abusing its position and acting against the interests of consumers can help the AMC's case. In addition to this, there is still very little trust in the market economy and therefore in what the implications of privatization and liberalization might be for prices. Again, being able to demonstrate that current prices are above a competitive level can be very helpful.

Another argument for an economic approach is the problem that firms can face in determining *ex ante* whether a competition authority is likely to consider a price to be excessive. This is an argument for excluding excessive prices from a law-based system based on formal prohibitions, where fines may be imposed on enterprises found to be in violation of the law. Of course, there are also difficulties *ex post* in determining whether prices have been excessive. One example is the need to allocate the costs of a multi-product firm to individual products, in order to determine whether it has been making unreasonable profits in one particular market. Another is the need to take account of the risks of failure, particularly in dynamic markets, and not simply to focus on the rates of return achieved by the winners. Despite these problems, under UK law it is possible for competition authorities to control excessive profits. EU law also prohibits excessive prices, but the number of cases is small and the European Court of Justice has overturned European Commission findings of excessive pricing.

The main reason for advising against price investigation and control might be a concern that the investigation of prices will encourage their regulation and that this will divert valuable resources from the promotion of competition. The AMC does not have unlimited resources and the regulation of prices is very time consuming. If this is the case, the key issue is then not whether the AMC should look at prices at all, but what action it should take if it concludes that there are significant barriers to entry and that prices are unreasonable. The AMC recognises that the regulation of prices can inhibit the development of competition, but faces considerable political pressure about price increases, even short-term increases, particularly in the case of 'vital' products such as bread. It has even been suggested that there would be concern about price increases in a competitive market given the low incomes of many people.

If the AMC is not actively involved in addressing the concerns of politicians and the populace, the danger is that there will be more not less price regulation. The Price Inspectorate can price regulate monopolies without consulting the AMC. The level of analysis carried out by the Price Inspectorate is very basic and there seems to be little discussion between the AMC and the Price Inspectorate on alternatives to price regulation. There is clearly a need for the AMC to take a lead in this issue, and to educate other government bodies about the costs of excessive intervention. This discussion will inevitably raise the issue of the division of responsibilities between the AMC and the Price Inspectorate.

Against this background, I believe that the AMC clearly needs to develop a robust approach to the question of excessive prices so that it is in a better position: to prepare strong cases to support the need for demonopolization of markets; to strengthen its position in discussions with other government bodies on the approach that should be taken to excessive prices; to resist pressures for price regulation as an automatic response to excessive prices; and to resist pressures for price regulation of enterprises which are not charging unreasonable prices.

## TECHNICAL PROBLEMS AND THE PROPOSED APPROACH

If these arguments are conceded, then some technical questions arise. Specifically, how is it possible to determine whether the prices charged by Ukrainian firms are excessive given the particular problems that exist in this and other transition economies? Determining whether prices are excessive is not straightforward in the West even with experienced economists and accountants working on cases. There is a considerable volume of literature on the technical problems that have to be addressed, and just some of the more widely encountered examples would include: the allocation of costs, transfer pricing, the use and measurement of the cost of capital, and international comparisons of prices.

The biggest problem in Ukraine is probably the lack of accounts prepared according to international standards. Most Ukrainian firms still prepare accounts according to Soviet-style conventions which were designed for taxation purposes rather than as a source of business information. The accounts of firms will not, therefore, necessarily give a reasonable picture of the financial position of the enterprise. An example of the problem is that these accounts are largely cash, rather than accrual based, which, when combined with a non-payment problem, can result in an understatement of revenue. Reported costs and revenues are further distorted by bartering which is a response to the problem of non-payment and the accumulation of debt. Under Soviet accounting conventions some production costs are not included in the profit and loss account, including land rent, expenditure on surveys or quality control, promotional expenditure, rejects or wastage. Another problem is alleged cases of accounts having been deliberately distorted by the inclusion of costs that are not officially 'allowed' in order to hide profits, although the scope for this is unclear. Evaluation of the capital base is usually on an historic cost basis adjusted by indices for inflation which can bear very little relation to the true value of the assets. For example, the value of the assets might exceed the replacement cost.

A key area of the Coopers and Lybrand work, therefore, involves identifying the adjustments that AMC must make to Soviet-style accounts. In the West, competition authorities will make special requests for accounting information that is not normally prepared by the firm, for example, line of business information or current rather than historic cost accounts. The limited number of trained accountants in AMCs and businesses is, however, a major constraint on the ability of the AMC to ask for special information. Obtaining line of business information is likely to be particularly difficult given the way in which accounts are prepared. One reason for this is that there has been very little need in the past for enterprises to be aware of the costs of individual product lines.

In addition to these measurement problems, there are also theoretical problems about how to determine whether profits are reasonable. The most common methods used by western competition or regulatory authorities for analysing profitability have been to compare the rate of return on capital employed (ROCE) with the average for the industry or comparable **sectors,** or to compare the ROCE with the firm's cost of capital.

The practical value of such inter-firm comparisons might be more limited in Ukraine. For a start, the AMC would need to make the same adjustments to the accounts of other firms to make any reasonable like-for-like comparison. In addition to this, this approach relies on the implicit assumption that the ROCE for the industry is a 'fair' return. This seems to be a very strong assumption in the case of Ukraine which has suffered from a dramatic fall in demand and production, widespread inefficiency, and limited competition in many industries.

Using the cost of capital as a measure of a reasonable level of profit is also based on some strong assumptions that might not be relevant to Ukraine. In a perfectly competitive market a firm can expect to earn a profit that is equal to its cost of capital and profits in excess of this would quickly attract new entrants into the market. The extent to which profits exceed the cost of capital is therefore a measure of market power. Even in the West, however, it is recognised that prices and profits will vary over time for many reasons, and that profits in excess of the cost of capital are not necessarily evidence of anti-competitive behaviour. It is therefore important to look at the level of profitability that has been achieved over a period of perhaps a few years, but whether analysis of historical performance is relevant in Ukraine is questionable when markets were highly regulated. The theory also relies on assumptions about perfect capital markets that allow enterprises to borrow or issue shares to fund investment. Clearly this is not the situation in Ukraine given the shortage of capital and the need to fund investment through retained profits.

An alternative approach to a direct analysis of profits, is to consider direct evidence of unreasonable prices by comparison of movements in prices in relation to costs. This can, however, also be difficult given the distortions created by actual and historic regulation of prices which means that prices might have been historically low. The comparison of prices between firms can also be helpful. This approach also avoids the theoretical arguments that arise where a firm is earning higher profits than other suppliers because it is more efficient and not because it is charging higher prices. With widespread problems of inefficiency and limited competition, this again raises questions about the extent to which comparisons between firms are helpful.

We are working with the AMC at the moment on the adjustments that might be made to the accounts of Ukrainian firms. When we have agreed what is practical, it will then be necessary to identify any outstanding problems and the circumstances when there might be a significant problem. We will also be working with the AMC on the information that is available on the cost of capital in Ukraine and other techniques that might be used to determine whether profits have been reasonable such as looking at how profits have been used.

Having addressed these measurement problems, we believe that the basic principles used in the UK and elsewhere in Europe are still relevant to the AMC. In particular, we would advise on the need to take a very broad look at the market and the behaviour of the players in the relevant market in order that the AMC can make a decision based on a complete picture rather than on the evidence about one aspect. We would therefore recommend that investigations cover the extent and nature of competition, and the behaviour of the enterprises and the implications of their behaviour for competition; how prices are determined, movements in costs and prices, and the profitability of the firm and by line of business; and comparisons between firms of prices, costs, profitability and productivity, and possibly, international comparisons.

The key differences between the approach in the West and Ukraine are likely to be in the detail of the investigation. For example, there will probably be less emphasis on historical data, and a less sophisticated approach to the analysis of profits and therefore the level of certainty surrounding the results.

Uncertainty surrounding the analysis is not a problem that is particular to Ukraine. In the UK, action is unlikely to be taken unless a firm has been able to sustain very high prices or profits for some time. In part this reflects theoretical arguments about the dangers of excessive intervention, but it also reflects the inevitable level of uncertainty in any investigation and the need for judgement. The same would be true for Ukraine and the AMC will have to persuade government that action should only be taken in gross and persistent cases of abuse.

We therefore return to the key issue, which is what action should be taken by the AMC when it establishes that prices are unreasonable. At the moment the natural response of the Price Inspectorate, local government and even the AMC is either to resort to some direct control over prices, or to impose fines. The AMC recognises that creating a competitive market is the most effective means of ensuring that prices are reasonable, and is also aware that price and profit regulation can inhibit the development of competition. There is, however, considerable concern about how rapidly competition will develop and therefore how long enterprises will be able to continue to charge excessive prices. A major element of our work with the AMC will be to discuss effective alternatives to price regulation, such as the removal of entry barriers, the liberalization of imports and reducing obstacles to internal trade, and, in some cases, considering splitting an enterprise into smaller units.

The AMC will also have to convince other elements of government that price and profit regulation should only be used in extreme circumstances. This will not be an easy task as there is still a considerable lack of understanding of how markets work which makes it difficult for officials to 'let go' and trust in the market.

Another issue will be the division of responsibility between the AMC and the Price Inspectorate. The Price Inspectorate could still have a role in the future implementing and monitoring price controls where these have been recommended by the AMC. This would have the advantage of addressing concerns about AMC resources being diverted into controlling prices which can be very time consuming. There would, however, need to be agreement on how the Price Inspectorate would itself determine the appropriate price or level of profitability. Current practice based on unadjusted Soviet-style accounts and profit norms is clearly not acceptable. The Price Inspectorate should not have the powers to initiate price controls without the approval of the AMC.

## CONCLUSIONS

For both economic and political reasons, our view is that the AMC should investigate allegations of excessive prices despite the technical difficulties. In reaching this conclusion we have taken into account the particular circumstances that exist in the transition economies including many industries where there is only limited competition, a cultural history of co-ordination between firms and high barriers to entry. In these circumstances, there is considerable concern about the ability of firms to abuse their position by charging excessive prices and therefore pressure for the AMC and other authorities to prevent this by controlling prices. We would stress, however, that: any investigation of pricing should be part of a wider investigation of the market; the aim of the investigations must be to identify markets where competition is not adequate and to take action to increase competition; and price regulation should only be imposed in extreme circumstances.

The conditions under which price control might be acceptable would seem to be: no effective competition between current producers; evidence of significant barriers to entry; and no scope in the short to medium term for lowering the barriers to entry. In these circumstances, there is either little scope for competition or competition might be very slow to develop.

In very sensitive markets there might be a need for some temporary price controls as competition develops. An example in the UK is the price controls currently proposed by OFTEL (the telecoms regulator) which provide some temporary protection for consumers in markets where competition is expected to develop in the near future. Given the implications for the development of competition, particularly in Ukraine where regulatory risks are particularly high, temporary regulation should only be used in extreme circumstances and there should be clear criteria for the removal of these controls within a reasonably short period. Price controls might be administered by the Price Inspectorate, but it should not be able to initiate investigations.

# 16
# Enterprise Restructuring in Ukraine

*Adam Rosevear*

## INTRODUCTION

The privatization process in many countries of the Former Soviet Union (FSU) is of an order unmatched by experience in any other part of the World. In Russia, about 122,000 enterprises were privatized between 1992 and 1996 (Goskomstat, 1996, quoted in Earle and Estrin, 1997). In Ukraine, privatization has been slower but by the end of March 1997, official figures showed that 50,547 enterprises had been privatized (State Property Fund, 1997). There is some doubt over the accuracy of these figures as they include companies where the State still holds a majority share. However, the scale of the ownership transformation is still unprecedented by Western standards. The privatization process in Ukraine is believed to have given majority employee ownership to many enterprises (Leshchenko and Revenko in this volume, Chapter 14). Therefore, Ukraine is suited for a study of the relationship between ownership and firm behaviour.

Theoretical considerations suggest that private and privatized firms would be likely to restructure more than state-owned firms, and that the pace of restructuring would also depend on the ownership structure and corporate governance of the firms concerned. Specifically, there would be an expectation that insider-ownership would be less conducive to restructuring than outsider ownership.

To a modest extent, these prior expectations are tested on the firms reviewed for this study. The firms concerned are a pilot sample of Ukrainian firms interviewed in the first half of 1997. In due course, based on a larger sample of firms, this work will be developed into a much fuller study.

# RESTRUCTURING

To move from a planned economy to a successful market type economy involves massive restructuring of industry. At the micro level, restructuring means that enterprise managers must take responsibility for re-orientating their firm towards the market. In the following analysis, employee-owned firms will be contrasted with managerially-owned firms, state-owned firms and investor-owned firms. Earle *et al.*, (1996) state that restructuring is implemented more effectively by outsider-owned firms. Outsiders owners do not have split objectives and they can thus focus on maximizing profits. In contrast, employee-owners may wish to maximize wages and employment (Blanchard *et al.*, 1991). In theory, manager-owned firms can be very effective at restructuring because of the high-powered ownership incentives – they receive the full benefit of improvements in performance. However, the quality of management and the links that they maintain with the State can retard restructuring (Earle *et al.*, 1996). Of all ownership types, state-owned firms are expected to restructure least, and private firms (both privatized and *de novo* firms) the most. However, other factors influence the restructuring process, such as the ability and incentives of managers, the hardness of the budget constraint and factors that affect regions and industrial sectors differentially.

In this chapter, the term restructuring will be used to denote all of the changes that an enterprise has made in order to be better able to serve its existing markets or to find new ones. Restructuring measures that merely involve an impact effect or, a reaction to a large economic shock can be seen as 'weak' restructuring. 'Weak' restructuring measures include reducing employment after a dramatic fall in output. This has been carried out by many firms in parallel to building up wage arrears and putting a large number of the workforce on unpaid leave. This indicates the lack of a strategic focus.

'Strategic' or 'strong' restructuring may also include reductions in workforce but this will be part of an overall strategy to reposition the business to serve its markets profitably. 'Strong' measures of restructuring show that the management is 'proactive' and not just reacting to events. 'Strong' measures include changes in product range, markets served and distribution systems. They also involve an insistence on a competitive price and quality from suppliers. 'Strategic' restructuring will implement improvements in product quality and service levels. It will also involve adjusting the management structure so as to facilitate communication between managers and workers. Inefficient managers will be fired and training programmes put in place. Lastly, 'strong' restructuring will involve a coherent disposal programme of non-core assets together with focused investment on the firm's core competencies.

# ENTERPRISE SURVEY

In order to examine how different ownership forms might affect the pace and extent of restructuring, a questionnaire was piloted in the first two weeks of

June 1997. The author questioned eight enterprises in Ukraine: six were in Kiev oblast and two were in L'viv. The size of the chosen sample does not make the survey a statistically random study across regions and industrial sectors. However, the main survey that followed later in 1997 was a random sample structured by region and industry. In each of the pilot firms, a senior manager, usually the Chief Accountant, was questioned over several hours about enterprise policy and the steps taken towards restructuring. In addition, quantitative data was taken from the company accounts from 1991, 1993, 1994 and 1995.

The following table details the share holding structure of the eight firms questioned.

**Table 1. Share Holding Structure**

|         | State | Managers | Workers | Outsider | Foreign |
|---------|-------|----------|---------|----------|---------|
| Firm 1  | 100   | 0        | 0       | 0        | 0       |
| Firm 2  | 30    | 26       | 18      | 0        | 26      |
| Firm 3  | 100   | 0        | 0       | 0        | 0       |
| Firm 4  | 100   | 0        | 0       | 0        | 0       |
| Firm 5  | 0     | 9.3      | 61.6    | 20.8     | 8.3     |
| Firm 6  | 100   | 0        | 0       | 0        | 0       |
| Firm 7  | 100   | 0        | 0       | 0        | 0       |
| Firm 8  | 3.1   | 8        | 12      | 76.9     | 0       |

*Source*:   Data collected by author (pilot survey).

An analysis of the questionnaire responses gives a picture of the restructuring measures taken in the sample firms. Firstly, statistics from 1991 to 1995 on the changes in employment, wages, costs and capital investment outline the situation of the firm. Secondly, this analysis is enriched by an in-depth qualitative survey answered by a senior manager on how much restructuring has taken place. Lastly, a comparison is made between different ownership structures and the progress of restructuring.

# Employment

As mentioned above, there has been a large drop in output in most Ukrainian firms since 1991. Consequently, one would expect firms to have reacted by reducing their employment significantly. This was broadly confirmed by the survey. Average employment for the sample has fallen by 28 per cent between 1991 and 1995 (see Chart 1).

Firms with different ownership structures reacted somewhat differently. Outsider-owned enterprises might be expected to adjust employment most rapidly towards the efficient level. Firm 8, the outsider-owned firm, had decreased employment the most. At the same time it had increased output and had full order books. It was also paying the remaining workers very high wages, up to 15 times the average Ukrainian salary.

The only worker-owned firm in the sample had decreased employment by an above average 37 per cent. This is in line with the worker ownership theory. Worker-owners will choose to either maximize employment or wages depending upon their preferences. The figures suggest that the workers in this company have chosen to trade lower employment for higher wages (see below).

**Chart 1**

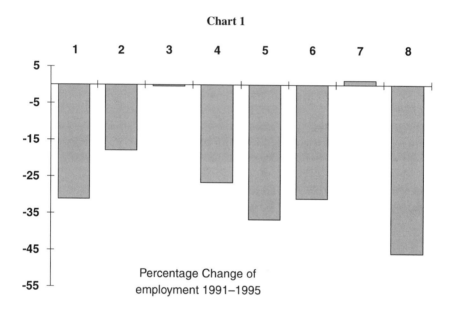

Percentage Change of
employment 1991–1995

In line with expectations, the two companies with either little or no change in employment were state-owned (Firm 3 and Firm 7). However, these enterprises were both bakeries and had not experienced the dramatic fall in demand for their products that four of the other firms had seen. Thus, one would expect that bakeries of all ownership types would have reduced employment less than in other industries. However, it is also interesting to note that the other three state-owned companies in the sample all decreased employment. Thus, even three out of five state-owned companies had performed this form of 'weak' restructuring.

The above findings refer to those workers who are registered as employed. While conducting the first interview, it came to light that many firms have 'workers' who do not work *and* are not paid. The questionnaire was quickly altered to inquire into how many workers were on unpaid involuntary leave. Having workers on involuntary leave confers a short-term advantage on the company as it does not have to give severance pay, although one might argue that without a drastic change in the fortunes of the company it is just delaying this cost, while incurring the costs of the social assets used by these excess workers. For the workers, however, they acquiesce in order to continue to benefit from the firm's social assets. This phenomenon reflects the management's wish to postpone the difficult decisions that restructuring entails. Although these 'unpaid' workers do offer the company a flexible workforce (at the cost of the social provision), the size of the pool of excess labour indicates that most companies are avoiding serious restructuring.

A senior manager at each enterprise was asked about optimal employment. How does the number of employees, excluding those on involuntary leave, compare to the 'efficient' number of employees needed to produce the current level of output, with the current technology. Chart 2 shows the results. Actual employment (earning a wage) is in excess of optimal employment despite the large number on involuntary leave. Only one company in the sample (Firm 1) replied that its employment level was about right. However, this state-owned company has 90 per cent of its work-force on unpaid leave. Thus, all of the firms questioned had excess workers.

**Chart 2**

Actual versus optimum employment

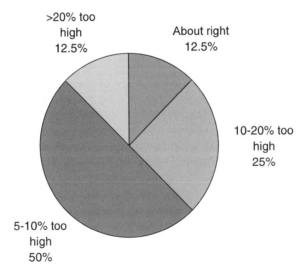

>20% too
high
12.5%

About right
12.5%

10-20% too
high
25%

5-10% too
high
50%

## Wages

Another interesting variable to investigate as a 'weak' restructuring measure is the behaviour of wages. Both the World Bank and Economist Intelligence Unit find that average wages in Ukraine fell between 1991 and 1994 before recovering somewhat in 1995.

This sample of eight firms shows the same pattern. In constant 1991 roubles, average monthly wages fell from 1084 in 1991 to 494 in 1994 before recovering to 618 in 1995 (a drop of 43 per cent). The drop between 1991 and 1994 occurred as money wages failed to keep pace with inflation during the period of hyper-inflation. In 1995, the increase was most likely just a partial catching-up of some of this lost ground. Certainly, the financial health of the enterprise sector further deteriorated in 1994 and 1995 as the 'inflation' profits (profits from any increase in the money value of stocks and work in progress) declined.

The wage differential between managers and workers was far less in the FSU than in Western economies. Senior managers were compensated by other benefits gained through their status as senior Communist party members. These benefits included the right to purchase goods in special shops and access to privileged education for managers' children. One would have expected that once these particular benefits had disappeared, managerial money wages would have risen in compensation. It is therefore surprising that between 1991 and 1994, managerial wages follow a similar pattern to average wages. The fall in managerial salaries is in fact even more pronounced. However, in 1995, the rise in managerial salaries is stronger than the rise in average salaries. Could this rise in managerial wages be the start of a trend, with a consequent rise in income inequality, or just a correction of the reduction in the wage differential between 1991 and 1994? Managerial salaries in the US and Europe are often related to the performance of the company, rewarding managers who achieve good results. If the rise in income inequality could be linked to the introduction of performance-related pay, this would be a positive factor for the Ukrainian economy. However, this is unnecessary in the case of manager-owned firms as they already have high-powered performance incentives as managers receive all the value added from their efforts.

**Chart 3**

Average wage

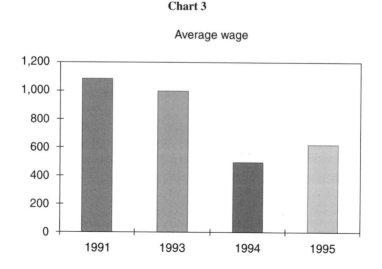

**Chart 4**

Managerial wages

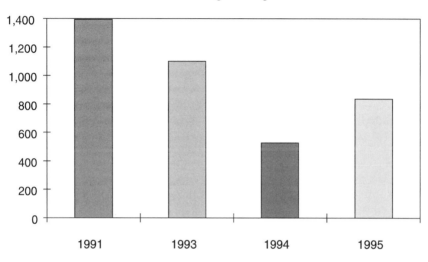

**Changes in Cost Structure in the Sample Firms, 1991–95**

A percentage breakdown of costs for the whole sample was prepared using information from the company accounts. The results are illustrated in Chart 5. As expected, the large decline in real wages (combined with the reduction in employment)
results in wages declining as a portion of costs from 17.8 per cent in 1991 to

**Chart 5**

Breakdown of costs

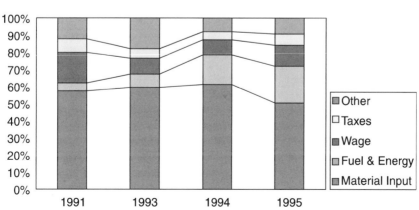

8.7 per cent in 1994, before bouncing back to 12.3 per cent in 1995. As expected, fuel and energy took an increasing proportion of costs as prices have moved progressively nearer to world market levels. Energy has risen from 4.6 per cent of costs in 1991 to 21.5 per cent in 1995. With regard to evidence of restructuring, one point of interest is the fall in the proportion of material inputs from 61.6 per cent in 1994 to 50.5 per cent in 1995. This could be a sign of better use of the available resources and a reduction in waste. This shows that initial 'weak' restructuring measures may have been implemented.

## The Age of the Capital Stock

The questionnaire highlighted the fact that the capital stock of the eight firms is very old. Chart 6 shows that only 5 per cent of the equipment had been purchased in the last 5 years and over 53 per cent of equipment was over 15 years old and surely obsolete in comparison with the world capital stock. For a firm to attempt 'strong' restructuring, this will necessarily involve investment in new energy-efficient, state of the art equipment. Indeed, the lack of investment over the last five years is testimony to the lack of 'strategic' restructuring.

**Chart 6**

Age of equipment

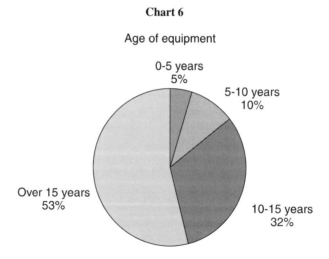

0-5 years
5%

5-10 years
10%

10-15 years
32%

Over 15 years
53%

The implementation of a capital expenditure programme requires financing. In the shallow debt markets and near non-existent equity markets of Ukraine, all firms will experience difficulties in obtaining investment finance. In addition, the ownership structure of the enterprise will impact on the ability of the firm to raise capital. An outsider-owned firm will be the most likely to have access to capital. Firstly, the 'outsider' had the necessary financial resources to purchase the firm in the first place, and one could rationally expect such new owners to have the necessary resources for capital investment. Secondly, it is likely to be favoured by debt and equity markets over other ownership forms.

Managerial ownership in the West has often been associated with support from debt markets (such as the junk bond market that fuelled the Management Employee Buy Out boom of the late 1980's). However, in order to buy the firm, the manager-owners are likely to have mortgaged both themselves and the future cash flow of the enterprise to the limit. Consequently they may not be judged to be good risks in the shallow capital markets of Ukraine. Thus, new financial resources may be scarce.

Employee-owned firms can experience difficulty in obtaining finance in the West. This problem is likely to be even worse in Ukraine. In addition, as with the managerial owners, the employees are likely to have depleted their personal financial resources in order to buy the firm. Thus, they would be extremely unlikely to have enough personal assets to invest more in the firm. Furthermore, the author encountered a marked distrust of outside finance on the part of employee-owned firms. One of these was not willing to borrow if the lender required any part of the firm as collateral, even if the investment would be very sure to succeed.

State-owned enterprises (SOE) used to have easy access to government funds. However, in a time of budgetary crisis the SOEs in the sample were experiencing difficulties in obtaining even emergency funding, let alone finance for new investments. State-owned enterprises often have privileged access to funds from state-owned and former state-owned banks.

The main source of funds for investment in Ukraine are likely to be internally generated. As these will be inadequate for the huge task ahead, it is likely that the transition has many more years left to run.

## RESTRUCTURING PROGRESS

The charts above illustrate that the firms in the sample have put off serious restructuring of their labour force and capital stock. In order to compensate for this relative inaction, wages have been cut and workers have been temporarily laid off. The firms were questioned over why they had not reduced employment to their perception of the optimal level. Five firms stated that they expected a recovery in their markets. Three firms cited the cost of severance pay and four also cited social reasons. One firm highlighted the fact that employees were also shareholders and thus, their freedom of manoeuvre was restricted. This shows that even after five years of crisis, seven of the firms were still unwilling to contemplate radical restructuring.

In order to capture an overall measure of how much managers think they have restructured their firms to meet the changing business environment, a series of questions were posed to a senior manager. Twenty-eight questions weighted towards 'strong' restructuring measures covered changes in the areas of 1) products, markets, quality; 2) inputs; 3) labour/management structure; 4) remuneration; 5) finance and asset disposal. The manager was asked to judge on a 1–5 scale how much had changed. At the extremes, 1 equalled 'no change', and 5 equated to 'everything had changed' (in the opinion of the manager). These responses were cross-checked with information received elsewhere in the questionnaire from the Company Accounts. The responses were then collated into a restructuring Index. Chart 7 shows the results. A higher number on the index indicates a higher level of restructuring.

**Chart 7**

Extent of restructuring

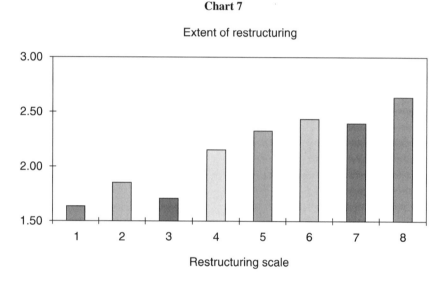

Restructuring scale

Chart 7 shows that Firm 8 has restructured the most. Indeed, this perception of its managers is confirmed by other data. This firm scores well with 'strong' measures of restructuring: the equipment is newer, the order books are full, the skill profile of the workforce has been upgraded and the firm is able to pay wages of up to 15 times the national average. Conversely, Firm 6 also scores highly even though it has lost its markets. However, it now faces a harder budget constraint as government subsidies have dried up. It has thus been forced to start restructuring. Firm 7, a successful bakery also scores quite highly. An explanation of this high number is that the leadership of the enterprise appeared, in the opinion of the author, to be dynamic, charismatic and as far as could be judged from the company accounts and the interview, effective.

One would expect that outsider owners would perform restructuring most effectively. In addition, one would expect outsider owners to embark on 'strong' longer term restructuring. In this small sample this has been the case: the 'outsider' owners of Firm 8 have replaced managers and made large changes to the firm strategy and investment programme. This strategy has paid off with full order books and confident plans for expansion. Firm 2, a construction company, scores very low on the restructuring Index. At first, this is surprising as a 26 per cent stake is not only 'outsider' owned, but is also foreign owned (by a German investment company). However, this investment house had bought the stake from the Ukrainian government but had not contacted the management in the three months after the stake acquisition. Where passive portfolio investors do not try to influence firm policy, the benefits of 'outsider' ownership can only be indirectly realised (through the possibility that they could sell the stake to another party). As such, this foreign investor can only have had an indirect influence on restructuring measures.

Employee-ownership theory indicates that employee-owners are well motivated but that they might award themselves high wages in lieu of ploughing back investment (Hannsman, 1990). One might also expect workers in poorly-performing divisions to be against any restructuring measures that would disadvantage them. The only majority-employee owned firm in the sample is Firm 5. This firm has restructured to an extent above the average in the sample. However, average wages leapt between 1994 and 1995 from third lowest in the sample to highest. This was even before workers officially took control of the firm. Therefore, it may turn out that the employee-owners will seek immediate returns from wages rather than take all the necessary restructuring measures that are likely to involve short-term pain.

The remaining five firms are state-owned. One might expect that these firms would have restructured the least. However, Firm 6 scores quite highly in the restructuring Index. This could be because it is facing a very tough budget constraint. Similarly, Firm 7 achieves an above average score. As outlined above, the quality of management seems to have affected the performance of this state-owned bakery. Thus, restructuring is also affected by the quality of management and the hardness of the budget constraint. Firm 1, a state-owned ceramic producer, achieves the lowest score on the Index. The management of this firm appear to be set against restructuring and are pinning their hopes on a resurgence in demand for their products. It is this firm that has 90 per cent of its registered work force on unpaid leave. The company is located on a large prime site in central Kiev. Asked whether or not they would consider a disposal of some of the unused land (once the question of ownership of land was settled in the Parliament) the answer was negative.

**Chart 8**

Ownership and restructuring

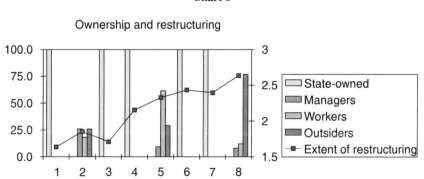

Later in 1997, a random sample of a further 150 companies was interviewed by the author. Study of this larger survey will enable more robust conclusions to be drawn on the correlations between ownership and restructuring at enterprise level. At this early stage, the tentative conclusions are that outsider-ownership is conducive to restructuring but that good management and a hard budget constraint are also significant.

# REFERENCES

Blanchard, O., Dornbusch, R., Krugman P., Layard, R. and Summers, L. (1991), *Reform in Eastern Europe*, Cambridge, Massachussets: MIT Press.

Earle, J. and Estrin, S. (1997), 'After Voucher Privatization: The Structure of Corporate Ownership in Russian Manufacturing Industry', June, London Business School, mimeo.

Earle, J., Estrin, S. and Leshchenko, L.L. (1996), 'Ownership Structures, Patterns of Control, and Enterprise Behavior in Russia', in Commander, S., Fan, Q. and Schaffer, M.E. (eds), *Enterprise Restructuring and Economic Policy in Russia*, Washington DC.: The World Bank.

Goskomstat (1996), *Russia in Figures 1996*, Moscow.

Hannsman (1990), 'Worker Ownership', *The Yale Law Journal*, Vol. 99.

Ukraine State Property Fund (1997), *Annual Report*, Kiev.

# 17
# The Political Economy of State-Building in Moldova

*Judy Batt, Mohammed Ishaq and Paul Hare*

## INTRODUCTION

The independent Republic of Moldova, formed in 1991 after the collapse of the Soviet Union, is a peculiarly fragile new state. The Moldovans are divided as to whether they in fact constitute a 'nation' at all, and this in turn has created uncertainty about the ultimate meaning and purpose of their 'national self-determination'. They speak a language whose literary standard is essentially no different from Romanian, and live on the territory of the former Soviet Republic of Moldova. In the inter-war period, much of this territory belonged to Romania. Language and history pose complicated questions for Moldovans and for the new Moldovan state. Does the fact that Moldovans speak Romanian mean that they are really Romanians, and therefore that their ultimate destiny is to re-unite with Romania? Is the idea of a separate Moldovan political identity to be dismissed as a 'deformation' of the Soviet period, or has their history shaped the Moldovans into a distinctive national group who now see their interests as best served by building a state of their own?

As if these difficult questions were not enough, the new state also faces the challenge posed by ethnic diversity. Moldovans constitute only 64.5 per cent of the population inhabiting its territory. The remainder comprises sizeable minorities of Ukrainians (14 per cent), Russians (13 per cent), and smaller but regionally concentrated minorities of Gagauzi (3.5 per cent) and Bulgarians (2 per cent), along with a Jewish population (1.5 per cent), drastically reduced by the holocaust of the Second World War and subsequent emigration. Ethnic diversity has been a problematic factor in nearly all the new states formed after the collapse of the communist federations in the early 1990s, where the national cultural revival of the majority and the achievement of separate statehood has alienated the minorities. In Moldova the minority backlash took the form of outright secessionist challenges posed by two separatist 'republics', set up by the Gagauz minority in the south and by the Russian-speaking elite on the left (east) bank of the Dniestr.

Coming to terms with the reality of ethnic pluralism is hard for any new state founded on the claim of its majority population to 'national self-determination', a claim based on the idea that each nation has a right to a state of 'its own'. The state is correspondingly assumed to be the property of the majority nation in the given territory, and this assumption sets up a mental block when it comes to considering the equal right to 'self-determination' of other national groups inhabiting the territory. While the majority may be prepared to concede 'minority rights', this rarely goes as far as recognising minorities as 'nations' with equal 'state-forming' status, which would imply a right, if not to secession, at least to an institutionally-entrenched, proportional 'share' in state power – in other words, to a form of federalism. Recognising the equal right of minorities to 'self-determination' is difficult not only because it is at odds with the nationalists' inherently unitary concept of the nation-state, but also because federalism is readily – and, in the light of Moldovan experience, understandably – seen as a threat to the territorial integrity of the new state, and even to the very existence of that state as an independent entity.

On the other hand, the failure of the majority nation to come to terms with the reality of ethnic diversity can itself become a threat to the survival of the new state. A doctrinaire, exclusive nationalism on the part of the majority, insisting on deference on the part of others to symbols confirming its 'right of possession' of the new state, and entrenching its hegemony by means of a centralized and unitary constitutional model, can provoke the very dangers of secession and disintegration that the majority nation itself most fears (for a more elaborate account of this dynamic, see Brubaker, 1995). This tendency is evident in most of the multi-ethnic states of post-communist Europe. What is unusual about the Moldovan case is the capacity of its post-communist political elite to learn and to evolve a more flexible stance which has opened the way to accommodation with the minorities. Specifically, the Moldovans came to see a territorial compromise with the Gagauzi as essential to the security and integrity of their state. This required an adjustment on the part of the Moldovans away from their original nationalist assumptions towards a more pluralistic concept of state-building.

The pact driven between the Moldovans and the Gagauzi at the end of 1994 falls short of full-blown federation on the model of, say the USA, Canada, or Germany, and – for reasons which will become clear below – the Moldovans themselves are reluctant to use the term 'federation' to describe their state. Nevertheless, the emerging political structures do correspond with Daniel Elazar's basic definition of 'federalism' as a set of principles for accommodating diversity, combining 'self-rule' with 'shared rule', a 'partnership, established and regulated by a covenant, whose internal relationships reflect the special kind of sharing that must prevail among the partners, based on mutual recognition of the integrity of each partner and the attempt to foster a special unity among them.' (Elazar,

1987: 5). If Moldova is to survive as an independent state, it seems that it will have to be based on a form of federalism.

This chapter aims to identify the factors which have propelled Moldova's evolution away from the nationalist unitary state formula, and then studies some key features of Moldova's early post-communist economic development in the light of the country's difficult political background. We open in by reviewing the peculiar history of the territory on which the Moldovan state now stands, and the ambivalence of the Moldovans themselves as to their political identity. Then in the next section, it is argued that the Moldovans' propensity for compromise was greatly reinforced by their weakness in the face of the challenges to their independence from the simultaneous revolts of the Gagauzi and the Russian minority, who formed the Transdniester Moldovan Republic (TMR), backed by communist 'neo-imperialists' and 'Great Russian' nationalists in Moscow. The following section discusses the post-communist economic situation and recent performance of Moldova, and some of the country's more striking reform achievements, linking these back to the political context. The final section contains conclusions.

# MOLDOVA AND THE MOLDOVANS

## Where is Moldova?

The territory on which present-day Moldova stands is quintessential European borderland, having been fought over, carved up repeatedly and transferred from one state to another. This accounts for the great variety of ethnic groups who have come over time to settle on the territory, and for their diverging attachments to the various states which historically have laid claim to it. To whom this land rightfully 'belongs' is therefore a question fraught with difficulty.

There did indeed once exist a distinct political entity, the Principality of Moldova, which was founded in the mid-fourteenth century but fell under Ottoman suzerainty a century later (Sellier and Sellier, 1991: 132–33). Subsequently, in 1538, its south-eastern part, between the Dniester and the Danube, was cut off and absorbed directly into the Ottoman empire. This area is still known by its Turkish name of Budjak. As the Ottoman empire weakened, the remaining territory of the Principality was further whittled away. In 1775 the Habsburg Empire annexed its north-western tip which became the Austrian province of Bukovina. In 1812, having defeated the Ottomans, the Russian empire annexed the eastern half of the Principality between the rivers Prut and Dniester, and rejoined it with Budjak, which it had meanwhile also acquired. Thus was created the Russian province of Bessarabia, on much – but not all – of which present day Moldova stands. Also, this time marks the arrival and settlement of the Gagauz and Bulgarian populations in the Budjak region, where they still live today.

The much-reduced Principality of Moldova remained as a separate political entity west of the Prut. It formed a close alliance with its Romanian sister, the

Principality of Wallachia, to win independence from both Ottoman and Russian domination in the course of the nineteenth century. In 1859, the election by the two principalities of a common Prince, Alexandru Ion Cuza, brought about *de facto* union which marked the birth of the modern Romanian national state. This new state then laid claim to all 'Romanian lands' still languishing under alien rule, including Bessarabia, Bukovina and Transylvania. These territories were all eventually acquired by Romania after the collapse of the Russian and Austro-Hungarian Empires at the end of the First World War (for a detailed account, see Hitchens, 1994: 279–91).

But the Soviet Union never accepted the incorporation of Bessarabia into Romania, and part of its long-term strategy to regain it was the establishment of a Moldovan Autonomous Soviet Socialist Republic (MASSR) on a strip of land on the left (east) bank of the Dniester, on Ukrainian territory, where a small population of Moldovans lived (30.1 per cent of the population in the 1926 census) alongside many Ukrainians and Russians. Some left-wing Moldovan émigrés from inter-war Romania played key roles in setting up and manning the MASSR. The Soviet Union succeeded in regaining Bessarabia and northern Bukovina as a result of the Molotov-Ribbentrop pact in June 1940, but they lost both again in 1941, and by 1942, Romania, with Axis support, had invaded a large area of Ukraine east of the Dniester including, but extending far beyond, the territory of the MASSR, to which it gave the name 'Transnistria'. This area across the Dniester had never before been included in the definition of the 'Romanian lands', and at the end of the war this returned to Soviet control along with the whole of Bessarabia and northern Bukovina.

The Moldovan Soviet Socialist Republic was originally formed in August 1940. Its borders were defined by an act of the Presidium of the USSR Supreme Soviet of November 1940, which substantially reshaped the territory. Northern Bukovina and much of Budjak in the south were again cut off from Bessarabia and transferred to the Ukrainian Soviet Socialist Republic. Soviet Moldavia thus consisted of the rump of Bessarabia with the addition of a strip of territory across the Dniester which had formed part of the former MASSR.

History has thus bequeathed an extraordinary legacy of confusion as to the political identity of the territory of present day Moldova. Should the territory return to Romania? If not, can it sustain itself against Russia? In either case, where do northern Bukovina and southern Bessarabia, the territories 'lost' to Ukraine after World War II, belong? If an independent Moldova is to be built, could it not also lay claim to western Moldova, now in Romania, as part of its historic heritage? Should it seek to keep hold of Transnistria, or let it break away? Merely posing these questions reveals the tenuousness and utter impracticality of any historically-based project of state-building. The borders which define it today are Soviet borders, and accepting them also requires coming to terms in some respects with the legacy of the Soviet period – in particular, with the inherited multi-national population. Torn between the rival external claims of Romania and Russia, and the rival internal claims of the Moldovan majority population and the non-Moldovan minorities, Moldovan statehood can be sustained only through a precarious balancing act, which presupposes a wholly new definition of Moldovan identity itself.

## Who are the Moldovans?

'[T]he Moldavians [...] can only be considered Romanians: they share exactly the same language, practise the same faith and have the same history. At every conceivable opportunity (in the 1870s, in 1918 and in 1941) the inhabitants of Soviet Moldavia freely opted for union with Romania and considered themselves as Romanian. Furthermore – and despite persistent Russian and Soviet attempts to prove the contrary – Moldavians never sought nor achieved an independent existence as a state. For all Moldavians, there are only two historic experiences: either union with Romania or Russian rule. Soviet Moldavia [...] is a territory without its own, separate nation, a political notion rather than an ethnic reality.' (Eyal, 1990:123–24)

This was how things looked to a leading Western analyst in 1990, the year which, in retrospect, marked the high point of the Moldovan national revival. In March 1990, elections were held in all republics of the Soviet Union; in Moldova, these produced a majority in the Supreme Soviet for the nationalist Popular Front of Moldova. Having adopted a version of the Romanian red, yellow and blue tricolour as the national flag, the Supreme Soviet declared Moldovan 'sovereignty' on 23 June, and many people inside and outside Moldova saw this as potentially the first step towards reunification with Romania.

But once Moldova achieved full independent statehood in the wake of the collapse of the USSR in August 1991[1], the momentum for reunification with Romania stalled, and the more time passes, the more attached the Moldovans seem to their new state. In March 1994, the government conducted a 'popular consultation' which posed the question, 'Are you in favour of the development of Moldova as an independent state, whole and indivisible, within the borders valid on the date of the proclamation of sovereignty and recognised by the UN, pursuing neutrality, co-operating for mutual advantage with all countries of the world, and guaranteeing the rights of all its citizens in accordance with international norms?'. Despite the boycott of the poll in Transnistria, where 18 per cent of the population live, a turnout of 75 per cent was recorded, and 95 per cent of the voters answered 'Yes' (Chinn and Roper, 1995: 32).

So language and history turned out to be less decisive than predicted in answering the question of Moldovan national political identity. Not only is the past open to a variety of possible interpretations, it does not stop at a given point. When, in apparent defiance of history, the Moldovans found themselves in possession of a state, a new historical fact was created around which a separate Moldovan national identity rapidly began to crystallize.

The Moldovan national revival of the late 1980s was from the start not a unified movement, but contained rival political agenda and rival interests which only fully emerged once statehood was acquired. The Popular Front of Moldova was formed in 1989 as a coalition between two informal groups of Moldovan intellectuals: the 'Democratic Movement in Support of Restructuring', which promoted political and economic reforms in line with Gorbachev's *perestroika*; and the 'Alexei Mateevici Literary-Musical Circle', which focused specifically on the demands for improved Moldovan-language education and on the status of the language itself in public life in the republic. According to Crowther, the general issues of reform propagated by the first group had little resonance with the Moldovan masses until they were linked with the more overtly nationalist agenda set by the second (Crowther, 1991:189). A series of mass demonstrations in late 1988 and throughout 1989 successfully demonstrated the power of the language issue to mobilize large numbers, strengthening the hand of nationalist intellectuals within the Popular Front. At the time the language issue anyway seemed to chime perfectly with the broader aims of *perestroika*, insofar as granting 'official' status to the language spoken by the Moldovans, the titular nation of the republic and the majority of its population, would bring the Soviet state closer to the people and so contribute to its 'democratization'.

But the Moldovan language issue had a special twist. Soviet rule in Moldova had seen the implementation of nationality policies aimed simultaneously at 'Russification' and at cultivating a distinct Soviet version of Moldovan identity, which would sever the historic and cultural links with Romania. The lynchpin of this policy had been to enforce the use of the Cyrillic script in the written language and to deny its identity with Romanian. The import of reading materials from Romania had been strictly controlled, and the few works by Romanian authors allowed to be published were first 'translated' into the Cyrillic script. History was comprehensively rewritten, and the interwar period, when Bessarabia had belonged to Romania, was referred to, if at all, as an unfortunate interlude of foreign occupation. The border with Romania was effectively closed, and personal contacts between Moldovans and Romanians drastically restricted.

The Popular Front now demanded that the use of the Latin alphabet be restored, and that it be formally recognised as the same as Romanian. The political implications of this seemed clear, as one émigré Romanian source explains:

> *'The truth is that once "Moldavian" was no longer written in the Cyrillic script, it became automatically Romanian. And once the language was Romanian, the biggest Soviet hoax of the century, the so-called Moldavian nation, vanished like a ghost in broad daylight.'* (Dima, 1991:142)

Compelling as this logic may seem to a nationalist intellectual, it is by no means evident from the available accounts of the mass demonstrations of 1988–89 that it was necessarily shared by the participants at the time. (An indication of the variety of demands made is given by Singurel, 1989) While the language issue was certainly associated with a 'rediscovery of history', the history which the Moldovans were most concerned to 'rediscover' was that of the Stalinist period of the late 1940s, when collectivization had been implemented with characteristic brutality, accompanied by mass deportations to Siberia of Moldovan peasants branded as 'kulaks', and famine in 1946–47 (see Gribincea, 1995:177–87).

But other, more immediate issues than these historical ones appear to have been raised with at least as much urgency by the demonstrators. The environment is singled out by many sources as having played a crucial role in propelling the Moldovan masses onto the streets (see Dima, 1991: 141–42; and Singurel, 1989). This tied in with a general dissatisfaction at the 'gigantomania', waste and corruption of the Stalinist pattern of development of both agriculture and industry in the republic. Industrialization had drawn in large numbers of immigrant workers whom the Moldovans resented as 'outsiders' who had jumped the queue in the allocation of housing (Dima, 1991:141).

While ethnic tensions certainly rose to the surface in 1989, and an anti-Russian agenda could easily be constructed out of the assortment of grievances generated by Soviet rule, these did not automatically add up to a pro-Romanian agenda. In fact, the question of the relationship with Romania was raised only obliquely, if at all. While the Popular Front leaders followed their Baltic counterparts in demanding the formal renunciation of the Molotov-Ribbentrop pact which had forced them into the USSR, in the Moldovan case, popular enthusiasm for the *status quo ante* – reunion with Romania – was checked by the fact that Romania itself was still languishing under the personal despotism of Nicolae Ceausescu, in an even more parlous condition than Moldova. In fact, the Soviet leadership did propose, as a gesture to mollify the Moldovans, to relax controls on the border with Romania, but this was met with a brusque rebuff from Ceausescu. Instead, barriers to the movement of persons and printed sources were strengthened on the Romanian side. Far from supporting the Moldovan national revival, Ceausescu feared it as a popular democratic challenge to his dictatorship (Eyal, 1990:138).

Nevertheless, the logic of linguistics and history continued to be considered compelling by the leadership of the Moldovan Popular Front, for obvious reasons. The primacy of language, culture and history in the definition of the 'nation' is characteristic of intellectuals, reflecting their professional pre-occupations and the nature of their vocation. The cultural intelligentsia were the most oriented towards Romania because this issue affected them most. They were the most likely to come into regular contact with Romanian literature and thought, and naturally aspired to resuming their place on the larger stage offered by Romania, seen as a more advanced, 'European' cultural milieu. But some Moldovan intellectuals and professionals feared that they would not be able to hold their own in competition with Romanians, and that reunification might lead to an invasion of 'carpetbaggers from Bucharest' who would sweep them aside (as had happened before in the inter-war period). As one Moldovan parliamentarian noted: 'People are asking themselves: "Suppose we unite [with Romania]. What do we do if, after a day or two, they begin treating us like second class citizens? What then? There is concern all round that if we unite, we will be marginalized and discriminated against."' (quoted by Socor, 1992a: 29)

What transformed the prospects of the Popular Front from an oppositional intellectual movement into a potent and effective challenge to Soviet power was the defection of a large section of the Moldovan party and state *nomenklatura* to its side. The mass demonstrations of 1989 provoked internal conflict within the Moldovan

Communist Party, hitherto a bastion of Brezhnevite traditionalism standing out against the tide of Gorbachev's *perestroika*. The leadership had been dominated for decades by Russians and highly Russified individuals with strong regional ties to Transnistria. All Bessarabians were treated with suspicion as potential pro-Romanian sympathisers, and former Romanian Communist Party members had even been refused entry to the CPSU. Thereafter, Bessarabian communists had been excluded from the top political posts. Gorbachev's *perestroika* and the accompanying political foment in Moldova provided this section of the élite with an opportunity for promotion which had hitherto been blocked. The replacement of Simeon Grossu by Petru Lucinschi as MCP First Secretary for the first time brought a Bessarabian to the top post.

While for the Popular Front, the language issue provided the catalyst for a wide-ranging attack on communist rule which some saw as the first step towards restoration of the territorial *status quo ante*, for the Bessarabian communist élite the language issue was a convenient lever firstly to dislodge the Transnistrian and Russian-speaking communist élite from power, and subsequently to enhance their own independence from Moscow. As the Soviet system disintegrated under the impact of Gorbachev's policies, these communists began to reinvent themselves as Moldovan nationalists and to make common cause with the Popular Front. Thus at this point the two groups had a shared interest in promoting the nationalist agenda, to assert the Moldovan majority's 'right of possession' of the republican state structures.

The formation of this coalition first appeared when the Moldovan Supreme Soviet passed the language law in August 1989, conceding almost all of the Popular Front's demands. Although the law accorded other language groups the right to use their their own languages in the localities where they lived, and conceded that Russian would continue to be used as the 'language of inter-ethnic communication', the idea of a 'shared' official status for Russian was rejected (see Zakonodatel' niye Akty..., 1990). All members of the administration were obliged to learn Romanian within five years and to use it at all times in their official capacity. As Eyal notes,

> '*There is little doubt that the Moldavians had won their most important victory. This had little to do with the language issue per se; rather, it amounted to extracting an open admission from their government that the republic was theirs and theirs alone, and that all other ethnic groups in Moldavia were not 'nations', but rather ethnic minorities whose rights should be respected but whose claims could not be considered as equal to the interests of the majority.*' (Eyal, 1990:133)

The March 1990 elections confirmed the consolidation of the nationalist coalition: the new Supreme Soviet was dominated by the Popular Front, which won some 40 per cent of the seats, supported by a further 30 per cent of deputies 'broadly sharing most of the Front's goals' (Socor, 1991a: 25). Almost all of them were in fact former communists. The Moldovan Communist Party First Secretary, Petru Lucinschi, failed to win the post of Chairman of the Supreme Soviet. This went instead to Mircea Snegur, a Front sympathiser and former collective farm chairman, who had previously held an administrative post in the Moldovan Ministry of Agriculture, eventually rising to become head of the Moldovan Communist Party Central Committee's agricultural section. When later the post of President of Moldova was created, Snegur was elected to it by the Supreme Soviet. A new government was installed under the reformist economist Mircea Druc.

The Supreme Soviet then proceeded to implement a series of measures which combined both radical political and economic reforms and the 're-nationalization' of Moldova. The Communist Party's 'leading role' was abolished: all parties and political movements were banned from organizing in state institutions, the police and the media. Officials and managers in senior positions were required to give up their Communist Party membership. The implementation of the 1989 language law was accelerated; russified and Soviet place names and Russified personal names were replaced with Moldovan ones; national literature and 'the history of the Romanians' were introduced into the core school curriculum; and a new national flag, the Romanian red, yellow and blue tricolour, was adopted.

On 23 June, the Supreme Soviet issued a declaration of 'sovereignty', asserting the primacy of Moldovan law over USSR law. A new citizenship law was introduced. Unlike the Baltic Republics, Moldovan citizenship was open to anyone resident on the territory on 23 June; but applications had to be made within one year, and dual nationality was not permitted. This challenged the non-Moldovans to come clean on their attitude to Moldovan statehood: 'the Russians had to stake their future on the continued existence of the Soviet Union, or else renounce Soviet citizenship and thus by their own actions contribute to the downfall of the Soviet state.' (Kolstoe, 1995:152) In September, military conscription was suspended in the republic. The Ministry of the Interior's police force were renamed the Carabinieri and the beginnings of a national army, the Republican Guard, were established.

When Gorbachev launched discussion of a new 'Union Treaty' in an effort to preserve the USSR on redefined terms, the Moldovans adopted the most radical position, favouring a loose, confederal 'association of sovereign states' with no central institutions (the so-called 'fifteen-plus-zero' formula – see Socor, 1991b: 18–20). At the end of the year, when Gorbachev proposed to put his version of the Union Treaty to a referendum throughout the USSR, deputies of the Moldovan Supreme Soviet denounced it as 'our own death warrant, which we are being invited to sign', and 'a legalization of the consequences of the Molotov-Ribbentrop pact.' (Socor, 1991b:19). Backed by a mass rally in Chisinau of an estimated 800,000 people organized by the Popular Front, which declared 'the right of Romanians in Soviet occupied territories…to determine the future of [those] territories', the Supreme Soviet voted to boycott the referendum (Socor, 1991b: 20).

But at the same time, contradictory signs were already emerging of diffidence on the part of the Moldovans towards Romania itself (Socor, 1991a: 27). The fall of the Ceausescu regime in December 1989 had been greeted with enthusiasm by leaders of the Popular Front, who went at once to Bucharest and voiced demands for unification. But this turned out to be very much a minority view, confined to a small number of intellectuals and students in Moldova. And despite the enthusiasm of the Romanian intelligentsia, the new Romanian government under Iliescu remained extremely cautious. His domestic critics saw this as evidence of his pro-Russian sympathies and personal ties with Gorbachev and the Soviet KGB. But there was a more practical reason – the catastrophic state of the post-Ceausescu Romanian economy, which had a sobering impact on the calculations of both Moldovans and Romanians.

The distinctively democratic and egalitarian flavour of Moldovan popular nationalism reappears at the end of the communist period. A growing unease among Moldovans at the undemocratic character of the post-Ceausescu regime in Romania began to become apparent as early as spring 1990 (Socor, 1992a: 31). And when the Iliescu regime became more overtly nationalist, and therefore more inclined to show an interest in Moldova, its increasingly obvious centralizing authoritarianism, and the patronizing attitude of the 'Greater Romanian' nationalist intellectuals, provided clear warning to the emergent new Moldovan political élites that unification might entail a new form of exclusion from power.

But in the meanwhile, the Moldovan national revival had generated a reaction among the Russian and Gagauz minority populations, leading to the formation of the two separatist movements which contested Moldovan 'ownership' of the state, and in particular, the Moldovans' right to unite the territory with Romania. These challenges brought the latent conflicts within the Moldovan national movement to a head.

## SEPARATIST CHALLENGES AND THE MOLDOVAN RESPONSE

The 'Gagauz Republic' and the 'Transdniester Moldovan Republic' were both formed in reaction against the Moldovan language law, the drive for Moldovan independence from Moscow, and the prospect of union with Romania. At first, they co-ordinated their activities closely and gave each other support, and sought help from the Soviet leaders in Moscow. But once the Soviet Union itself dissolved, the significant differences in interests and political resources between them came to the fore.

The Gagauz population is concentrated in the Budjak region, in five of the southern *raiony* of Moldova. Of the total of 197,768 Gagauzi recorded in the 1989 Soviet census, 153,458 (78 per cent) live in Moldova. Almost all the rest live across the border in the Odessa oblast of Ukraine. The area is extremely poor, and suffers from a serious water shortage and polluted water supplies. The Gagauzi were one of the most disadvantaged ethnic groups in Soviet Moldova. With no provision for education in their own language, they became the most highly Russified of all the non-Russians in Moldova. Cultural facilities also hardly existed: for example, between 1957 and 1990, only 33 books were published in the Gagauz language (King, 1995b: 21–22). In 1989, 73 per cent gave Russian as their second language; while 91 per cent of them claimed to some knowledge of the Gagauz language, it is far from clear how ready they were to function in it for all purposes. Intermarriage with non-Gagauzi and total Russification of education in the Gagauz area meant that families of the younger generation even used Russian at home.

The Moldovan language law therefore provoked a strong reaction among the Gagauzi because for them, the abandonment of Russian posed an immediate threat to their access to education and their capacity to operate in public life. It was not just that the Gagauzi did not see any compelling reason to shift from Russian to Romanian, but that, at least for the time being, going over from Russian to the Gagauz language was not seen as a practical option either.

In May 1989, a Gagauz movement for cultural revival, the 'Gagauz Halki', appeared. At first this movement had in fact aligned itself with pro-*perestroika* forces, and was represented at the founding meetings of the Popular Front in June of that year. But the Gagauzi rapidly discovered the incongruity of their aims with those of the increasingly exclusive form of nationalism propagated by the Popular Front leadership. When the language law was passed, Gagauz leaders, mainly local party and administrative officials as well as the Gagauz Halki, met in Comrat, the main regional centre in the south, and declared 'independence'. Later in the year, they proclaimed the formation of a 'Gagauz Autonomous Soviet Socialist Republic' on MSSR territory, whose chief purpose was to retain Russian as the official language in their region.

For the Russians of Moldova, the language law was equally inconvenient. A survey in 1992 revealed that only 6.5 per cent of them professed a full command of Moldovan, while 23.5 per cent could understand and read it; 52.5 per cent could only pick out certain phrases, while 15.5 per cent admitted to total ignorance (Kolstoe, 1995:145–46). Because Russian had hitherto been the sole language in which public affairs had been conducted in the republic, the adoption of the language law immediately challenged their positions in the structures of political, economic and administrative power. It was both a symbolic and and practical blow to their dominant status in the republic.

Russian opposition began with the formation of the *Edinstvo* (Unity) movement in April 1989, to defend the unity of the USSR. In August, strikes broke out in the large factories of Chisinau and Transnistria, most of whose workforce was Russian, in protest at the language law. A 'Union of Working Collectives' was formed, which was to provide the organizational nucleus of the Transdniester Moldova Republic (TMR), formed in 1990. The leadership of this movement, however, did not spring up from below, but was in the hands of communist *nomenklatura* élites, mainly Russian and russified Ukrainians, who staffed the local party apparatus, the local Soviets, and the large enterprises concentrated in Transnistria, most of which were All-Union enterprises directly controlled from Moscow rather than Chisinau (Kolstoe, 1995:157). They were supported by the mainly Russian and Russified anti-*perestroika* wing of the Moldovan Communist Party, which had broken away and withdrawn its deputies from the Moldovan Supreme Soviet in 1990; and had the sympathy of officers of the Soviet 14th Army, stationed in Transnistria.

All of these groups had a very large material stake in opposing *perestroika* and maintaining the USSR. Thus for them, the language issue was an opportunity to mobilize mass support among the Russians for their own broader pro-Soviet ideological and political agenda. But the territory they claimed was not wholly, or even mainly, inhabited by Russians. According to the 1989 census, the largest national group in Transnistria was still the Moldovans, who constituted 40 per cent; 28 per cent were Ukrainian, and the Russians came third with 23 per cent. Because the Ukrainians were highly Russified, the TMR leaders claimed to act in the name of the 'Russian-speaking' majority. But they could not claim to speak on behalf of the majority of Russians, two-thirds of whom still lived on the right bank, in Bessarabia.

The consolidation of these two secessionist 'republics' proceeded in parallel and in direct reaction to the consolidation of the Moldovans' own hold on the republican institutions and the overtly nationalist overtones which accompanied their moves towards independence from Moscow. When the Moldovans declared 'sovereignty' in June 1990, the Gagauzi reiterated their demand for autonomy, adopted a new national flag and anthem, and set up a new university in Comrat to meet the need for higher education in Russian of their young people now excluded from the established Moldovan universities, which had gone over almost at once to Romanian as the sole language of instruction.

The response of the Moldovan Supreme Soviet, now fully under the control of the Popular Front, was symptomatic of the nationalist hubris which then gripped it: it ruled the Gagauz actions unlawful on the grounds that the Gagauzi were 'not indigenous', and constituted a mere 'ethnic group', not a 'nation' with a right to a national territory. In response, the Gagauz 'National Congress' was convened, declaring the secession of the 'Gagauz Republic' and announcing its application to be re-attached to the USSR as an independent constituent republic of the federation. Elections to a Gagauz Supreme Soviet were set for October. In September, the TMR followed suit by proclaiming secession from Moldova. The response of the Popular Front was to appeal over Moldovan TV against the dismemberment of 'ancestral Moldavian land', and the Moldovan Supreme Soviet Presidium followed this up by outlawing all attempts to form separate republics on Moldovan territory, which, in their view, manifested 'ignorance of law and history'.

Meanwhile, the Popular Front set about raising an irregular volunteer force of Moldovan 'patriots', who were bussed into the Gagauz area in order to prevent the elections taking place. But the Gagauzi had also acquired arms, *via* their supporters in the TMR who had by this time gained access to weapons from the Soviet 14th Army, and were running them across Ukrainian territory from Transnistria. The stage seemed set for bloodshed. This finally impelled Moscow to intervene, and USSR Ministry of the Interior forces were sent in to keep the peace – also allowing the Gagauzi to hold their elections after all. Moldovan President Snegur, who had declared a state of emergency, was forced to accept this *fait accompli*. A total of six *raiony* in the south – in only two of which the Gagauzi constituted more than half of the population – were now beyond the writ of Chisinau.

In early 1991, the Gagauzi and the TMR held referendums on the Union Treaty, in defiance of the Moldovan boycott, and voted almost unanimously in favour of staying in the USSR (Chinn and Roper, 1995: 311). The conditions in which this ballot was held were far from satisfactory (see Socor, 1991c). This phase of the unfolding drama culminated in the attempted coup in Moscow on 21 August 1991, which propelled the Moldovan Republic to declare full independence. The Gagauz Republic and the TMR first publicly supported the coup leaders, and, when the coup collapsed, declared their own independence from Moldova. But at this point, with the dissolution of the USSR, the dynamics of the conflict began to change.

Firstly, with independence, the underlying divisions within the Popular Front came to the surface, and President Snegur began to develop a strategy for accommodation with the secessionists. Throughout 1991, he had actively promoted a 'multi-cultural' agenda, focusing on the development of mother-tongue education for the Ukrainians, Bulgarians and Gagauzi, designed to peel them away from the Russians. A draft law on local self-government issued in January 1991 included the possibility of a separate Gagauz region, albeit with limited political status. By the end of the year, Snegur was also suggesting a deal on the Moldovan constitution, which might include a clause recognising a 'special status' for Gagauzia and Transnistria, including their right to exercise 'self-determination' should Moldova change its 'international status', i.e., reunite with Romania.

In the course of 1991, the position of the Gagauzi had also shown signs of shifting. Two pro-Soviet Gagauz leaders were sidelined by more pragmatic Gagauz regionalists in March 1991, and in May a new Gagauz proposal for 'autonomy' was submitted to the Moldovan Supreme Soviet. In August, the Gagauz declaration of independence from Moldova was accompanied by a proposal for the formation of a 'confederation' between Bessarabia, Gagauzia and Transnistria. This looked at first like an anti-Moldovan proposal, but with hindsight it can be interpreted as a sign of Gagauz willingness to come to terms with the new political reality. The newly formed independent Ukraine promptly blocked the land bridge between the TMR and Gagauzia, across which arms and men had hitherto passed. Gagauzia was far too small to go it alone, and once the USSR ceased to exist, the Gagauzi had little real option but to seek to rejoin Moldova.

The turning point came with the culmination of the conflict with the Transnistrians in 1992. Detailed accounts of the course of events can be found elsewhere (see especially Kolstoe *et al.*, 1993). Our focus here is on how this propelled the Moldovans to compromise with the Gagauzi. The TMR politically was a very different animal from the Gagauz Republic. It was inextricably tied to the USSR and all it had stood for, and when this dissolved in the autumn of 1991, the TMR suffered a major setback. Having declared its support for the Moscow coup, it pitted itself against the triumphant new independent Russian government installed in Moscow under Yeltsin, who at first was sympathetic to Moldovan independence. The new situation was read by the Moldovans as a propitious opportunity to regain control over Transnistria. On 29 March 1992, President Snegur issued an ultimatum to the TMR leaders, and on 19 June, Moldovan forces recaptured Bendery, a mainly Russian city on the right bank of the Dniester. But they were unable to hold it: on the night of 20–21 June they were driven back by TMR forces, bolstered by some Cossack irregulars, and, crucially, by soldiers and tanks of the former Soviet – now Russian – 14th Army stationed on the territory, acting, it seems, independently of Moscow (Kolstoe *et al.*, 1993: 987–88).

This defeat proved a turning point for the Moldovans, fully revealing the costs of pressing their claim to independent statehood in national terms. Separatist movements now controlled large areas. The loss of Transnistria was an especially bitter blow. The bulk of Moldova's industrial capacity was located there, along with vital energy facilities. All Moldova's communications infrastructure connecting it to the former USSR, vital for trade links, ran through Transnistria. Moreover, the conflicts with the minorities had drawn Moscow back into Moldovan affairs, and had contributed to the fateful reawakening of Russian 'patriotic' feelings in Moscow. Even pro-*perestroika* Russian democrats, previously sympathetic to Moldova's independence, now rallied to the side of the Transnistrians, whose cause became identified with the larger one of defending the Russians stranded beyond Russia's borders by the collapse of the USSR. Thus Chisinau found itself with no real option but to agree to Russia's proposal for the establishment of a 'peace-keeping force', comprising Moldovan, Russian and TMR units. While the lengthy communiqué which announced this agreement in July 1992 declared respect for the sovereignty, independence and territorial integrity of Moldova, nevertheless the TMR continued to exist and to build up its organizational and institutional structures. The price Chisinau would have to pay for the recovery of Transnistria seemed likely to include not only the formal federalization of the state, but the permanent stationing of Russian troops on its territory, with all that would imply for its independence (see 'Moldova...', 1995).

Thus July 1992 marked a watershed in Moldovan politics. The tentative, rather *ad hoc* moves towards compromise already indicated by President Snegur were now consolidated into a coherent strategy under a new 'Government of National Consensus', led by Andrei Sangheli, which took shape in the late summer of 1992. The basic ingredients of the concept of 'national consensus' were the commitment to independent Moldovan statehood and territorial integrity; the recognition of the Moldovans' affinity with the Romanians as cultural, but not political; and the willingness to negotiate on cultural and administrative autonomy for the national minorities (Socor, 1992b: 5–6).

This government was able to muster the support of some 180–190 parliamentary deputies, out of the roughly 240 who still took up their seats (about 80 deputies, mostly from the Gagauzia and Transnistria, had permanently withdrawn). The parliamentary scene was by now highly fragmented into loose and constantly shifting clubs of deputies, but what is clear is that the government enjoyed the support of representatives of the Moldovan former *nomenklatura*, mainly collective farm chairmen and local government officials, centrist Moldovan intellectuals who had parted company with the Popular Front, and former communists from the Bessarabian Russian and Ukrainian minorities, and about half of the Gagauz and Bulgarian deputies from the Budjak region (Socor, 1992b: 8).

The picture was clarified by the general election of 27 February 1994 (see King, 1995a:11). This was won by the Agrarian Democratic Party, which took 43.2 per cent of the vote and gained 54 seats in the new 101-member parliament. This party was a regrouping of the Moldovan former *nomenklatura* élites, especially those rooted in the rural areas, who had formed the bedrock of support for the 'Government of National Consensus'. The election fully demonstrated their capacity to mobilize the rural majority of Moldovan voters. By contrast, the two successors to the Popular Front were much less successful: the Christian Democratic Popular Front, which remained true to the cause of immediate reunification with Romania, won 7.5 per cent of the vote and 9 seats, while the Bloc of Peasants and Intellectuals, also committed to reunification but in a more gradual way, won 9.2 per cent of the vote and 11 seats. The main opposition force was the Socialist-Unity (*Edinstvo*) bloc, with 22 per cent of the vote and 27 seats, composed mainly of former communists promoting closer relations with Russia and full integration in the CIS, supporting the establishment of a permanent Russian military base in Moldova, and stoutly defending the use of Russian in government and education.

The composition of the new parliament allowed President Snegur and Prime Minister Sangheli to move rapidly towards a compromise with the Gagauzi. Many laws passed in the first flush of Moldovan nationalism were rescinded. The implementation of the language law was suspended. In March 1994, the 'popular consultation' confirmed that the majority of the Moldovan people wanted Moldova to remain an independent state, and a new constitution was adopted in July 1994. This, while preserving the status of Moldovan as the 'state language', using the Latin alphabet, also guaranteed the right 'to the preservation, development and functioning of the Russian language and other languages spoken on the territory of the country' (Article 13), and committed the State to 'provide, in correspondence with the law, for the right of the individual to choose the language of education and training' (Article 35). It also included in Article 111 reference to 'special status of autonomy' for 'settlements on the left bank of the Dniester river as well as certain settlements in the south of the Republic of Moldova', subject to the support of three-fifths of the parliamentary deputies. This opened the way to the drafting of the 'Law on Special Status for Gagauzia (Gagauz Yeri)', which passed its second reading in December 1994, and was promulgated by President Snegur on 13 January 1995 (see Socor, 1994; King, 1995b).

The law defined Gagauzia as 'an autonomous territorial unit' constituting 'a component part of the Republic of Moldova', but with the right to 'full self-determination' (i.e., secession) in the event of a change in Moldova's 'international status' (i.e., reunification with Romania). Gagauzia would have three official languages – Gagauz, Moldovan, and Russian – and would have the right to display its own flag and symbols alongside those of the Moldovan Republic. It would elect its own assembly, with a four-year term of office, and its executive would be headed by a directly-elected governor, the Bashkan, who would also hold an *ex officio* post as Deputy Prime Minister in the government of Moldova. The Gagauz assembly would draw up its own constitution, and would have wide powers over culture, education, the local economy, health, social welfare, housing, and the environment. Gagauzia would have its own budget, but the crucial issue of finance was left only vaguely defined.

In March 1995, 30 settlements (3 towns, 27 villages) decided by local referendum to join to form Gagauzia. On 28 May and 11 June, two rounds of elections produced a 34-seat assembly and the first Gagauz Bashkan, Georgi Tabunshchik, who had formerly been the Communist Party first secretary of Comrat *raion*. The political complexions of both assembly and Bashkan appear to favour co-operation and mutual understanding with the Moldovan parliament: the new Gagauz political élite closely resembles its Moldovan counterpart in almost everything except language, being composed largely of former *nomenklatura* local 'notables', men of a strongly pragmatic orientation, administrative experience and the will to 'make things work'. The largest single group of deputies is made up of representatives of 'workers' collectives' (11), but there are also 8 deputies belonging to the Party of Communists of Moldova, reconstituted in 1993 after the 1991 ban on the Communist Party had been lifted. This party claims to have cut all ties with Russia and presents itself as 'social democratic'. It has much in common in terms of domestic policy (as opposed to foreign policy) with the Socialist-Unity bloc in the Moldovan parliament. Several deputies are from the Moldovan Agrarian Democrats (and several Gagauzi represent their constituencies in the Moldovan parliament on the Agrarian Democrat benches). Two members of the Gagauz parliament are more radical nationalists, and the rest are independents.

It was not until 1 January 1996 that a separate Gagauz budget was established. In an interview in May 1996, the Speaker of the Gagauz assembly, Peter Pashali, indicated that so far the Gagauzi had no complaints against the Moldovan government on this score, fully recognising the parlous condition of the finances of the Republic as a whole. It is hard to give an accurate estimate of Gagauzia's financial provision in 1996 because of the radical overhaul of the assignment of taxes between Chisinau and the *raions* which has taken place in the meanwhile. It does seem to be the case, however, that Gagauzia's subvention went up in 1996, while total subventions went down. Gagauzia is allowed to retain 30 per cent of VAT collections (like other poorer *raiony*), and also retains 70 per cent of profit tax from republican enterprises (in contrast to the standard deal which allows *raiony* to retain 50 per cent). Like other *raiony*, it retains 100 per cent of the profit tax on municipal enterprises and 100 per cent of the land tax.

Progress towards a settlement with the TMR has become ever more bogged down in the increasingly complex politics of Russia, and is to that extent dependent more on external developments than on any further concessions the Moldovan government might reasonably be expected to make. But meanwhile, the majority of Russians living on the right bank show signs of adjusting with growing confidence to the new reality of independent Moldova. Citizenship in Moldova appears to be quite tolerable, on condition that the language law is not fully implemented, and the prospect of union with Romania becomes ever less likely. The relatively good performance of the Moldovan economy in recent years, particularly in establishing the new currency and controlling inflation, contrasts favourably with that of Russia. Moldova retains its attractions for its Russian citizens as a pleasant place to live. While there have indeed been grumbles at the shrinkage of places in Russian language schools (Kolstoe, 1995:150–51), Russian language education is still provided but inevitably not on the previous scale. And many Russian parents are choosing to send their children to Moldovan schools in order to prepare them practically for future life in independent Moldova.

## THE MOLDOVAN ECONOMY: THE EARLY POST-COMMUNIST YEARS

Like the other former Soviet republics, Moldova inherited serious problems from the former Soviet Union such as: a costly social security system (largely because of pensions); weak institutions; and an inadequate legal system. Furthermore the republic was adversely affected by: the disruption of trade with the former Soviet republics; the emergence of large inter-enterprise arrears (similar to those in Ukraine); an inefficient payments system; high inflation; and the demise of state orders.

As a result, in the early years of independence Moldova's economy was in serious decline, and attempts to address the economic problems were impeded by: political turmoil; inter-ethnic strife; and an uncertain relationship with Russia. In particular the armed conflict in the separatist Trans-Dniester region occupied much of the mind and energies of the government until mid-1992. Although the armed conflict has ended, separatist tendencies in the rebel Dniester region have not dissipated, and the region's constant rebellious behaviour manifests itself in the form of demands for a separate currency and a separate foreign policy.

Despite the immediate problems that were facing the country its commitment to a free market economy, incorporating economic reforms, was typified by its adoption of a programme of structural reforms in early 1992 encompassing: a property law; a privatization law; a law of Agrarian reform; a bankruptcy law; a foreign investment law; and an anti-monopoly law. The country also affiliated itself with key international organizations and institutions. On August 12, 1992, Moldova became a member of the International Monetary Fund (IMF), and the World Bank. It also joined the European Bank for Reconstruction and Development (EBRD), and the United Nations.

## Macroeconomic Stabilization

Macroeconomic stabilization is one of the prerequisites of moving to a market economy.[2] But trying to achieve macrostability during the transition to a free market is challenging. The volatile nature of the economic environment, and the introduction of new institutions are likely to complicate macroeconomic policy. The overall aim has to be to maintain a non-inflationary monetary policy during a period in which the velocity of money is likely to be changing suddenly and unpredictably, prompted not least by changes in the fiscal system. In transition economies where financial markets are not well developed, monetary policy may have little initial effect on the real economy, but controlling inflation is essential to maintaining the credibility of the government, and the transition process itself. It is also critical that the financing of the fiscal deficit is not achieved through the printing of money, since this can lead to bouts of very rapid inflation, and even hyperinflation. Given this conception of macroeconomic stabilization, we now review the Moldovan experience in the 1990s. Table 1 summarizes some of the main economic indicators of the Moldovan economy, to introduce to the discussion.

**Table 1.   Moldova: Main Economic Indicators (% Change Over Previous Year Unless Otherwise Indicated)**

| Year\Item | GDP | Industrial Production | Agricultural Production | Inflation (CPI) | Exports ($ mn) | Imports ($ mn) | Budget balance (% of GDP) |
|---|---|---|---|---|---|---|---|
| 1990 | −2.4 | 3.2 | −12.9 | 4.2 | | | 3 |
| 1991 | −17.5 | −11.1 | −10.1 | 98.0 | | | 0 |
| 1992 | −29.0 | −27.1 | −16.4 | 1208 | 868 | 905 | −4.2 |
| 1993 | −1.2 | 0.3 | 9.9 | 1283 | 451 | 631 | −6.4 |
| 1994 | −31.2 | −27.7 | −24.3 | 330 | 618 | 672 | −8.7 |
| 1995 | −3.0 | −6 | 5 | 30 | 741 | 773 | −5.5 |
| 1996 | −8.0 | | | 23.5 | 830 | 862 | −3.4 |
| 1997* | 5.0 | | | 12 | | | |

*Source*:   *Moldovan Economic Trends*, various issues; EBRD *Transition Report* and *Transition Report Update*, various issues.
*Note*:   1997 figures are forecasts; from 1994, most of the data do not include the Transdniestr region.

Between the end of 1990 and the end of 1993 GDP fell by an estimated 50 per cent. Declines in real GDP in Moldova have been fairly sustained, levelling off recently with the resumption of very modest growth. In 1991 real GDP fell by 17.5 per cent from the previous year. In 1992 it fell by 29 per cent, followed by falls of 1.2 per cent in 1993 and 31.2 per cent in 1994. The spectacular fall of over 30 per cent in 1994 was attributable largely to the poor harvest which hit agricultural production particularly badly. Despite these catastrophic falls in GDP and production, officially recorded unemployment in Moldova has been surprisingly low, remaining below 2 per cent of the labour force. However, there is a great deal of underemployment within Moldova's factories and farms, and any of those not recorded as unemployed are most likely employed in the second, or 'grey' economy, earning incomes are also largely unrecorded in official statsistics. Conservatively, these unrecorded incomes could easily amount to 20 per cent of GDP.

Moldova is not well endowed with natural resources and the economy is primarily agricultural. Among the major crops are wheat, corn, sugar beets, vegetables and fruit, and wine. Agricultural production, which is the mainstay of the Moldovan economy, fell by over 40 per cent between 1990 and 1992, but recovered substantially in 1993 to register an increase of 9.9 per cent. But it fell by a further 24.3 per cent in 1994 because of a poor harvest. Moldova has a comparative advantage in its agriculture and food processing industries, provided that it can secure access to suitable new markets. Although agricultural production has declined substantially since 1991, it still remains the largest and potentially most profitable area of the economy. The importance of the agricultural sector is indicated by the fact that in 1995 it accounted for 46.1 per cent of total employment, by far the largest sector.

Moldova's trade was badly hit by the dissolution of the Soviet Union, but after some years of trade deficits the situation has returned to a more balanced one. There remain some serious problems of identifying and gaining access to new markets and, in the longer term, reorienting and restructuring Moldovan production to meet the demands of these markets.

The first few years of Moldovan independence were characterized by very high rates of inflation, as Table 1 shows. In 1992 average inflation had reached 1200 per cent . Although it had fallen considerably by 1994, it remained very high. Since 1994 Moldova's performance has been much more satisfactory. Inflation dropped from over 300 per cent in 1994 to around 30 per cent by the end of 1995, and was continuing to fall.

As with most countries in the former Soviet bloc, increases in inflation were initially stimulated by price liberalization; Moldova liberalized the prices of most industrial goods and some consumer goods and services[3] in January 1992. The drop in the Moldovan inflation rate, in recent times, reflects both the success of anti-inflationary policy measures as well as the depressed state of the economy. As far as specific policies are concerned there have been reductions in the budget deficit, and since the end of 1993 a tight monetary policy. Moldova's more liberal trade and exchange rate policy also helped in the stabilization of the price level. Many restrictions on imports and exports were removed, allowing the exchange rate to reflect the changes in the demand and supply of foreign currency. Increasing competition from imported goods put pressure on domestic prices.

The strong Leu (see below for details of the introduction of a new currency), and the continued vigilance of Moldova's National Bank, ensured that price rises moderated in 1996. However, some continued upward pressure on prices is likely to remain because of necessary increases in electricity charges. The government will have to charge consumers higher prices for energy in order to reflect higher prices paid to Russia, and other suppliers, and also in order to meet its energy debt to Russia. Already Moldova's gas debts to Russia are mounting. They stood at US$400m at the beginning of May 1996, up from US$282m in January 1996. But unless the debt is settled or an agreement reached, Moldova may face cutbacks in energy supplies. In this context, the failure of industrial consumers to pay their bills, and the fact that the government still charges domestic customers low prices, are not helpful. In May 1996 the government did take some measures to redress the problem by raising electricity prices by 50 per cent for private customers, and 10 per cent for industry.[4] However, this is only a first step along a difficult, and politically sensitive path.

*Fiscal and Budgetary Policy*

As has been the case with countries in transition in general, Moldova has experienced severe fiscal problems.[5] This has been due to: a fall in the country's GDP which *ceteris paribus* reduces revenues and increases expenditures; and the changing role of the economy. But since 1992, steps have been taken to address some of the problems in the fiscal sphere. Major tax reforms in 1992 included the introduction of VAT, and restructuring of the personal income tax. In 1993 there was further reform with several new taxes including road tax, some import tariffs, and an extension of the VAT base. A progressive enterprise profits tax was also introduced. The system of tax administration has been strengthened, though there are still problems over tax collection. New legislative changes mean that tax administrators can impose fines, and directors have the responsibility for the prompt payment of their enterprise obligations. Other reforms such as increasing the coverage of the budget, simplifying the budget system, and increasing the accountability to the authorities have also been introduced.

As far as budgetary policy is concerned, the consolidated budget (which comprises the state budget and local budgets) has been in constant deficit since independence. Arrears in the budget have mainly been the result of problems in the collection of VAT and profits tax. The deficit is financed through a combination of internal financing (an active market on three month government securities has been created and has been operational since mid-March 1995), and foreign loans. The consolidated budget revenues accounted for 16.8 per cent of Moldova's GDP in 1993, 24.3 per cent in 1994, and 26.2 per cent in 1995.

Moldova at present faces continued challenges in the fiscal sphere. Problems include the fact that not all expenditures are covered by the consolidated budget, and the existence of extra-budgetary funds. The most important extra budgetary fund is the social fund which administers the pensions and family support. The fund is financed by a payroll tax, which is made up of 35 per cent of the total wage bill paid by enterprises, and an additional 1 per cent of the wage bill paid by workers. At present there are significant arrears to the fund due to the inability of enterprises to pay wages, tax evasion, and late payments. Recent figures reveal that arrears to pensioners from the social fund were around 310 million lei, of which 230 million lei were pension arrears, and 80 million lei were arrears in income support and social protection payments. Economic agents' payment arrears to the social fund were around 430 million lei. A scheme is under-way which aims at reducing the overall indebtedness by paying pensioners in food and consumer goods which are currently held as stocks by enterprises. In addition, with the continuing restructuring of enterprises there will be an increase in open unemployment which will require further social expenditures.

## Monetary Policy

Moldova experienced difficulties in establishing an independent central bank, a new currency, and learning how to conduct monetary policy in a small highly open economy. The IMF helped by organizing training courses for central bankers, as did some European central banks. Bank staff are on average very young, and this may have helped the bank in facilitating rapid reforms, since there were few people set in old ways of doing things.[6] However, on the negative side there was the potential for some serious mistakes.

In mid-1991 a new national two-tier banking system was established. The direction of credit operations of the new central bank initially remained greatly influenced by the government, and parliament. In 1993 the central bank's powers were enhanced. At present the functions of the National Bank of Moldova are: (a) Lender to the government; (b) Issue currency, and control inflation; (c) Supervise the activity of commercial banks on the basis of the existing international standards; (d) Monitor the balance of payments position, and responsibility for the maintenance of the stability of the exchange rate.

The National Bank is independent of the government, but the supervision of the banking sector has been hampered by the slow introduction of international accounting standards. The governor is responsible to parliament and reports every six months to the Finance and Budget Committee. Parliament can sack the governor but only in very exceptional circumstances when serious misbehaviour has occurred, and when two-thirds of parliament votes for it. The parliament is considered reasonably balanced. The governor is therefore free to act as a tough central banker and maintain monetary discipline.

To assess the stringency of Moldova's monetary policy stance, we can examine the annual velocities of circulation of M2 and M3, calculated by taking the arithmetic mean of the monthly observations of these monetary aggregates over the years 1993–95. In 1993 the velocity of M2 was 11.6, and M3 10.8. In 1994 the velocity of M2 had increased to 12.1 but for M3 had fallen to 10.3. However in 1995 both the velocities of circulation for M2 and M3 had fallen considerably to 9.0 and 7.9 respectively, an indication also of more stable prices, thus lowering the opportunity cost of holding money.

The money multiplier is another important monetary indicator. The value of the money multiplier depends on two key ratios: the banks' desired ratio of cash reserves to total deposits, and the private sector's desired ratio of cash in circulation to total bank deposits. In the case of Moldova the money multiplier has been relatively low. This reflects the fact that the private sector's desired ratio of cash to bank deposits has been high, thus giving the banks a smaller deposit with which to create a multiplied deposit expansion, and secondly because of the fact that banks' desired ratio of cash to deposits has also been high, leading them to create less deposits for any given cash reserves. In other words the commercial banks have had significant excess reserves in their accounts with the central bank. Currently the central bank has set a required reserve ratio equal to 8 per cent for the commercial banks, in line with international norms.

Moldova does have a problem of bad debt. The riskiness of loans adds a significant risk premium to the lending rates charged by commercial banks. Factors which contribute to the riskiness of loans in Moldova include the bad financial situation of many enterprises, and the unclear legal framework especially with regard to the bankruptcy law.

Overall it can be said that currently broad money is controlled fairly tightly. At present credit and monetary growth are not excessive. Although figures for broad money depict a largely upward trend this is not particularly excessive. A tight monetary policy has been place since 1995, and is supported by banking reform. To finance the government deficit government bonds are sold to the commercial banks in bi-monthly auctions rather than reverting to the wholesale printing of money. The central bank has tried to keep interest rates as moderate as possible without compromising its tight monetary policy. Control over the commercial banks is very strict, and new commercial banks must have statutory capital of at least US$ 4 million.

## Economic Reforms

Moldova has received financial assistance since independence to help facilitate economic reforms, and soften any adverse shocks which have afflicted the economy as a result of the adoption of a transition programme. The IMF memorandum signed by the government in October 1993 set out three major tasks: reducing inflation; stabilizing the new currency; and decreasing the budget deficit. In 1993 Moldova even received praise from the international financial community for its economic reform programmes.

The situation today is far from satisfactory. Moldova has made some progress, particularly on the stabilization front but reforms in other areas have not advanced as much. Structural change in Moldova lags behind privatization and macroeconomic reform-both hailed by the World Bank and IMF as among the most progressive in the former Soviet Union.[7] Moldova's backlog of unpaid wages and pensions is one of the country's most serious economic problems, and a key source of social unrest. On July 1st 1996 wage arrears amounted to 262.5 million lei. The situation has been so desperate that an increasing proportion of salaries is given in the form of payments in kind. In addition, as mentioned before, arrears to pensioners amounted to 310 million lei at the beginning of August 1996. Indeed the political situation in the country remains uncertain. The population has taken to the streets to air its grievances and protest at grinding poverty. The average official monthly wage of US$33 buys just 44 per cent of a basket of basic consumer goods, according to the Labour Ministry.

In Transdniestr conditions are even worse. No multilateral aid or foreign investment has reached the region. The government has been unable to pay wages in the region, and Smirnov (the region's leader) has resorted to desperate measures, declaring a state of emergency in January 1996, and increasing police powers. The situation in Transdniestr remains unresolved, as explained above. The World Bank classified Moldova in the category of intermediate reformers[8] still some way behind the Baltic states, Romania, Hungary, Poland, and the Czech Republic – who were rated in the category of leading and advanced reformers – but on a par or ahead of Russia, Kazakhstan, and the other Central Asian Republics.

The IMF recognises that Moldova still has much progress to make, and in view of this agreed in 1996 to lend it US$200million to support economic reforms over three years.[9] This was subject to: consumer price rises being around 15 per cent; a modest rise in real incomes (25 per cent), although quite how this would be achieved was not made clear; and a 5 per cent average growth rate in GDP. The overall message from the IMF is that the government must demonstrate its commitment to a wide-ranging reform programme.

In the area of privatization the results have been promising but there have been some obstacles. Privatization has progressed, with non-state employment accounting for 47 per cent of the labour force. Two thirds of the non-agricultural sector has been privatized. In addition nearly all housing has been privatized. Privatization in the agricultural sector has been slower, with some important issues remaining to be resolved. All industry has passed through the first stage of privatization, commercialization, followed by ownership changes based on free distribution *via* the use of privatization bonds.

The privatization process in Moldova can be briefly summed up along the following lines. privatization is regulated by the State Privatization Programme set forth in 1993. This programme includes full privatization by vouchers of small, medium, and large scale enterprises, and the privatization of housing. After initial problems in getting the programme started because there was no asset valuation of the state property to be privatized, and there was no listing of citizens who had rights to own vouchers, the practical implementation of the programme began in June 1994. Enterprises whose property belongs to the state are privatized by declaration of the Ministry of Privatization and State Property. Enterprises subject to privatization estimate the book value of their assets. The property valuation of a given enterprise depends upon the type of enterprise. Three categories of enterprises are distinguished: state enterprises; leased enterprises; and joint-stock companies. The state privatization programme 1995–96 was adopted with the main aim of completing privatization. The programme called for privatization by vouchers, and at the same time provides the basis for privatization using private savings. The end of November 1995 saw the completion of the mass privatization programme.

Altogether, 2235 companies, of which 1137 were large or medium-sized enterprises, and some 1098 small enterprises, have been privatized under the programme. Parliament in fact extended the mass privatization programme until November 1996. The government has recently started to privatize for cash.

However, the state still has large holdings in many firms and these are to be sold off in the next stage. There has always been some element of doubt about the strength of Moldova's commitment to privatization. Its reform programme, presented to parliament in a heavily amended form in 1992, envisaged the transition from a socialist economy to a market economy based on private ownership but with a *significant* role for the government. A major impediment to the privatization effort has been the PMR'S refusal to participate (the PMR is the self-declared separatist Transdniestr Moldovan Republic). The PMR represents only about 12 per cent of Moldova's total territory, and 14 per cent of the population, but in 1991 it accounted for the production of all electrical machines, gas containers, and over half the production of electricity. The Moldovan authorities cannot even obtain accurate accounting information on these enterprises. This in turn has made negotiating agreements with the IMF very difficult.

## The Political Dimension of Reforms

Post-Soviet politics in Chisinau have been dominated by a divide between pro-Romanian and pro-Moldovan forces.[10] Relations with Russia and other parts of the former Soviet Union have been as controversial as relations with Romania. Questions of national identity, and relations with Romania and Russia in particular have defined the primary dividing lines among political groupings, as discussed above. This has made it difficult to steer political debate towards privatization, land reform, and industrial restructuring.

Most political groups or parties in Moldova have been so pre-occupied with the crucial questions of statehood, national identity, and separatism that the economy has not really figured as a prominent issue, despite the fact that the general standard of living is very low. In other words election platforms have been dominated by questions of national identity and ethnic grievances, rather than the state of the economy.

This apparent neglect of the economy may not prove dangerous or costly for Moldova's long term transition to a market economy so long as the economy continues to make the significant progress that it has been doing of late. But politicians will need to do more to soften the impact on society of harsh economic measures. It would be interesting to see what progress the Moldovan economy could make if the government was able to concentrate all or more of its energies on economic management, and less on questions of statehood and ethnicity. The fact is that economic restructuring still lags behind macrostabilization, and a successful transition cannot be achieved with progress on only one area.

What is even more worrying is the fact that poverty and falling living standards are more prevalent in the secessionist regions. That means there is a potentially explosive mixture of poverty and separatism which is likely to harden the separatist stance. It is difficult to see what more the government can do. Some would even go as far as to argue that it has already conceded far too much to the separatists, perhaps more than any other 'new state'.

However, in a curious way, political factors have aided economic change, despite the fact that politicians' attention was mostly directed elsewhere. For the parliament in Moldova has not suffered or has not had to contend with the factional and ideological divisions on economic matters on the scale that, for example, afflicted Ukraine, and there have been no major anti-reformist groups calling for a return to command economy principles (perhaps with the exception of Transdniestr's self proclaimed president, Smirnov, who leads a local government committed to central planning).

Even potential rivals to the incumbent Snegur for the presidency, such as Petru Lucinschi, have come out in favour of continued economic reforms.[11] Furthermore, although politicians have mostly regarded the economy as a secondary issue, recent positive developments indicate that the they have not only displayed their commitment to far reaching reforms but they have demonstrated an ability to put those commitments into practice. Thus, while the role of politics in managing the economy has been quite modest, the measures that the key political actors have taken have had encouraging results. Clearly, however, politicians will need to devote more time and energy to economic matters in order to enable Moldova to build on its recent macrostabilization achievements. The task of not only managing the economy but overhauling a whole economic system in order to meet the requirements of transition still presents a considerable challenge for Moldova.

## CONCLUSIONS

Moldova offers a particularly striking example of the costs of attempting to build a unitary nation-state in a multi-national context. The problem, however, is that the alternative, federalism, has been badly discredited in most of the post-communist world by the failure of all three federal states in the region, the USSR, Yugoslavia and Czechoslovakia. The fact that in Moldova, the political élite came to change its mind, and shifted towards the acceptance of a quasi-federal compromise, has much to do both with the strength of the opposition it faced in the TMR, and the unformed nature of Moldovan national identity which allowed room for flexibility. Both of these conditions seem to be unique to Moldova, suggesting that a similar shift towards federalism is not likely to be repeated in other new post-communist states where majoritarian nationalists are set upon unitary state-building in the face of minority opposition.

Moreover, it was unfortunate but perhaps inevitable that by the time the Moldovan élite had come to recognise the need for a quasi-federal compromise, the position of the TMR had become entrenched and Moscow's position had hardened, with the result that the question of whether federalization will secure Moldova's territorial integrity remains open.

In the face of their multiple internal and external challenges, the Moldovans have concluded not only that their best interests are served by remaining independent from Romania, but also that their own independence cannot be sustained without accommodation and respect for the equal rights of the other national groups with whom they now recognise they must share the territory and the state.

There is no doubt that the Republic of Moldova has made significant progress on macroeconomic stabilization since 1994. In the period immediately after independence Moldova found itself facing all the difficulties associated with its established ties to other parts of the Soviet Union. The break up of the Soviet Union meant the loss of previously secure markets, the exposure of the economy to severe shocks, and the emergence of economic problems such as unemployment and open inflation, with neither the networks or the 'culture' to deal with these problems adequately. The situation was compounded by political factors such as internal strife, and the emergence of divergent political groupings.

However, despite these initial problems the benefits of reform have begun to materialize. Inflation has come down dramatically since 1994, an outcome in which the exercise of a restrictive monetary policy had no small part to play. The circulation of money has been kept under control, and National Bank credits to both the government and commercial banks have also been brought under control. The comparative stability of the new currency, the Leu, has further aided this process. Progress with inflation, however, has not yet been matched by correspondingly positive progress in the area of growth, though sectors are starting to grow again and at least the declining path of GDP has been arrested. The budget deficit as a percentage of GDP has begun to fall but expenditures still remain high while tax evasion continues to deplete fiscal revenues. Recent legislative changes in order to tackle such problems will help fiscal management of the economy.

Outside the domain of macro-stabilization, serious economic problems still remain, and these will have to be tackled. Unemployment is still rising. The privatization process is far from complete, and given the widespread poverty in Moldova, it is difficult to see where citizens will find the money to make a success of the final stage of privatization called 'privatization for cash'. Foreign debt continues to climb, and the country has been unable to attract significant foreign direct investment thus far. Nevertheless, Moldova's unusually creative approach to finding a 'political settlement' in the country gives grounds for cautious optimism about the country's prospects in the economic sphere as well.

# NOTES

1. Strictly, August 1991 was the month of the unsuccessful coup against Gorbachev. The USSR was formally dissolved on Christmas Day, 1991.
2. For a general discussion on the 'standard' transition package, see R. Portes' 'Introduction', *European Economy*, special edition No. 2, Brussels: European Commission, 1991.
3. See *IMF Economic Reviews: Moldova*, No. 2, 1993.
4. See *Economic Intelligence Unit (EIU), Country Report, Moldova*, 3rd quarter, 1996.
5. This was established at interviews conducted with staff at the National Bank of Moldova, May 1996.
6. For more on taxation in transition economies, see EBRD, *Transition Report*, 1994, chapter 6.
7. *Financial Times*, Feb 29, 1996, p. 5.
8. *EIU, Economies in Transition: Regional overview*, 2nd quarter, 1996. p. 9.
9. East European Markets, July 19, 1996.
10. For more on this see King, *Post Soviet Moldova: A borderland in Transition*.
11. *EIU, Country Report, Moldova*, 3rd quarter, 1996.

# REFERENCES

Batt, J. (1996), 'Moldova: Nation-State or Multi-National Federation?', CREES mimeo.

Brubaker, R. (1995), 'National minorities, nationalizing states and external national homelands in the New Europe', *Daedalus*, Vol. 124, No. 2, pp. 107–33.

Chinn, J., and Roper, S. (1995), 'Ethnic mobilization and reactive nationalism: the case of Moldova', *Nationalities Papers*, Vol. 23, No. 2, pp. 291–325.

Crowther, W. (1991), 'The Politics of Ethno-National Mobilization', *The Russian Review*, Vol. 50, No. 2, pp. 183–202.

Dima, N. (1991), *From Moldavia to Moldova: the Soviet-Romanian Territorial Dispute*, Boulder, Colorado: East European Monographs.

Elazar, D. (1987), *Exploring Federalism*, Tuscaloosa: University of Alabama Press.

Eyal, J. (1990), 'Moldavians', in G. Smith (ed.), *The Nationalities Question in the Soviet Union*, London: Longman, pp. 123–41.

Fane, D. (1993), 'Moldova: breaking loose from Moscow' in I. Bremmer and R. Taras (eds), *Nations and Politics in the Soviet Successor States*, Cambridge: Cambridge University Press, pp. 121–53.

Gribincea, M. (1995), *Basarabia in primii ani de ocupatie Sovietica*, Cluj-Napoca, Editura Dacia.

Hare, P., Ishaq, M. and Saul E. (1996), 'The legacies of Central Planning and the Transition to a Market Economy: Ukrainian Contradictions', Forthcoming in *Soviet to Independent Ukraine: A Troubled Transformation*, edited by Taras Kuzio

Hitchens, K. (1994), *Romania 1866–1947*, Oxford: Clarendon Press.

Kaminski, B. (1996), 'Economic Transition in Russia and the New States of Eurasia', vol. 8, New York: M.E. Sharpe.

Kemme, D. (1991), *Economic Transition in Eastern Europe*, and the Soviet Union: Issues and Strategies, Occasional papers series no. 20. New York: Institute for East-West Security Studies.

King, C. (1995a), *Post-Soviet Moldova: a Borderland in Transition*, London: RIIA Post-Soviet Business Forum.

King, C. (1995b), 'Gagauz Yeri and the dilemmas of self-determination', *Transition*, Vol. 1, No. 19 (20 October), pp. 21–22.

Kolstoe, P. (1995), *Russians in the Former Soviet Republics*, London: C. Hurst and Co.

Kolstoe, P., *et al.*, (1993), 'The Dniester conflict: between irredentism and separatism', *Europe-Asia Studies*, Vol. 45, No. 6, pp. 973–1000.

*Konstitutsiya Respubliki Moldova* (1994), Chisinau: Moldpress.

'Moldova: a test case for Russia and the "Near Abroad"?' (1995), *Transition*, Vol. 1, No. 19 (20 October), pp. 4–25.

*Monitorul Oficial al Republicii Moldova* (1995), No. 3–4, pp. 46–50.

Portes, R. (1991), 'Introduction' in *European Economy*, special edition No. 2, Brussels: European Commission.

Rothschild, J. (1974), *East Central Europe between the Two World Wars*, Seattle and London: University of Washington Press.

Sellier, A. and Sellier J. (1991), *Atlas des Peuples d'Europe Centrale*, Paris: Editions La Decouverte.

Singurel, G. (1989), 'Moldavia on the barricades of perestroika', *Radio Liberty Report on the USSR*, Vol. 1, No. 8 (24 February), pp. 35–48.

Socor, V. (1990), 'Gagauz in Moldavia demand a separate republic', *Radio Liberty Report on the USSR*, Vol. 2, No. 36 (7 September), pp. 8–13.

Socor, V. (1991a), 'Political power passes to democratic forces', *Radio Liberty Report on the USSR*, Vol. 3, No. 1 (4 January), pp. 24–28.

Socor, V. (1991b), 'Moldavian parliament endorses confederation', *Radio Liberty Report on the USSR*, Vol. 3, No. 9 (1 March), pp. 18–20.

Socor, V. (1991c), 'Moldavia resists pressure and boycotts referendum', *Radio Liberty Report on the USSR*, Vol. 3, No. 13 (29 March), pp. 9–14.

Socor, V. (1992a), 'Why Moldova does not seek reunification with Romania', *Radio Liberty Report on the USSR*, Vol. 1, No. 5 (31 January), pp. 27–33.

Socor, V. (1992b), 'Moldova's new "Government of National Consensus"', *Radio Liberty Research Report*, Vol. 1, No. 47 (27 November), pp. 5–6.

Socor, V. (1994), 'Gagauz autonomy in Moldova: a precedent for Eastern Europe?', *Radio Liberty Research Report*, Vol. 3, No. 33 (26 August), pp. 20–28.

*Vedomosti Narodnogo Sobraniya Gagauzii* (1995), No. 1.

Verdery, K. (1996), 'Civil society or nation? "Europe" in the symbolism of postsocialist politics', in *What was Socialism, and What Comes Next?*, Princeton: Princeton University Press.

Williamson, J. (ed.) (1993), *Economic Consequences of Soviet Disintegration*, Washington, DC: Institute for International Economics, Washington.

*Zakonodatel'niye Akty Moldavskoi SSR o Pridanii Moldavskomu Yazyku Statusa Gosudarst-vennogo i Vozvrate yemu Latinskoi Grafiki*, (1990), Chisinau: Carte Moldove-nesca.

# Part V

# Outcomes

# 18
# The Institutional Framework of Privatization and Competition in Economies in Transition (Overview)

*Silvana Malle*[1]

Amongst the numerous issues discussed in this volume in the light of empirical research, some preliminary findings and assessments are highly interesting for the understanding of the transitionary developments in the first years of transformation to the market and of the results of policy measures – both those results that were expected and those that failed to materialize. One can draw attention to the following important points:

- competition was more relevant than privatization for transformation first, and growth, next;
- the transfer of state ownership to private owners did not always bring about restructuring and changes in behaviour;
- the new private sector is more important for the resumption of growth than the privatization of state-owned enterprises (SOEs);
- mass privatization was not the only way to achieve fast privatization.

That private enterprise is not always competitive and that competition is what matters to increase efficiency is the core of Jo Stiglitz's approach to economic transformation, an approach shared by Saul Estrin and by many contributors to this volume, who have offered evidence in support of this position. However, to be fair to the eclectic discourse of institutional economics, one should also remember that for Stiglitz one main advantage of the private enterprise over the state enterprise is that the transaction costs needed to obtain state subsidies are higher for the former – which can be taken to mean that budget constraints do, indeed, hit harder in private business. Apart from the attractiveness of Stiglitz *versus* Stiglitz's arguments in support of or against privatization as a means for improving efficiency, however, one needs to stress that the very dimensions of the problem of privatization in post-communist economies render any comparison with apparently similar problems in advanced market economies rather difficult to accept without qualifications.

Any balanced assessment less than a decade from the start of transition can but point to the difficulties of determining the successes and failures of privatization as their points of reference go far beyond what econometric studies can yet capture. The demise of state ownership, the rejection of nationalization, the decentralization of economic power in Europe have combined constitutional (political) and systemic (economic) changes. These changes take time. The recent study conducted by the World Bank on 26 countries, which is based on econometric evidence, is a robust analytical step forward in the effort to identify the policy measures which counted for success in transition, but this study is not exempt from the limitation of selecting a time horizon which may not be the most appropriate; although nobody can say what horizon should be the appropriate one, since the experience of the transformation from state-owned economies to economies based on private business is unique.

Some countries have resumed growth only two years from the start of transformation, such as Poland, some later. The average time span for the resumption of growth by 1995 was three-and-a-half years, also according to the analysis of Stanley Fisher *et al.*, (1966: 45–66). But, apart from the difficulty of explaining theoretically the difference between two and five years for the resumption of growth, a difference which matters in building medium-term strategies, the question remains whether the number of observations is sufficient to argue that transformation has been accomplished or that growth is sustainable. By 1994 Bulgaria had achieved positive growth, along with the Central European Countries (CECs), and kept growing in 1995. It became clear in 1996 that this growth was not sustainable with an estimated output fall of more than 10 per cent. The sustainability of growth in the Baltic countries is also uncertain, with growth in Latvia, for instance, having turned negative in 1995 after a modest 1 per cent increase in 1994, and estimated rates of growth in the area in general for 1996 and 1997 are still quite modest (OECD, 1996a).

Major banking failures indicate that microeconomic restructuring is far from complete and impinges on still fragile macroeconomic stabilization. While growth continues to be positive in the CECs, all these countries have nonetheless been badly hit by the recession in western Europe and in Germany in particular. In some countries, even the most successful, the rapidly increasing deficit in the trade balances, not always due to increasing imports of investment goods, could be a worrying sign that the real appreciation of the domestic currency is hardly sustainable with the existing standards of price and quality competitiveness in industry. On a larger scale, low levels of savings and highly expensive social benefits and pensions are major problems for the sustainability of growth all over the region. All in all it would be reasonable to agree from the visible results so far that transformation is not yet completed and that more or less important reversals could still occur in any field.

From the point of view of their impact on growth, it would also be too early to assess the successes and failures of any of the schemes of privatization so far implemented on the way to a market economy or to discard privatization as a policy measure. First, privatization, whether implemented or not, had a political dimension in all countries. Second, its results would need to be assessed through a prism, one side of which is represented by efficiency, while equity, inter-branch and inter-enterprise reallocation of resources, corporate governance, the enforcement of legally protected individual property rights and individual material responsibility represent other, equally important, facets. Thirdly, it would be dangerous, given its future macroeconomic implications, to suggest that privatization can be postponed indefinitely. What we see now are the embryos of what is slowly developing, so that it might be difficult to recognize the customary features and behaviours of an institutionally well-crafted market economy.

Market economies need an impartial judiciary, enforceable contracts and good administrators in order to sustain investment, and in particular large-scale foreign investment, as Martin Cave (Chapter 3) has recalled. They all need time. What one needs to observe now is whether there exists on the part of the individual governments a commitment to transformation, or resistance to further reforms. As pointed out by Judy Batt and Kataryna Wolczuk (Chapter 2), the sheer volume of legislation which needs to be passed results in laws of poor quality. The quality, scope and implementation of commercial and civil legislation are important. They should be the filters for a reasonable economic assessment.

That the privatization of large-scale companies in most post-communist countries has not necessarily brought about restructuring of the same companies is a strong finding of the research presented in this volume. In the light of experience so far, it appears that the adjustment of supply to market demand has proceeded in its own way, whether with, without or alongside privatization. Harder budget constraints have, altogether, been more important than privatization as such. This means that macroeconomic stabilization policies directed at cutting budget deficits and budget subsidies have mattered first. At the same time, in the light of the structural changes which occurred along with stabilization policies, one needs to add some qualifications when stressing, as Mario Nuti (Chapter 5) rightly does, the comparatively higher importance of the new private sector in the resumption of growth in Poland (but not only in that country).

That all enterprises, both state and private, were exposed to harder budget constraints has mattered in improving efficiency and labour productivity. But what was crucial in the Polish case, and has been missing in the Russian case, was the dynamism of the new small-scale business sector. This, however, poses the problem of how new business got hold of the necessary resources, capital and land, to start. The likely answer is: from the state, in one (legal) way or another. Thus, if privatization was not the direct means of transformation, it must nonetheless have been an important indirect channel for the reallocation of resources out of state firms or manager-employee-owned firms (MEBOs), one of the most common forms of privatization in Poland, but also in other countries. To this extent MEBOs, even if not the most promising form of management from the point of view of efficiency, may be seen as an important stage in the process of redistribution of property rights *à la* Coase, as it provides both for social consensus and for increased flexibility in the use of resources. This also confirms that one needs to discriminate among different forms of privatization from the point of view of their comparative potential in mobilizing resources across enterprises and branches.

The possibility of selling the enterprise's assets or part of the assets is important at the initial stage of transition even if it does not contribute directly to its own efficiency, because it is the only way, apart from foreign direct investments (FDI), to set up the initial physical capital. Similarly, the possibility of renting or, even better, selling part of the enterprise's premises is crucial for the starting up of any business. From this point of view, a crucial element is institutional progress in mobilizing real estate since this market is determinant for competitiveness in all markets. Along with other newly independent states (NIS), Russia has not yet made the necessary progress in this field. The fact that Russian enterprises own neither the land on which they are built nor their own premises must be seen as a dramatic obstacle to the setting up of any business, including small-scale trading. Renting premises compared with owning them is a far less attractive option in countries where contracts are hard to enforce, the possibility of eviction is low and the breaching of agreements common. The obstacle to effective competition in former Soviet Union (FSU) countries caused by the lack of a cadastre, the most important institution for the enforcement of property rights, is not always fully appreciated in transformation policy and recommendations.

It is also in this context that the potential of different forms of privatization to meet new business needs should be assessed. While direct sales through the negotiation of detailed contracts may indeed provide the new owners with a reasonable certainty about the acquired property, including land, mass privatization schemes, in general, overlook these problems. What is often the most valuable asset in privatizable enterprises, the land on which they are built, is not part of the privatization deal. Further transfers of property rights are then complicated to the extent that sellers themselves may be ignorant of what they own *de facto*.

The immediate failures of mass privatization, on which attention is increasingly drawn, are epitomized by Derek C. Jones (Chapter 13) as a 'disappointing slow degree of change in key areas such as managerial turnover', and a 'dramatic consolidation of managerial power'. This finding is supported by Russian research showing that in a high number of cases, even when they are not dominant owners, managers are effectively in control (Klepach *et al.*, 1996). While this fact is not in itself negative, it turns out to be worrying when control does not lead to active production strategies. This, indeed, seems to be less true for management-controlled than for employee-controlled companies (63 per cent of active survival strategies by the former compared to 73 per cent passive strategies by the latter) according to Russian findings. While the end-results of mass privatization could indeed turn out to be more positive some years from now, a satisfactory explanation of why the effects of active survival strategies, if such they are, are not yet visible on a larger scale with the resumption of industrial growth, is missing.

The point has been made in Chapter 7 (Takla) that the correlation between export growth and privatization is not corroborated by empirical evidence. With overwhelming state ownership in raw materials and heavy industry, the sectors in which the transformation countries had some competitive advantages through stocks of unsold output after the dissolution of COMECON, this is perhaps not surprising. However, this finding should not be used to infer that privatization does not matter for competition in the international market. Divergent developments in Hungary and in Romania suggest that privatization does indeed matter for the balance of trade. By forming joint ventures early and then selling a large number of enterprises to foreign investors (in Hungary foreign participation represents 58 per cent of the value of privatized enterprises), Hungary was able to attract a larger volume of foreign direct investment (FDI). While the immediate impact of such developments may result in a worsening trade balance through imports of investment goods, as it did in Hungary in 1994, in the medium term this contributes to the strengthening of the economic foundations and to sustainable growth. In Hungary, from 1995 onwards, foreign investments started accounting for some 70 per cent of exports. Besides, Hungary has now become the largest recipient of greenfield FDI and positive developments in the trade balance are now contributing importantly to relieve the pressure of foreign debt and interest rates on the utilization of internal resources. Romania, on the contrary, found itself in a position of having to sustain increasing imports of energy for unrestructured energy-intensive state-owned companies and having to conduct a crazy exchange rate policy with lower exchange rates for importers enforced through a politically friendly banking system at the expense of the economy as a whole. In one year, from 1995 to 1996, with artificially sustained growth, inflation doubled, entailing both a worsening budget and foreign trade deficit.

When taking into account the necessary qualifications and comparative evidence on general economic developments, the argument that privatization, in the sense of the transfer of property rights from the state to other entities, while not necessarily implying restructuring, is a necessary step forwards, seems to be more well-founded than either excessively commendatory or gloomy assessments. Gains in efficiency are not necessarily visible at the level of the existing enterprises and products mix or branches. It is well known that industry was overexpanded in communist economies; that it will need to shrink is also commonly accepted. One should also expect, and perhaps research should give more focus to this, the transformation of industrial enterprises into trade or service business. While the company profile may change, it is important at the initial stage of transformation that it provides, if nothing else, room for new activities. In all countries in transformation, trading and services have indeed expanded and they are by and large private. This would have hardly been possible had not privatization made room for the redistribution of resources through a more decentralized level of decision-making on the holding of company assets. Only ten years ago in communist countries, the enterprises could not even write off a desk without obtaining the authorization of higher entities such as their branch ministries. There was not only an economic rationale in the extensive model of growth, but also an administrative one perhaps less evident, but nevertheless very real, which should not be forgotten at least for a balanced assessment of what has been done and what still needs to be done from an institutional point of view.

Another important point which emerged in the conference that gave rise to this book is that, contrary to largely held views, privatization need not to be mass privatization in order to be fast. As correctly pointed out by Paul Hare and Anna Canning (Chapter 6), Hungary has privatized almost all industry while resisting the option of mass privatization. After some hesitation in 1993 and 1994, pressed by the problems of growing current account and budget deficits, Hungary increased the pace of direct sales. This raises the question, addressed to the conference, that with fast privatization there will soon be nothing to privatize and that in the future these sources of off-the-budget revenues will not be available. However, while it is correct to maintain that privatization revenues should not be accounted as budget revenues, the fact that these revenues can be used to repay part of the public debt is not irrelevant for macroeconomic stabilization in countries in transformation which are faced with the need to increase the primary budget surplus, even with heavy social costs, in order to make up for the rising burden of interest rates on the general budget deficit. Furthermore, while the option of negotiating the cancellation of part of the debt is open, in principle, to any country, it is also important that a country be recognized in the international community as an honourable debtor. Foreign investors are aware of this. The record of Hungary as the major receiver of FDI among the European countries in transformation cannot be disjoined from its commendable attitude towards its external creditors.

Whether through voucher schemes or through direct sales, *de facto* privatization has been gradual in all countries (see recent OECD Surveys of the Czech Republic, Slovakia, Poland, Hungary). Not only does much property remain under state (political) control, but large-scale privatized enterprises continue, through old connections, to enjoy privileged access to capital and this is then reflected in the mounting volume of bad debts in most countries in transformation which also include new non-performing loans.

This point, which emerges in the studies contained in this volume, is often overlooked in research on privatization. Whether schemes of mass privatization or direct sales have been adopted, a large share of industry still remains in state hands: in Poland, considered to be the most successful country in transition, by the end of 1995 the value of production of the 6.6 per cent of SOEs included in the total number of enterprises in manufacturing was 47.1 per cent of the total. The number of SOEs fell to 4081 by mid-1996 from 8453 in 1990 (OECD, 1996b: 71–72). Most mining, quarrying and utilities are still in state hands. In Russia, one of the least successful countries in transition, in which a mass privatization was completed by June 1994, 45 per cent of property still remained state-owned by the end of 1996. The most valuable assets have not yet been fully or even partly privatized. A creeping re-nationalization could even start through the scheme of state credit to some enterprises and groups of enterprises guaranteed by enterprises' equity shares.

While this could be taken as additional evidence for arguing that privatization did not principally affect gowth one way or another – though the above caveat remains – it also provides evidence for the enormous tasks which still remain for transformation. If property is to remain in state hands while problems of macroeconomic stabilization are not yet solved (even in Poland inflation is still about 20 per cent and the budget deficit is still significant and threatened by the maturity of the remaining foreign debt), a solution must be found for the adequate financial and decision-making decentralization of management and investment policies. In Poland many of the branches under state control are still heavily subsidized, sometimes in a less transparent way through the creation of holdings. If further privatization is to be implemented this should be done with determination, to avoid the temptation of setting up golden ghettos for so-called strategic sectors.

Many countries resist bankruptcies. While it is unlikely that bankruptcies would occur on a mass scale for social reasons, the fact that this institution is the best market means to reallocate resources of non-viable firms to useful activities while protecting creditors' rights should be better understood in the countries themselves and, perhaps, also in research dealing with transformation. Bankruptcies would also help to break the vicious circle of inter-enterprise debt arrears which in some countries – Russia is one of the most dramatic examples – are, indeed, obstacles to competition.

The development of inter-enterprise debt arrears often goes along with the reassertion of old conglomerates or with the creation of new ones, such as the financial-industrial groups (FIGs). This phenomenon has been well described for Lithuania by Rasa Morkûnaitë (Chapter 12), but is not unique to that country. David Stark, in an article published in one issue of *Transition* in 1995, has vividly described the emergence of 'rekombinants' in Hungary. This phenomenon is more striking, perhaps, in Russia, although this volume has not paid much attention to it. By August 1996 there were 37 FIGs registered in Russia and some 150 effective organizations of the same type dispersed over the country. Altogether they produce an estimated 50 per cent of the total industrial output (Radygin, 1996). This form of organization received a further stimulus through the shares-for-loan scheme which permitted some major Russian banks to become trustees of state-owned shares, and eventually owners of some large-scale companies, in exchange for credit to the govenment budget.

One should know more about the effective nature and behaviour of such structures, whether their stategy is one of survival or an aggressive one. At any rate, it is likely that these groups are formed to resist competition and put pressure on federal or local governments for support. The law contemplates the possibility for them of obtaining state guarantees on the issue of bonds. In some regions promissory notes issued by enterprises and groups of enterprises are used to pay for local tax. It would be interesting to know to what extent these pratices are widespread and, if state guarantees have been issued, which type of agreement or other financial consideration has been used.

What forms of industrial organization are emerging and evolving in countries in transformation is an issue that matters in dealing with markets and competition; whether this organization is open to outsiders, whether foreign direct investments have access to the country and under what conditions. While the studies in this volume have focused on employee-owned enterprises and their possible developments, the formation of holdings and other groups has not attracted much attention, although formal and informal groupings are important in these countries to the extent that, through vested interests in the *status quo*, they can be strong enough to resist further improvement towards effectively competitive markets. This could be a welcome theme for a further volume on transformation.

## NOTE

1. The views expressed in this chapter are those of the author and do not necessarily represent the views of OECD.

## REFERENCES

Fisher, S. *et al.*, (1966), 'Stabilization and Growth in Transition Economies: the Early Experience', *Journal of Economic Perspectives*, Vol. 10(2), Spring 1966.
Klepach, A. *et al.*, (1996), 'Corporate Governance in Russia in 1995–1996', RECEP Working Paper, Moscow.
OECD (1996a), *Economic Outlook*, Autumn.
OECD (1996b), *Economic Survey of Poland*, pp. 71–72.
Radygin, A. (1996), 'O razvitii finansovo-promyshlennykh grupp v Rossii', Institut ekonomicheskikh problem perekhodnogo perioda, Newsletter, October 1996.
Stark, D. (1995), 'The Hidden Character of East European Capitalism: Recombinant Ownership', *Transition*, Vol. 6(11–12), Nov–Dec.

# Index